# HEART'S DELIGHT

## *Recipes from the Heart*

Edited by
*Elaine Finley*
*Rebecca Germany*
*Susan Harper*
*Pam McQuade*

*ISBN: 157748-522-X*



Published by Barbour Publishing, Inc., P.O. Box 719, Uhrichsville, OH 44683 http://www.barbourbooks.com

ecpa Member of the Evangelical Christian Publishers Association

Printed in the United States of America.

# INTRODUCTION

A home-cooked meal is truly a *Heart's Delight.*

Old-fashioned home-cooking has certainly become a special treat in many households today, with schedules full and time at a premium. A traditional dinner has always been a heart-warming way to get the family together for good, wholesome food and conversation, but putting a home-cooked meal on the table can sometimes be a challenge. That is where *Heart's Delight* can help!

We have gathered over 700 recipes from people just like you who all happen to be members of **Heartsong Presents,** one of the world's largest Christian romance book clubs. The members gladly sent us their favorite old-fashioned, down-home, proven recipes that are delicious, easy, and sure to please. From appetizers to desserts, you'll have a home-cooked meal put together in no time.

So from their homes to yours, enjoy these classic recipes, and cook to your *Heart's Delight.*

*Delight theyself also in the LORD: and he shall*
*give thee the desires of thine heart.*
Psalm 37:4

# CONTENTS

# BREAKFAST

# BREAKFAST

## BREAKFAST CASSEROLE
Ella Weaver, Pollok, TX

**8 flattened crescent rolls**
**Cooked and drained sausage**
**1 cup hash browns**
**6 eggs, beaten**
**Cheese, grated**

OVEN 350°

Grease 5x11-inch pan. Layer with rolls, sausage, hash browns and eggs. Top with grated cheese. Bake at 350° for 45 minutes or until done.

## BREAKFAST CASSEROLE
Gay Waneck, Smithville, TX

*"This is very popular for brunches, and if I am going to take it to work, I mix it up the night before and when I get up the next morning, I let it bake while I am getting ready; then it is still warm when we eat it at work. It's also nice to mix up the night before, if you have guests and want a leisurely time with them in the morning."*

**1 pound sausage, cooked and drained**
**6 eggs, beaten**
**1 teaspoon salt**
**1 teaspoon dry mustard**
**1 cup grated cheese**
**1 cup milk**
**2 slices day-old bread, torn**

OVEN 350°

Combine all ingredients in two-quart casserole dish. Bake uncovered at 350° for 45 minutes.

## BACON AND CHEESE BREAKFAST PIZZA
Amber Walter, Penns Creek, PA

**Pastry for single crust pie (9-inch)**
**½ pound bacon, cooked and crumbled**
**2 cups (8 ounces) shredded Swiss cheese**
**4 eggs**
**1½ cups (12 ounces) sour cream**
**2 tablespoons chopped fresh parsley**

OVEN 450°

Roll pastry to fit into a 12-inch pizza pan. Bake at 450° for 5 minutes. Sprinkle bacon and cheese evenly over crust. In a bowl, beat eggs, sour cream, and parsley until smooth; pour over pizza. Bake until puffy and light brown.

## BREAKFAST PIZZA

Lanita Coorde, Eltopia, WA

**1 family-size Boboli (Italian bread)**
**1 to 2 tablespoons margarine, melted**
**1 to 2 teaspoons garlic powder**
**6-ounce can tomato paste**
**2 tablespoons picante or salsa**
**6 to 8 eggs**
**¼ cup shredded cheddar cheese**
**10 to 11 slices Canadian bacon, quartered**
**½ cup Parmesan or mozzarella cheese, grated**

OVEN 400°

Spread Boboli with melted margarine, add garlic powder. Mix together tomato paste and picante or salsa; spread on bread. Scramble eggs with cheddar cheese, cooking until soft curds. Spread on bread. Arrange quartered bacon slices in rows on pizza. Cover with parmesan or mozzarella cheese. Bake at 400° for 10–15 minutes.

## SAUSAGE CHEESE GRITS CASSEROLE

Carolyn Anne Taylor, Gaffney, SC

**4 cups water**
**1 teaspoon salt**
**1 cup quick grits**
**4 eggs, slightly beaten**
**1 pound sausage, browned**
**1½ cups (6 ounces) grated sharp cheddar cheese, divided**
**1 cup milk**
**½ cup margarine**

OVEN 350°

Preheat oven to 350°. Grease 3-quart baking dish; set aside. Bring water and salt to boil in large saucepan. Slowly stir in grits. Cook 4–5 minutes, stirring occasionally. Remove from heat. Stir small amount of grits mixture into eggs. Return all to saucepan. Add sausage, 1 cup cheese, milk, and margarine. Blend well. Pour into prepared baking dish. Sprinkle with remaining ½ cup cheese. Bake 1 hour or until cheese is golden brown. Let cool 10 minutes.

## GRITS CASSEROLE

Iva Kay Jacobson, Horton, KS

**4 cups boiling water**
**1 cup grits (not instant)**
**1 stick butter**
**½–¾ pound sharp cheese, grated**
**2 eggs, beaten**
**1 teaspoon salt**
**½ teaspoon paprika**
**½ teaspoon garlic salt**

OVEN 375°

Cook grits in boiling water 5 minutes. Add butter, cheese, garlic salt, paprika, salt, and eggs. Pour into greased baking dish. Bake 40 minutes at 375°.

Makes a 9x13-inch baking dish full.

# BREAKFAST

## OVERNIGHT SAUSAGE SOUFFLE
Sarah Hight, Lakewood, WA

**1 pound link pork sausage, cut up**
**6 slices bread, cubed**
**1 cup grated medium cheddar cheese**
**4 eggs**
**½ teaspoon salt**
**½ teaspoon dry mustard (optional)**
**2 cups milk**

OVEN 325°

Fry sausage and cut into pieces. Alternate layers of bread cubes, sausage, and cheese in a 2½-quart casserole dish. Beat eggs and add milk; then salt, dry mustard, and milk. Pour egg mixture over the other ingredients. Cover and refrigerate overnight. Bake in a 325° oven for 45 minutes to 1 hour.

## CREPE PEON
Margaret Walker, Tucson, AZ

**Flour tortillas, 1–2 per person**
**1 egg, beaten**
**⅝ cup milk**
**2 tablespoons butter**

Rather than making your own, or using pre-made crepes, take any size flour tortilla; dip in beaten egg mixed with ⅝ cup milk and cook in butter or margarine lightly like French toast. It is sturdier than a "real crepe" and works great.

Variation:
Roll any ingredients inside crepe for any occasion: ice cream, cheese with fruit, nuts, veggies or tuna, crab, egg, ham, salad, etc. Anything to suit your imagination.

## BERTA'S BAVARIAN APPLE PANCAKES
Karen Rivera, Ridgewood, NY

*"My best friend Donna and I got this recipe from her German mother-in-law. She's "old-fashioned" and doesn't use "recipes," making everything from her head. She kept saying, "Well, you have to know how to cook."*

**3 eggs**
**1 teaspoon vanilla extract**
**4 teaspoons sugar**
**Lite oil for frying**
**1 cup flour**
**1 cup milk**
**4 apples, peeled and shredded**
**4 tablespoons cinnamon and sugar mixed for sprinkling**

Beat together eggs, vanilla, and 4 teaspoons sugar. Add milk, mix in flour. Stir in apples. Fry in oil in very hot pan. Spoon ⅓ cup mixture into oil. Turn over when edges are dry and bubbles form. Sprinkle with cinnamon and sugar mixture.

## SAUSAGE BREAKFAST BAKE

Elizabeth Hunt, Ithaca, MI

**2 cups pancake mix (or 1½ cups prepared baking mix and ½ cup cornmeal)**
**1¼ cups milk**
**2 eggs**
**2 tablespoons salad oil**
**8-ounce package smoky links, cut into bite-size pieces**
**14-ounce jar spiced apple rings**

OVEN 350°

Combine all ingredients and beat until smooth with a rotary beater. Turn into a 9x13-inch baking dish. Stir smoky links into batter. Arrange apple rings in the batter, in areas where the "cake" pieces will be cut. Bake at 350° for 35 minutes. Serve with apple maple syrup.

**Apple Syrup:**

**Apple syrup from jar of spiced apple rings**
**4 teaspoons cornstarch**
**¾ cup maple-flavored syrup**
**4 teaspoons butter**

Pour apple syrup into a cup and add water to make ⅔ cup. Pour into saucepan and add cornstarch and maple flavored syrup. Cook until bubbly and add butter.

## PANCAKES

Faye C. Galway, Radford, VA

**1¼ cups plain flour**
**1¼ cups buttermilk**
**1 egg, beaten**
**1 teaspoon sugar**
**½ teaspoon salt**
**½ teaspoon baking soda**
**1 tablespoon liquid shortening**
**1 teaspoon baking powder**

Mix ingredients and fry on hot griddle.

## DOUGHNUT MUFFINS

Madeline Carter, Brooklin, ME

**1 egg, beaten**
**½ cup milk**
**⅓ cup oil**
**1 teaspoon vanilla**
**1 teaspoon lemon juice**
**1½ cups all-purpose flour**
**2 teaspoons baking powder**
**½ cup sugar**
**1 teaspoon nutmeg**
**½ teaspoon cinnamon**

**Topping:**

**3 teaspoons sugar**
**¼ teaspoon nutmeg**

OVEN 400°

Beat together egg, milk, oil, vanilla, and lemon juice. Add flour, baking powder, sugar, nutmeg, and cinnamon. Mix together sugar and nutmeg for topping and spread over top of muffins. Bake at 400° for 15 minutes. (Muffins in a regular muffin tin will take 20 minutes.)

# BREAKFAST

## WAFFLES WITH MAPLE SYRUP

Phyllis Lance, McMinnville, TN

**3 cups sifted all-purpose flour**
**4 teaspoons baking powder**
**1 teaspoon salt**
**2 teaspoons sugar**
**2/3 cup melted butter or shortening**
**2 cups melted butter**
**2 cups milk**
**4 eggs, separated**

Using electric mixer, beat egg whites until fluffy, set aside. Beat egg yolks 1 minute, add milk and beat 1 minute. Add sifted dry ingredients and beat 1 minute. Add melted butter and beat 15 seconds. Fold in stiffly beaten egg whites. Pour on hot waffle iron.

**Homemade maple syrup:**
**2 cups sugar**
**¼ cup brown sugar**
**2 pounds white corn syrup**
**1 cup water**
**1 teaspoon vanilla**
**1 teaspoon maple flavoring**

Mix together and bring just to boiling point (enough to melt sugars.) Add vanilla and maple flavorings. Stir well and serve over waffles or pancakes. This keeps well in the refrigerator.

## BREAKFAST GRANOLA

Nancy L. Staurseth, Poplar, WI

**7 cups oatmeal (not quick)**
**1 cup wheat germ**
**½ cup honey**
**½ cup oil**
**½ cup brown sugar**
**½ cup water**
**1 teaspoon vanilla or orange flavoring**

OVEN 225°

Mix well oatmeal and wheat germ. Bring to boil honey, oil, brown sugar, and water. Remove from stove and add flavoring. Pour liquid over oats mixture and mix well. Bake 1 hour at 225° in double cake pan. Stir once or twice during baking. Should be crisp.

Add other ingredients to taste such as raisins, dates, dried fruit, coconut, pumpkin, sunflower and/or sesame seeds, orange peel. Applesauce is a good topping.

# BREADS

# BREADS

## BREAD MACHINE OATMEAL BREAD

Fern Anderson, Carlton, MN

*"This is a very simple but really good recipe for the bread machine."*

**1¼ cups + 2 tablespoons water**
**1 tablespoon oil**
**½ cup molasses (mild)**
**1 teaspoon salt**
**3 cups bread flour**
**1 cup quick-cooking oats**
**1½ teaspoons yeast**

Follow machine instructions.

Yield: 1½-pound loaf.

## BISHOP'S BREAD

Melinda Kubat, Erie, PA

*"This recipe for this delicious bread has been passed down in my family for years. My grandma, Ruth Hammer, always made this at Christmas. It is a holiday tradition and a wonderful memory."*

**1½ cups sifted flour**
**1½ teaspoons baking powder**
**¼ teaspoon salt**
**⅔ cup chocolate chips**
**2 cups coarsely chopped walnuts**
**1 cup diced dates**
**1 cup halved glazed maraschino cherries**
**3 eggs**
**1 cup granulated sugar**

OVEN 350°

Mix all ingredients together until moist. Mixture will be thick. Put in greased and floured bread pan. Bake at 350° until done, approximately 1 hour.

## CHEW BREAD

Dixie LaMarr, Gibsonville, NC

*"This recipe is enjoyed by everyone. I prefer it without the chocolate chips, however, children like it better with them."*

**½ cup margarine**
**1 box light brown sugar**
**3 eggs, well beaten**
**2 cups self-rising flour, sifted**
**1 teaspoon vanilla**
**1 cup nuts, chopped (pecans or walnuts)**
**½ cup chocolate chips (optional)**

OVEN 300°

Cream margarine; add sugar, eggs, and flour. Add nuts. Pour into 8x12-inch greased baking dish. Bake at 300° for 40 minutes.

## HAWAIIAN BREAD

Mary Lib C. Joyce, High Point, NC

**1¼ cups pre-sifted plain flour**
**1 cup sugar**
**½ teaspoon salt**
**1 teaspoon baking soda**
**½ cup corn oil margarine**
**3 small ripe bananas, mashed**
**2 eggs, well beaten**

OVEN 350°

Mix together flour, sugar, salt, and baking soda. Using pastry cutter, cut margarine into flour mixture, until like cornmeal. Add bananas and eggs. Stir well together and pour into 8x8-inch pan sprayed with cooking spray. Bake at 350° for 35 minutes until it begins to pull away from side of pan. Cool. Cut into 3 loaves. Freezes well.

Variation: Add ¼ cup chopped maraschino cherries and ½ teaspoon almond extract. Add nuts if desired.

## HOMEMADE BREAD

Robin Steed, Portland, IN

**2 tablespoons yeast (2 packages)**
**3 cups warm water**
**7 cups flour, whole wheat and unbleached**
**½ cup oil**
**½ cup honey**
**2 tablespoons lecithin**
**2 teaspoons salt**
**¼ cup gluten flour**
**½ teaspoon ginger**
**Cooking spray**

OVEN 250°–350°

Mix yeast and ginger and stir. Add all the flour, stir. Let sit 15 minutes. Add remaining ingredients. Stir. Heat just over 1 minute at 250°, then turn off. Place dough on lightly floured surface. Knead 7 minutes. Add flour as needed. Place dough in oiled and sprayed bowl. Spray dough top with cooking spray and cover with towel. Put in oven. Let rise 45–60 minutes. Cut and separate dough into 3 equal parts. Roll out then roll into a loaf. Tuck ends under and place in loaf pans. Place all 3 pans in oven to rise 30–60 minutes, 2 inches above pan. Bake at 350° for 15–20 minutes, then cover tops with foil and continue baking at 300° for 20–25 minutes. Place on cooling racks. Brush lightly with melted butter and cover, for soft crust. Place in plastic bags or wrap and freeze.

Makes 3 loaves.

# BREADS

## BANANA NUT BREAD

Lois Kelly, Erie, PA
Anita Barisich, Independence, KS
*"I use 1/3 cup more sugar and leave out the milk."*

**2/3 cup sugar**
**1/2 cup soft shortening**
**2 eggs**
**3 tablespoons sour milk**
**1 cup very ripe mashed bananas**
**2 cups sifted flour**
**1 teaspoon baking powder**
**1/2 teaspoon baking soda**
**1/2 teaspoon salt**
**1/2 cup chopped nuts**

OVEN 350°

Mix together sugar, shortening, and eggs. Stir in milk and bananas. Sift together flour, baking powder, baking soda, and salt; stir into other mixture. Blend in nuts. Pour into well-greased loaf pan. Let stand 20 minutes before baking. Bake at 350° for 50–60 minutes. Double recipe for two loaves. This bread is very moist.

## COUNTRY FAIR EGG BREAD

George Clanton, Weldon, CA

**1 1/2 cups scalded milk**
**1/2 cup butter**
**1/2 cup sugar**
**2 packages yeast**
**1/2 cup lukewarm water**
**2 eggs, beaten**
**9 cups sifted flour (approximately)**

OVEN 350–425°

Pour the scalded milk over the butter and sugar. Cool. Dissolve the yeast in the lukewarm water and let stand until it bubbles, about 5 minutes. Add the yeast and the beaten eggs to the cooled milk. Gradually add the flour, beating it in thoroughly. Do not add any more flour than is necessary to make an easily handled dough, as the bread should be light and tender.

Turn out onto floured board and knead until smooth and elastic. Place in greased bowl, cover, and let rise until doubled in size (about 1 1/2 hours). Punch down and turn out onto a lightly floured board. Shape into 3 loaves and place in greased 8-inch loaf pans. Cover and let rise until dough is just to the tops of the pans. Bake in a 425° oven for 10 minutes, then lower the heat to 350° and bake 40 minutes longer, or until bread is done.

Makes 3 loaves.

## BANANA NUT PUDDING BREAD

Norma Bigley, Mesa, AZ

**1 package banana cake mix**
**1 package banana instant pudding (or vanilla)**
**1/2 cup Crisco oil**
**1 cup water**
**4 eggs**
**2 mashed bananas**
**Nuts**

OVEN 350°

Blend all ingredients in large bowl. Bake at 350° in loaf pan about 30 minutes.

## SOUR CREAM NUT BREAD

K. Joyce Gess, Sanford, FL

**2 ½ cups buttermilk biscuit mix**
**⅔ cup sugar**
**1 cup chopped nuts**
**1 cup sour cream**
**⅓ cup milk**
**2 eggs, lightly beaten**
**1 teaspoon vanilla**

OVEN 350°

Preheat oven to 350°. Grease bottom of a bread loaf pan. In a large bowl, combine biscuit mix, sugar, and nuts. Stir in sour cream, milk, eggs, and vanilla, blending well. Pour into prepared pan. Bake for 50–55 minutes. Cool in pan 10 minutes. Remove from pan, cool on wire rack.

## IRISH BROWN BREAD

Una McManus, Columbia, MD

**Editor's Note:** Author of numerous books, including *Love's Tender Gift, Abiding Love*, and *Wild Irish Roses* for Heartsong Presents, Una has written under the pen names of Elizabeth Murphey and Cara McCormack. She is a native of Ireland with relatives still living there.

**1¾ cups flour (whole wheat, or half white and half whole wheat)**
**½ cup brown sugar plus 1 tablespoon molasses**
**½ teaspoon baking soda**
**1 teaspoon salt**
**5½ tablespoons margarine (or butter)**
**1 cup oatmeal (or ⅓ cup bran; ⅓ cup cracked wheat; ⅓ cup wheat germ)**
**1 egg, beaten**
**Buttermilk or regular milk**
**Raisins (optional)**

OVEN 400°

Mix dry ingredients. Rub in margarine. Mix in egg and enough milk to make stiff, not liquid, dough. Spoon into greased loaf pans (one regular size or two small) and bake uncovered for 45 minutes at 400°. The small loaf pans turn out nice loaves with lots of crust. Great for parties and holiday meals. Serve with butter, sharp cheddar cheese, and lots of strong, hot, Irish tea.

## JULEKAGE (CHRISTMAS BREAD)

JoAnn A. Grote, Montevideo, MN

*"My family is of Scandinavian heritage. The majority of "Christmas foods" served in our home are of Scandinavian origin. One of our favorites is Julekage, a Christmas bread. In my Heartsong,* Love's Shining Hope, *Scandinavian neighbors shared Julekage with the heroine, Pearl, at Christmas. The following recipe was handed down from my mother-in-law. I especially enjoy this toasted and spread with butter."*

**Editor's Note:** JoAnn has authored several Heartsong Presents romances, including *The Sure Promise* and *Sweet Surrender.*

**2 cakes or packages of yeast**
**1 cup milk (3/4 cup milk and 1/4 cup water if dry yeast is used instead of cake yeast)**
**1/2 cup sugar**
**2 eggs**
**1 teaspoon salt**
**6 cardamom seeds, ground**
**4 cups flour**
**1/8 lb. butter**
**2/3 package candied fruit**
**Black raisins**
**White raisins**

**Powdered sugar frosting:**
**3 cups powdered sugar**
**1/3 cup soft butter**
**1 1/2 teaspoons almond flavoring**
**2 tablespoons milk**

OVEN 350°

Scald and cool milk. When milk is lukewarm, dissolve yeast in milk. Mix in sugar, slightly beaten eggs, salt, cardamom, and two cups flour. Melt butter and add to mixture. Mix well. Add remaining flour, but keep dough "sticky." Mix in candied fruit and a good handful each of black and white raisins, packing in as much fruit as the mixture will hold. Knead on floured board until smooth. Put into a greased bowl to raise. (Dough should rise to twice its original size. Due to the fruit, this can take 2 hours or longer.)

After dough is risen, cut dough down with a knife while dough is in bowl, instead of punching or kneading. Let rise again, about 45 minutes. Divide dough into two parts and pound down. Shape into loaves and let rise to about twice its size again. Bread can be baked in bread pans or formed into round loaves and baked on a greased cookie sheet or in a greased pie pan. Bake 30–40 minutes at 350°.

Bread may be frosted with a powdered sugar frosting while bread is still warm.

Frosting: Cream together sugar and butter. Stir in flavoring and add milk, until desired consistency is reached.

## PEACH BREAD

Margo Stevenson, Kankakee, IL

**½ cup butter, room temperature**
**1 cup sugar**
**2 eggs**
**1 teaspoon vanilla**
**1¾ cups flour**
**1 teaspoon baking soda**
**1 teaspoon baking powder**
**½ teaspoon salt**
**¼ cup sour cream**
**1 cup mashed peaches (drained well, if canned)**
**½ cup ground almonds**

OVEN 350°

Preheat oven to 350°. Grease and flour 8½x5½-inch loaf pan. Cream butter and sugar until fluffy. Add eggs, vanilla, peaches, and sour cream; mix well. Add dry ingredients and mix well. Pour into prepared pan and bake 50 minutes, until toothpick inserted in center comes out clean.

## STRAWBERRY BREAD

Marie Honeycutt, Shelby, NC

**3 cups all-purpose flour**
**1 teaspoon salt**
**1 teaspoon baking soda**
**1 tablespoon cinnamon**
**2 cups sugar**
**3 eggs, well beaten**
**1¼ cups oil**
**2 packages frozen strawberries, thawed and drained**
**1¼ cups chopped nuts**
**Red food coloring, if desired**

OVEN 350°

Combine dry ingredients. Make well in center. Pour in eggs and oil. Stir until dry ingredients are moistened. Add berries and nuts. Mix well. In lightly greased 8-inch pans bake at 350° for 60–70 minutes.

Makes 2 loaves.

## FRUIT LOAF

Pauline R. Herr, Minburn, IA

**2 cups sugar**
**1 cup water**
**1 lump butter**
**Vinegar**
**Honey**
**2 cups mixed nuts, chopped fine**
**1 pound dates, chopped fine**
**1 pound coconut, chopped fine**
**½ pound figs, chopped fine**

Boil sugar, water, butter, vinegar, and honey until it threads. Mix well with syrup in large bowl. Turn out on piece board and mix in powdered sugar. Mix well with hands, form into loaf then roll into several long rolls and set away to cool. Cut into thin slices to serve. Keeps well. Can be frozen.

# BREADS

## PINEAPPLE NUT BREAD
Beverly Chadwick, Baldwinsville, NY

**¾ cup sugar**
**2 eggs**
**½ cup margarine or shortening**
**2 cups flour**
**1 teaspoon baking powder**
**1 teaspoon baking soda**
**½ teaspoon nutmeg**
**½ teaspoon salt**
**1 teaspoon vanilla**
**½ cup chopped nuts**
**16-ounce can crushed pineapple, drained**

OVEN 350°

Mix ingredients in order listed. Stir just until moist. Bake in greased loaf pan at 350° for 35–40 minutes. Garnish with a few chopped maraschino cherries.

## CRANBERRY APPLE BREAD
Denise Ryberg, Windom, MN

**2 cups chopped, peeled apples**
**¾ cup sugar**
**2 tablespoons oil**
**1 egg**
**1½ cups flour**
**1½ teaspoons baking powder**
**½ teaspoon baking soda**
**1 teaspoon cinnamon**
**1 cup fresh or frozen cranberries**
**½ cup chopped walnuts**

OVEN 350°

Preheat oven to 350°. Grease a bread loaf pan. Combine apples, sugar, and oil in a medium bowl. Add egg and mix well. Combine dry ingredients in separate bowl. Add apple mixture, mixing just until dry ingredients are moist. Stir in cranberries and walnuts. Spread butter evenly in loaf pan. Bake for 1 hour or until toothpick inserted in center comes out clean.

## NO KNEAD BREAD
Virginia Harger, Ely, MN

**1½ cups scalded milk**
**½ cup shortening**
**½ cup sugar**
**1 teaspoon salt**
**1½ cups water**
**3 packages dry yeast**
**½ teaspoon malt powder**
**3 eggs**
**9 cups flour, separated 4 cups and 5 cups**

OVEN 350°

Mix together scalded milk, shortening, sugar, and salt; cool to lukewarm by adding water. Add dry yeast. Stir. Add malt powder, eggs, and 4 cups flour. Mix on low speed until blended; then mix on high for 3 minutes. Work in 5 more cups flour. Shape into loaves to rise—OR—roll out divided dough ¼ at a time and spread with melted butter, brown sugar, and cinnamon to taste. Roll up and seal with water. Let rise in loaf pans and bake at 350° for 1 hour to 1 hour and 15 minutes.

## BECKY'S LEMON BREAD

Heidi Rhude, Henderson, NV

**Lemon peel and pulp from 1 lemon, chopped finely**
**½ cup shortening**
**1 cup sugar**
**2 eggs (or 4 egg whites)**
**1¼ cups flour**
**1 teaspoon baking powder**
**¼ teaspoon salt**
**½ cup milk**
**1½ cups chopped nuts**

**Glaze:**
**½ cup sugar**
**Lemon juice**

OVEN 350°

Prepare and set aside lemon juice and pulp. In mixing bowl, cream sugar, shortening, and eggs, one at a time. Mix together flour, baking powder, and salt. Add to the egg mixture alternately with milk. When mixture is creamy, add chopped lemon and ½ cup chopped nuts. Spoon into a greased and floured bread loaf pan. Bake at 350° for 1 hour. While bread is baking, make glaze from the lemon juice and sugar. When bread is done prick holes in the top with a fork and pour glaze over bread while it's hot.

## HARDTACK

Sue Westmark, St. Cloud, MN

**1½ cups buttermilk**
**¾ cup oil**
**1 teaspoon baking soda**
**½ cup sugar**
**2 cups quick oatmeal**
**3 cups flour**
**½ teaspoon salt**

OVEN 400°

Mix all ingredients together and let stand for 20 minutes or so. Using about 1 cup mixture at a time, roll out very thin. Prick with a fork or roll with a spiked rolling pin. Cut into roughly 2x4-inch pieces. Put on greased cookie sheet and bake until light brown. Watch closely.

## GERMAN SWEET BREAD

Barbara Jeanloz, Norwalk, CT

**2 cups flour (some can be whole wheat flour)**
**1 cup sugar**
**1 cup milk**
**¼ pound margarine (or butter)**
**1 teaspoon baking powder**
**2 eggs**
**Cinnamon (optional)**

OVEN 350°

Cream together margarine and sugar. Add flour then other ingredients and mix well. Pour into greased bread pan (loaf pan). Bake at 350° for 1 hour. Serve hot or cold.

# BREADS

## GRANDMA'S SWEET BREAD

Deborah LeBrun, Saint Cloud, MN

**1 cup sugar**
**3 cups flour**
**½ cup margarine**
**1 teaspoon baking soda**
**1 teaspoon baking powder**
**½ cup sour cream**
**½ cup half-and-half**
**1 teaspoon vanilla**
**Nutmeg**

OVEN 375°

Cream sugar and margarine. Add sour cream and milk. Add remaining ingredients; mix well. Chill in refrigerator overnight. Roll in a figure eight shape. Bake on ungreased cookie sheet at 375° until light brown.

Makes 3½–4 dozen.

## ROSETTA'S AND LAURA'S PUMPKIN BREAD

Laura Burnette, Dayton, KY

**1½ cups sugar**
**1½ cups flour**
**1 teaspoon baking powder**
**1 teaspoon baking soda**
**1 teaspoon salt**
**¼ teaspoon cinnamon**
**Cloves**
**Nutmeg**
**½ cup salad oil**
**½ cup water**
**2 eggs**
**½ cup chopped nuts**
**1 cup pumpkin**
**1 tablespoon applesauce**

OVEN 350°

Sift dry ingredients together. Beat eggs, stir in oil, water, pumpkin, and applesauce. Add this mixture to dry ingredients, mix thoroughly, add nuts. Bake in greased and floured 9x5x3-inch loaf pan for 1 hour in 350° oven.

## PUMPKIN LOAF

Barbara Howell, New Bern, NC

**3 cups sugar**
**3 eggs**
**3 cups self-rising flour**
**2 cups or 1 can pumpkin**
**1 cup oil**
**1 teaspoon nutmeg**
**1 teaspoon cloves**
**1 teaspoon cinnamon**
**½ teaspoon salt**

OVEN 350°

Blend sugar and oil; add beaten eggs. Add pumpkin then dry ingredients. Grease two loaf pans. Bake at 350° for 1 hour to 1 hour and 15 minutes.

## PUMPKIN ROLL

Debra White Smith, Jacksonville, TX

*"This is a wonderful holiday recipe which impresses the socks off of anybody who sees it! Happy rolling!"*

**Editor's Note:** *The Neighbor* and *Texas Honor* in the Heartsong Presents series were written by Debra. She is a wife and mother who donates the majority of her writing profits to adoption programs. She also loves the time she volunteers for the blind.

**3 eggs**
**1 teaspoon lemon juice**
**⅔ cup pumpkin**
**1 cup sugar**
**¾ cup flour**
**1 teaspoon baking powder**
**2 teaspoons cinnamon**
**1 teaspoon ginger**
**½ teaspoon nutmeg**
**½ teaspoon salt**
**1 cup chopped nuts**

**Filling:**

**1 cup sifted powdered sugar**
**8 ounces cream cheese, softened**
**4 tablespoons butter, softened**
**½ teaspoon vanilla**

OVEN 375°

Beat eggs on high speed. Blend in sugar, pumpkin, and lemon juice. Stir in dry ingredients. Spread on a wax paper-lined cookie sheet. Top with nuts and bake at 375° for 15 minutes. Heavily dust a clean dish towel with powdered sugar, peel off the wax paper from the pumpkin roll, and roll it and the towel up together like a cinnamon roll. Allow to cool for 1–1½ hours. Blend the filling ingredients until smooth. Unroll the towel and roll, spread filling evenly over flat surface. Then re-roll without the towel. Should resemble a jelly roll. The powdered sugar coating makes it very attractive.

## PUMPKIN NUT BREAD

Teresa Hershberger, Virginia Beach, VA

**4 eggs**
**1 cup water**
**3 cups flour**
**1 teaspoon ground cloves**
**½ teaspoon baking powder**
**1 cup chopped pecans**
**1 cup cooked pumpkin**
**3 cups white sugar**
**½ teaspoon salt**
**1 teaspoon cinnamon**
**2 teaspoons baking soda**

OVEN 325°

Mix all ingredients together. Pour into bread pans; bake at 325° for 45 minutes to 1 hour.

# BREADS

## PUMPKIN BREAD

Laurie Gilbertsen, Elk River, MN

**2⅔ cups sugar**
**⅔ cup shortening**
**4 eggs**
**16-ounce can pumpkin (2 cups)**
**⅔ cup water**
**3⅓ cups all-purpose flour**
**2 teaspoons baking soda**
**1½ teaspoons salt**
**½ teaspoon baking powder**
**1 teaspoon cloves**
**1 teaspoon cinnamon**
**⅔ cup coarsely chopped nuts**
**⅔ cup raisins**

OVEN 350°

Preheat oven to 350°. Grease bottoms of two 9x5x3-inch loaf pans, or three small loaf pans. Mix sugar and shortening in large bowl. Mix in eggs, pumpkin, and water. Blend in flour, baking soda, salt, baking powder, cinnamon, and cloves. Stir in nuts and raisins. Pour into pans. Bake about 1 hour and 10 minutes, or until done.

## ZUCCHINI BREAD

Julie E. Giddings, Crossville, TN

**3 eggs**
**2 tablespoons vanilla**
**1 cup salad oil**
**2 cups sugar**
**3 cups shredded zucchini**
**3 cups flour**
**½ tablespoon baking powder**
**1 teaspoon salt**
**1 teaspoon baking soda**
**1 teaspoon cinnamon**

OVEN 350°

Mix well, eggs, vanilla, oil, sugar, and zucchini. Add flour, baking powder, salt, baking soda, and cinnamon. Blend well. Pour into 2 greased loaf pans. Bake at 350° for 1 hour. Done when toothpick in center comes out clean.

## ZUCCHINI BREAD

Mandy Brock, Munsing, MI

**3 eggs**
**2 cups sugar**
**1 cup regular oil**
**2 teaspoons vanilla**
**3 cups flour**
**2 cups grated raw zucchini**
**1 teaspoon salt**
**1 teaspoon baking soda**
**¼ teaspoon baking powder**
**3 teaspoons cinnamon**
**1 cup coarsely chopped walnuts or raisins**

OVEN 350°

Beat eggs until light and fluffy. Add sugar, oil, zucchini, and vanilla. Mix lightly but well. Combine dry ingredients in separate bowl; add to egg and zucchini mixture. Stir until well blended. Stir in nuts or raisins. Pour into 2 greased and floured 9x5-inch bread pans. Bake for 60 minutes or until toothpick inserted in center comes out clean. Cool on racks slightly before removing from pans.

## ZUCCHINI PINEAPPLE BREAD

Cheryl A. Bardaville, St. Louis, MI
Joyce E. Sarver, Columbus, OH

*"I have had bread frozen for up to 3 years and it still tastes great! For a great treat slice frozen bread ½-inch thick and spread with Philadelphia pineapple cream cheese or strawberry cream cheese; great plain as well."*

**3 eggs**
**1 cup oil**
**1–2 cups sugar**
**2 teaspoons vanilla**
**3 cups flour**
**2 teaspoons baking soda**
**1 teaspoon salt**
**¼–½ teaspoon baking powder**
**1½ teaspoons cinnamon**
**¾ teaspoon nutmeg**
**2 cups zucchini, shredded**
**1 cup (8¼ ounce can) crushed pineapple, well drained**
**1 cup raisins or currants**
**1 cup nuts**

OVEN 325°

Do not preheat oven. In a large mixing bowl, beat eggs, oil, sugar, and vanilla until thick. Sift flour, baking soda, salt, baking powder, and spices together and stir into first mixture. Stir in remaining ingredients. Pour into two 5x9 greased and floured loaf pans and bake at 325° for 1 hour, or 45 minutes for small loaf pans, or until toothpick comes out clean. When completely cooled wrap in foil. Keep in refrigerator, or freeze.

Makes 2 loaves.

## ZUCCHINI BREAD WITH PEANUT BUTTER

Rose Richart, Plymouth, FL

**3 eggs**
**2½ cups sugar**
**1 cup oil**
**½ cup peanut butter**
**3 cups flour**
**3 teaspoons cinnamon**
**1 teaspoon salt**
**1 teaspoon baking soda**
**1 teaspoon baking powder**
**3 teaspoons vanilla**
**2 cups grated zucchini**
**1 cup nuts**

OVEN 350°

Combine ingredients. Bake at 350° for 50–60 minutes. Can be baked as bread or as muffins.

## DARK ZUCCHINI BREAD

Ruth Dews, East Canton, OH

**3 eggs**
**1 cup vegetable oil**
**1½ cups sugar**
**2 cups grated zucchini**
**2 teaspoons vanilla**
**2 cups flour**
**¼ teaspoon baking powder**
**3 teaspoons cinnamon**
**1 teaspoon salt**
**2 teaspoons baking soda**
**1 cup chopped nuts**

OVEN 350°

Stir together all ingredients. Pour into small individual pans and bake at 350° for 20–30 minutes.

## LENA'S CORN BREAD

Lena Nelson Dooley, Hurst, TX

**Editor's Note:** Lena is the author of *Home to Her Heart* for Heartsong Presents, but her writing extends to curriculum, scripts, articles, software manuals, international business reports, and much more.

Combine and stir together:

**⅔ cup cornmeal**
**1⅓ cup flour**
**⅓ cup sugar**
**1 teaspoon salt**
**4 teaspoons baking powder**

In mixing bowl, mix together well:

**1 cup milk**
**1 egg**
**¼ cup oil**

OVEN 375°

Stir dry ingredients into liquids. Bake at 375° for about 15 minutes if making muffins. Can also pour into square cake pan and bake about 25 minutes.

## BROCCOLI CORN BREAD

Donna Thompson, Kingsport, TN

**1 box prepared corn bread mix**
**3 eggs, beaten**
**1 onion, diced**
**1 cup cottage cheese**
**10-ounce package taco cheese**
**½ cup butter, melted**
**1 box frozen chopped broccoli**

OVEN 350°

Mix all ingredients together. Put in 9x13-inch pan. Bake at 350° for 45 minutes. Delicious served with soup or salad.

## JALAPENO CORN BREAD

Lois Bentley, Raccoon, KY

**3 cups corn bread mix**
**½ cup vegetable oil**
**1 large onion, grated**
**1½ cups grated cheddar cheese**
**2 cups whole or evaporated milk**
**3 eggs**
**1 cup canned cream style corn**
**½ cup chopped jalapeno peppers (may be omitted)**
**3 ½-ounce jar pimentos, chopped**

OVEN 400°

Preheat oven to 400°. Mix all ingredients well. Pour into greased 9x13-inch pan. Bake until brown, about 45 minutes.

Yield: 24 squares.

## MEXICAN CORN BREAD

Patricia Robertson, Tucson, AZ

**1 cup cornmeal**
**¼ cup sugar**
**1 teaspoon salt**
**1 cup flour**
**1 egg**
**1 cup milk**
**¼ cup vegetable oil**
**1 can cream style corn**
**1 small can diced green chilies**
**½ pound grated longhorn cheese**
**1 cup cottage cheese**

OVEN 450°

Combine dry ingredients, add egg, milk, oil, corn, and cottage cheese. Stir lightly and pour half of batter in well-greased 9x13-inch pan. Layer green chilies and cheese on top of batter. Add rest of batter and bake at 450° for 20–25 minutes.

## SOPAPILLAS (FRY BREAD)

Ricki Lackey, Farmington, NM

**4 cups flour**
**1 teaspoon salt**
**4 teaspoons baking powder**
**2 tablespoons shortening**
**1½ cups water (approximately)**
**Vegetable oil for frying**

Mix flour, salt, and baking powder, work shortening into flour, add enough water to make a soft dough (not sticky). Knead well, let stand 30 minutes. Halve the dough, roll out until ⅛-inch thick. Cut into 3-inch squares or equivalent of 3-inches deep. Fry at 365°. When grease is hot, drop in squares and hold or keep dunking until square puffs up. Fry until golden brown then turn over and fry other side. Serve with honey or shake in cinnamon and sugar until coated. Just great served with pinto beans and Mexican food.

# BREADS

## NAVAJO FRY BREAD
Pauline Teakell, Cuba, NM

**2 cups flour**
**2 teaspoons baking powder**
**½ teaspoon salt**
**½ cup powdered milk**
**½-inch melted lard or shortening**
**Warm water**

Sift together flour, baking powder, and salt. Blend in powdered milk. Add enough warm water to make a soft dough. Knead until dough is not sticky. Cover and let stand for 1 hour. Pinch off a handful of dough and roll into circle ½- to ¼-inch thick. Fry in lard or shortening in heavy skillet. Brown both sides. Should brown quickly. Drain on paper towels.

May be served plain or with honey or roll a hot dog in the circle of dough to cook in the skillet. Recipe may be doubled.

## GRANDMA'S POPOVERS
Rachel Munger, Cheshire, CT
*"This was my husband's mother's recipe. She went to be with the Lord at age 99!"*

**1½ cups flour**
**1½ cups milk**
**¾ teaspoon salt**
**3 eggs**
**6 tablespoons butter, margarine or drippings**

OVEN 450°

Combine ingredients in blender. Mix on high until smooth and creamy. Pour into oven-safe glass custard cups filled ½ full or muffin tins, preheated with about ½ tablespoon butter or margarine, or drippings from roast beef. Bake at 450° for 15 minutes. Reduce heat to 350°, bake until "popped" high and golden brown. May be pricked with fork to let steam escape and returned briefly to oven.

Yield: 12 popovers.

## BLUEBERRY MUFFINS
Sue Ellen Slabach, Sturgis, MI

**2 cups flour**
**3 teaspoons baking powder**
**1 cup milk**
**1 egg, slightly beaten**
**½ cup sugar**
**⅓ cup vegetable oil**
**1 cup blueberries**

OVEN 350°

Mix flour, sugar, and baking powder. In a separate bowl, beat egg; add milk and oil; mix with fork. Make a well in flour mixture and pour in milk and oil mixture. Stir well. Add blueberries. Spoon batter into greased muffin tins or, for easier clean-up, use paper muffin cups. Sprinkle with sugar. Bake at 350° until golden. Serve with butter.

Makes 12 large muffins.

## YEAST BISCUITS

Amy Davis, Smithville, OK

**1 package yeast**
**1 cup hot water (115°)**
**2 tablespoons oil**
**1 tablespoon honey**
**1 teaspoon salt**
**2¼ cups all-purpose flour**

OVEN 350°

Preheat oven to 350°. Dissolve yeast in water. Add all other ingredients. Mix well. Make into biscuits. Let rise until double. Bake 30 minutes.

## BALLOON BISCUITS

Vivian Messenger, Ft. Wayne, IN

*"These are fun to make and even more fun to eat. The kids can help with these too."*

**4 tablespoons butter, melted**
**½ cup sugar**
**¼ cup cinnamon**
**2 packages (10 each) refrigerated biscuits**
**20 large marshmallows**

OVEN 425°

Spray a large baking sheet with nonstick vegetable oil spray. Mix sugar and cinnamon in a small bowl. Roll or pat each biscuit to enclose a marshmallow. Pinch to seal, coat with butter then with sugar. Place seam down on baking sheet. Bake on middle rack of oven at 425° for 8–10 minutes until golden brown. When done the marshmallows will have disappeared, leaving sweet hollow shell.

Variations: Use chunks of banana instead. The bottom will be sticky, chewy, and yummy!

## FAVORITE BISCUITS

Anne Whittemore, Johnson City, TN

**2 cups flour**
**1 tablespoon baking powder**
**½ teaspoon salt (optional)**
**1 tablespoon honey (optional)**
**4 tablespoons margarine**
**1 cup yogurt (plain)**

OVEN 450°

Combine dry ingredients. Mix. Cut up margarine. Use fork to chop and combine thoroughly. Add yogurt. Knead and pat out on floured bread board. Cut, bake in 450° oven for 10 minutes.

# BREADS

## RICH MUFFINS

Sally Gordin, Modesto, CA

**2 cups flour**
**½ cup sugar**
**1 tablespoon baking powder**
**½ teaspoon salt**
**2 eggs, beaten**
**½ cup oil**
**½ cup milk**

OVEN 400°

Sift flour with sugar, baking powder, and salt into a mixing bowl. Combine eggs, oil, and milk in separate bowl. Make a well in center of dry ingredients. Add liquids, all at once. Mix only until dry ingredients are moist. Fill well-greased muffin tins ⅔ full. Bake at 400° for 15–20 minutes or until golden brown.

Makes 12.

## CORN MUFFINS

Hettie Powers, Fort Mills, SC

**1½ cups yellow cornmeal**
**½ cup all-purpose flour**
**2 tablespoons granulated sugar**
**2 teaspoons baking powder**
**½ teaspoon baking soda**
**½ teaspoon salt**
**1¼ cups buttermilk**
**¼ cup unsweetened applesauce**
**2 egg whites**
**2 tablespoons vegetable oil**

OVEN 400°

In large bowl combine first six ingredients. Combine applesauce, milk, egg whites, and oil. Stir into dry ingredients just to moisten well. Fill greased or "PAMmed" muffin cups ⅔ full. Bake at 400° for 18–20 minutes. Cool in pan 8–10 minutes.

## WHOLE WHEAT BANANA MUFFINS

Cynthia McClimans, Jamestown, NY

**3 extra-ripe bananas**
**⅓ cup oil**
**½ cup honey**
**2 eggs, beaten**
**1¾ cups whole wheat flour**
**½ teaspoon salt**
**1 teaspoon baking soda**
**¼ cup hot water**
**½ cup nuts or raisins, or both (optional)**

OVEN 350°

Beat oil, honey, bananas, and eggs; add water. Mix in dry ingredients. Bake at 350° 20 minutes in muffin tins. Use cupcake liners to avoid extra clean-up!

## APPLESAUCE MUFFINS

Carolyn Anne Taylor, Gaffney, SC

**4 cups plain flour**
**2 cups sugar**
**1 cup margarine, softened**
**2 teaspoons baking soda**
**2 cups applesauce**
**3 teaspoons cinnamon**
**1 teaspoon ground cloves**
**2 teaspoons allspice**
**2 eggs**
**1 teaspoon vanilla**

OVEN 375°

Mix softened margarine with eggs. Add applesauce and dry ingredients to this. Bake at 375° until brown, 10–15 minutes. Can keep batter in refrigerator 2 weeks.

Makes 4–5 dozen.

Variation:
Nuts and raisins can be added just before baking.

## AEBLESKIVER (DANISH APPLE PANCAKE MUFFINS)

Melinda Krise, Anchorage, AK

**2 eggs, separated**
**2 cups milk**
**2 teaspoons baking powder**
**¼ cup melted butter**
**2 tablespoons sugar**
**2 cups all-purpose flour**
**¼ teaspoon salt**
**1 apple, diced**

Beat egg yolks. Add sugar and milk. Sift together flour, baking powder, and salt. Add dry ingredients. Stir in melted butter. Fold stiffly-beaten egg whites into batter leaving it lumpy. Don't stir batter after adding egg whites. Heat monk's pan, or a heavy duty muffin pan with deep wells, with 1 teaspoon butter in each muffin cup. When butter is bubbling add batter. When outside of the batter is crusty add a cube of apple; use something sharp to flip each aebleskiver. When brown on both sides. Serve with butter and syrup.

## PUMPKIN MUFFINS

Mrs. Joseph Dulek, Rock Island, IL

**1¼ cups sugar**
**1¼ cups pumpkin**
**½ cup melted margarine**
**2 eggs**
**1½ cups flour**
**2 teaspoons baking powder**
**1 teaspoon cinnamon**
**¼ teaspoon ground nutmeg**
**¼ teaspoon salt**
**1 cup milk**
**½ cup raisins**
**¼ cup chopped pecans or walnuts**

OVEN 400°

Combine sugar, pumpkin, and margarine. Blend in the eggs. Combine dry ingredients and add alternately with milk, mixing well after each addition. Stir in raisins and nuts. Spoon into well-greased miniature muffin cups. Pour filling ⅔ full. Sprinkle with combined 2 tablespoons sugar and ¼ teaspoon cinnamon. Bake for 25 minutes.

Makes approximately 5 dozen.

# BREADS

## SWEET BLUEBERRY MUFFINS

Louise Rochon, Mountain Top, PA
*"Easy, quick, fluffiest muffins I ever had!"*

**1½ cups flour**
**½ cup sugar**
**2 teaspoons baking powder**
**½ teaspoon salt**
**¼ cup vegetable oil**
**1 egg**
**½ cup milk**
**¾ cup blueberries**

OVEN 400°

With electric mixer, mix all ingredients thoroughly. Stir in berries last. Bake in greased muffin tins at 400° for 25 minutes.

## BANANA-CHOCOLATE CHIP MUFFINS

Kimberly Day, Lynchburg, VA

**⅔ cup sugar**
**1 tablespoon baking powder**
**½ teaspoon salt**
**2 cups flour**
**⅓ cup butter, melted**
**1 egg, beaten**
**1 cup milk**
**2 or 3 three bananas, chopped**
**1 cup mini-chocolate chips**

OVEN 375°

Sift together the first 4 ingredients (dry ingredients). Stir in butter, egg, and milk until blended. Fold in bananas and chocolate chips. Spoon into greased or paper-lined muffin tins. Bake at 375° for 15–20 minutes.

Yield: 1–1½ dozen.

## CHERRY CHOCOLATE CHIP MUFFINS

Adwina Jarvis, Wautoma, WI
*"These freeze well. Will keep for 2 months in freezer. I take them out as I need them."*

**2 cups flour**
**½ cup sugar**
**1 teaspoon baking soda**
**½ teaspoon cinnamon**
**¾ cup vegetable oil**
**2 eggs**
**2 teaspoons vanilla**
**20-ounce can cherry pie filling**
**½ cup milk chocolate chips**
**⅓ cup nuts**

OVEN 350°

Combine all ingredients, fill cupcakes a little over half full. Bake at 350° for 30 minutes.

Makes about 20 cupcakes.

## CORNMEAL ROLLS

Eileen Kessinger, Beckley, WV

**1/3 cup cornmeal**
**1/4 cup sugar**
**1/2 teaspoon salt**
**2 cups milk**
**1/3 cup water**
**1 package dry yeast**
**1/2 cup butter or margarine**
**2 eggs, beaten**
**4 cups flour**

OVEN 350°

Mix meal, salt, sugar, and milk. Cook until slightly thick. Remove from heat, add butter or margarine and cool. Dissolve yeast in warm water. Add to mixture. Add eggs and flour a little at a time. Turn out onto floured board and knead. Let rise until double. Pan to preference. Bake at 350° about 15 minutes until golden brown. Dip in butter.

## STONEGROUND CORNMEAL ROLLS

Christi Hawkins, Red Oak, TX

**1/3 cup stoneground cornmeal**
**1/2 cup sugar**
**2 teaspoons salt**
**1/2 cup shortening**
**2 cups milk**
**1 package active dry yeast**
**1/4 cup warm water**
**2 eggs, beaten**
**4 cups flour**
**Melted butter**

OVEN 375°

Cook cornmeal, sugar, salt, shortening, and milk in medium saucepan until as thick as cooked cereal. Cool to lukewarm. Add yeast dissolved in lukewarm water, then eggs. Beat. Add flour to form dough. Knead. Place in covered bowl and let rise 1 hour. Punch down. Knead. Roll and cut out biscuits. Sprinkle butter and cornmeal on top. Bake at 375° for 15 minutes.

## FEATHER ROLLS

Debbie Graber, Eureka, NE

**1 1/2 cups warm water**
**1/4 cup sugar**
**1/2 cup mashed potatoes (hot)**
**1/3 cup oil**
**1 teaspoon salt**
**1 tablespoon instant yeast**
**4 1/2–5 cups bread flour**

OVEN 350°

In a large bowl mix water, sugar, potatoes, oil, salt, yeast, and 2 cups of flour. Add remaining flour and stir by hand. Dough should be a little bit sticky. Cover and put in refrigerator overnight. Three hours before serving, take out of the refrigerator with oiled hands, form into 20–24 small rolls. Place on greased cookie sheet. Let rise until doubled. Bake at 350° until golden, 15–20 minutes. Do not overbake. Brush tops with margarine when out of the oven. These are very fluffy and light rolls.

# BREADS

## PERFECT SUNDAY DINNER ROLLS

Geneva Lee, Overland Park, KS

**1 package dry yeast, dissolved in ¼ cup warm water**
**2 eggs**
**4 cups flour**
**½ cup sugar**
**1 cup warm water**
**½ cup oil**
**1 teaspoon salt**

OVEN 375°

Add sugar to yeast and water. Beat eggs in warm water; add oil and salt. Add to yeast and sugar mixture. Gradually add flour. This will be a sticky dough and will rise at least twice its size, so use a large bowl. Let stand overnight and make out dough in the morning by dividing in 4 parts. Roll each part one at a time onto floured surface to make a circle. Cut like a pizza and roll from large end to small. Place on greased pan, let stand until you return home from church. Bake at 375° for 8 minutes.

## NO KNEAD REFRIGERATOR ROLLS

Leann Termin, Strafford, MD

**2 packages active dry yeast**
**2 cups warm water (110°–115°)**
**½ cup sugar**
**2 teaspoons salt**
**6½–7 cups flour**
**1 egg**
**¼ cup soft shortening or oil**

OVEN 400°

Dissolve yeast in water. Add sugar, salt, and half of flour to yeast. Beat eggs with shortening and remaining flour until smooth. Cover and place in refrigerator at least 2 hours. Two hours before baking cut off amount needed and return to rest. Shape into rolls and place on greased baking sheet. Rise 1½–2 hours. Heat oven to 400°. Bake 12–15 minutes. Dough will keep in refrigerator for 5 days.

## CHEESE SCONES

Eleanor Ness, Alberta, Canada

**3 cups flour**
**5 teaspoons baking powder**
**¼ teaspoon salt**
**4 teaspoons sugar**
**½ cup butter**
**Grated cheddar cheese (approximately 1½ cups)**
**1¾ cups milk**

OVEN 425°

Preheat oven to 425°. Blend butter into dry ingredients, add cheese and stir into dry ingredients with fork. Add milk. Scoop onto baking sheet with greased ice cream scoop. Bake approximately 15 minutes.

## SCONES

Gail Gaymer Martin, Lathrup Village, MI

**Editor's Note:** Scones were a treat for the heroine in Gail's first book that was titled *Seasons* and released by Heartsong Presents. Gail is a retired teacher and well-known for her numerous articles.

**1½ teaspoons baking powder**
**1½ teaspoons salt**
**½ teaspoon ground ginger**
**2 cups all-purpose flour (plus extra for dusting)**
**½ cup granulated sugar**
**¾ cup unsalted butter, cut into small pieces**
**1 cup sultanas (golden raisins) or any dried fruit, such as cherries, cranberries, or diced apricot**
**2 large eggs**
**3–4 teaspoons milk**

Sift dry ingredients in bowl and stir in sugar. Rub in butter until the mixture is like fine bread crumbs. Stir in the dried fruit.

These are to be cooked on a black iron griddle, heavy frying pan, or electric frying pan.

Beat the eggs and add them. Stir in just enough milk to make a firm but sticky dough. Turn the dough onto a floured board, sprinkle with flour, and roll it to ½-inch thickness. Cut into rounds. Re-roll the trimmings and cut more rounds. Brush heavy frying pan with oil and heat over medium heat. Frying scones for about 5 minutes on each side until they are well browned. Serve warm with butter or preserves. Also good plain. You may store and eat them cold as well.

## CARAMEL ROLLS

Penny Hoots, Good Rich, ND

*"My family begs for this treat. It's a treat for me also because it's so easy and so yummy. I've given this recipe out to whomever I serve it!"*

**4 cans refrigerator biscuits**
**½ cup ice cream**
**½ cup white sugar**
**½ cup brown sugar**
**½ cup margarine**

OVEN 350°

Cut biscuits in half and roll in cinnamon and sugar. Put in 9x13-inch pan sprayed with cooking spray, mix rest of ingredients in microwave until melted, mix until smooth. Pour over biscuits and bake at 350° for 25–30 minutes or until brown. Invert on large pan and enjoy!

# BREADS

## QUICK MIX CINNAMON ROLLS

Christine Mason, Garner, NC

**2¼ cups prepared baking mix**
**⅔ cup milk**
**2 teaspoons cinnamon**
**1 cup sugar**

OVEN 450°

Heat oven to 450°. Stir ingredients until soft dough forms. Turn onto surface dusted with baking mix. Knead 10 times. Roll dough ½-inch thick. Butter surface entirely. Sprinkle cinnamon and sugar mixture onto buttered dough. Starting with dough closest to you, roll into long tube. Seal with water. Cut into 1 dozen rolls. Bake 10 minutes on ungreased cookie sheet.

## EASY CINNAMON ROLLS

Margaret Tackett, Fayetteville, AR

*"These are very easy to make. Every time I make them they disappear in no time. People always request these when we have dinner at church and at the family reunions."*

**1 package yellow cake mix**
**5 cups flour**
**2½ cups warm water**
**3 packages yeast**

OVEN 350°

Mix cake mix and flour in large bowl. Add yeast to warm water and add to flour mixture. Mix well. Place in large greased bowl and let rise until doubled. Punch down and divide in half. Roll out on floured board in rectangle shape to ¼-inch thickness. Brush with melted butter then sprinkle on sugar and cinnamon. (Optional: add chopped nuts and coconut.) Roll up and seal, cut into 1-inch rolls. Put on ungreased cookie sheet or baking dish. Cover and let rise again until double and bake in 350° oven for approximately 15–20 minutes. Let cool slightly and frost with icing.

**Icing:**

**1 pound powdered sugar**
**Milk**
**½ teaspoon vanilla**

Mix powdered sugar with small amount of milk, just to make spreadable. Add approximately ½ teaspoon vanilla. Spread on top of rolls while still warm.

## MAYONNAISE ROLLS

Eileen Heatwole, Stuarts Draft, VA

**2 cups self-rising flour**
**1 cup milk**
**4 tablespoons mayonnaise**

OVEN 400°

Stir all together, fill muffin pans about ¾ full and bake at 400° for 20 minutes.

Makes 1 dozen.

Variation: Add garlic and cheese to mix or herbs. Makes a quick easy bread.

## HOLIDAY BUNS

Dorothy A. Lewis, El Paso, TX

**4 cups warm water**
**1 cup sugar**
**1 package yeast**
**1 egg**
**3 teaspoons salt**
**1 cup oil**
**10 cups flour**

OVEN 350°

Combine water, sugar, and yeast. Let stand 10 minutes, covered. Mix in remaining ingredients and let rise until double. Put in baking pans, for round rolls. Bake at 350° for 20 minutes.

Variation: For raisin bread, add 1 cup raisins and 2 teaspoons cinnamon.

## PINEAPPLE SWEET ROLLS

Clarice Watts, Lamar, MO

**1 package yeast**
**2 tablespoons warm water**
**1 cup milk**
**½ cup sugar**
**1½ teaspoons salt**
**¼ cup shortening**
**1 egg, beaten**
**3½ cups flour**

**Filling:**

**1 can crushed pineapple**
**½ cup brown sugar**
**¼ teaspoon cinnamon**
**4 teaspoons cornstarch**
**1 tablespoon butter**
**1 cup toasted, grated coconut**

OVEN 350°

Dissolve yeast in warm water. Heat milk to a boil. Remove from heat. Add sugar, salt, and shortening, stirring well. Let cool. Add dissolved yeast, beaten eggs, and flour, beating well. Knead dough lightly. Let rise in warm place for an hour. Roll out into rectangle. Spread with pineapple filling.

Filling: Combine pineapple, brown sugar, cinnamon, and cornstarch; heat until thick and clear. Remove from heat and add butter and coconut. Let filling cool before spreading over dough. After filling is spread over dough, roll up. Slice; place slices in greased pan. Let rise for one hour. Bake at 350° for 20 minutes.

Makes 18–20 rolls.

# APPETIZERS

# APPETIZERS

## CHICKEN FINGERS

Barbara Leslie, Newborn, GA

**3 cups cornflakes**
**½ teaspoon poultry seasoning**
**¼ teaspoon ground black pepper**
**3 tablespoons fat-free egg substitute**
**3 tablespoons skim milk**
**1 pound boneless skinless chicken breasts**
**Non-stick cooking spray**

OVEN 400°

Place cornflakes in food processor and process into crumbs. Combine cornflake crumbs, poultry seasoning, and pepper. Stir to mix well; set aside. Combine egg substitute and skim milk in dish. Mix well and set aside. Cut chicken breast into strips. Dip in egg mixture first and then in cornflake mixture. Coat large baking sheet with non-stick cooking spray. Spray strips lightly with cooking spray. Bake at 400° for 15 minutes.

## BARBECUE BEEF CUPS

Retta Burch, Silver Springs, FL

**¾ cup chopped beef**
**½ cup barbecue sauce**
**1 can refrigerator biscuits (10 count)**
**¼ cup shredded cheddar cheese**
**1 teaspoon onion flakes or fresh onions**

OVEN 400°

In a large skillet, brown beef; drain excess grease. Add onion flakes and sauce. Separate biscuits and place in ungreased cups of muffin pan. Press each biscuit in middle to form a cup. Spoon a drop of sauce beef mixture into each biscuit cup and top with cheese. Bake in 400° oven for 8–10 minutes.

Makes 8–10 servings.

## DEVILED EGGS

Laureen Springer, Oklahoma City, OK

**14 hard-cooked eggs**
**¾ cup low-fat or fat-free mayonnaise or salad dressing**
**4 packets sugar substitute sweetener**
**½ teaspoon vinegar**
**½ teaspoon mustard**
**¼ teaspoon salt**
**Paprika**

When eggs are cool, cut in half lengthwise. Mix yolks with all other ingredients except paprika. Fill egg whites with mixture. Sprinkle yolk filling with paprika.

## BOLOGNA SANDWICH SPREAD

Tracie Peterson, Topeka, KS

*"We like this recipe because it is fast, easy, and cool for those busy, warm days of summer."*

**Editor's Note:** Tracie has been voted favorite Heartsong Presents author for three years in a row. She has written over thirty books, including some under the pen name of Janelle Jamison.

**1 pound bologna (or ham)**
**2 hard-cooked eggs**
**½ cup pickle relish**
**½ cup mayonnaise or salad dressing**
**2 teaspoons mustard**
**½ cup Colby cheese (optional)**

Grind together the bologna, eggs, and cheese. When everything is finely ground, mix in the relish, salad dressing, and mustard. Serve chilled on your favorite bread.

## PIZZA PINWHEELS

Joanna Cann, Midway, GA

**2 10-ounce packages refrigerator pizza dough**
**½ cup bottled pizza sauce**
**2 ounces shredded mozzarella cheese (about ½ cup)**
**4 cherry tomatoes, halved**
**1 egg yolk**

OVEN 425°

Preheat oven to 425°. Lightly oil 1 or 2 baking sheets. On lightly floured surface, unroll each package of dough, forming two squares. Cut each square into 4 smaller squares; transfer to baking sheets. Spread pizza sauce evenly over squares to within ½-inch of sheet's edges. Starting from corners of squares, cut toward middle of dough; stop ½-inch from center. Fold every other point into center; press to secure. Over each pinwheel center sprinkle 1 tablespoon cheese and top with tomato half. Combine egg yolk with 1 tablespoon water; brush over dough. Bake 12–15 minute, until crust is golden and cheese bubbles.

## TEQUITAS

Gerry Lowrance, Belen, NM

**3–6 pounds extra lean ground beef**
**1 package Shillings Chil-O Mix**
**1 package Williams chili mix**
**8 ounces Velveeta cheese**
**1 family size can tomato sauce**
**Approximately 12 dozen corn toruntilas (depends how much meat is in each tequita)**

Brown ground beef. Add chili mixes and tomato sauce. Simmer 20–30 minutes. Add chunks of cheese; stir until melted. Turn off heat. Heat toruntilas by placing them (one or two at a time) in hot vegetable oil, turn, and remove immediately; drain on paper towels. Roll meat mixture in toruntila and fasten with toothpick. Store in freezer until ready to cook; then drop frozen tequitas in deep oil and cook until crispy. Serve with a side of taco sauce or salsa to dip tequitas in.

# APPETIZERS

## WHITE TORUNTILA ROLL

Nadine Guin, Wharton, TX

**4 white flour toruntilas, burrito size**
**8 ounces cream cheese, softened**
**4-ounce can mild chopped green chilies**
**Very thinly sliced ham, turkey, or other meat, chopped very fine to resemble deviled meat consistency**
**Picante sauce or pimiento to your taste**

Mix cream cheese, chilies, chopped meat, picante, and/or pimiento well. Spread the filling to about ½-inch of edge of toruntilas. Roll the toruntila and wrap in plastic wrap. Chill well. Slice in ½-inch slices and serve. (Best when chilled overnight).

## MEXICAN HORS D'OEUVRES

Susan Cowan, Noblesville, IN

**8 ounces cream cheese, softened**
**1 ripe avocado, mashed**
**1 tablespoon lemon juice**
**2 tablespoons mayonnaise**
**½ cup sour cream**

**Topping suggestions:**
**Finely chopped green onions**
**Shredded lettuce**
**Chopped tomatoes**
**Sliced green olives**
**Shredded cheddar cheese**

Mix together until smooth. Spread on large plate or tray; chill. Layer on topping suggestions, all or some. Sprinkle with chili powder. Serve with toruntila chips.

## STUFFED MUSHROOMS

Dorothy Traer, Oxford, AL

**1 pound fresh mushrooms, washed, stems removed**
**½ cup butter, melted**
**¾ cup of Italian-style bread crumbs**
**¼ cup grated Parmesan cheese**
**4 ounces shredded mozzarella cheese**

OVEN 375°

Combine butter, bread crumbs, and parmesan cheese with fork. Stuff each mushroom cap with bread crumb mixture until all is used. Top each cap with mozzarella cheese. Arrange caps on lightly greased baking sheet and bake at 375° until mozzarella is melted and golden. Serve hot.

## STUFFED MUSHROOMS

Esther L. Covey, Ridgecrest, CA

**1 can crabmeat**
**8-ounce box large mushrooms**
**½ cup butter**
**1½ cups bread crumbs**
**1 lemon**

OVEN 350°

Clean mushrooms. Chop stems into small pieces, sauté mushrooms in melted butter in saucepan with crabmeat until tender. Remove pan from heat, add bread crumbs. Fill mushroom caps with mixture. Bake at 350° for 10 minutes. Sprinkle with juice of lemon.

## RYE HORS D'OEUVRES

Mary Finlayson, Greenville, FL

**1 pound sausage**
**1 pound ground beef**
**1 pound processed cheese, melted**
**1 tablespoon oregano**
**½ teaspoon garlic salt**
**½ teaspoon Worcestershire sauce**
**2 packages party-style rye bread**

Brown meats and drain on paper towel. Mix all ingredients together. Spread rye bread slices on cookie sheets. Spread meat mixture on bread and broil until the meat mixture is bubbly. Freezes well.

## SALMON PUFFS

Miriam Clark, Savannah, GA

**1 small onion, chopped**
**1 can salmon, deboned**
**1 can cream of chicken soup**
**1 egg**
**¾ cup self-rising cornmeal**
**¾ cup self-rising flour**
**Black pepper to taste**

Mix all ingredients well. Drop by teaspoonfuls into frying pan with 350° oil. Brown on both sides of puffs. Remove from frying pan and place on a platter, padded with paper towels, to drain.

Serves a large number.

# APPETIZERS

## PARTY HAM ROLLS

Penny Combs, Castlewood, VA

**1 package prepared biscuits**
**½ cup margarine**
**½ tablespoon poppy seed**
**½ teaspoon Worcestershire sauce**
**½ tablespoon mustard**
**1 tablespoon onion flakes, or minced**
**Baked and sliced ham**
**Swiss or mozzarella cheese**

OVEN 350°

Melt margarine; add poppy seed, Worcestershire sauce, mustard, and onion. Pour over biscuits and let set overnight. Bake 15–20 minutes at 350°, or until cheese melts.

## MINI-HAM PUFFS

Tracey Ellis, Charlotte, NC

**2½-ounce package processed ham**
**1 small onion**
**½ cup shredded Swiss cheese**
**1 egg**
**⅛ teaspoon ground black pepper**
**1½ teaspoon Dijon mustard**
**8-ounce refrigerated crescent rolls**

OVEN 350°

Preheat oven to 350°. Chop ham and onion finely. Place in bowl and stir in cheese, egg, pepper, and mustard. Spray mini-muffin pan with vegetable oil spray. Unroll crescent rolls and press dough into one large rectangle. Cut rectangle into 2 pieces. Place dough pieces in muffin pan cups. Use small scoop when filling cups. Bake for 15 minutes, or until lightly browned.

Makes 24 appetizers.

Variation: Mini-Ham Squares. Spread the crescent roll dough on a 13-inch baking stone, pinching seams to seal. Spread ham mixture on crust and bake at 350° for 20 minutes. Cut into small squares to serve.

## HAM-IT-UP CRESCENT SNACKS

Mary Wyatt, Walker, LA

**8-ounce can crescent dinner rolls**
**4 4x7-slices or 8 3¾x3¾-slices ham**
**4 teaspoons prepared mustard**
**4 ounces (1 cup) shredded Swiss or cheddar cheese**
**2 tablespoons sesame seed**

OVEN 375°

Heat oven to 375°. Unroll dough into rectangles. Firmly press diagonal slices with mustard. Sprinkle with cheese. Start at short side and roll up each rectangle, press edges to seal, coat rolls with seeds. Cut each of the 4 rolls into 5 pieces. Bake 15–20 minutes.

## SUGAR DOGS

Beth Kissell, Cheyenne, WY

*"This is an excellent appetizer to make. It's easy and inexpensive. These are wonderful."*

**3 packages hot dogs, cut in thirds**
**1 pound bacon, each piece cut in half**
**2-pound bag brown sugar**

Wrap piece of hot dog in bacon strip. Secure with a toothpick. Put hot dogs in Crock-Pot. Pour bag of sugar over top. Cook on low until sugar melts. Serve hot.

## MAPLEY APPETIZERS

Dorothy Bradt, Flint, MI

**13½-ounce can pineapple chunks, drained, reserve juice**
**16 ounces smoked sausage links**
**4 teaspoons cornstarch**
**½ teaspoon salt**
**½ cup maple syrup**
**⅓ cup water**
**⅓ cup vinegar**
**1 large green pepper, cut into small squares**
**1 jar maraschino cherries, drained**

OVEN 250°

Cut sausage into small pieces and brown in skillet. Blend cornstarch, salt, pineapple juice, maple syrup, water, and vinegar. Heat to boiling, stir constantly. Add pineapple, sausage, green pepper, and cherries. Cook 5 minutes. Keep warm for serving.

## HOLIDAY CRACKERS (OYSTER SNACK CRACKERS)

Belinda Hogue, Grand Prairie, TX
Jan Nash, Louisville, KY

**16 ounces plain oyster crackers**
**1 package ranch dressing dry mix**
**¼–½ teaspoon lemon pepper seasoning**
**½–1 teaspoon dill weed**
**¼–½ teaspoon garlic powder**
**¾–1 cup salad oil or olive oil**

Combine ranch dressing mix and oil; add dill weed, garlic powder, and lemon pepper. Pour over crackers, stir well to coat. Place in warm oven for 20 minutes. Stir well halfway through. Place in airtight container. Great with soups or just to eat as a snack!

# APPETIZERS

## SALMON PARTY BALL
Clarinda Biggs, Steelville, MO

**16-ounce can salmon**
**8 ounces cream cheese, softened**
**1 tablespoon lemon juice**
**2 teaspoons grated onion**
**1 teaspoon prepared horseradish**
**¼ teaspoon salt**
**¼ teaspoon liquid smoke**
**½ cup chopped pecans**
**3 tablespoons snipped parsley**
**Assorted crackers**

Drain and flake salmon, removing bones and skin. Combine salmon, cheese, lemon juice, onion, horseradish, salt, and liquid smoke; mix. Chill several hours. Combine pecans and parsley. Shape salmon mixture into a ball; roll salmon ball in nut mixture. Chill. Serve with assorted crackers. Trim plate with cherry tomatoes and parsley, if desired.

Makes 3 cups of spread.

## CHEDDAR CHEESE CRACKERS
Essie Denton, Sikeston, MO

**3 tablespoons toasted sesame seed**
**¼ teaspoon cayenne or red pepper**
**½ cup margarine, softened**
**1 cup all-purpose flour**
**½ teaspoon dry mustard**
**½ pound shredded cheddar cheese (2 cups)**

OVEN 350°

Preheat oven to 350°. Toast sesame seed in a skillet over low heat. Combine flour, pepper, mustard, margarine, and cheese; work with hands or spoon into a stiff dough. Roll into small balls, about 1 tablespoon. Dip balls into sesame seed. Place on ungreased cookie sheet. Press flat with glass dipped in flour. Bake until light golden brown.

## CHEESE BALL
Laurie Whitstine, Rayville, LA

**2 8-ounce packages cream cheese, softened**
**1 bunch green onions, chop (about 4)**
**1 small can chopped black olives**
**1 small can prepared ham, crumbled with broth**
**1 cup chopped pecans**
**10-ounce package medium cheddar cheese, shredded**

Mix cheese in medium-sized bowl with chopped onions, black olives, and crumbled ham. Add about ½ of the chopped pecans and shredded cheese. Mix all ingredients together. Shape into 2 balls. Pour remainder of pecans and cheese on a plate and roll the balls in it until they are covered. Chill and serve with crackers of your choice.

## APRICOT CHEESE BALL

Pam Fisher, Pittsburgh, PA

**8 ounces cream cheese, softened**
**1/3 cup apricot preserves**
**1–2 tablespoons chopped chives**
**2 teaspoons minced dried onions**
**Dash parsley**
**Chopped walnuts**

Combine ingredients, except for nuts. Roll cheese ball in nuts.

## CHEESE BALL

Ester M. Jones, Wilsonville, AL

**2 8-ounce cream cheese, softened**
**1 cup butter**
**4 cups grated cheese**
**2 packages ranch salad dressing (dry)**
**Nuts**

Mix all together; shape into balls. Roll in nuts.

## HAWAIIAN CHEESE BALL

Rebecca Germany, Scio, OH

**Editor's Note:** Managing editor for the Heartsong Presents series and author of two novellas.

**2 8-ounce cream cheese, room temperature**
**½ cup cheddar cheese**
**1 teaspoon seasoned salt**
**2 tablespoons onion, finely chopped**
**2 tablespoons green pepper, finely chopped**
**8-ounce can crushed pineapple, well drained**
**½ cup pecans, chopped**

Blend all ingredients, except pecans. Shape into balls. Roll balls in pecans. Serve with assorted crackers.

## CHEESE BALL

Lucy Atkins, Union, WV

**8 ounces cream cheese, softened**
**1 tablespoon milk**
**2 teaspoons Worcestershire sauce**
**½ medium onion**
**1 tablespoon margarine**
**½ teaspoon garlic salt**
**Dash salt and pepper**
**½ pound grated sharp cheddar cheese**
**Pecans, chopped (optional)**
**Parsley (optional)**

Mix all ingredients together and shape into a ball. Roll in chopped pecans or parsley.

# APPETIZERS

## PARTY MIX

Debra Graber, Loogootee, IN

*"You can use this mix for a big crowd or put it in baggies for your family to eat individually. You can also freeze either way so that it lasts longer and stays fresh."*

**1 bag Cheetos Crunchy Cornies**
**1 box Cheeze-Its crackers**
**1 bag pretzel sticks**
**1 bag corn chips**
**1 box fish crackers**
**1 can cocktail peanuts**
**1½ cups melted butter**
**4 tablespoons Worcestershire sauce**
**1 tablespoon Accent seasoning**
**1 tablespoon seasoned salt**
**½ teaspoon celery salt**

OVEN 200°

Mix all ingredients together. In a small pan add butter, Worcestershire sauce, Accent, seasoned salt, and celery salt. Mix well. Spread into single layer on cookie sheets. Bake at 200° for 2 hours. Stir every 20 minutes while baking.

## HOT SPINACH BALLS

Marianne Krivacek, Cleveland, OH

*"These appetizers are always a hit."*

Catherine M. Switzer, Arnold, PA

**4 large eggs, beaten**
**2 10-ounce packages frozen chopped spinach (squeeze dry)**
**1 cup onion, minced**
**¾ cup grated Parmesan or Romano cheese**
**¾ cup butter or margarine, melted**
**½ teaspoon thyme**
**¼ teaspoon nutmeg**
**¼ teaspoon pepper**
**½ teaspoon garlic salt**
**2½ cups herb-seasoned stuffing mix (crumb type)**

OVEN 350°

Stir all ingredients, except stuffing, until well blended. Add stuffing mix. Let stand 20 minutes until slightly firm. Shape into balls using a rounded teaspoon for each ball. Arrange on ungreased cookie sheet. Bake at 350° for 20 minutes, until lightly brown.

Balls may be cooled, wrapped, and frozen. Reheat on cookie sheet at 350° for approximately 10 minutes.

Makes approximately 112 balls.

## EASY SALSA

Debbie Graber, Eureka, NE

**2 14- or 16-ounce cans diced tomatoes**
**4-ounce can diced green chilies**
**1 teaspoon cumin**
**1 teaspoon seasoned salt**
**½ teaspoon garlic powder**
**½ teaspoon lemon or lime juice**
**½ green bell pepper**
**½ onion**
**½ jalapeno pepper**
**Few sprigs fresh cilantro**

Place all ingredients in blender and process quickly until vegetables are chopped. Refrigerate for 2 hours to blend flavors. Serve with toruntila chips.

## GRANOLA

Kristen Kellett, Yakima, WA

**6 cups oats**
**2 cups whole wheat flour**
**1 teaspoon salt**
**2 teaspoons cinnamon**
**½ cup sunflower, pumpkin, or sesame seeds**
**1 cup ground nuts (optional)**
**1 teaspoon maple flavor**
**1 tablespoon vanilla flavor**
**1 teaspoon almond flavor**
**1–1½ cups fruit juice**
**¾ cup ripe bananas, blended**
**½ cup dried fruit (optional)**

OVEN 170°

Combine dry ingredients. Combine liquids, then add to dry ingredients. Mix with hands until evenly moistened and crumbly/chunky. Spread in single layer on cookie sheet. Bake at 170° overnight (8 hours). Add fruit last ½ hour.

Makes 13 cups.

## SALSA

Sally Stoller, Paulding, OH

**12 cups tomatoes, peeled and chopped**
**4 large green peppers**
**2 jalapeno peppers**
**5 medium yellow onions**
**2 bunches green onions**
**2 tablespoons onion salt**
**2 (10- or 12-ounce) cans tomato paste**
**1 tablespoon salt**
**2 tablespoons garlic salt**
**4 tablespoons lemon juice**
**⅓ cup brown sugar**
**1½ cups vinegar**
**3 tablespoons black pepper**

Chop fine, put in large kettle. Boil 20 minutes at medium heat. Pour into hot jars.

Makes 9–12 pints.

## TACO DIP

Kim Mace, Kotzebue, AK

**8 ounces cream cheese, softened**
**1 pound hamburger, browned, drained**
**1 cup salsa sauce**
**1 can refried beans**
**1 cup shredded cheddar cheese**
**Sliced olives**

OVEN 350°

Spread cream cheese in bottom of 9-inch pie pan. Mix browned hamburger with salsa and put on top of cream cheese. Spread beans on top; put shredded cheese on top of beans. Lay sliced olives on top and bake at 350° for 25 minutes. Serve with toruntila chips.

# APPETIZERS

## MEXICAN DIP

Susan Cowan, Noblesville, IN

*"This dip has long been a favorite with my family and friends at gatherings and I have often shared the recipe with others."*

**8 ounces cream cheese, softened**
**1 ripe avocado, peeled and mashed**
**1 tablespoon lemon juice**
**2 tablespoons mayonnaise**
**4 ounces sour cream**

**Toppings:**
**Green onions, finely chopped**
**Lettuce**
**Tomatoes**
**Cheddar cheese**
**Green olives, sliced**

Blend all ingredients together until smooth, chill. Spread on large plate then layer with suggested vegetables. Sprinkle with chili powder to taste. Serve with your favorite corn chips.

## BEAN-BEEF DIP

Donna Rheault, Hume, CA

**1 large can refried beans**
**1 can roast beef in gravy**
**1 jar chunky salsa**
**1 small can diced chilies**

Shred roast beef, mix with other ingredients. Heat and serve with tortilla chips.

## BEAN DIP

Patty Burling, Bucyrus, OH

**1 can Hormel Chili No Beans**
**8 ounces cream cheese, softened**
**Shredded cheddar cheese**

Mix cream cheese with Chili No Beans. Sprinkle with shredded cheddar and microwave until cheese melts. Serve with tortilla chips.

## CREAMY TACO CHEESE DIP

Sandra Deweese, Beebe, AR

**½ pound ground beef**
**1 small onion**
**½ can Rotel diced tomatoes**
**½ block Velveeta cheese**
**1 can ranch style beans**
**8 ounces sour cream**
**½ package taco seasoning**
**1 can pitted black olives**

Brown beef and small onion; drain well and set aside. Heat Rotel until bubbling hot. Add cheese, beans, sour cream, and taco seasoning. When mixture is hot, mix in browned beef, onion, and olives.

## BEEF DIP

Melrose Ferrell, Zebulon, NC

*"Very good for party food. Serve with Triscuit crackers or any mild cracker. Serve warm or cold."*

**1 cup sour cream**
**2 8-ounce packages cream cheese, cut up**
**2 2½-ounce packages chipped dried beef**
**2 tablespoons minced onion**
**4 tablespoons milk**
**½ cup green pepper**
**Garlic to taste**
**Pepper to taste**
**Crackers of choice**
**Butter or margarine**
**Nuts, chopped**

OVEN 350°

Mix all ingredients in blender. Pour into 8x8-inch glass dish. Top with crumbled crackers and nuts coated in margarine or butter. Bake at 350° for 35 minutes.

## HOLIDAY SPINACH AND ARTICHOKE DIP

Wanda Stubblefield, Chattanooga, TN

**1 pound sour cream**
**1 package ranch dip mix**
**14-ounce can artichokes, drained and chopped**
**2 10-ounce packages frozen chopped spinach, thawed and well drained**
**2-ounce jar diced pimientos, rinsed and drained**
**2 round loaves sourdough bread**

OVEN 400°

Mix well sour cream, artichoke, pimientos, and spinach; set in refrigerator 1 hour. Cut top off bread and clean out the inside, being careful not to tear open. Save filling; cut up and toast for dippers. Spoon mix into hollowed bread. Bake at 400° for 20–25 minutes. Cover with foil if browning too much. Serve hot or cold. Great next day.

## SHRIMP MOUSSE

Virginia Harger, Ely, MN

**1 can tomato soup, diluted**
**2 8-ounce packages cream cheese, softened**
**3 ounces lemon-flavored gelatin**
**½ cup mayonnaise**
**1 cup celery, chopped fine**
**½ cup hot water**
**½ cup green (or winter) onions, chopped**
**8-ounce can small shrimp, chopped**

Heat soup. Whip cream cheese and mayonnaise. Add chopped shrimp and soup to cheese mixture; blend well. Separately dissolve gelatin in hot water. Combine all ingredients and mix well. Chill in 5-cup mold. Serve with favorite dipping vegetable, crackers, and chips.

## OLD-FASHIONED SHRIMP DIP

Donna Feusi, Loomis, CA

*"This recipe is from my husband's grandmother and it was always a special treat when she made it."*

**1 can tomato soup**
**8 ounces cream cheese**
**1 package unflavored gelatin**
**½ cup water**
**1 cup mayonnaise**
**2 cans deveined shrimp, broken lightly**
**¾ cup finely chopped celery**
**¾ cup finely chopped green onions**
**Salt and pepper to taste**

Dissolve gelatin in water. Bring soup to boiling in double boiler. Completely dissolve cream cheese and gelatin in soup. Cool. Add mayonnaise, celery, onions, and seasonings. Let firm about 5 minutes in the refrigerator. Add shrimp. Put in well-greased mold until firm. Unmold dip. Serve with crackers.

## VEGETABLE DIP

Pam Silverthorn, Sidney, MI

**1 cup sour cream**
**1 cup mayonnaise**
**2 drops hot sauce**
**1 teaspoon seasoning salt**
**1 tablespoon Beau Monde herb mix**
**½ teaspoon garlic salt**
**1 tablespoon parsley flakes**

Mix well. Let set for couple of hours for flavors to blend.

## CARAMEL CREAM CHEESE

Jayne Richards, Karab, UT

**8 ounces cream cheese, softened**
**1 cup brown sugar**

With a mixer, mix cream cheese with brown sugar until smooth. Serve with sour apples, popcorn, or other dipping item.

## CHEDDAR SHRIMP DIP

Dot Mauldin, Laurens, SC

**4 ounces drained shrimp, chopped**
**4 ounces grated sharp cheddar cheese**
**¾ cup mayonnaise**
**¾ tablespoon Worcestershire sauce**
**1 small onion, chopped**
**Dash garlic salt**
**Dash hot sauce**

Mix ingredients. Serve with crackers.

## HOT SAUCE

Treva Fitts, Bowie, TX

**4 cups tomatoes, peeled, quartered**
**½–¾ medium purple onion**
**¾–1 medium bell pepper**
**1 large jalapeno (remove seeds)**
**Juice of one lime**
**2½ teaspoons salt (heaping)**
**¾ teaspoon sugar**
**1 teaspoon red pepper (cayenne)**
**3 large pods of garlic**
**¾ teaspoon celery seeds**
**½ teaspoon dry mustard**
**1 teaspoon black pepper**
**2 teaspoons Tabasco**
**1 capful of vinegar**
**6–8 leaves cilantro**

Mix all in blender on frappe.

## FRUIT DIP

Connie Hudson, Middleport, OH

*"My family loves this cool treat!"*

**8 ounces cream cheese, room temperature**
**7-ounce jar marshmallow cream**

Beat cream cheese with mixer until creamy. Add marshmallow cream and whip until mixed well. Refrigerate.

Serve with strawberries, kiwi, grapes, apples, bananas, and peaches or on graham crackers.

## AUNT LIDIE'S MACAROON FRUIT DIP

Arlie Roerdink, Cedar Grove, WI

*"I like it as a spread on toasted bread! This is my family's favorite."*

**½ pint sour cream**
**1 cup light brown sugar**
**½ pound crushed macaroon cookies (2 cups)**

Beat sour cream and brown sugar until fluffy. Add crushed macaroons and mix well. Store in refrigerator.

# APPETIZERS

## FRUIT 'N SAUCE

Marie Honeycutt, Shelby, NC

**2 cans pineapple chunks**
**2 cans sliced peaches**
**2 cans mandarin oranges**
**3 or 4 bananas**
**1 small box vanilla pudding (not instant)**

Drain pineapple, peaches, and oranges, reserving 2 cups juice. Place juices in pot with pudding mix. Bring to boil and remove from heat. Cool and pour over fruit. Chill.

## REFRIGERATOR PICKLES

Inona Coburn, Phoenix, AZ

*"These pickles are a delightful addition to a relish tray."*

**1 cup sugar**
**1 cup vinegar**
**1 tablespoon salt**
**2 cucumbers (approximately)**

Mix sugar, vinegar, and salt in a pan. Bring to a boil. Boil just until the sugar and salt are dissolved, about 1 minute. Remove from heat. Cool. Slice cucumbers into thin slices. Put in a quart jar. Pour in the cooled vinegar solution. Put in refrigerator. The cucumbers will fill the jar. The brine might not completely come to top of jar. But in a few hours the cucumber slices will "wilt" a bit so all will be covered. Tip the jar upside down a couple of times during the first 3 or 4 hours. Keep refrigerated until gone.

## APPLE BUTTER

Mrs. Donald Hoskins, Clarinda, IA

**16 cups cooked apple pulp**
**1 cup cider vinegar**
**9 cups sugar**
**4 cinnamon sticks (approximately 2 inches each)**

OVEN 350°

Boil all ingredients in a Crock-Pot until it is thick, several hours. Or put ingredients in a roaster pan and cook in 350° oven. Stir often and be careful as it pops very easily.

## CASSIA BUD SWEET DILLS

Judy Battleshaw, Jackson, MI

**43- to 46-ounce jar kosher dill pickles, drained and sliced**
**2 cups sugar**
**½ cup vinegar**
**¼ cup water**
**1 top Cassia Buds or ½ crushed cinnamon stick**
**½ teaspoon pickling spice**

Put dill slices in jar or container. Boil sugar, vinegar, and water until clear; watch closely. To pickle slices add Cassia Buds or cinnamon stick. Then add pickling spice. Pour syrup over pickles. Refrigerate. Pickles will be ready the next day.

## FRUIT SLUSH

Carol Kyllonen, Lewisburg, PA

**1 medium can frozen orange juice**
**½ cup lemon juice**
**2 cans crushed pineapple, with juice**
**3 cups water**
**2 cups sugar**
**3–4 diced bananas**
**10-ounce jar maraschino cherries**

Mix together and put in freezer until slushy or freeze and take out and thaw until slushy.

## FROZEN SLUSHY

Geraldine Stock, New Oxford, PA

*"This snack is very healthy. It makes the perfect snack for afternoons. Can be served anytime. Kids just love this."*

**1 can fruit juice (can mix several kinds together)**

Put in a freezer container and freeze. Take out about ½–¾ hour before using, to allow to thaw. Do not thaw to liquid stage. Thaw until fruit juice is in the slushy stage. Serve in small containers, dishes, or small 3-ounce paper cups.

# APPETIZERS

## HOT CHOCOLATE

Patricia Racic, Brandon, FL

**1-pound can Quick, or powdered chocolate drink mix**
**1 pound sugar**
**8-quart box powdered sugar**
**3- to 6-ounce jar powdered creamer**

Sift all ingredients together and store in container. Put 4 heaping teaspoons in cup of boiling water.

## LIME SHERBET PUNCH

Elizabeth Hunt, Ithaca, MI

**46-ounce can pineapple juice**
**1 large bottle ginger ale**
**1 pint lime sherbet**

Place in punch bowl. Add scoops of lime sherbet.

## FRUIT SLUSH WITH APRICOTS

Marilyn Walz, Colby, KS

*"Low-fat, high fiber, delicious, nutritious, cool summer treat. Can be a salad or dessert."*

**12-ounce can frozen orange juice, thawed**
**1 #2-can crushed pineapple**
**1 #2½-can apricots**
**6 bananas**
**1 jar maraschino cherries or 16-ounce package strawberries, juice included**

Mix juice (adding no water or sugar), bananas, and apricots in blender. Add remaining ingredients and stir in large bowl. Put in 9-ounce clear plastic cups and freeze. Thaw 15–30 seconds in microwave to serve. Amount and ingredients are flexible according to your needs.

## 1979 CRANBERRY TEA

Kathryn Banning, Buena Vista, CO

*"This recipe is from a dear Christian woman who is now with the Lord. Good to serve at your holiday parties. Put it in Crock-Pot on low and you don't have to worry about it the rest of the evening while you enjoy your party."*

**1-pound package cranberries, or 1 quart cranberry juice**
**1 quart water**
**2 quarts water**
**1 cup hot cinnamon candy**
**½ cup lemon juice**
**1¼ cups orange juice**
**2 cups sugar, or sweetened to your taste**
**10 cloves (whole)**

Cook cranberries until they are tender; strain and use juice. Add 2 quarts more water. Add other ingredients, heat together, and serve.

## ORANGE SPICED TEA

Octavia Yates, Clayton, OK

*"This is a great drink when the weather outside is cold. Good served with buttered toast or hot buttered biscuits."*

**1 cup powdered orange drink mix**
**1 heaping cup lemon instant tea (unsweetened)**
**3 cups sugar (or equal amount of sugar substitute)**
**1 teaspoon cinnamon**
**½ teaspoon nutmeg (can substitute cloves)**

Mix all ingredients together. Put 3 heaping teaspoons of mix to one medium mug of hot water (boiling water is best). Use more or less to suit your taste.

## ENGLISH WASSAIL

Kathleen Yapp, Gainesville, GA

**Editor's Note:** Kathleen's publishing accomplishments include *A Match Made in Heaven* and *Golden Dreams* for Heartsong Presents.

**3 oranges**
**3 quarts apple cider**
**2 cinnamon sticks (3 inches long)**
**½ teaspoon nutmeg**
**½ cup honey**
**⅓ cup lemon juice**
**2 teaspoons lemon rind**
**5 cups pineapple juice**
**Whole cloves**

OVEN 325°

Stud oranges with cloves about ½-inch apart. Place in baking pan with a little water; bake slowly for 30 minutes. Heat cider and cinnamon sticks in large saucepan. Bring to a boil. Simmer, covered, 5 minutes. Add remaining ingredients and simmer uncovered, 5 minutes longer. Pour into punch bowl, float spiced oranges on top. Use cinnamon sticks for stirring. Or put in Crock-Pot on high to keep hot.

## PERKY PUNCH

Nichole Stiffler, Blairsville, PA

*"Perfect for special occasions or a hot summer day!"*

**1 small can frozen orange juice**
**1 small can frozen lemonade**
**1 package strawberry Kool-aid (unsweetened)**
**1 package cherry Kool-aid (unsweetened)**
**1 tall can Hawaiian Punch**
**2 12-ounce bottles ginger ale**

Prepare orange juice and lemonade according to directions on cans. Add Kool-aid using half amount of water and all two cups sugar required. Add Hawaiian Punch. Pour into punch bowl; add ginger ale, and ice cubes.

## RHUBARB STRAWBERRY SAUCE
Rachel R. Schaffner, Bethlehem, PA

**2 cups water**
**2 cups rhubarb**
**¾ cup granulated sugar**
**3-ounce box wild strawberry-flavored gelatin**

Put water, rhubarb, and sugar in saucepan and cook until rhubarb is soft. After rhubarb is boiled, remove from stove, and add gelatin. Mix well. Put in bowl and cool. Refrigerate until firm. Serve with dinner.

Serves 8.

## FRESH CRANBERRY SAUCE
Kristin Powell, Canton, MA

**1 pound fresh cranberries (4 cups)**
**2 cups water**
**2 cups granulated sugar**

Cook cranberries in water 5–10 minutes or until all skins pop open. Strain through fine sieve to remove skins and seeds, pressing pulp through with juice. Stir sugar into pulp, boil about 3 minutes. Refrigerate.

Makes about 1 quart.

## CRANBERRY RELISH
Cheryl A. Bardaville, St. Louis, MI

**2 12-ounce bags cranberries**
**2 cups sugar**
**1 cup orange juice**
**16-ounce can sliced peaches, drained**
**8-ounce can crushed pineapple**
**1 cup walnuts, broken and crushed**
**1 cup golden raisins**

Cook sugar, cranberries, and orange juice to boil, stirring constantly. Reduce heat. Simmer uncooked until berries pop open. Remove from heat. Cut up peaches and add with nuts, pineapple, and raisins. Store covered and refrigerated.

Makes 2 quarts.

## SQUASH RELISH

Mrs. T. K. Whiteside, Robert Lee, TX

**12 cups grated squash**
**5 tablespoons salt**
**4 cups chopped onions**
**2 cups chopped bell peppers**
**5 cups sugar**
**2½ cups white vinegar**
**2 teaspoons pickling spices**
**1 teaspoon celery seeds**
**1 teaspoon turmeric**

Combine squash and salt; let stand overnight. Rinse. Mix spices in little bag; add to rest of ingredients, let boil 5 minutes.

Makes about 6 pints.

## PEACH MARMALADE

Lois Alspaugh, Newmanstown, PA

**5 cups peaches (smashed)**
**5 cups sugar**
**1 small can crushed pineapple**
**6-ounce package apricot-flavored gelatin**

Boil fruit, sugar, and pineapple for 15 minutes. Stir in gelatin and boil until dissolved. Pour into containers and freeze.

## STRAWBERRY FIG JAM

Cathryn Stallings, Maben, MS

**3½ cups mashed figs**
**3 cups sugar**
**1 small package strawberry-flavored gelatin**

Mix well, bring to a boil, and cook 5 minutes. Pour into sterilized jars and seal.

## STRAWBERRY PRESERVES

Julie Darby, Kansas City, MO

**2 quarts strawberries, heaping**
**6 cups sugar**

Cover strawberries with boiling water, let stand 2 minutes; drain. Put in kettle with 4 cups sugar and boil for 2 minutes. Once a rolling boil starts, set kettle aside and let bubbling stop. Add 2 cups sugar, cook at a rolling boil for 15 minutes. Leave in kettle 15 minutes then pour into shallow pan. Shake pan often. Preserves should not be more than 1½-inch deep. Let stand overnight. Pack cold in sterilized jars and seal.

# APPETIZERS

## BLUSHING PEACH JAM

Sherry Tatman, Brooklyn Center, MN

- **1½ pounds (2 cups) peaches, peeled, pitted, crushed**
- **¼ cup lemon juice**
- **2 cups red raspberries (measure before crushing)**
- **7 cups sugar**
- **1 package powdered Sure-Jell**
- **1½ teaspoons margarine**

Add 2 tablespoons lemon juice to crushed peaches. Let stand. Crush berries and add remaining 2 tablespoons lemon juice. Combine peaches and raspberries. Add margarine. Put in heavy kettle. Add Sure-Jell. Bring to full rolling boil. Add sugar and follow Sure-Jell recipe from there.

## JALAPENO PEPPER JELLY

DiAnn Mills, Houston, TX

**Editor's Note:** DiAnn debuted in the Heartsong Presents series with *Rehoboth.*

- **1½ cups chopped green peppers**
- **½ cup chopped fresh jalapeno peppers**
- **1½ cups white vinegar**
- **6 ounces Certo or Sure-Jell**
- **6 cups sugar**
- **4 drops green food coloring**

Mix green peppers, jalapenos, and white vinegar in blender until mushy. The more jalapeno pepper seeds used, the hotter the jelly. Put mush into large cooking pot. Add sugar and bring to a boil, stirring often. Remove from heat, add food coloring, and let stand 10 minutes. Stir in Certo and pour into sterilized jars.

### BAKER'S NOTE

Before handling jalapenos, spray hands with PAM or use rubber gloves.

## BARBECUE SAUCE

Joyce Taillon, Wooster, OH

- **6 tablespoons margarine**
- **1 teaspoon Tabasco sauce**
- **2 cups catsup**
- **⅔ cup concentrated lemon juice**
- **2 tablespoons mustard**
- **2 teaspoons onion powder**
- **2 teaspoons Accent (optional)**
- **¼ cup Worcestershire sauce**
- **¼ cup molasses**
- **½ teaspoon salt**

Combine ingredients in a saucepan and simmer 15 minutes. Refrigerate. Great on chicken, beef, pork, and hot dogs.

Makes 1 quart.

# SALADS

# SALADS

## FREEDA'S CHERRY SALAD

Cay Sergent, Halfway, MO

**1 can sweetened condensed milk**
**1 large container whipped topping**
**1 can cherry pie filling**
**16-ounce can crushed pineapple**
**1 cup chopped pecans**
**2 cups miniature marshmallows**

Mix ingredients together. Chill and serve.

## SALAD DRESSING

Helen Pogue, Fredericktown, MO

**1 cup sugar**
**2 teaspoons salt**
**4 teaspoons prepared mustard**
**¼ cup celery**
**¼ cup onion**
**½ cup vinegar**
**1 cup salad oil**

In blender, chop or grind until mixed well. Keeps several weeks in refrigerator.

## CHERRY PIE SALAD

Sherry Davis, Choctaw, OK

*"Great for church dinners or special family get-togethers."*

**13-ounce can sweetened condensed milk**
**1 large can crushed pineapple, drained**
**2 cans cherry pie filling**
**16-ounce whipped topping**
**½ cup chopped nuts (optional)**

In a large bowl, mix condensed milk and drained pineapple together. Add cherry pie filling and nuts. Mix well. Fold in whipped topping. Refrigerate until time to serve.

## CHERRY SALAD

Ada Norgaard, Tyler, MN

**1 can cherry pie filling**
**1 large can crushed pineapple, drained**
**9 ounces whipped topping**
**1 can sweetened condensed milk**
**3-ounce package dry cherry pie filling (no water)**
**Small package marshmallows (optional)**

Mix all ingredients together.

## LIME AND COTTAGE CHEESE SALAD

Evelyn Peeples, Water Valley, MS

*"Mighty refreshing."*

**1 package lime gelatin**
**1 cup canned milk (undiluted)**
**1 tablespoon lemon juice**
**1 cup cottage cheese**
**½ cup finely chopped celery**
**¾ cup boiling water**
**9-ounce can crushed pineapple, with juice**
**½ cup mayonnaise**
**½ cup broken nut meats (optional)**

Dissolve gelatin in boiling water. Cool slightly; then stir in milk and cool until syrupy. Fold in other ingredients and chill until firm. Cut into squares and serve on lettuce leaf.

## SUMMER DELIGHT GELATIN SALAD

Dorothea Hulet, Banks, OR

**1 package lemon gelatin**
**1 package lime gelatin**
**2 cups boiling water**
**¼ teaspoon salt**
**2 tablespoons lemon juice or vinegar**
**2 cups crushed pineapple**
**1 cup evaporated milk**
**2 tablespoons horseradish**
**1 cup chopped nuts**
**1 cup salad dressing**
**¾ cup cottage cheese**
**Paprika**

Mix together lemon gelatin mix, water, salt, and lemon juice; cool, then add pineapple and milk. Add horseradish, nuts, Miracle Whip, and cottage cheese; let set. When set, add 2 cups hot water to lime gelatin. Let set until cool. Pour over salad. Sprinkle with paprika.

## LITE LIME SALAD

Alta Brown, Medina, NY

**24-ounce carton lime Light n' Lively cottage cheese**
**2 3-ounce packages of sugar-free lime gelatin**
**20-ounce cans crushed pineapple, well drained**
**2 8-ounce containers lite whipped topping**

Place cottage cheese in a large mixing bowl. Stir in the powdered contents of gelatin packages. Add pineapple and whipped topping. Stir well. Refrigerate.

# SALADS

## ORANGE-PINEAPPLE SALAD

Mrs. Paul E. Nester, Meadows Dan, VA

**15-ounce can crushed pineapple, undrained**
**6-ounce package orange-flavored gelatin**
**2 cups buttermilk**
**1 cup flaked coconut**
**1 cup chopped pecans**
**12-ounce carton whipped topping**

Place pineapple in saucepan; bring to a boil, stirring constantly. Remove from heat. Add gelatin and stir until completely dissolved. Stir in buttermilk, coconut, and pecans. Cool. Fold in whipped topping and pour into a 9x13-inch casserole dish. Chill until firm.

## ORANGE SALAD

Fern Sweeter, Foley, MN

**3 cups water**
**3-ounce package vanilla pudding (cooked type)**
**3-ounce package tapioca pudding (cooked type)**
**3-ounce package orange gelatin**
**12-ounce container whipped topping**
**1 large can drained mandarin oranges**
**20-ounce can crushed pineapple, drained**

Bring pudding, gelatin, and water to boil. Cool. Add fruit and fold in whipped topping.

## GAIL'S ORANGE SALAD

Gail Habelman, Easley, SC

**1 small box orange gelatin**
**1 small cottage cheese**
**1 large whipped topping**
**1 can mandarin oranges, drained**
**½ small package miniature marshmallows**

Pour dry gelatin over whipped topping, mix well. Add cottage cheese and fold in oranges, pineapple, and marshmallows.

## ORANGE-CARROT GELATIN SALAD

Marie Piper, Grandview, TX

**3-ounce package orange gelatin**
**1 cup boiling water**
**8-ounce can crushed pineapple**
**11-ounce can mandarin oranges, drained**
**1 cup grated carrots**

Dissolve gelatin in boiling water. Drain pineapple, reserve juice. Add enough cold water to juice to measure 1 cup. Stir in gelatin. Chill until partially set. Add pineapple, oranges, and carrots. Pour in serving bowl. Chill until firm.

Serves 4–6.

## ORANGE SALAD

Carol Blaylock, Duncanville, TX

**2 3-ounce packages tapioca pudding**
**3-ounce package orange gelatin**
**1 large can pineapple chunks or tidbits, with juice**
**2 cans mandarin oranges, with juice**
**1 teaspoon orange drink mix (optional, but makes nice color)**
**1–2 teaspoons lemon juice (optional)**
**2 bananas (optional)**

Drain fruit, heat approximately 3 cups of juice in large pan, add water if you don't have enough liquid. Mix pudding with another 1¼–1½ cups juice/water mixture. Pour pudding/juice mixture into hot juice, stirring continuously, cook until almost clear. Add gelatin, orange drink mix, and lemon juice; stir well. Cool slightly. Add pineapple and oranges. Allow to cool completely for several hours. Add bananas just before serving.

Serves 8.

## ORANGE-APRICOT SALAD

Judith Fillingim, Columbus, GA

**2 3-ounce boxes orange gelatin**
**2 cups boiling water**
**1 cup whipped topping**
**12-ounce can apricot nectar**
**1 can mandarin oranges, drained**

Dissolve gelatin in boiling water. Add apricot nectar. Chill until it begins to set. Fold oranges and whipped topping into gelatin mixture. Pour into mold and chill.

# SALADS

## APRICOT GELATIN
Brenda Hart, Dunbar, PA

**2 small boxes apricot gelatin**
**¾ cup sugar**
**2 small jars of strained apricot baby food**
**1 can crushed pineapple**
**8 ounces cream cheese, softened to room temperature**
**2 small packs whipped topping mix**

Heat gelatin, sugar, apricots, and undrained pineapple until gelatin is dissolved. Do not boil! Beat cream cheese. Pour gelatin mixture into cream cheese and beat together. Allow to cool. Whip whipped topping mix according to directions on package. Fold into cooled gelatin and cream cheese mixture. Pour into 9x13-inch dish and refrigerate overnight.

## GLENDA'S BLUEBERRY SALAD
Nadine Guin, Wharton, TX

**2 4-serving size or 1 8-serving size blackberry or raspberry-flavored gelatin**
**2 cups boiling water**
**2-ounce can crushed pineapple, undrained**
**21-ounce can blueberry pie filling**

**Topping:**
**8 ounces cream cheese, softened**
**1 pint sour cream**
**½ cup sugar**
**1 teaspoon vanilla**

Dissolve gelatin in boiling water. Add pineapple. Stir in pie filling. Pour into large glass bowl or individual serving cups and refrigerate until jelled. Prepare topping: mix together cream cheese and sour cream. Stir in sugar and vanilla. Spread topping on top.

## CARAMEL APPLE SALAD
Laurie Haugen, Edmore, ND

**3-ounce package instant butterscotch pudding, powder only**
**8 ounces whipped topping**
**10-ounce can pineapple, crushed or tidbits, with juice**
**1 cup miniature marshmallows**
**3 cups apple (cut up)**

Mix altogether, refrigerate, and enjoy.

## "BEST EVER" DRESSING
Lois Willett, Steilacoom, WA

**2 tablespoons sugar or 2 teaspoons sugar substitute**
**2 tablespoons vinegar**
**¼ cup orange juice**
**2 tablespoons vegetable oil (can use light mayonnaise instead)**
**2 tablespoons catsup**
**Garlic powder and salt and pepper**

Blend all ingredients and chill.

## ENGLISH WALNUT APPLE SALAD

Johnnie Reynolds, Goodlettsville, TN

*"Very pretty and tastes great."*

**4 or 5 large, sweet apples, sliced**
**¾ cup English walnuts, chopped**
**1 cup sugar**
**2 tablespoons flour**
**1 cup water**
**1 tablespoon butter**
**1 tablespoon vinegar**
**Few drops red food coloring**

Mix sugar, flour, butter, and water in saucepan; cook until thick. Remove from heat and cool. When cooled add vinegar and food coloring. Pour over apples and nuts. Mix. Cover and store in refrigerator until ready to serve.

## MARSHMALLOW APPLE SALAD

Jean Hamm, South Webster, OH

*"Given to me by a friend, years ago."*

**3 apples, cut up in cubes, skins on**
**½–1 cup grapes, cut in half**
**½ cup nuts**
**1 cup marshmallows**
**1 cup whipped topping**

**Dressing for salad:**
**1 cup pineapple juice**
**¾ cup sugar**
**1 heaping tablespoon flour**
**2 eggs, separated**
**1 tablespoon butter**

Combine salad ingredients. Dressing: Heat juice and butter until warm. Blend flour, sugar, and egg yolks; then egg whites beaten stiff and pineapple juice. Cook on medium-low heat or use double boiler until thick. Cool. Add a cup of whipped topping just before serving. Better to add dressing to apple mixture just before serving or at least ½ hour before serving.

## TAFFY APPLE SALAD

Connie Steele, Bellville, WV

*"Really tastes like taffy apples!"*

**8-ounce can crushed pineapple with juice**
**2 tablespoons flour**
**½ cup sugar**
**1 large container whipped topping (or extra large container)**
**5 Granny Smith (sour) apples, diced with skins on**
**½–1 cup Spanish peanuts, with skins**

Cook pineapple with juice, flour, and sugar until thick. Cool completely in refrigerator. Add apples, whipped topping, and peanuts.

# SALADS

## GRAPE SALAD

Pat Powell, Orange Park, FL

**10 ounces peas, cooked slightly, drained**
**½–1 cup finely diced celery**
**1–2 cups diced turkey, chicken, ham**
**½ pound each, red and green seedless grapes**
**1 cup salad dressing**
**1 teaspoon ginger**
**2 tablespoons lemon juice**
**Small package almonds, sliced or slivered**

Mix together, except almonds. Set at least 1 hour before serving. Add slivered or sliced almonds just before serving.

## CINNAMON SALAD

Mrs. George DePasse, Henryetta, OK

**4-ounce package gelatin, cherry or raspberry**
**1 cup hot water**
**½ cup red cinnamon candies**
**½ cup boiling water**
**1 cup apples, chopped**
**1 cup celery, chopped**
**¾ cup pecans, chopped**

Dissolve gelatin in 1 cup hot water. Add cinnamon candies to ½ cup boiling water, stir to dissolve. Add enough water to make 1 cup liquid. Combine gelatin and candy mixture. Chill until partially set. Add remaining ingredients. Chill until firm. Can be doubled for more.

## PARADISE SALAD

Nikki Miller, Morgantown, IN

**24-ounce regular or low-fat cottage cheese**
**12-ounce carton regular or fat-free whipped topping**
**6-ounce box gelatin (I use strawberry flavor)**
**2 20-ounce cans crushed pineapple, drain well**

Mix cottage cheese and dry gelatin, then mix in whipped topping. Add pineapple. Mix well and chill.

Make the night before you want to use it for full flavor. Keeps in the refrigerator for 2 weeks. I use low-fat cottage cheese and fat-free whipped topping for a great low-fat salad.

## STRAWBERRY NUT SALAD

Delilah Nuckols, Northport, AL

**2 3-ounce packages strawberry gelatin**
**1 cup boiling water**
**16 ounces frozen strawberry**
**20-ounce can crushed pineapple**
**1 cup chopped pecans**
**3 chopped bananas**
**8 ounces sour cream**
**¼ cup mayonnaise or salad dressing**

Combine gelatin and boiling water; stir in nuts, strawberries, and pineapple; set aside. Stir bananas into gelatin mixture, spoon half of mixture into 7x11-inch baking dish, and refrigerate until almost jelled. Combine sour cream and mayonnaise, spread over strawberry, then layer top with remaining strawberry mixture. Refrigerate.

## TANGY FRUIT SALAD

Catharine Kramer, Greenwood, DE

**20-ounce can pineapple chunks, juice drained and reserved**
**3 4-ounce packages instant vanilla pudding mix**
**¼ cup dry orange-flavored instant breakfast drink**
**11-ounce can mandarin oranges, drained**
**16-ounce can fruit cocktail, drained**
**2 bananas, sliced**
**1 apple, or pear cut into chunks**

In small bowl, combine reserved pineapple juice, pudding mix, and breakfast drink; set aside. In a large bowl combine all fruit. Fold juice mixture into fruit. Refrigerate before serving.

Yield: 6–8 servings.

## CRUNCHY FRUIT SALAD

Terri Smith, Dayton, OH

**2 bananas**
**2 oranges, pared and sectioned**
**1 cup strawberries, cut into halves**
**½ cup sour cream**
**1 tablespoon orange juice**
**1 cup granola**

Slice bananas into 1 quart bowl. Cover completely with oranges and strawberries. Cover and refrigerate at least 1 hour, but no longer than 24 hours. Just before serving, mix sour cream, honey, and orange juice. Fold into fruit until well-coated. Sprinkle with granola.

# SALADS

## CHEESY FRUIT SALAD

Gladys Milstead, Pennellville, NY

**20-ounce can pineapple chunks, drain and reserve juice**
**1 tablespoon cornstarch**
**1 egg, beaten slightly**
**¼ cup sugar**
**1 tablespoon mayonnaise or salad dressing**
**¼ pound American cheese, diced**
**4-ounce package marshmallows, cut up or 2 cups miniature marshmallows**
**2 bananas, diced**

Mix together cornstarch, egg, and sugar; cook until thick. Cool; then add mayonnaise, cheese, marshmallows, bananas, and pineapple chunks. Mix all together. Refrigerate.

Serves 6–8.

## FRUIT SALAD

Mrs. Richard Hennings, Dubuque, IA

**7 tablespoons sugar**
**2 tablespoons flour**
**2 eggs, beaten**
**½ teaspoon prepared mustard**
**#2-can chunk pineapple**
**1 tablespoon butter**
**12 marshmallows, cut up**
**1 small bottle maraschino cherries, cut in half**
**1 or 2 sliced bananas**

Take juice of pineapple and other ingredients minus the chunk pineapple and boil in saucepan until thick (use medium heat and stir often so it will not scorch). When thickened remove from heat and add butter and cool. When cool, mix with pineapple, marshmallows, and bananas (added last for they turn dark).

## MOLDED FRUIT SALAD

Lena Parks Mahone, Spottswood, VA

*"This salad holds up well even under hot conditions."*

**2 3-ounce packages orange or lime gelatin**
**8-ounce package cream cheese (low-fat works fine)**
**1 cup small marshmallows**
**15- or 16-ounce can crushed pineapple, or fruit cocktail, with juice**
**2 cups boiling water**
**½ cup mayonnaise**

Dissolve gelatin in boiling water. Add cream cheese, marshmallows, and mayonnaise. Will be smooth and creamy if mixed in a blender. After blended, add pineapple or fruit cocktail, including juice. Spray mold (4–5 cup mold) with vegetable oil. Cool salad in mold until completely jelled.

## FRUIT GRAPES

Deborah LeBrun, St. Cloud, MN

**1 pound red grapes (seedless)**
**¾ cup brown sugar**
**½ large tub whipped topping**
**1 cup sour cream**
**1 pound green grapes**
**1 small package slivered almonds**

Mix sugar, whipped topping, and sour cream. Add grapes and slivered almonds.

## FROZEN FRUIT SALAD

Alice Becker, Russell, KS

**2 ripe bananas**
**16-ounce can pineapple juice**
**2 tablespoons lemon juice**
**1 cup orange juice**
**½ cup mayonnaise or salad dressing**
**10-ounce can mandarin oranges, undrained**
**¼ cup sugar**
**Iceburg lettuce**

Combine in blender: bananas, pineapple juice, and lemon juice. Blend 1 minute on low speed until smooth. Add and whirl ½ minute on low: orange juice, mayonnaise or salad dressing, oranges, and sugar. Freeze. Serve frozen salad on lettuce leaf.

Pour into six 6-ounce molds, or 9x9x2-inch pan. Freeze 4 hours or until firm. Cut. Serve on lettuce leaf. Serve as a dessert or as a salad.

## FRUIT WHIP

Ida Mae Shown, Knoxville, TN

**8-ounce package cream cheese**
**1 can sweetened condensed milk**
**8-ounce whipped topping**
**#2-can fruit cocktail, drained**
**#2-can mandarin oranges, drained**
**#2-can chunk pineapple, drained**
**Any fruit or nuts desired**

Beat cream cheese and milk until smooth. Add whipped topping and fold in drained fruits and nuts if desired (I use pecans). Chill and serve.

# SALADS

## HONEY FRUIT SALAD

Gloria A. Babish, Greenville, PA
Bettina Geesaman, Knoxville, TN

**⅓ cup honey**
**½ cup mayonnaise (can be light)**
**½ cup chopped English walnuts**
**3 cored, unpeeled apples, chopped**
**2 bananas, peeled and sliced**
**11-ounce can mandarin oranges, drained**
**1 cup seedless grapes**
**1 tablespoon lemon juice**
**1 cup shredded lettuce**

Blend honey and mayonnaise until smooth. Toss remaining ingredients (except lettuce) with lemon juice. Stir in honey mixture; refrigerate. Just before serving toss in lettuce.

Makes about 7 cups.

## WATERMELON SALAD

Johnnie C. Reynolds, Goodlettsville, TN

**6-ounce package raspberry gelatin**
**2 cups boiling water**
**1 cup miniature marshmallows**
**1 cup crushed pineapple, drained**
**1 cup diced cantaloupe**
**1 cup seedless white grapes**
**1½ cups cubed watermelon**

Dissolve gelatin in water; add marshmallows, stirring until dissolved. Chill until slightly thickened; fold in remaining ingredients. Spoon into an 8-cup mold; chill until firm.

Yield: 6–8 servings.

## MINTY MIXED MELON

Bettina Geesaman, Knoxville, TN

**2 cups chopped cantaloupe, about 1 large**
**2 cups chopped honeydew melon, about 1 medium**
**2 cups chopped watermelon, about ½ small**
**1 cup sliced strawberries**
**1 teaspoon grated lime peel**
**2 tablespoons chopped fresh, or**
**2 teaspoons dried, mint leaves**
**2 tablespoons honey**

Mix all thoroughly in a bowl. Cover and refrigerate at least 2 hours or until chilled.

Serves 6.

## CRANBERRY SALAD SUPREME

Alice M. Turk, Deckerville, MI

**3-ounce package raspberry gelatin**
**1 cup boiling water**
**16-ounce can whole cranberry sauce**
**3-ounce package lemon gelatin**
**1 cup boiling water**
**3-ounce package cream cheese**
**⅓ cup mayonnaise**
**8-ounce can crushed pineapple**
**½ cup whipped cream**
**1 cup miniature marshmallows**
**2 tablespoons chopped nuts**

Dissolve raspberry gelatin in 1 cup boiling water. Stir in whole cranberry sauce. Turn into 9x9x2-inch baking dish. Chill until partially set. Dissolve lemon gelatin in 1 cup boiling water. Beat together cream cheese and mayonnaise, then gradually add lemon gelatin. Stir in undrained pineapple. Chill until partially set. Whip cream, fold in lemon mixture and marshmallows. Spread on top cranberry layer. Top with chopped nuts. Chill until firmly set.

## CLARA'S BEST FRESH CRANBERRY SALAD

Linda Herring, Monohans, TX

**Editor's Note:** Linda is the author of several books for Heartsong Presents that include *Dreams of the Pioneers.*

**1 pound fresh cranberries**
**Rind of one orange, grated**
**1 small can crushed pineapple**
**1½ cups sugar**
**1 cup crushed pecans (optional)**
**1 large box any kind of red gelatin**
**1 cup boiling water**
**1 package plain gelatin**
**½ cup cold water**
**1 large package cream cheese**

Dissolve the red gelatin. Dissolve the plain gelatin in ½ cup cold water. Put in blender or food processor. Add fresh cranberries until well crushed. Add the cream cheese and sugar. Pour into a large bowl and add all remaining ingredients. Let chill and serve.

Serves 8 or more.

## SPICED CRANBERRY RING

Mrs. Don L. Johnson, Brookfield, MO

**2 3-ounce packages raspberry gelatin**
**2 cups boiling water**
**⅛ teaspoon salt**
**¼ teaspoon cinnamon**
**Dash of ground cloves**
**2 6-ounce cans "whole-berry" cranberry sauce**
**1 cup apples, diced**
**½ cup diced celery**
**½ cup chopped walnuts**

Dissolve gelatin and salt in boiling water. Stir in cinnamon and cloves. Add cranberry sauce, fold in apples, celery, and walnuts. Pour into 6-cup mold, chill until firm, about 4 hours. Unmold. Garnish as desired. Peach, pear, and apricot halves work well.

Serves 12.

# SALADS

## FROZEN CRANBERRY SALAD

Margaret R. Dyson, Kernersville, NC
Kari Farwell, Quincy, MI

**2 3-ounce packages cream cheese, softened (can use low-fat or fat-free)**
**2 tablespoons mayonnaise or salad dressing (can use low-fat or fat-free)**
**2 tablespoons sugar**
**14-ounce can cranberry sauce, jelled (Option: whole cranberry sauce)**
**8-ounce can crushed pineapple, drained**
**½ cup pecans or walnuts, chopped**
**2 cups whipped topping**
**2 cups flaked coconut (optional)**
**Pinch of salt**

In medium bowl, blend cream cheese and salad dressing. Fold in whipped topping; set aside. In a large mixing bowl, combine pineapple, nuts, coconut, and cranberry sauce. Gently combine with cream cheese mixture. Spread into 9x13-inch pan. Cover and freeze. Thaw 10–15 minutes before serving. Cut into squares.

## STRAWBERRY PRETZEL SALAD

Lori L. Murray, Westville, OK
Anita Thomason, Grayson, GA
Anita VanSoest, Greeley, CO

**2½ cups crushed pretzels**
**1½ sticks melted margarine**
**8 ounces cream cheese**
**1 small bowl whipped topping**
**1 cup sugar**
**2 small packages strawberry gelatin**
**2 cups boiling water**
**20 ounces frozen strawberries**

Mix pretzels and margarine. Spread in 9x13-inch pan. Bake 10 minutes. Stir once, let cool. Cream together sugar, cream cheese, and whipped topping. Spread over pretzels. Mix gelatin with boiling water. Add strawberries. Pour over cream cheese mixture when it starts to set up. Place in refrigerator until gelatin sets up.

## CRANBERRY SALAD

June Warkentin, Reedley, CA

**1 pound fresh cranberries, ground**
**1 cup sugar**
**¾ pound marshmallows, ground**
**1 pint whipped cream**
**1 cup pineapple, drained and crushed**

Grind cranberries, stir in sugar and mix well. Grind marshmallows and add to mixture. Whip the cream and mix all ingredients together. Pour into pan or dishes. Place in freezing part of refrigerator. Let stand overnight. Makes a large salad.

Serves 12.

## STRIPED COOKIE SALAD

Laurel Ceroll, Custer, SD
Debbie Wagenbach, Burlington, IA

**2 cups buttermilk**
**8–16 ounces whipped topping**
**2 packages vanilla instant pudding**
**2 small cans mandarin oranges**
**Fudge-striped cookies, frozen and broken into pieces**

Mix everything together except cookies. Put in refrigerator until ready to use. Stir in cookies before serving.

## HOMESTEAD SALAD

Bonnie Cook, Inola, OK

**1 large package frozen mixed vegetables**
**3 stalks celery**
**½ cup chopped onion**
**½ chopped pepper**
**1 can of red kidney beans**

**Marinated dressing:**
**¾ cup sugar**
**½ cup vinegar**
**½ cup water**
**1 teaspoon salt**
**1 tablespoon prepared mustard**

Cook frozen vegetables, drain, cool. Mix onion, celery, and peppers; add beans. Combine dressing ingredients, cook stirring constantly until thickened. Add cool dressing and refrigerate 8–10 hours. Keeps well several days.

## WATERGATE SALAD

Retha Kempf, Hughesville, MO

**15-ounce can crushed pineapple, with juice**
**3-ounce package pistachio instant pudding, or any other flavor you want**
**1 cup miniature marshmallows**
**8 ounces whipped topping**
**½ cup chopped pecans**

In large mixing bowl place crushed pineapple with juice. Sprinkle the pistachio pudding over pineapple and add the rest of ingredients; mix together. Put in serving bowl, chill until firm and ready to serve.

# SALADS

## OVERNIGHT LAYERED SALAD

Beverly Camp, Montoursville, PA

**1 head lettuce, cut into wedges**
**2 stalks celery, cut in 4-inch pieces**
**1 small onion, chopped**
**2 carrots, shredded**
**10-ounce package frozen peas, thawed**
**3 hard-boiled eggs, sliced**
**1½ cups mayonnaise**
**2 tablespoons sugar**
**4 slices bacon, cooked hard, crumbled**
**½ cup grated cheese**

Layer first 6 ingredients in a 9x13-inch dish. Mix mayonnaise and sugar and spread over entire top of salad. Cover and chill overnight. Before serving top with bacon and cheese.

## YUM YUM SALAD

Darlene Mindrup, Glendale, AZ

*"When I first went to meet my husband's family, I was introduced to some rather unusual foods. My yet-to-be husband insisted that this salad was a must. This was the first recipe I asked for after we were married."*

**Editor's Note:** Author of four Heartsong Presents romance novels, Darlene is a "radical feminist turned radical Christian."

**6-ounce package strawberry gelatin**
**1 small can crushed pineapple**
**¼ cup sugar**
**1 cup grated American process cheese (Velveeta; other cheese does not work)**
**½ pint whipping cream, whipped**
**2 cups miniature marshmallows**

Prepare gelatin according to directions on package. Let cool. Combine pineapple with sugar in saucepan. Heat until sugar is dissolved. Combine gelatin, pineapple mixture, and cheese. Let cool second time. When slightly thickened, fold in whipped cream and marshmallows. Chill until set.

## LAYERED SALAD MEDLEY

Wilma Brouwer, Zephyrhills, FL

**1 large head of lettuce, shredded**
**⅓ cup green onion, chopped**
**⅓ cup celery, sliced**
**6-ounce can water chestnuts, sliced**
**10 ounces frozen peas, not thawed**
**2 cups mayonnaise**
**1½ tablespoons sugar**
**¾ pound bacon, fried and crumbled**
**3–4 hard-boiled eggs**
**3 tomatoes, sliced**
**Parmesan and Romano cheeses**

Place lettuce in 9x13-inch casserole, sprinkle next 3 ingredients on top in layers. Break peas apart and sprinkle on top while frozen. Spread mayonnaise over top like frosting. Sprinkle with sugar. Cover and refrigerate overnight. Before serving add layers of bacon, egg, and tomato slices. Sprinkle with cheese, do not toss salad, cut into squares.

## HEAVENLY BROCCOLI SALAD

Elaine Mershon, Grants Pass, OR

*"This is a cold salad that must be refrigerated for at least 8 hours before it is served."*

**½ cup finely chopped celery**
**½ cup raisins, rinsed and drained**
**½ jar bacon bits**
**⅓ cup unsalted sunflower seed kernels**
**1 bunch broccoli florets**
**1 small red onion, chopped (optional)**
**Seedless red grapes, in season, (optional)**

**Dressing:**
**½ cup mayonnaise**
**¼ cup sugar**
**1 or 2 tablespoons cider vinegar**

Cut broccoli into small florets. Make sure onion and celery are in small pieces. Mix all salad ingredients together. Mix all dressing ingredients together well. Mix salad ingredients and dressing together well. Cover and refrigerate until ready to use.

## LAYERED SALAD

Frances Callaway, Rincon, GA

*"You can use any kind of leftover meat or canned vegetables. Great with broccoli or cauliflower too. Really is a meal in itself!"*

**1 head lettuce, cut small**
**2 cucumbers, diced**
**2 tomatoes, diced**
**1 medium onion, diced**
**6 radishes, sliced thin**
**1 medium bell pepper, diced**
**1 pound bacon, fried and crumbled**
**Salt and pepper to taste**
**3-ounce can English peas, drained**
**3-ounce can whole kernel corn, drained**
**1 pint mayonnaise**
**1 pound grated cheddar cheese**

Arrange salad ingredients, one at a time, layering as you go. Spread mayonnaise over salad ingredients and sprinkle cheddar cheese on top. Serve in a large oven-safe dish or oblong pan, with egg turner.

## SEVEN-LAYERED SALAD

Marie Quimby, Rio Rancho, NM

**1 head lettuce, washed, drained, cut into bite-size pieces**
**2 green peppers**
**2 cans sweet peas, drained**
**1 large onion, chopped**
**1 package shredded cheddar cheese**
**Miracle Whip**

Layer lettuce on bottom of salad bowl. Cover lettuce with layer of peas, green pepper, onion, Miracle Whip, cheese, then bacon bits. Cover and refrigerate overnight.

# SALADS

## 12-LAYER SALAD

Marie Schwartz, Berne, IN

**1 each of five different 3-ounce packages gelatin: cherry, lemon, orange, lime, and strawberry**
**16 ounces sour cream**

Add 1 cup boiling water to cherry gelatin. Take out ½ cup and add ⅓ cup sour cream, slowly. Pour in 9x13-inch pan. Chill 20 minutes or until firm. Add 3 tablespoons cold water to remaining gelatin and pour on top of first layer. Chill this until firm. Repeat all this with each flavor of gelatin, fixing in order given. May add whipped topping on top.

## FROSTED PEACH GELATIN

Wendy Wilcox, Covington, IN

**2 packages peach gelatin**
**2 cups boiling water**
**2 cups 7-Up, or other lemon-lime soda**
**1 cup peaches, drained, reserve juice**
**2 large bananas**

**Frosting:**
**½ cup sugar**
**3 tablespoons flour**
**1 egg**
**2 tablespoons butter**
**1 cup whipped topping or the whole container**

Make gelatin and add the 4 ingredients, let set. Frosting: Combine sugar and flour. Add reserved juice and egg. Heat over medium heat until thick, cool, then add whipped topping. Spread over gelatin mixture.

## CHURCH DINNER SALAD

Betty Warren, Crowley, TX

**¼ cup water**
**1 tablespoon unflavored gelatin**
**1½ cups sugar**
**1 teaspoon salt**
**1 cup vinegar**
**1 teaspoon celery salt, or seed**
**1 cup salad oil**
**¼ cup water**
**1 bell pepper**
**6–8 cups chopped cabbage (about 1 medium head)**
**2 large carrots**
**1 onion, chopped**

Mix ¼ cup water and gelatin, set aside. Bring to boil, ¼ cup water, sugar, salt, vinegar, and celery. Mix with gelatin while still hot. Set back and cool completely. When cool, add salad oil. Mix with mixer about 2 minutes. Prepare vegetables. After dressing is thoroughly mixed, pour over vegetables and mix well. Refrigerate 24 hours before serving.

## GINGER ALE SALAD

Elaine Mershon, Grants Pass, OR

*"I prefer to use canned fruits in juice instead of heavy syrup. This is my version of a recipe in the 1931* Joy of Cooking.*"*

**1 small can mandarin oranges**
**16-ounce can pineapple chunks**
**1 small jar maraschino cherries**
**15-ounce can grapefruit sections**
**½–1 cup seedless grapes (if in season, and if desired)**
**2 envelopes unflavored gelatin**
**4 tablespoons cold water**
**½ cup sugar**
**⅛ teaspoon salt**
**1 pint ginger ale**
**Juice of 1 lemon**

Drain all 3 fruits and reserve juice. Mix juices together. Drain, seed, and slice cherries in half. If you use grapes, wash and quarter. Peel and seed red grapes. Soak gelatin powder in cold water. Bring ½ cup of the reserved juice to a boil. Dissolve gelatin mixture in juice. Stir in sugar, salt, ginger ale, and lemon juice; stir well. Refrigerate until partially set then fold in chilled fruits. Pour into a wet salad mold and chill until set. Unmold onto a plate of lettuce. Serve plain or with a mixture of mayonnaise and whipped cream.

Serves 10.

## QUICKIE COOL SALAD

Shirley Bowen, Winamac, IN

**24 ounces cottage cheese**
**1 container whipped topping**
**1 can crushed pineapple, drained**
**1 package dry red or green gelatin (for holiday)**

Mix all together. Serve.

## CHOW MEIN NOODLE SALAD

Dorothea Hulet, Banks, OR

**1 package frozen peas, cook and cool**
**4 hard-boiled eggs, chopped**
**7-ounce can Spam, cubed**
**½ cup green pepper, diced**
**1 tablespoon green onion, chopped**
**1 cup mayonnaise**
**3-ounce can chow mein noodles**

Combine all ingredients, add mayonnaise and chill overnight. Just before serving add chow mein noodles.

# SALADS

## ROMAN PASTA SALAD

Pamela Owen, Crofton, KY

**1 pound thin spaghetti, or other shapes of pasta**
**2 large tomatoes**
**1 large onion**
**1 large cucumber**
**1 large green pepper**
**16 ounces Italian dressing**
**1 envelope Italian dressing mix**

Cook and cool pasta, set aside. Cut and dice vegetables. Mix vegetables with Italian dressing. Add to cool pasta, refrigerate overnight.

## NAPA SALAD

Virginia Harger, Ely, MN
Lois Jones, Elida, OH

**1 head Napa cabbage, shredded**
**2 bunches green onions, chopped**
**½ cup butter**
**2 packages Ramen noodles, broken (discard season packet)**
**Croutons (optional)**
**2 tablespoons sesame seeds**
**½–1 cup sliced almonds**
**¾ cup peanut oil**
**½ cup sugar**
**¼ cup rice vinegar**
**2 tablespoons soy sauce, more to taste**
**Garlic salt (optional)**

Combine cabbage and green onion in large serving bowl. In fry pan melt butter and add Ramen noodles, sesame seeds, and almonds; brown these together. In another pan boil peanut oil, sugar, rice vinegar, and soy sauce to make dressing. Pour dressing over combined cabbage and noodles, toss, and serve.

## BLT PASTA SALAD

Suzanne Beam, Tipton, IA
*"This is a wonderful summertime salad."*

**7-ounce package elbow macaroni, cooked and drained**
**8 slices bacon, cooked and crumbled**
**1 cup mayonnaise**
**⅓ cup chili sauce**
**¼ cup lemon juice**
**2 teaspoons chicken-flavored instant bouillon**
**2 teaspoons sugar or sweetener**
**1 large tomato, chopped**
**¼ cup sliced green onions**
**4 cups sliced lettuce**

Combine mayonnaise, chili sauce, lemon juice, bouillon, and sugar. Stir in tomato and onions, cover and chill. Just before serving stir in lettuce and bacon. Refrigerate leftovers.

Makes about 8 cups.

## SHELL "MAC" SALAD

Irma L. Lumsden, Marble Hill, MO

**1-pound box small shell macaroni**
**2 large green peppers, diced**
**2 large purple onions, diced**
**3 cups grated carrots**

**Dressing:**

**1 can condensed milk**
**½ cup white vinegar**
**½ cup vegetable oil**
**½ cup sugar**
**2 cups mayonnaise**

Boil macaroni until tender, drain and rinse under cold water. Toss together with veggies. Mix dressing ingredients and add to macaroni mixture.

## TACO SALAD TOSS

Julie Darby, Kansas City, MO

**2 cups chopped lettuce**
**1-pound can (2 cups) dark red kidney beans, drained**
**1 medium avocado, mashed**
**½ cup dairy sour cream**
**2 medium tomatoes, chopped, drained**
**1 tablespoon canned green chilies, chopped**
**2 tablespoons Italian dressing**
**1 teaspoon chili powder**
**1 teaspoon instant minced onions**
**¼ teaspoon salt**
**Dash of pepper**
**½ cup cheddar cheese, cut up**
**½ cup corn chips**
**Ripe olives (optional)**

Combine lettuce, kidney beans, and tomatoes and chill. Add next 5 ingredients. Mix well. Season with salt and pepper. Blend avocado and sour cream. Toss salad with avocado/sour cream dressing, top with cheese and corn chips. Garnish with ripe olives if desired.

## TACO SALAD

Barb Stachowski, Minneapolis, MN

**1 pound hamburger, fry and drain**
**1 package taco seasoning (1¼-ounce)**
**1 small head lettuce, broken up**
**1 medium onion, diced**
**1 green pepper, diced**
**3 small tomatoes, chopped**
**1 cup shredded cheddar cheese**
**1 can kidney beans**
**14-ounce package tostito chips, broken**
**1 bottle ranch dressing w/bacon**

Mix taco seasoning into hamburger. Cool in refrigerator. Just before serving mix in remaining ingredients and toss with dressing.

# SALADS

## THREE-BEAN SALAD

Elizabeth Hunt, Ithaca, MI

**1 can yellow beans, drained**
**1 can green beans, drained**
**1 can red beans, drained**
**1 small onion, chopped**
**½ cup red or green peppers**
**¾ cup (or less) sugar**
**⅔ cup vinegar**
**⅓ cup salad or olive oil**
**Salt and pepper**

Stir together. Put in a covered dish and refrigerate. Use slotted spoon to serve.

## CARROT-AMBROSIA SALAD

Mildred Sasher, North Fort Myers, FL

**1 pound carrots, scraped and shredded**
**8-ounce carton sour cream**
**20-ounce can crushed pineapple, drained**
**¾ cup golden raisins**
**¾ cup flaked coconut**
**¾ cup mini marshmallows**
**2 tablespoons honey**

Combine all ingredients, tossing well. Cover and chill at least 2 hours.

Makes 6–8 servings.

## FRESH BROCCOLI SALAD

Mrs. Florence E. Kelley, Hollywood, FL

*"Everyone asks me to bring this to covered dish dinners!"*

**1 package fresh broccoli**
**3 stalks celery (or 1 big Vidalia onion)**
**1 cup raisins**
**½ cup bacon bits (or 6 crispy bacon slices, cooked and crumbled)**
**1 tablespoon vinegar**
**1 teaspoon sugar**
**3 tablespoons mayonnaise**

Chop florets of broccoli and celery. Add other ingredients. Mix with mayonnaise. Cool an hour or more.

## BROCCOLI SALAD

Jeanne Durham, Gladwin, MI

*"A friend gave me this recipe and we love it!"*

**2 bunches broccoli (raw, use florets)**
**½ cup raisins (optional)**
**1 red onion**
**1 pound bacon, cooked, crumbled, and drained on paper towel**

Mix together broccoli, raisins, onion, and bacon. Separately mix together mayonnaise, vinegar, and sugar. Combine with mayonnaise mixture.

## MARINATED SALAD

Barbara Gates, Murphysboro, IL

**1 head cauliflower**
**1 bunch broccoli**
**1 can black olives**
**1 can mushrooms**
**1 can water chestnuts**
**Cherry tomatoes**
**Carrots**
**Celery**
**Other raw vegetables of your choice**
**1 package dry Italian dressing mix**

Pour Italian dressing mix and bottled dressing (more or less to taste) over all, mix well. Refrigerate 24 hours before serving.

## TREE SALAD

Melissa Barefoot, Alum Bank, PA

**1 head broccoli**
**1 head cauliflower**
**8-ounce package mild cheddar cheese**
**1 pound bacon, cooked until crisp**
**¼ cup salad dressing (Miracle Whip)**
**¼ cup sugar**
**2 teaspoons vinegar**

Cut up broccoli and cauliflower into bowl. Put in cheese. Crumble bacon into bowl. Mix Miracle Whip, sugar, and vinegar (if you like a lot of dressing, make a double batch). Pour into broccoli and cauliflower, mix well.

# SALADS

## BROCCOLI-CAULIFLOWER SALAD

Lois Gillaspie, Olney, IL

**1 bunch broccoli, cut into small bite-size pieces**
**1 cauliflower, cut into small bite-size pieces**

**Dressing:**
**¾ cup Green Goddess dressing**
**1 tablespoon sugar**
**1 tablespoon apple cider vinegar**
**¾ cup mayonnaise**
**½ cup bacon bits**
**Onion if desired**

* Green Goddess dressing is hard to find, so use this recipe if you need to.

Yields 2 cups.

To make your own Green Goddess salad dressing:

**1½ cups mayonnaise**
**¼ cup chives, chopped**
**2 tablespoons tarragon vinegar**
**2 tablespoons parsley, diced**
**1 tablespoon tarragon, crushed**
**1 green onion, chopped**

Mix broccoli and cauliflower together with dressing. Cover and let set overnight.

## CORN SALAD

Tammy Melson, Booneville, MS

**2 cans whole kernel corn**
**1 onion, diced**
**1 bell pepper, diced**
**1 large cucumber, peeled and diced**
**Pinch of salt**
**¼–½ teaspoon pepper**
**3 or 4 large tablespoons mayonnaise**

Mix all together and chill.

## CORN BREAD SALAD

Claudine Young, Ashgrove, MO

**1 small box corn bread mix**
**¼ cup chopped onion**
**¼ cup chopped celery**
**¼ cup chopped green pepper**
**½ cup chopped ripe tomato**
**Mayonnaise or salad dressing**

Bake corn bread according to directions, cool. Crumble bread into mixing bowl. Mix vegetables with crumbs. Moisten with mayonnaise or salad dressing. Chill about 3–4 hours.

## CAULIFLOWER-PEA SALAD

Nelda Isenhour, Kernersville, NC

**1 large head broccoli**
**1 large head cauliflower**
**¼ cup chopped onion**
**10-ounce package frozen peas**
**1 pint, or less, mayonnaise**
**1 jar bacon bits**
**2 tablespoons Salad Supreme or Salad Delight**
**4 ounces shredded cheese**

Cut cauliflower into bite-size pieces and spread in a 9x13-inch pan or dish. Sprinkle onion over cauliflower. Slightly thaw frozen peas; spread over cauliflower and onion. Spread mayonnaise over vegetables. Spread bacon bits over mayonnaise. Add Salad Supreme. Over all, sprinkle shredded cheese and let stand for at least 24 hours in refrigerator. Lightly toss when ready to serve.

## RANCH CRUNCHY PEA SALAD

Tammy Leisher, Milwaukee, WI

**10-ounce package frozen baby peas, thawed**
**1 cup diced celery**
**1 cup chopped cauliflower**
**¼ cup diced green onions**
**1 cup cashew halves**
**½ cup sour cream***
**1 cup prepared ranch dressing***
**Bacon, cooked and crumbled (for garnish)**

Combine all ingredients, garnish with cooked, crumbled bacon. Chill before serving.

*I use fat-free sour cream and lite ranch dressing to lower fat content.

## BLACK-EYED PEA SALAD

Mary Welton, Austin, TX

**3 tablespoons chopped onion**
**½ teaspoon red pepper**
**2 tablespoons white vinegar**
**3 tablespoons oil**
**¼ teaspoon salt**
**1 tablespoon sugar**
**4 15-ounce cans black-eyed peas, drained**

Mix all ingredients together, except peas, until sugar is dissolved. Pour over black-eyed peas and refrigerate. Will keep in refrigerator for several days.

# SALADS

## APPLE-CABBAGE COLESLAW

Juanita Hampton, Broken Bow, OK

**½ large cabbage, shredded**
**1 red apple, chopped with peel**
**½ cup fat-free salad dressing**
**Pinch of salt**
**½ tablespoon white vinegar**
**6 packages Sweet 'n Low sweetener**
**2 tablespoons skim milk**

Place shredded cabbage and chopped apples in large bowl. Mix together salad dressing, salt, vinegar, Sweet 'n Low, and milk. Pour over cabbage and apples. Mix well. Chill before serving. Keeps several days in refrigerator.

## COLLEEN'S "TASTES-LIKE-MORE" POTATO SALAD

Colleen L. Reece, Auburn, WA

**Editor's Note:** Colleen is one of Heartsong Presents' all-time favorite authors, and she has authored numerous books, with both historical and contemporary themes.

**4 medium potatoes, cooked and cooled to handling temperature (best to use White Rose potatoes)**
**1 medium onion (better yet, several green onions with tops), chopped**
**4 hard-boiled eggs, cooled and chopped**
**4 dill pickles, chopped fine**

Toss lightly with a pre-stirred blend of mayonnaise, prepared mustard, a little dill pickle juice, and pepper. Good served right away or chilled. Refrigerate.

Variations: Black or ripe olives, cherry tomatoes, and/or fresh parsley can be used for garnish.

## LETTUCE SLAW

Susan Roberts, Bloomingdale, OH

**1 head lettuce**
**1 head cauliflower, cut up**
**1 tomato, diced**
**1 can black olives, sliced**
**1 purple or red onion, sliced, broken into rings**
**Mayonnaise**
**⅓ cup Parmesan cheese**
**1 cup crumbled bacon**
**1 tablespoon sugar**

Mix lettuce, cauliflower, tomato, olives, and onion with enough mayonnaise to lightly coat. Refrigerate for a couple of hours. Mix well Parmesan cheese, bacon, and sugar. Add just before serving.

## SAUERKRAUT SALAD

Virginia Byers, Brea, CA

1 pound sauerkraut
1 cup celery, chopped
1 medium onion, chopped
1 small can (1 ounce) pimientos, chopped
½ cup vinegar
½ cup salad oil
1 cup sugar

Place kraut in strainer and scald. Let cool, add all ingredients. Chill overnight. Stir once or twice.

## PICNIC POTATO SALAD SPUD

Angela Flores, Phoenix, AZ

2 baked potatoes
2 tablespoons chopped onion
1 hard-boiled egg, chopped
1 celery, chopped
2 tablespoons pimiento, chopped
2 tablespoons chopped pickle
⅓ cup mayonnaise
1 teaspoon mustard
1 teaspoon vinegar or juice from sour pickle
¼ teaspoon salt
2 shakes of black pepper
Powdered paprika to decorate

Cool potatoes, cut thin slice from top, remove pulp, and dice. Combine potato, onion, pickle, celery, pimiento, and egg; stir lightly. Combine mayonnaise, mustard, vinegar, salt, and pepper; mix thoroughly. Combine potato mixture and mayonnaise mixture together; mix well. Heap into potato shells. Sprinkle with paprika; chill.

## HONG KONG CHICKEN SALAD

Debbie Baluka, Colstrip, MT

6 ounces cooked and shredded chicken (boneless, skinless chicken)
3 cups shredded Romaine lettuce
1 cup fresh bean sprouts
3–4 green onions, slivered lengthwise and cut into 1-inch pieces
1 cucumber, chopped into ½- to 1-inch pieces

**Dressing:**

1½ tablespoons rice vinegar
4 teaspoons salad oil
1 teaspoon sugar
⅛ teaspoon pepper
¼ teaspoon salt
2 teaspoons dark sesame oil

Make dressing ahead of time and chill. Just before serving add dressing to chilled salad.

## FLYING FARMER CHICKEN SALAD
Jan Brouwer, Lansing, IL

**5 cups cooked chicken, cut in chunks**
**2 tablespoons salad oil**
**1 teaspoon salt**
**2 tablespoons orange juice**
**2 tablespoons vinegar**
**Mayonnaise**

Mix and pour over chicken. Let stand in refrigerator overnight. Add remaining ingredients and lightly toss.

## BUFFET CHICKEN SALAD
Mrs. John H. Clement, Chesapeake, VA

**2 whole fryers**
**20-ounce can white grapes, drained**
**20-ounce can pineapple chunks (drained)**
**11-ounce can mandarin oranges, drained**
**1 cup chopped celery**
**1 cup mayonnaise**
**2 tablespoons soy sauce**
**1 cup toasted almonds, slivered**

Boil chicken in lightly salted water until very tender. Chill and remove all skin and bones. Cut in bite-size pieces. Add celery and fruit. Mix soy sauce and mayonnaise and blend with first 4 ingredients. Sprinkle toasted almonds over the top.

Serves 8.

## LO-CAL ITALIAN DRESSING
Lucile Foote, Minoa, NY

**½ cup water**
**½ cup vinegar**
**2 teaspoons cornstarch**
**1 tablespoon vinegar**
**¼ teaspoon dry mustard**
**¼ teaspoon paprika**
**1 teaspoon salt (or No Salt salt substitute)**
**Sugar**
**½ teaspoon sweet basil**
**⅛ teaspoon instant minced garlic**
**Pepper to taste**

Bring water and ½ cup vinegar to boil. Remove from heat and stir in cornstarch dissolved in 1 tablespoon vinegar. Return to low heat and stir until just boiling. Remove and beat in other ingredients—OR—Beat all ingredients in microwave-safe pint container. Microwave on high about 3 minutes, stirring twice during cooking.

Makes 1 cup.

# VEGETABLES

# VEGETABLES

## ASPARAGUS CASSEROLE

Ingrid W. Hutto, Gilbert, SC

**1 can asparagus, reserve juice**
**1 can cream of chicken soup**
**4 pieces of bread, toasted**
**Cheddar cheese**

OVEN 400°

Break toasted bread in bottom of dish. Put drained asparagus on top of bread. Mix asparagus juice with cream of chicken soup. Pour over mixture. Top with cheese. Bake at 400° for 45 minutes to 1 hour.

## ASPARAGUS DELIGHT

Kay Harjo, Bellville, KS

*"Kids even like it!"*

**1 can cream of asparagus soup**
**1 can cream of celery soup**
**1½ cans milk**
**1 stick margarine or butter**

Mix together and simmer over low heat until creamy. Serve with snack crackers.

## BAKED SWEET POTATOES

Sandy Clark

**6–8 large sweet potatoes**

OVEN 425°

Wash potatoes, cut ends and scars off. Preheat oven to 425°. Wrap each potato in aluminum foil. Place loosely on cookie sheet, bake for 45 minutes or until fork passes easily through (center oven rail). Unwrap potatoes, butter generously, and enjoy! Refrigerate any left-overs and re-warm when needed.

Option: Add cinnamon with butter.

## GRANDMA'S SWEET POTATO CASSEROLE

Julie Malterer, Uhrichsville, OH

**Editor's Note:** Julie has been in charge of Heartsong Presents customer service department since the beginning in 1992.

**3–6 cups mashed sweet potatoes**
**½ cup margarine, melted**
**2 eggs**
**1 cup sugar**
**1 tablespoon vanilla**
**1 cup brown sugar**
**⅓ cup flour**
**1 cup chopped nuts**

OVEN 350°

Mix sweet potatoes, ½ cup melted margarine, eggs, sugar, and vanilla together in a bowl. Pour into buttered casserole. Mix remaining ingredients with ⅓ margarine. Sprinkle over potato mixture. Bake at 350° for 20 minutes.

## SWEET POTATO CASSEROLE

Marjorie Osborn, Robinson, IL

**1 large can sweet potatoes**
**¾ cup sugar**
**2 eggs**
**1 teaspoon vanilla**
**1 stick margarine, melted**
**½ cup evaporated milk**

**Topping:**
**1 cup brown sugar**
**⅓ cup flour**
**1 cup chopped nuts**
**⅓ cup margarine**

OVEN 350°

Mash potatoes with juice. Mix all ingredients with potatoes and pour into greased 9x13-inch pan. Mix topping ingredients together until crumbly and sprinkle on top of mixture. Do not stir. Bake at 350° for about 40 minutes.

## PECAN SWEET POTATOES

Mary Williams, Bonnie, IL

**6 medium sweet potatoes, baked, cooled, peeled**
**½ cup brown sugar**
**½ cup chopped pecans**
**1 cup orange juice**
**1 tablespoon orange peel**
**1½ tablespoons butter, cut up**
**½ teaspoon salt**

OVEN 350°

Lightly spray 9x13-inch baking pan with vegetable spray. Slice potatoes in ¼-inch slices; layer in pan, set aside. In small bowl, combine brown sugar, pecans, and orange peel. Pour mixture over sweet potatoes. Pour orange juice over all. Dot with butter. Season with salt to taste. Cover and refrigerate until ready to use. Bake at 350° for 45 minutes, uncover and cook 15–20 minutes longer.

# VEGETABLES

## SWEET POTATO SOUFFLE

Selma Stenholm, Evanston, IL

**5 fresh sweet potatoes, approximately**
**½ cup granulated sugar**
**3 tablespoons butter**
**2 eggs**
**¼ teaspoon cinnamon**
**½ teaspoon vanilla flavoring**
**Approximately ½ cup milk or to desired consistency**

**Topping:**
**Brown sugar**
**Chopped pecans**
**Marshmallows**

OVEN 350°

Cook potatoes until tender, then puree. Add ingredients with milk to desired consistency. Bake at 350° for 1 hour. Top with chopped pecans and brown sugar last 10 minutes of baking time. Or: top with marshmallows the last 5 minutes of baking time.

## SWEET POTATO CASSEROLE

Nikki Miller, Morgantown, IN

**2 large or 4 small cans sweet potatoes, drained**
**1 cup sugar**
**2 eggs**
**1 teaspoon vanilla**
**½ cup butter or margarine, melted**

OVEN 350°

Mix all ingredients and pour into 9x13-inch casserole dish. Add topping.

**Topping:**
**2 cups brown sugar**
**⅔ cup flour**
**1 cup chopped pecans or almonds**
**⅔ cup margarine or butter, softened**

Bake at 350° for 30–35 minutes.

## HOMINY CASSEROLE

Carolyn Butcher, Carthage, TX

**3 small cans yellow hominy, drained**
**1 can cream of mushroom soup**
**8-ounce jar jalapeno processed cheese**
**3 green onions, finely chopped**
**1 cup corn chips, crushed**

OVEN 300°

Mix all ingredients. Sprinkle crushed corn chips on top. Bake for 20 minutes in casserole dish at 300°.

## CREAMY SCALLOPED POTATOES

Carol Fields, Magnolia, TX

**8 medium potatoes**
**12 slices American cheese**
**1 can cream of chicken soup**
**1 can water**

OVEN 350°

Peel potatoes, slice into thin slices (crosswise). Use four for first layer in oblong dish. Salt and pepper to taste. Put six slices of cheese on top of potato layer, spread ½ can of soup over cheese. Repeat. Pour 1 can of water over top slowly. Cover with foil and bake 45 minutes to 1 hour at 350° until done.

## GRILLED PARMESAN TATERS

Carlene Bennett, Wichita, KS

**1 pound small red potatoes, cut into ½-inch cubes**
**¼ cup chopped onion**
**2 teaspoons oil**
**1 tablespoon Parmesan cheese**
**1 teaspoon oregano**
**½ teaspoon garlic salt**
**¼ teaspoon pepper**
**Heavy duty foil**

Place taters in bowl, add onion and oil, toss. Put in center of foil. Combine dry ingredients and sprinkle over taters. Fold foil into pouch, put on grill for 18–20 minutes or until taters are tender.

Serves 4.

## MAKE-AHEAD MASHED POTATO CASSEROLE

Sharon Johnston, Independence, KS

**12 large potatoes, peeled and boiled in salted water, drained**
**8 ounces sour cream**
**8-ounce package cream cheese**
**1 teaspoon onion powder**
**¼ cup melted margarine or butter**
**Paprika**

OVEN 350°

Mix together all ingredients except butter and paprika. Mash or whip until fluffy, adding milk if necessary. Spread in buttered 9x13-inch casserole and top with melted butter and paprika. Bake at 350° for 1 hour. May be kept in refrigerator or frozen for future use.

## HASH BROWN POTATO CASSEROLE

Lorie Weidhaas Bell, Arlington, TX
Sonia Sweeney, Columbus, GA
Marge Porter, Gulf Breeze, FL
Eunice Van De Hoef, Englewood, CO
Margaret Swagger, Lake City, MN
Kimberly Kunkle, Manheim, PA

**2-pound bag frozen hash browns**
**1 stick margarine or butter**
**½–1 teaspoon salt**
**½ teaspoon pepper**
**1 can cream of chicken soup (can use reduced fat/sodium)**
**1 pint sour cream (can use low-fat)**
**¼ cup chopped onion**
**8–10 ounces shredded cheddar cheese**
**1 cup cornflakes**
**3 tablespoons melted butter**
**2 cups ham, diced and cooked (optional)**

Mix all ingredients except cornflakes and melted butter. Pour in large baking dish. Sprinkle top with cornflakes and butter. Bake at 350° for 1½ hours.

Variation:
Julia Nooney, Feura Bush, NY
*"Whenever I take this to potluck suppers I've learned to also take a few copies of the recipe with me. Even using reduced or fat-free ingredients, this makes a filling dish."*

Add 1 can cream of potato soup (can use reduced fat or low-sodium type).

## POTATO CASSEROLE

Gay Waneck, Smithville, TX
*"Great when you need a "take-out" dish."*

**2 cups mashed potatoes, whipped smooth**
**8 ounces cream cheese**
**Onion, chopped**
**2 eggs**
**1 can French fried onions**

OVEN 350°

Add cream cheese, onion, and eggs to potatoes; beat all until smooth. Pour into casserole dish, sprinkle with French fried onions. Bake about 20 minutes at 350°.

## SCALLOPED POTATOES

Betty Hendren, Harrodsburg, KY

**6 medium potatoes, sliced thin**
**6 tablespoons butter (corn oil margarine)**
**2 tablespoons flour**
**2 cups milk (½ or 1%)**
**¾ cup grated cheddar cheese**
**Salt and pepper to taste**

OVEN 375°

Place sliced potatoes in oven dish sprayed with cooking spray (PAM). Melt butter over low heat. Add flour, stir until smooth. Add salt and pepper to taste, milk, and cheese; stirring constantly until thickened. Pour over potatoes and bake uncovered at 375° for 1 hour.

Serves 6.

## QUICK AND EASY SCALLOPED POTATOES

Evangeline Frodahl, Ocean City, MD

**4 cups peeled and sliced (thinly) potatoes**
**½ medium green pepper, cut in strips**
**10-ounce can condensed cream of mushroom soup**

In a two-quart glass casserole dish combine potatoes and green pepper, cover with glass lid. Microwave on high 10–12 minutes, stirring once. Stir in soup and recover. Cook on high 5–6 minutes or until tender, stirring once. Sprinkle with paprika or cheese if desired. Let stand covered 2 minutes.

Makes 4–6 servings.

## ROASTED POTATO BITES

Mrs. Lesley Ellis, Pascagoula, MS

**12 to 15 small red potatoes**
**1 cup shredded cheddar cheese**
**½ cup real or light mayonnaise**
**½ cup minced green onion**
**½ pound bacon, cooked, crumbled**
**2 tablespoons chopped fresh basil**

OVEN 375°

Bake potatoes until tender. Allow to cool enough to handle. Cut crosswise in half. Slice a small slice from bottom so they stand upright. Scoop out potatoes leaving ¼ in shell. Combine scooped potatoes with rest of ingredients. Spoon in potato shells. Bake 3–5 minutes or until brown. Serve hot.

## OVEN BAKED POTATOES

Louise Sisk, Ridgecrest, NC

*"My family enjoys these potatoes so much that I keep some mixture in the refrigerator for a quick meal helper."*

**6–8 potatoes cut into wedges**
**¼ cup cooking oil**
**2 tablespoons Parmesan cheese**
**¼ teaspoon pepper, or less**
**1 teaspoon garlic salt**
**½ teaspoon paprika**

OVEN 375°

Cut potatoes into four to six wedges, depending on size. Mix potatoes and cooking oil. Mix the remaining ingredients, put just a little of mixture at a time in plastic bag, shake four to five pieces of potatoes and place on sprayed baking sheet. Repeat until all potatoes are coated. Bake at 375° for 45 minutes or until tender.

# VEGETABLES

## POTATO AND APPLE WHAT?

Laurie Boyd, Mesa, AZ

**2 medium red delicious apples**
**2 red potatoes**
**2 medium onions**
**½ cup raisins**
**Dash of mace**
**1 tablespoon molasses**
**1 teaspoon cinnamon**
**1 teaspoon garlic powder**
**Approximately ½ cup water**

Cut apples into bite-size chunks. Clean and cut potatoes into bite-size chunks; put into pan with water. Turn heat on low. Cut onions and add to pot. Add garlic powder, cinnamon, and mace; bring to boil. Boil uncovered until tender. Add raisins and molasses and let sit about 2 minutes. Eat it hot or cold. Will look grayish but tastes great!

## PARTY POTATOES

Waneita Pearl, Linton, IN

*"I entered this recipe in a potato contest a number of years ago, and won ten pounds of potatoes every week for a year. I supplied the church dinners with potatoes that year."*

**6 medium potatoes, boiled, peeled, cut for mashing**
**3 ounces cream cheese**
**1 small sour cream**
**Salt to taste**
**Paprika**
**Butter or margarine**

OVEN 375°

Boil and mash potatoes. Add cheese and sour cream, beat. If not thin enough add some milk. Salt to taste. Pour in baking dish. Dot with butter; sprinkle top with paprika. Bake in 375° oven 30 minutes or until brown on top. This can be made early and baked later.

## PARTY POTATOES

Margie Goble, Long Beach, CA

**6 large potatoes**
**½ stick margarine**
**1 can cream of chicken soup**
**1 pint sour cream**
**¾ cup chopped green onions, with tops**
**1½ cups cheddar cheese, grated**
**½ cup bread crumbs**

OVEN 375°

Boil potatoes in jackets, cool, and grate with large grater. Melt margarine and remove from heat. Add to undiluted soup, sour cream, onions, and cheese. Fold this mixture into potatoes. Put in greased casserole. Top with crumbs and bake at 375° for 45 minutes.

## CHEESY POTATOES

Sally Gordin, Modesto, CA

**32-ounce bag frozen hash browned potatoes**
**1 can creamy chicken mushroom soup or cream of mushroom soup**
**½ pint sour cream**
**½ cup milk**
**1 cube margarine, melted**
**1 cup cheddar cheese, grated**

OVEN 350°

In a bowl, mix together hash browned potatoes with soup, sour cream, and milk. When mixed well, add melted butter and about ½ of the grated cheese. Spread into a greased 9x13-inch pan and top with remaining cheese. Bake at 350° uncovered for about 45 minutes.

Serves 6–8.

## COLCANNON

Una McManus, Columbia, MD

**Editor's Note:** Author of numerous books, including *Love's Tender Gift, Abiding Love*, and *Wild Irish Roses* for Heartsong Presents, Una has written under the pen names of Elizabeth Murphey and Cara McCormack. She is a native of Ireland with relatives still living there.

**3 pounds potatoes**
**1 small head cabbage or 1 bunch kale (called curly kale in Ireland)**
**1 cup milk (more or less as needed)**
**½ to 1 cup chopped onions (chopped green onions can be substituted)**
**½ stick margarine or butter**
**Salt and black pepper**
**½ to 1 cup shredded cheddar cheese**

OVEN 350°

Boil spuds and mash. Chop cabbage or kale very fine and steam with onions (or boil in potato water). Onions could also be sautéed, if you have the time. Chopped green onions could be left raw, but should be chopped very fine. Mix mashed potatoes, cabbage/kale, onions, salt and pepper, margarine/butter, and milk together. Mix well. Transfer into greased dish and bake in 350° oven for 20–30 minutes. If you do not want crusty top, cover with foil. During last five minutes, sprinkle with shredded cheese. Good as side dish, or as a whole lunch served with vegetable soup.

## LOUISIANA FRIED TATERS

Eleanor Vaughan, Nashville, IN

**4 large potatoes, diced, unpeeled**
**1 large onion, diced**
**Salt and pepper to taste**
**1 small yellow squash**
**1 large red tomato, diced**

Fry potatoes and onion until half done. Salt and pepper to taste. Add squash and fry until all done. Add tomato, cook until tomato is just warm. Serve hot.

# VEGETABLES

## $20.00 POTATOES

Brenda Krug, Baltimore, MD

**6–7 potatoes, boiled and peeled**
**¼ cup butter**
**10-ounce can cream of mushroom soup**
**3 tablespoons minced onion**
**2 cups sour cream**
**1½ cups shredded cheddar cheese**
**1 teaspoon salt**
**½ teaspoon pepper**
**½ cup cornflakes**

OVEN 350°

Grate potatoes in bowl; heat butter and soup in pan, stirring until smooth. Stir in onion, sour cream, cheese, and salt and pepper. Add to potatoes, mix well, spoon in baking dish. Top with cornflakes and melted butter. Chill or bake at 350° for 1 hour.

## LEFSE

JoAnn A. Grote, Montevideo, MN

*"In the 1930s, my grandparents ran a café in a small town on the Minnesota prairie near the setting for my Heartsongs. Lefse was served on every table at every meal. One day my grandmother came out to the dining room to find a traveling salesman with a round of lefse on his lap. He'd never seen lefse before and thought it was a new kind of napkin!"*

**Editor's Note:** JoAnn has authored several Heartsong Presents romances, including *The Sure Promise* and *Sweet Surrender.*

**5 cups white potatoes, peeled**
**½ cup sour cream**
**1 teaspoon salt**
**¼ cup butter, melted**
**2¾ cups flour**

Cook potatoes until done. Drain. Put through ricer and cool completely. Mix cream, salt, and butter in bowl. Alternately add potatoes and flour, mixing well. (You may wish to use your hands to mix.) If mixture is too moist, add more flour. Divide dough in half. Make 2 long rolls. Place in refrigerator at least 30 minutes. Preheat electric griddle to 410°. Slice dough into 1 to 2-inch pieces. Roll into very thin rounds (about 8 inches in diameter) on floured board. (Use only enough flour on board to keep dough from sticking on board. Too much flour will toughen the lefse). Bake until little brown spots appear. Turn and bake on other side. Rounds should be soft when done. Cover baked rounds immediately to prevent them from drying out. Store in tight containers in refrigerator.

Makes about 16 rounds.

In the past, lefse was often wrapped around a piece of meat. Today, it is commonly eaten as a sweet. The rounds are cut into four pie-shaped pieces. The piece is then spread with butter and either white or brown sugar. The pieces are rolled to make them easier to eat.

## CORN CASSEROLE

Mary Anne Tarrant, Bullard, TX

*"This dish has become a favorite at family and church dinners."*

**1-pound can whole kernel corn**
**1-pound can cream style corn**
**8 ounces sour cream (or 1 cup milk)**
**1 egg, beaten**
**3 tablespoons chopped onion**
**1 small box quick corn muffin mix**
**½ stick margarine**
**½ teaspoon parsley**
**½ teaspoon salt**
**½ teaspoon pepper**

OVEN 350°

Combine all ingredients. Bake in greased 7x11-inch casserole dish in 350° oven for 45 minutes.

Serves 10.

## CORN FRITTERS

Susan Hunsicker, Lehighton, PA

**1¼ cups flour**
**1 teaspoon baking powder**
**1½ teaspoons salt**
**2 eggs**
**2 cups chopped, fresh corn**
**Milk**

Combine ingredients, batter should be thick. Add more flour to batter if needed. Drop into hot oil, using small tablespoon.

## CORN SOUFFLE

Amy Winkler, Cincinnati, OH

**1 stick margarine, melted**
**1 can creamed corn**
**1 can whole kernel corn, drained**
**1 box corn meal mix**
**8 ounces sour cream**

OVEN 375

Mix ingredients together and bake in greased dish. Bake at 375° for 45 minutes, covered.

## MOCK FRESH FRIED CORN

Irene Monroe, Knoxville, TN

*"So fresh tasting you're sure to see the corn silk!"*

**3 cans shoe peg corn (white) juice and all, Green Giant brand**
**4 tablespoons flour**
**½ pint whipping cream, do not whip**
**Salt and pepper to taste**
**½ stick margarine**

OVEN 350°

Mix flour with corn, add salt and pepper and whipping cream. Cut margarine and put in corn. Bake at 350° for 30–40 minutes.

# VEGETABLES

## QUICK CORN CASSEROLE

Rosey Dow, Grenada, West Indies

**Editor's Note**: Rosey is the author of *Megan's Choice* and *Em's Only Chance* in the Heartsong Presents series. She, her husband, and children are missionaries in Grenada.

**1 cup quick baking mix**
**3 tablespoons butter or margarine**
**2 cups whole kernel corn**
**2 tablespoons flour**
**1 cup evaporated milk**
**1 tablespoon sugar**
**2 eggs**
**⅛ teaspoon pepper**
**¼ teaspoon salt**

OVEN 350°

Cut butter into baking mix. Set aside for topping. Run frozen corn under warm water to thaw, or drain canned corn. Place all ingredients except corn and topping into blender. Blend five seconds, until egg is incorporated. Add corn and blend 2 seconds. Some large pieces of corn should remain. Do not overblend! Pour corn mixture into buttered 9x9-inch casserole dish. Sprinkle on topping. Bake at 350° for 30 minutes, until knife inserted in center comes out clean.

Serves 4.

## GREEN BEAN CASSEROLE

Jan Willman, Noblesville, IN

**2 quarts green beans, drained**
**2 cans cream of mushroom soup**
**Large can French fried onion rings**
**Milk**
**Salt and pepper**

OVEN 350°

Mix beans, soup, and salt and pepper to taste with enough milk to slightly dilute soup. Spread in cake pan and sprinkle with onion rings. Bake at 350° until bubbly and onion rings are slightly brown.

## PINTO BEANS

Elsie M. Brown, Doniphan, MO

*"This recipe is from my friend Dollie Scott."*

**2 cups pinto beans, washed**
**4 cups water**
**1 pound ground beef**
**1 medium onion, chopped**
**1 cup diced tomato**
**Salt and pepper to taste**
**Chili powder to taste**

Put beans in pan with 4 cups water. Bring to a boil and cook 5 minutes. Turn off heat and let stand for 1 hour. Drain and put in 2 cups of fresh water; cook beans until they start to get tender. Brown ground beef and onion. Add tomatoes to the beans. You can now season with salt, pepper, and chili powder if you like. (It is good with chili powder.) Let simmer with meat and spices until beans are done and flavors are well mixed. You can serve them with cornbread or over rice!

## CHEESY GREEN BEANS

Paula M. Barben, Maple Shade, NJ

**3 cans of sliced green beans**
**16-ounce jar processed cheese**
**1 pound bacon**

OVEN 325°

Cook bacon until crisp and set aside. Drain green beans and put into a baking dish. Microwave the processed cheese and pour onto the green beans. Crumble the bacon and add to the mixture. Mix well. Put into 325° oven until bubbly and hot. Serve immediately.

## LENTIL-RICE CASSEROLE

Melva Jane Proechel, Hastings, MN

*"When I take this casserole to a gathering of people it always disappears. It rates an A+ in our recipe collection. Hope you like it as well."*

**3 cups chicken broth**
**¾ cup uncooked lentils**
**½ cup uncooked brown rice**
**1 small onion, chopped**
**½ teaspoon basil**
**¼ teaspoon oregano**
**¼ teaspoon thyme**
**¼ teaspoon garlic powder**
**¾ cup mozzarella, cheddar, or Colby cheese, grated**

OVEN 300°

Mix all ingredients together in large casserole dish. Cover and bake at 300° for 2–2½ hours. Top with cheese 20 minutes before baking is over.

## PINTO BEAN CASSEROLE

Betty Myers, Lexington, NC

**1 to 1½ pounds hamburger**
**1 medium onion, chopped**
**1 can tomato soup**
**1 can pinto beans**
**1 can chili beans**
**½ package Mexican cornbread mix**

OVEN 350°

Cook hamburger and onions, then drain grease off. Press in bottom of 9x13-inch baking dish. Spread tomato soup over meat mixture, then pour beans over this. Mix cornbread as directed on package and spread over beans. Bake at 350° about 1 hour or until bread is cooked and light brown.

## CHEESE SQUASH CASSEROLE

Rhonda Holston, Carrier, MS

**3 cups cooked squash, drained**
**1 pound ground beef, browned and drained**
**8 ounces processed cheese spread**
**1 roll Ritz crackers, crushed**
**2 eggs, beaten**
**1 tablespoon butter**
**1 can Rotel tomatoes**
**1 medium onion**
**1 bell pepper**
**1 can cream of mushroom soup**
**Salt and pepper**
**1 can French fried onions, for topping**

OVEN 350°

Sauté onion and bell pepper in butter. Combine all ingredients together adding salt and pepper to taste. Put in 9x13-inch casserole dish; top with fried onions. Bake at 350° for 30 minutes.

## SQUASH DRESSING

Crystal Hill, Belton, TX
Marie Nowell, Nashville, TN

**2 cups cornbread**
**2 cups yellow squash, cooked and mashed**
**1 cup diced onion**
**1 stick margarine**
**2 cups diced chicken**
**Salt and pepper to taste**
**1 can cream of chicken soup (do not dilute)**
**1 can sliced mushroom**
**1 teaspoon sage**
**½ cup egg, beaten, or 2 eggs**

OVEN 350°

Sauté onion in margarine. Mix all ingredients and bake at 350° for 30–40 minutes, until brown on top.

## CRESCENT ROLL ZUCCHINI PIE

Mary Welch, Wendell, NC

*"My garden has been so full this year. I've made lots of these great pies!"*

**4 cups thinly sliced zucchini**
**1 cup chopped onion**
**¼ to ½ cup margarine**
**1 teaspoon salt**
**½ teaspoon pepper**
**¼ teaspoon oregano**
**2 eggs, beaten**
**8 ounces mozzarella cheese**
**1 package refrigerator crescent rolls**
**2 teaspoons mustard**

OVEN 375°

Cook and stir zucchini, onion, and margarine for 10 minutes. Stir in salt, pepper, and oregano. Combine eggs and mozzarella cheese, stir into zucchini mixture. Spread crescent rolls into 10-inch greased pan and spread crust with mustard. Bake at 375° for 18–20 minutes or until set. Let stand for 10 minutes before serving.

## SUMMER ZUCCHINI CASSEROLE

Lolita McDowell, New Philadelphia, OH

*"This carefully guarded recipe is a favorite dish among family and coworkers."*

**Editor's Note:** Lolita loves to sell books, including inspirational romance books, to Christian bookstores. She is a longtime employee of Barbour Publishing.

**1 medium zucchini, chopped**
**2 white potatoes, chopped**
**2 green peppers, chopped**
**2 carrots, chopped**
**1 celery stalk, chopped**
**3 or 4 tomatoes, sliced**
**⅓ cup raw rice (not instant)**
**1¾ cups shredded cheddar cheese**

Combine the following and let stand while chopping the vegetables:

**⅓ cup olive oil**
**2 tablespoons wine vinegar**
**2 tablespoons parsley**
**3 teaspoons salt**
**¾ teaspoon pepper**
**1 teaspoon Tabasco, to taste**

OVEN 350°

Spray large casserole dish with cooking spray. Cover bottom of pan with a layer of tomatoes followed by half of the chopped vegetables. Then add another layer of tomatoes. Sprinkle the rice over the top and add the rest of the vegetables topped by a final layer of tomatoes. Pour oil mixture over all and bake at 350° for 1½ hours. Sprinkle the cheese on top at the end of the baking time and let it melt.

## ZUCCHINI SQUASH CASSEROLE

Mable Purviance, Missoula, MT

**2 pounds zucchini squash**
**1 onion, chopped**
**1 bell pepper, chopped**
**1 carrot grated**
**1 stick margarine**
**8-ounce package herb dressing mix**
**1 can cream of chicken soup**
**½ pint yogurt**

OVEN 350°

Cook squash and onions until tender, then mash. Add pepper, carrots, soup, and yogurt; mix well. Melt margarine and add to dressing mix. Put ⅔ of dressing mix with squash. Pour into a greased casserole dish and put the remaining ⅓ dressing on top. Bake at 350° for 35 minutes.

Takes a large casserole dish. This can be prepared ahead of time and frozen.

# VEGETABLES

## ZUCCHINI HALF SHELLS

Carolyn Taylor, Gaffney, SC

**6 small zucchini, cut ends off and cut in half lengthwise**
**¼ cup butter, melted**
**1 tablespoon grated onion**
**1 beef bouillon cube, crushed**
**2 tablespoons water**

Melt butter in large skillet, add grated onion and bouillon cube. Add zucchini cut side down; cook until golden. Turn; add 2 tablespoons water. Cover and cook over low heat about 10 minutes.

Serves 5–6.

## BUTTERED SQUASH

JoAnn Lee, Garland, TX

*"It is very good and good for you."*

Take fresh crook-neck squash; wash and cut it. Use plenty of cut up onions, butter, salt, and pepper. Add water and bake in microwave oven until done; serve.

## CABBAGE CASSEROLE

Kristi Gregory, Whitehouse, TX

**1½ pounds ground meat (browned and drained)**
**1 head of cabbage**
**1 small bag of carrots, sliced**
**16-ounce can tomato sauce**
**1 cup rice**
**½ cup sugar**
**Salt and pepper to taste**

OVEN 350°

Brown and drain ground meat. Boil cabbage for 10 minutes (in small strips). Cook rice as box directs and set aside. Add carrots, tomato sauce, sugar, rice, and cabbage to meat in 9x13-inch Pyrex dish. Bake at 350° for 1–1½ hours.

Serves 6.

## BROCCOLI AND CAULIFLOWER CASSEROLE

Lucy McGinnis, Bella Vista, AR

**16 ounces frozen broccoli**
**8 ounces frozen cauliflower**
**½ cup chopped onion**
**½ cup sliced celery**
**1 tablespoon butter**
**1 can cream of mushroom soup**
**8-ounce jar processed cheese food spread**
**8-ounce can sliced chestnuts, drained**
**1½ cups quick cook rice (dry)**
**1 cup milk**
**½ cup butter**
**Slivered almonds**

OVEN 350°

Cook broccoli and cauliflower until tender and crisp, drain. Sauté onions, celery, and almonds in 1 tablespoon butter. Combine remaining ingredients and pour into greased 2½ quart (9x13-inch) pan. Bake at 350° for 40 minutes.

## BROCCOLI AND RICE CASSEROLE

Nikki Miller, Morgantown, IN
Lynn Campbell, Greensburg, PA

**20 ounces frozen chopped broccoli, thawed**
**1 can cream of mushroom soup**
**1 small jar processed cheese food**
**1 stick margarine**
**1 cup diced celery**
**1 cup chopped onion**
**1½ cups quick-cooking rice (uncooked)**

OVEN 350°

Heat soup, cheese, margarine, celery, and onion just enough to melt the cheese and margarine. Add uncooked rice and broccoli. Stir well. Pour into greased 9x13-inch pan (cooking spray works great for pan). Bake at 350° for 35 minutes.

## BROCCOLI SOUFFLE

Janine Brian, Lemoore, CA

**2 packages frozen broccoli**
**¾ cup mayonnaise**
**1 egg, beaten foamy**
**2 cans cream of mushroom soup**
**1 small onion, chopped**
**1 package yellow cheese (1 pound) grated**
**1 package croutons**

OVEN 350°

Cook broccoli as instructions direct. Drain. Mix egg and mayonnaise with broccoli. Put in buttered casserole by layers: broccoli, onions, soup, cheese, croutons. Repeat until all ingredients are used. Bake 1 hour at 350°.

## BARBECUED BEANS

Janette Cole, Wood Lake, MN

**1 pound hamburger**
**1 onion, chopped**
**4 1-pound cans pork and beans in tomato sauce**
**1 tablespoon Worcestershire sauce**
**Salt and pepper to taste**
**2 tablespoons vinegar**
**2 tablespoons brown sugar**
**½ cup ketchup**
**Dash chili powder**

OVEN 350°

Brown hamburger and onion; drain off fat. Add remaining ingredients. Bake at 350° for 35 minutes, or make in a large frying pan; cook on low heat stirring often, until boiling. Simmer about 10–15 minutes.

# VEGETABLES

## BARBECUED GREEN BEANS

Susan Underwood, Fuquay-Varina, NC

**4 slices bacon, cut up**
**¼ cup brown sugar**
**¼ cup onion, chopped**
**1 tablespoon Worcestershire sauce**
**½ cup ketchup**
**2 16-ounce cans green beans, drained**

OVEN 350°

Brown bacon and onions, then add ketchup, brown sugar, and Worcestershire sauce. Simmer 2 minutes. Place beans in 2 quart casserole dish. Pour sauce over beans. Don't stir. Bake at 350° for 20–30 minutes.

## SHARON'S SCRUMPTIOUS BEANS

Sharon Long, Hendersonville, TN

**3 16-ounce cans pinto beans**
**2 16-ounce cans chili beans**
**16-ounce can diced tomatoes**
**1 medium onion, chopped**
**1 pound ground beef, cooked and drained**
**Salt and pepper to taste**

Cook ground beef and drain. In slow cooker, combine all ingredients and cook for 2–3 hours.

## MOM'S BEST BAKED BEANS

Lois Davis, Grove Hill, AL

**1 pound ground whole hog or venison sausage**
**1 large green bell pepper, chopped**
**1 large onion, chopped**
**32-ounce can pork and beans (I use Showboat Pork 'n Beans brand)**
**1 small bottle barbecue sauce (I use Kraft Barbeque Sauce brand)**
**Garlic powder**
**Cajun seasoning**

OVEN 350°

Cook sausage (we prefer venison), drain, and crumble. Sauté pepper and onion together. Mix all ingredients in large casserole. Season to taste with garlic powder, cajun seasoning, salt, and pepper. Bake at 350° for 1½ hours.

## ROGER'S BAKED BEANS

Donna Wright, Rocklin, CA

*"I usually double the recipe. Great for pot lucks! Just remember to bring along paper towels or insulated cups to put it in."*

**6 slices bacon, chopped up**
**1 medium onion**
**1 can kidney beans**
**1 can baked beans (I use B&M brand)**
**1 can butter beans**
**¼ pound processed cheese spread (I use Velveeta brand)**
**½ cup sugar**
**⅓ cup brown sugar**
**2 tablespoons Worcestershire sauce**

OVEN 350°

Drain and set aside cooked bacon and onion. Mix remaining ingredients of beans, cheese, sugars, and sauce then stir in the bacon and onions. Bake 1 hour at 350° or place in Crock-Pot and simmer all day.

## WESTERN BEANS

Evelyn Case, Derby, KS

**8 slices bacon, reserve grease**
**3 medium onions, chopped**
**#303-can green beans**
**#303-can butter beans**
**1 cup sliced carrots**
**1 #2½-can pork and beans or kidney beans**
**¾ cup brown sugar**
**½ cup vinegar**
**½ teaspoon dry mustard**
**½ teaspoon salt and pepper**

OVEN 350°

Combine brown sugar, vinegar, dry mustard, salt, and pepper for a sweet and sour sauce. Fry bacon and sauté onion in 3 tablespoons bacon grease. Discard remaining grease. Combine all ingredients and bake at 350° until cooked down. (You may want to double sweet and sour sauce.)

## SPICY APPLE BEAN BAKE

Mrs. T. Hobbs, Topeka, KS

**40-ounce can baked beans (or pork 'n beans)**
**1-pound can kidney beans**
**2 large apples, chopped**
**½ cup raisins**
**1½ cups chopped onion**
**1 cup chopped green pepper**
**1 pound lean ground beef, browned (or 3 cups leftover meat)**
**1 cup catsup**
**½ cup sweet pickle relish**
**½ cup brown sugar**
**1 teaspoon dry mustard**
**½ cup molasses**
**4 slices crisp bacon (optional)**

OVEN 275°

Mix in 3-quart casserole. Cover and bake at 275° for 2½ hours.

# VEGETABLES

## BETTER THAN BAKED BEANS

Marguerita Bates, Joplin, MO

*"This is wonderful and easy for people who don't like to cook. We like to dip our dinner meat into the sauce."*

**1 can pork and beans**
**1 teaspoon parsley flakes**
**1 tablespoon blackstrap molasses (the best!), or brown sugar**
**Dash of onion (optional)**
**½ teaspoon celery seed**
**¼ to ½ cup barbecue sauce**

Cook five minutes on the stove over medium heat.

## ONION PIE

Marilyn White, Lake Jackson, TX

**4 tablespoons, plus 2 teaspoons margarine, divided**
**1 cup crushed Ritz brand crackers**
**2 cups sweet onion, thinly sliced**
**2 eggs**
**¾ cup milk**
**¾ teaspoon salt**
**¾ teaspoon pepper**
**¼ cup grated cheddar cheese**
**Paprika**
**Fresh parsley**

OVEN 350°

Preheat oven to 350°. Melt 4 tablespoons margarine; mix in cracker crumbs. Press crumbs into pie plate to make crust. In large skillet, melt 2 teaspoons margarine. Sauté onions until clear but not brown. Spoon onion mixture into crust. In a small bowl beat eggs with milk, salt, and pepper. Pour over onions. Top with cheese and paprika. Bake for 30 minutes. After baking, sprinkle parsley on top.

## GREEN CHILI PIE

Pat Cookman, Gaston, OR

**1 onion, chopped**
**1 can green chilies, chopped**
**1 can cream of chicken soup**
**1 can evaporated milk**
**2 cups grated cheddar cheese**
**1 package corn tortillas**
**1 tablespoon butter**

OVEN 325°

Sauté onions in butter; add chilies; then add soup and evaporated milk; warm thoroughly. In 2-quart casserole dish tear up and layer 3 tortillas, add layer of mixture then cheese and repeat 2 more times, top with cheese. Bake in 325° oven for 20 minutes. Serve with tacos.

## BARBECUED KRAUT

Margaret Floth, Sullivan, IN

**2 cans sauerkraut, reserve juice**
**2 cans tomatoes**
**1 cup firmly packed brown sugar**
**½ pound bacon (I use Bacon Bits brand)**

OVEN 350°

Use juice of 1 can kraut; add 1 can tomatoes. Stir in brown sugar. Fry bacon crisp and sprinkle over top. Bake 1–1½ hours at 350° (or until juice is gone.)

## VEGETABLE MEDLEY

M. Tanner, Camden, AR

**1 potato**
**1 squash**
**1 cup sliced okra**
**1 onion, sliced and separated (less if desired)**

Peel potato, quarter, and slice thinly. Slice squash, quartering if large. Place all vegetables together. Add salt and pepper to taste; lightly coat with cornmeal. Fry in ¼-inch oil, turning as necessary to cook thoroughly. Cover.

(Either squash or okra may be omitted.)

## HOMEMADE BEETS

Millie Hummel, Reading, PA

**5 or 6 raw red beets**
**1 cup red beet juice**
**1 cup vinegar**
**½ cup brown sugar**
**1 teaspoon salt**

Wash beets, cut tops off only (do not peel). Cook with skin on until beet is done. Reserve the juice. Scrape shell off; cut into slices or cubes; put vinegar, salt, reserved juice, and sugar together; mix. Pour over beets.

# VEGETABLES

## BAKED GARDEN VEGETABLES

Doris E. Schwanke, Porter, TX

**1 cup carrots, julienned**
**2 cups potatoes, peeled, sliced**
**1 package frozen baby lima beans**
**2 medium zucchini, quartered and sliced**
**2 cups bok choy, coarsely chopped (may use cabbage)**
**3 tablespoons fresh parsley, minced**
**¼ teaspoon Spike (salt-free seasoning)**
**½ teaspoon sea salt**
**¼ cup butter (not margarine)**
**Fresh ground black pepper**

OVEN 325°

Preheat oven. Place (layer) all vegetables in a heavy casserole. Dot with butter, sprinkle with parsley and seasonings. Cover casserole and bake 45–60 minutes or until tender. Toss with additional butter if desired. Serve with fresh diced tomatoes.

Serves 4, generously.

## EGGPLANT SOUFFLE

Alice Huntley, Lake Panasoffkee, FL

**1 eggplant, cooked, drained and mashed**
**½ can undiluted cream of mushroom soup**
**1 cup soft bread crumbs**
**½ cup grated cheese**
**2 teaspoons grated onion**
**1 tablespoon ketchup**
**1 teaspoon salt**
**2 eggs, separated**

OVEN 375°

Combine ingredients, except egg whites. Beat whites stiff and fold in. Pour into 2-quart casserole. Bake at 375° for 45 minutes or until knife in center comes out clean.

## EASY EGGPLANT PARMESAN

Diane K. Bailey, Millerton, PA

**2 medium-sized eggplants**
**2 large eggs**
**2 tablespoons butter**
**1¼ cups dried bread crumbs**
**2 tablespoons Parmesan cheese**
**8-ounce package mozzarella cheese, shredded**
**1½ to 2 cans of your favorite spaghetti sauce**

OVEN 375°

Cut eggplants lengthwise into ½-inch thick slices. Beat eggs with butter until blended. Dip eggplant slices into egg mixture, then bread crumbs. Arrange on cookie sheet and broil 10–12 minutes until tender, turning once. Repeat with remaining slices. In 9x13-inch pan, spoon 1 cup sauce, top with eggplant, then with more sauce, and half the mozzarella cheese. Repeat layering. Sprinkle Parmesan cheese on top. Bake 40 minutes, covered. Garnish with parsley.

## STUFFED PEPPERS

Carol Meister, Little Rock, AR

**1 pound ground beef**
**1/3 cup chopped onion**
**16-ounce can tomatoes, cut up**
**½ cup uncooked long-grain rice**
**½ cup water**
**1 teaspoon Worcestershire sauce**
**½ teaspoon salt**
**Dash pepper**
**6 green peppers, tops cut off, insides cleaned**

OVEN 350°

Sauté beef and onion until brown. Add tomatoes, rice, water, Worcestershire sauce, salt, and pepper, and simmer covered for 15 minutes. While this is cooking, cut tops off peppers, clean insides out and cook 5 minutes in salted water. Stuff cooked peppers. Bake in dish 20–25 minutes at 350°.

Serves 6.

## CARROT HASH BROWNS

Trudy Norris, Akron, OH

**2 tablespoons butter**
**1 teaspoon safflower oil**
**3 medium carrots, finely grated**
**3 medium potatoes, finely grated**
**½ small onion, finely grated**
**½ teaspoon salt**

In a large skillet melt butter and oil. Add carrots, potatoes, and onion. Add salt. Sauté until browned on one side. Flip over and sauté on other side until browned. Break apart into small chunks or serve in wedges.

Serves 3.

## CARROT SOUFFLE

Ann Milstid, Ballwin, MO

*"I am a recipe collector and love to cook. I have given this recipe to family and friends more than any other recipe I have. It is delicious and will go with any meat. You can even top it with Cool Whip and use it as a dessert!"*

**2 pounds cooked carrots**
**2 cups sugar**
**6 eggs**
**2 sticks margarine**
**6 tablespoons flour**
**2 teaspoons baking powder**
**2 teaspoons vanilla**

OVEN 350°

Blend or mash carrots; gradually add other ingredients; add baking powder and vanilla last. Beat or whip until smooth. Place in casserole. Bake 30–45 minutes at 350°, until firm.

# SOUPS

# SOUPS

## BUSY DAY SOUP
JoAnn Black, Arlington, TX

**2¼ cups tomato juice**
**1 pound hamburger**
**1½ cups diced potatoes**
**1 cup diced celery**
**1 cup diced carrots**
**½ cup diced onion**
**¼ cup uncooked rice**
**1 can corn**
**1 can diced tomatoes**
**2 teaspoons salt**
**¼ teaspoon pepper**
**2 teaspoons Worcestershire sauce**
**¼ teaspoon chili powder**
**5 cups water**

Brown hamburger. Place all ingredients in large soup pot. Cover and simmer 1–1½ hours until vegetables are done.

## GRANDMA'S MILK OR RIVEL SOUP
Joanie Troyer, Eureka, IL

*"This recipe is a favorite of mine and my children when their dad (my husband) is away at Minister's Week. This was handed down from my great-grandmother Sarah (Flohr) Lind, born in 1880."*

**2 quarts milk**
**1 cup flour**
**1 large egg**
**1½ teaspoons salt (I use ½ teaspoon salt)**
**2 to 3 tablespoons cream (or 1 to 2 tablespoons butter)**

Heat milk to boiling point in top of double boiler or a heavy kettle. Add salt. Make rivels: cut together egg and flour to cherry stone size rivels. Drop rivels into hot milk. Keep milk at boiling point for 3–5 minutes.

## CHICKEN & CRACKER BALL SOUP
Marian Whitehorn, Tempe, AZ

**Chicken (any parts)**
**1 box salted or unsalted crackers**
**3 cans chicken stock**
**6 eggs**
**2 cups milk**
**Salt and pepper if wanted**

Cover chicken with water. Add chicken stock, cover, and simmer until chicken is done. Remove and debone; set aside. Crush crackers in blender or use rolling pin until like sand. Put in bowl, add eggs, mix slowly. Add milk until moist. Roll into balls, larger than marbles, smaller than ping-pong balls. Bring soup to boil. Add balls, cover for 15 minutes. Replace chicken.

## SOPA DE LA CASA

Tiffany and Joanie Troyer, Eureka, IL

**8 slices bacon, diced and fried**
**1¼ cups finely chopped onion**
**1¼ cups finely chopped celery**
**2 green peppers, finely chopped**
**2 cloves garlic, minced**
**2 14½-ounce cans broth**
**31-ounce can refried beans**
**½ teaspoon pepper**
**2 tablespoons chili powder ( I use canned California green chilies)**
**Tortilla chips**
**Monterey Jack cheese, shredded**

In a heavy pot cook bacon until crisp. Drain ½ of bacon drippings (I drain all). Add onion, celery, green pepper, and garlic. Sauté until tender. Blend in broth, refried beans and seasoning. Bring to boil; remove immediately. Garnish with chips and cheese.

Yields: 8 cups.

## GRANDDADDY'S SOUP

Waunda Hagan, Tampa, FL

*"This is a wonderful hearty soup and our family calls it Granddaddy's Soup because this is what he made."*

**2 Chorizzo (Spanish sausage) sliced**
**½ pound white bacon**
**1 pound ham, cut into bite-size pieces**
**1 pound beef stew, cut into bite-size pieces**
**2 large potatoes, cut up**
**2 large cans white beans, or gallon size**
**2 packages frozen turnip greens, with roots**
**1 large onion**
***Small piece of sour pork (optional)**
**Salt and pepper to taste**

In large pot put all ingredients except greens, potatoes, and beans. Cover with water and bring to boil. Lower heat and simmer until meat is tender. Add greens, potatoes, and beans. Cook until tender. (Better the next day.)

*This is just a piece of salt pork that has been left out and turned yellow. It put a tang in the soup. Can be bought in Tampa but you can put some in airtight container and put on shelf. Lasts years! Also soup can be made with collard greens but we like the turnip best.

## LENTIL SOUP

Doreen Walgren, Seaside, OR

**1 pound bacon**
**2 cups, or 12-ounce package, lentils**
**2 cups onion**
**2 cups diced celery**
**3 medium carrots**
**8 cups beef stock**
**½ cup flour (in bacon drippings)**
**2 cups diced potatoes**

Sauté bacon with onion until golden, add lentils and flour. Mix well. Add broth and diced vegetables. Boil, simmer 2 hours. Salt and pepper to taste.

## HAMBURGER SOUP

Wanda McCain, Cement, OK

**1 pound ground beef**
**½ teaspoon salt**
**¼ teaspoon oregano**
**¼ teaspoon basil**
**1 tablespoon soy sauce**
**1 small onion, diced**
**(or 1 package onion soup mix)**
**1 large or 2 small cans tomato soup**
**6 cups water**

Brown beef in skillet; drain off fat. In a large pot put browned meat, salt, oregano, basil, soy sauce, onion or soup mix, tomato soup, and water. Add desired vegetables (carrots, potatoes, celery, etc.) and cook until tender. Bring to a slow boil, then turn down to simmer. You can add a few egg noodles, macaroni, spaghetti, and beef bouillon cubes.

## HEARTY HAMBURGER SOUP

Jennifer Thiel, Trumbull, NE

**2 pounds lean ground beef**
**1 medium sized onion, diced**
**1½ cups diced carrots**
**1 cup diced celery**
**2 cups tomato juice**
**2 quarts water**
**2 teaspoons salt**
**¼ teaspoon pepper**
**¼ cup rice or barley**
**2 cups diced potatoes**

Brown meat, lightly. Add all other ingredients except potatoes and simmer 1 hour in a heavy kettle. Add potatoes and simmer 1 hour longer. Freezes well.

## CHEESEBURGER RICE SOUP

Naomi Marner, Abbeville, SC

*"Your kids will love this on a cold day. So will you!"*

**2 pounds hamburger**
**4 cups cooked rice**
**1 cup carrots**
**1 onion (small) chopped**
**16 ounces sour cream**
**1 cup celery chopped**
**Small box processed cheese spread**
**4 cups milk**
**4 tablespoons chicken seasoning cubes**
**Salt and pepper to taste**

Cook onions, carrots, and celery until tender. Add fried hamburger, rice, milk, and cheese. Add sour cream last and do not boil.

## HODGEPODGE CROCK-POT SOUP

Betty Miskotten, Hamilton, MI

**1 pound ground beef**
**1 chopped onion**
**Salt and pepper**
**1 can tomato soup**
**1 can mixed vegetables**
**1 can kidney beans**
**1 can SpaghettiO's**
**½ to 1 soup can water**

**Optional:**
**1 can Great Northern Lima Beans**
**1 can minestrone soup**

Brown meat and onion; drain. Add remaining ingredients. Cook in Crock-Pot for 2–3 hours.

Note: Lower salt and cholesterol by using ½ pound ground round. Use special packages (low salt & fat) of other ingredients.

## TACO SOUP

Virginia Byers, Brea, CA

**1 small can pinto beans**
**1 pound ground beef**
**1 envelope (1¼ ounces) taco seasoning**
**14½ ounces stewed tomatoes**
**15 ounces kidney beans, undrained**
**1 cup water**
**Shredded cheddar cheese (about 1¼ cups per serving)**
**Sliced onions**
**Sour cream, corn, or tortilla chips for garnish (optional)**

Brown ground beef in large Dutch oven. Drain fat. Add taco seasoning, tomatoes, beans, and water; heat until soup comes to a boil and is heated through. Ladle into individual bowls, top with cheese. If desired also top with onions, corn chips, and sour cream.

Yield: 5 cups.

## TACO SOUP

Sherry K. Davis, Choctaw, OK

**1 pound lean ground beef or turkey**
**1 large can diced tomatoes**
**1 package Hidden Valley Ranch Salad Dressing mix (powder original with buttermilk)**
**1 small onion, chopped**
**1 package taco seasoning**
**1 can each of kidney beans, black beans, pinto beans, white beans, and garbanzo beans, with liquid (may substitute other beans for garbanzo beans)**

Brown ground beef or turkey and onion. Drain off fat. Add tomatoes, seasonings, and beans with liquid. Bring to boil and let cook until ready to serve. Serve with hot corn bread or chips. If you like it spicy, add a can of Rotel tomatoes.

## CHEDDAR CHOWDER

Sharon Gilmer, Brookfield, MO

**2 cups boiling water**
**2 cups diced potatoes**
**1 cup diced carrots**
**1 cup diced celery**
**½ cup chopped onion**
**1 cup ham, cubed**
**1 small can whole corn**

**White Sauce:**
**¼ cup margarine**
**¼ cup flour**
**2 cups milk**
**2 cups shredded cheddar cheese (Velveeta brand works well)**

Combine and simmer until tender, not soft, do not drain. Make a white sauce with margarine, flour, and milk. Add cheese and blend until melted. Add to undrained vegetables slowly (can curdle), then simmer about 15 minutes. Add salt and pepper to taste. Great with corn bread!

## HARVEST CHOWDER

JoAnn A. Grote, Montevideo, MN

**Editor's Note:** JoAnn has authored several Heartsong Presents romances, including *Love's Shining Hope* and *Sweet Surrender.*

**4 strips bacon**
**½ cup chopped onion, fresh or frozen**
**1 small clove garlic, minced**
**1 teaspoon basil, crumbled**
**10-ounce package frozen corn**
**10-ounce package frozen peas and carrots**
**1 cup frozen hash browns**
**1- to 1¾-ounce can chicken broth**
**¾ teaspoon salt (optional)**
**¼ teaspoon pepper**
**1 tablespoon cornstarch**
**2 cups half-and-half (I have used whole milk instead)**
**2 tablespoons chopped parsley (optional)**

In large saucepan (I use Dutch oven), cook bacon until crisp. Remove bacon and add onion, garlic, and basil to drippings. Cook slowly until onion is tender. Add chicken broth, corn, peas and carrots, hash browns, salt, and pepper. Bring to boil, cover and reduce heat to simmer. Cook over moderate heat for 10 minutes or until vegetables are tender. Mix in cornstarch. Add half-and-half. Cook, stirring until soup comes to a full boil. Crumble bacon and add as garnish to chowder. Also add parsley as garnish.

Makes 1½ quarts chowder, enough for 6–8 servings.

## POTATO SOUP

Ann McKinney, Ft. Worth, TX

**2 medium potatoes, diced**
**1 large onion, diced**
**1 can low-fat cream of chicken soup**
**Velveeta brand light cheese, cut into strips**

Put ingredients in saucepan with lots of water. (Adjust to taste, lots of soup or mostly potatoes.) Salt and pepper to taste. Simmer until potatoes and onions are done. Add Velveeta Light and stir until cheese is melted. (Stirring is necessary to keep cheese from sticking to pan.) Remove from heat and serve.

## HOMEMADE POTATO SOUP

Janet Hayman, Zephyrhills, FL

*"My children love this potato soup. When my youngest son comes to visit, he always asks for me to make a pot of potato soup for him."*

**6 potatoes, peeled and cut into bite-size pieces**
**1 onion, chopped**
**1 carrot, pared and sliced**
**1 stalk celery, sliced**
**4 chicken bouillon cubes**
**1 teaspoon parsley flakes**
**Ham, cut up into bite-size pieces**
**5 cups water**
**1 teaspoon salt**
**Pepper to taste**
**⅓ cup butter**
**13-ounce can evaporated milk**

Put all ingredients except milk into pan. Cook until all vegetables are done. Stir in evaporated milk and heat to boiling point. If desired mash potatoes with masher before serving.

## CREAM OF POTATO SOUP

Millie Hummel, Reading, PA

**1 very small onion, diced**
**10 pounds of potatoes, pared and diced small**
**2 teaspoons parsley**
**2 teaspoons celery salt**
**1 teaspoon salt**
**1 stick butter**
**½ pint half-and-half**

Put potatoes and onion in covered pot, in enough water to cover them. Add parsley, celery salt, and regular salt. Cook until potatoes are done, and water is almost cooked off. Turn off burner and add butter and half-and-half, stir in. Then add diced egg.

## CHEESY POTATO SOUP

Lucy Johnson, Martinsville, IL

**4 chicken bouillon cubes**
**4 cups water**
**1 cup diced onions**
**1 cup diced carrots**
**3 cups diced potatoes**
**1 pound processed cheese food, diced**
**3 cups milk**
**1 package California blend vegetables (optional)**
**2 cups broccoli tops (optional)**

Combine first five ingredients plus optional choices, and cook for 20 minutes. Add cheese last ten minutes, stirring until melted. Add milk. Continue to simmer until hot, being careful not to scorch. Reheat in double boiler. Can be frozen.

Serves 8.

## POTATO-CHEESE SOUP

Roseanne Schmidt, Millers, MD

*"Our favorite soup! There are never leftovers."*

**3 medium potatoes, diced**
**1 small onion, chopped fine**
**Milk**
**3 tablespoons butter or margarine, melted**
**2 tablespoons parsley, snipped**
**¾ teaspoon salt**
**2 tablespoons flour**
**Dash pepper**
**1 cup cheddar cheese, shredded**

In a 2-quart saucepan, add potatoes and onion to 1 cup salted boiling water. Cover and cook about 20 minutes or until potatoes are tender. Mash potatoes slightly; do not drain. Measure mixture and add enough milk to make 5 cups. Blend melted butter, flour, parsley, salt, and pepper. Stir into potato mixture in saucepan; cook and stir until thickened and bubbly. Add cheese. Cook and stir until cheese is partially melted. Serve immediately.

## POTATO CHEESE CHOWDER

Monah Pittman, Bixby, OK

**6 slices bacon**
**4–5 cups potatoes**
**2 cups onions**
**1 cup green pepper**
**1 cup picante sauce**
**3 cups water**
**Salt, pepper, and garlic powder to taste**
**1 pound processed cheese food cut into 1-inch cubes**

Fry bacon in large soup kettle. Set bacon aside and reserve 2 tablespoons of bacon drippings. Discard remaining drippings. Add onions and pepper to drippings in kettle and cook over medium heat until soft. Add all remaining ingredients except cheese and cook until potatoes are done. Remove from heat. Add cheese and stir until melted. Serve topped with crumbled bacon.

## 15-BEAN SOUP

Debbie Linehan, Lusby, MD

**4 small onions, chopped**
**2 ham hocks, or ham bone**
**⅔ cup catsup**
**⅓ cup molasses**
**¼ cup sugar**
**¼ teaspoon dry mustard**
**1 teaspoon soy sauce**
**15-beans package**

Soften beans overnight or bring to a boil and let sit for one hour. In fresh water, simmer beans, ham, and onions for 2 hours. Combine remaining ingredients in separate bowl. Add to beans and cook for another 30 minutes.

## CARROT AND GINGER SOUP

Loree Lough, Ellicott City, MD

**Editor's Note:** Loree has also been known as Cara McCormack and Alesha Carter. To name a few of her Heartsong Presents books: *Pocketful of Promises, Priscilla Hires a Husband,* and *The Wedding Wish.*

**1 can chicken broth**
**2 packages sliced carrots**
**6 medium cubed potatoes**
**1 medium diced onion**
**½ stick margarine**
**2 tablespoons ginger**
**1 tablespoon parsley**
**1 teaspoon orange peel**
**1 cup sour cream**
**1 cup water**
**½ cup skim milk**

Sauté onions and ginger in butter. Add carrots, potatoes, broth, and water. Simmer until vegetables are soft. Add spices. Puree. Return to pot. Add sour cream, milk, salt, and pepper to taste.

Serves 6–8.

# MAIN DISHES

## EASY CHICKEN POT PIE
Mrs. Henry Clark, Savannah, GA

**Filling:**
**2 cups chicken, cooked and diced**
**1 medium onion, chopped**
**4 boiled eggs, sliced**
**2 cans mixed vegetables, drained**
**1 can cream of chicken soup**
**1 can cream of celery soup**
**½ cup chicken broth**

**Crust:**
**1 cup sweet milk**
**1 cup mayonnaise**
**1 cup self-rising flour**

OVEN 350°

Preheat oven to 350°. Layer chicken, onion, and egg in large, greased, oblong casserole dish or pan. Mix remaining ingredients and pour over layers of chicken, onion, and egg. Mix crust ingredients and spread evenly over soup and vegetable mixture for top layer. Bake 1–1½ hours or until crust is golden brown.

## CHICKEN POT PIE
Hannah Hale, Williamston, NC

**3 cups chicken, cooked and deboned**
**1¼ cups chicken broth**
**1 can cream of celery soup**
**1 can peas**
**1 can sliced carrots**

Place chicken in large casserole dish. Top with peas and carrots. Mix broth and soup. Pour over vegetables. Salt and pepper to taste.

**Topping:**
**1 teaspoon salt**
**¼ teaspoon pepper**
**2 teaspoons baking powder**
**1 cup plain flour**
**1 stick margarine**
**1 cup milk**

OVEN 375°

Mix dry ingredients. Cut butter into flour mixture. Add milk. Blend well. Pour over chicken. Bake at 375° for about 30 minutes.

## CHICKEN DISH
Nancy Azner, Jamestown, NY

**3 cups chicken breast, cooked and cut up**
**1 package quick-cooking rice, combination long grain and wild rice with herbs and seasoning**
**1 can cream of celery soup**
**1 small onion**
**1 can drained French-style beans**
**1 cup mayonnaise**
**1 can drained water chestnuts**
**Salt and pepper to taste**

OVEN 350°

Mix all together. Put in 2½- to 3-quart casserole dish. Bake at 350° for 30 minutes.

## OVERNIGHT CHICKEN

Mary Sutley, Franklin, PA

**2 cups cooked chicken, cut up**
**2 cups uncooked macaroni**
**2 cups milk**
**1 can mushroom soup**
**1 can cream of chicken soup**
**1 cup cheese**
**Onion, cut up**

OVEN 350°

Mix all ingredients using your own seasoning. Refrigerate overnight or for 4 hours. Bake at 350° for about 1 hour.

## 'NITE BEFORE CHICKEN

Sharon Dalton, Richland Center, WI

**4 whole chicken breasts, cooked and deboned**
**7-ounce package macaroni (2 cups uncooked)**
**2 cans cream of chicken soup**
**2 cups milk**
**8 ounces grated cheddar cheese**
**1 small onion, grated**
**4 hard-boiled eggs, chopped**
**Parmesan cheese**
**Paprika**

OVEN 350°

Mix all ingredients except Parmesan cheese and paprika. Place in large greased 9x13-inch casserole. Sprinkle with cheese and paprika, cover and put in refrigerator overnight. Bake at 350° for 60 minutes.

## OVEN BARBECUED CHICKEN

Tricia Kibbe, Grayling, MI

**6 chicken breasts, boned and skinned**
**¼ cup brown sugar**
**⅛ teaspoon garlic powder**
**1 teaspoon onion powder**
**1 cup ketchup**
**½ cup water**
**½ cup apple cider vinegar**
**2 teaspoons Worcestershire sauce**

**Mixture:**
**¼ cup fat-free Parmesan cheese**
**1 teaspoon oregano**

OVEN 375°

Wash chicken and set aside. Mix together all ingredients, except for chicken, in saucepan and heat to boiling. Pour over chicken. Bake 20 minutes at 375°, turn over chicken, cover with sauce. Sprinkle with mixture, bake another 15–20 minutes.

## CREAMY BAKED CHICKEN BREASTS

Vivian Messenger, Ft. Wayne, IN

**4 boneless chicken breasts**
**4 slices Swiss cheese**
**1 can cream of chicken soup (thin with water to pour)**
**2 cups herb-seasoned stuffing crumbs**
**½ cup butter (optional)**

OVEN 350°

Lay chicken in baking dish. Add a cheese slice on each. Pour soup over all. Sprinkle with crumbs on top. Drizzle butter on top. Bake at 350° uncovered for 50–55 minutes.

## HAWAIIAN HAYSTACKS

M. L. Cherry, Riverside, CA

**2 cans cream of chicken soup**
**1 cup chicken broth**
**2 cups diced, cooked chicken**
**2 cups cooked rice**

Combine soup and broth to make gravy. Stir to blend. Add chicken and simmer 8–10 minutes. Serve gravy over rice.

Guests may add any or all of the following to their haystack. Place each in separate bowls:

**9-ounce can chow mein noodles**
**3 chopped tomatoes**
**1 cup chopped celery**
**½ cup chopped green peppers**
**½ cup chopped green onion, or may use red sweet onion**
**20-ounce can pineapple chunks**
**1 cup grated cheese**
**½ cup coconut**
**½ cup halved maraschino cherries**
**1 cup mandarin oranges**

## PHONEY ABALONE

Darla Fraser, Burney, CA

*"I've never tried abalone but I am told this tastes a lot like it. It's a different way of fixing the old standby of chicken."*

**5 boneless, skinless chicken breasts**
**1 bottle clam juice**
**2 teaspoons garlic salt**
**1½ teaspoons parsley**
**2½ cups cracker crumbs**
**2 tablespoons grated Romano cheese**

Pound chicken until thin. Mix garlic salt, parsley, and clam juice in medium bowl. Add chicken and cover with a tight lid. Shake to cover all chicken. Refrigerate 24 hours. Mix Romano cheese and cracker crumbs. Coat chicken with cracker mixture and brown in frying pan with small amount of oil.

## CHICKEN AND PEPPERS

Diana Shawver, McCall, ID

**2 chicken breasts, boned, cut into 1-inch squares**
**1 envelope onion soup mix**
**3 tablespoons cooking oil**
**3 tablespoons soy sauce**
**1 clove garlic, minced**
**3 teaspoons cornstarch**
**2 sweet peppers (1 green, 1 red), cut into 1-inch squares**
**3 ribs celery cut into ½-inch slices**
**8 green onions cut into ½-inch strips**
**¾ cup cold water**
**½ teaspoon sugar**

In medium bowl combine chicken, onion soup, 1 tablespoon oil, 1 tablespoon soy sauce, garlic, and 1 teaspoon cornstarch; marinate 20–30 minutes. In large skillet heat remaining oil; cook peppers and celery over high heat for 3 minutes, stirring frequently. Add green onions, cook 2 minutes; remove from pan. Add chicken to skillet and cook 3 minutes. In small bowl, mix remaining soy sauce and cornstarch with water and sugar. Add to skillet with vegetables; simmer 3 minutes.

Makes 4 servings.

## CHICKEN-ETTI

Jackie Arbogast, McAlisterville, PA

**8-ounce package of spaghetti (cooked), broken into two-inch pieces equaling 2 cups**
**3 or 4 cups of cut up chicken**
**¼ cup green peppers**
**2 cans cream of mushroom soup**
**1 cup chicken broth**
**¼ teaspoon celery salt**
**¼ teaspoon pepper**
**1 onion grated**
**¾ pound processed cheese spread, grated (makes 2 cups)**

OVEN 350°

Keep about 1 cup of the grated cheese for the top of the casserole. Bake 1 hour at 350°.

## SAVORY POPPYSEED CHICKEN

Carole Keller, Coopersburg, PA

**2 cups chicken, cooked and diced,**
**1 can cream of chicken soup**
**8 ounces sour cream**
**2 tablespoons ground poppyseeds**
**1 sleeve of Ritz-type crackers, crumbled**
**1 stick butter or margarine, melted**

OVEN 350°

Combine soup and sour cream, then set aside. Mix crumbled crackers with melted butter and poppyseeds; stir well. Put into 2- or 3-quart casserole dish. Place chicken on top and pour soup mixture over all. Sprinkle with cracker crumbs. Bake at 350° for 25 minutes or until bubbly and browned on top. Great with rice!

## SMOKED CHICKEN

Gwen Metzger, New Manchester, IN

*"This chicken is absolutely the most heavenly tender chicken I've ever eaten!"*

**1 chicken (12 pieces)**
**1 cup Tender Quick (or slightly less)**
**8 to 10 cups water**
**3 tablespoons Liquid Smoke**

OVEN 350°

Dissolve Tender Quick in water, pour over chicken and let stand 2 days in brine. Drain, rub on Liquid Smoke and let stand overnight. Bake at 350° for 18–20 minutes per pound. (Bake covered.)

## CLASSIC CHICKEN DIVAN

Cheryl A. Bardaville, St. Louis, MI

**2 10-ounce packages frozen broccoli spears**
**¼ cup butter**
**6 tablespoons flour**
**½ teaspoon salt and pepper**
**2 cups chicken broth**
**½ cup whipping cream**
**3 tablespoons dry white wine**
**3 chicken breasts, halved and cooked**
**¼ cup grated Parmesan cheese**

OVEN 350°

Cook broccoli, using package directions; drain. Melt butter. Blend in flour, salt, and pepper. Add chicken broth; cook and stir until mixture thickens and bubbles. Stir in cream and wine. Place broccoli crosswise in 8x12-inch baking dish. Pour half the sauce over broccoli. Top with chicken. To remaining sauce add cheese, pour over chicken. Sprinkle with additional Parmesan cheese. Bake for 20 minutes or until heated through. Broil just until sauce is golden, about 5 minutes.

## CRUNCHY CHICKEN BAKE

Michelle Kalmanek, Pensacola, FL

**1 envelope Lipton Cream of Chicken flavor Cup-a-Soup**
**⅓ cup hot water**
**1 whole chicken breast (skinless and boneless) about 1 pound**
**¾ cup crushed herb seasoning mix**
**1 tablespoon butter or margarine, melted**

OVEN 375°

Preheat oven to 375°. In bowl, blend Cup-a-Soup with hot water. Dip chicken in soup mixture, then in crumbs; place in shallow baking dish and drizzle with butter. Bake 45 minutes or until tender.

Makes about 2 servings.

## BETTER 'N FRIED CHICKEN

Carolyn Anne Taylor, Gaffney, SC

**1½ pounds fryer chicken**
**½ cup powdered milk**
**2½ teaspoons paprika**
**½ teaspoon garlic salt**
**1 teaspoon poultry seasoning**
**¼ teaspoon pepper**

OVEN 350°

Remove skin and all visible fat from chicken. Put all ingredients in a plastic bag with chicken pieces and shake. Bake at 350° for 1 hour.

## LEMON-PEPPER CHICKEN

Laurie Whitstine, Rayville, LA

**5 boneless chicken breasts**
**1 stick margarine**
**Lemon-pepper seasoning**
**1 can cream of mushroom soup**
**Cooked rice**

Melt margarine on medium heat. Place chicken breasts in skillet of melted margarine, sprinkle liberally with lemon-pepper seasoning. Cover with lid and let it cook about 5 minutes. Turn the breasts over and sprinkle with seasoning again. Turn the breasts over again, in 5–7 minutes, to keep from burning. Cook them approximately 20–25 minutes, if frozen. When they are brown and done, remove from skillet. Open soup and stir into butter and drippings left. Stir well, brown. (Everything will be loosened from bottom of skillet.) Add 2½–3 cups water to mixture until it looks like gravy. Serve over cooked rice.

## OVEN-BAKED CHICKEN

Karen Wilhelm, Salisbury, NC

**1 stick margarine, melted**
**½ cup mayonnaise**
**2 teaspoons dry mustard**
**Pepperidge Farm brand corn bread mix**

OVEN 350°

Dip chicken in the mixture of melted margarine, mayonnaise, and mustard. Roll in corn bread mix and put on aluminum foil on baking sheet. Bake at 350° for 30 minutes or until fork inserts easily in meat.

# MAIN DISHES

## CHICKEN RUBEN

Jeanette Talbert, Dunnellon, FL
Verena Gibbs, Omaha, NE

**4 chicken breasts, split and boned (8 pieces)**
**¼ teaspoon salt**
**⅛ teaspoon pepper**
**16-ounce can sauerkraut, drained and pressed**
**4 slices (4x6-inch) Swiss cheese**
**1½ cups bottled Thousand Island dressing**
**1 tablespoon chopped parsley**

OVEN 325°

Place chicken in greased baking dish. Sprinkle with salt and pepper. Place sauerkraut on top of chicken. Top with Swiss cheese. Spread dressing over mixture and cover with foil. Bake at 325° for 1½ hours. Sprinkle with chopped parsley.

Serves 6–8.

## VINEYARD CHICKEN

Rebecca Hendricks, Telford, PA

**4 boneless, skinless chicken breasts, halved**
**2 tablespoons flour**
**¼ teaspoon dried basil**
**¼ teaspoon dried tarragon**
**¼ teaspoon paprika**
**Salt and freshly ground pepper**
**1 tablespoon butter**
**1 tablespoon safflower oil**
**2 garlic cloves, minced**
**½ cup cooking wine or lemon juice**
**1 cup halved red grapes**
**1 can chicken broth**

Mix flour, basil, tarragon, paprika, salt, and pepper in Ziploc bag; toss chicken pieces in bag, one at a time. Add butter, oil, and garlic to fry pan. Brown chicken over medium high for several minutes. Turn, heat, and simmer; add broth and cooking wine. Cook until reduced liquid. Add grapes. Serve over rice.

Serves 4.

## CHEESY CHICKEN

Carla Hinkle, Upland, PA
Melissa Barefoot, Alum Bank, PA

**5 (or more) pieces of chicken**
**1 can cream of chicken or cream of mushroom soup**
**Cheese slices (regular or sharp, your choice)**
**Butter**
**Garlic salt**

OVEN 350°

Place chicken in shallow pan, pour soup over top, place cheese slices on top of soup. Put butter on each piece and then sprinkle with garlic salt. Bake in 350° oven for 1 hour. Tastes great over rice or noodles.

## HOT CHICKEN SUPREME

Mary M. Kyker, Telford, TN

**3 whole chicken breasts, cooked and diced**
**1½ cups chopped celery**
**1 cup shredded sharp cheddar cheese**
**½ cup mayonnaise**
**¼ cup slivered almonds, toasted**
**¼ cup chopped pimiento**
**2 teaspoons chopped onion**
**½ teaspoon poultry seasoning**
**½ teaspoon grated lemon rind**
**3-ounce can Chinese noodles (chow mein)**

OVEN 350°

Combine all ingredients except noodles, stir well. Spoon chicken mixture into greased 1½-quart casserole and top with noodles. Bake at 350° for 30 minutes.

## TERIYAKI CHICKEN

Debbie Baluka, Colstrip, MT

*"It's beautiful garnished with orange slices, fresh parsley, and maraschino cherries. With leftover sauce I add some chopped green onions to our pover the rice. Serve with steamed white rice and broccoli. Fortune cookies are nice touch for dessert."*

**1 cut up chicken**
**½ cup white sugar**
**½ cup soy sauce**
**1 teaspoon garlic, crushed kind**
**½ teaspoon salt**
**½ teaspoon ginger**

OVEN 350°

Mix together sugar, soy sauce, garlic, salt, and ginger; dip chicken into mixture. Bake at 350° for 30 minutes, each side; totaling 1 hour.

## CRESCENT ROLL CHICKEN

Jean Greene, North Little Rock, AR
Evelyn Whetstone, Spencerville, PA

**3 chicken breasts, cooked, boned and cut into small pieces**
**1 can cream of chicken soup**
**½ cup grated cheddar cheese (optional)**
**½ cup milk**
**1 can crescent rolls**

OVEN 350°

Combine cheese, soup, and milk. Pour half in 9x13-inch pan. Separate rolls; place as much cut-up chicken in each roll as will fit; roll up, tucking in edges. Place in pan. Spoon other half of sauce over rolls. Sprinkle grated cheese over all (optional). Bake at 350° for 25–30 minutes or until lightly browned.

Note: If using 29-ounce can of chicken soup, use more cheese and 2 packages of crescent rolls.

## CHICKEN ROLL-UPS

Doris Schwanke, Porter, TX

**1 package flour tortillas**
**4 cups leftover chicken, cut in bite-size pieces**
**1 can cream of chicken soup, undiluted**
**1 can Rotel tomatoes, with chilies**
**8 ounces sour cream**
**1 cup shredded cheddar**

OVEN 350°

Warm tortillas in microwave for easier handling. Spoon chicken in center of tortilla and roll up tightly. Place seam side down in baking dish. Continue until all chicken is used. Mix together soup, tomatoes, and sour cream until well blended. Spoon over roll-ups allowing to cover completely and run down the sides. Spread cheddar on top. Bake at 350° 30 minutes until cheese is melted.

Makes 10.

## CHICKEN BAR-B-QUE SAUCE

Diane Bailey, Millerton, PA

**12 halves of chicken**
**1 cup oil**
**1½ cups vinegar**
**¼ cup salt**
**½ teaspoon pepper**
**3 teaspoons poultry seasoning**
**1 egg**

Mix sauce ingredients together and shake, or beat, well. You can cook your chicken in a pit, on a grill, or in the oven. I skin mine and then just keep basting with the sauce occasionally. It is delicious, and if you're not cooking for a crowd, keep the sauce in refrigerator for later use.

## BAKED STEAK

Jenny Duff, Las Vegas, NV

*"This is incredibly easy to make and tastes fantastic, the steak is tender like roast beef. My husband's favorite meal."*

**3 pound round steak**
**2 teaspoons butter**
**1 small onion, cut into rings**
**1 cup ketchup**
**1 tablespoon Worcestershire sauce**
**¼ cup water**

OVEN 350°

Place meat into a shallow baking pan. Spread butter over the meat and top with the onion rings. Mix remaining ingredients and pour over meat. Cover pan with foil and bake at 350° for 2½ to 3 hours.

## STEAK & SQUASH

Connie Pyles, Bogata, TX

**2 pounds round steak, cut into cubes**
**6–8 large yellow squash, sliced**
**1 onion, chopped (optional)**
**Salt and pepper to taste**

Cut steak into cubes. Add a little oil to skillet. Put steak cubes in skillet and let brown. Add sliced squash and onions. Add 1 cup of water to skillet and let simmer covered over medium heat. Stir occasionally until done and juice is cooked down. Cooking time: 30 minutes. Remove, cover, and let brown 2 minutes.

## POOR MAN STEAK

Elaine Davis, Crossville, TN

**2 pounds lean ground beef**
**1 chopped onion**
**2 cups crushed crackers**
**1 can evaporated milk**
**2 teaspoons salt**
**1 teaspoon pepper**
**2 cans mushroom soup**

OVEN 350°

Mix all except soup in baking loaf pan, press this and let set in refrigerator all night. Cut into slices and fry on each side, then put in a baking dish and put some soup on each slice. Rinse cans with a little water and add to meat mixture. Bake at 350° for 1 hour. Use more soup if needed and use as gravy.

## DEER STEAK AND GRAVY

Deborah Hopkins, Booneville, MS

**3 pounds deer steak**
**1 medium onion**
**1 bell pepper**
**1 cup flour**
**2 teaspoons salt**
**1 teaspoon pepper**
**½ cup oil**
**1 can cream of mushroom soup**

Slice onion and pepper in rings. Brown onion and pepper lightly in oil. Remove and drain. Mix flour, salt, and pepper. Pound into trimmed deer steaks. Brown on both sides. Drain off oil. Place onion and pepper rings on top of steak and spread soup on top of all. Add water to almost cover meat. Simmer adding water as needed until tender.

# MAIN DISHES

## FOOLPROOF ROAST

Robbie Sauvie, Columbus, GA
*"Perfect for Sunday."*

**1 roast**
**Favorite vegetables**

Wrap roast with all of your favorite vegetables: carrots, celery, onion etc., in heavy duty foil, sealed tightly. Place this in a Dutch oven or large baking pan. Pour 1 cup water for every pound of roast into the Dutch oven or pan. Place the pan in the cold oven then turn it on to the highest temperature setting for 1 hour, not to broil. Do not open the oven! After 1 hour, turn the oven completely off and leave it for 3–4 hours. Again, it is very important that you *do not open the oven.* You should serve up a perfectly cooked roast every time without worry of the house burning down while you are away.

## ROUND STEAK STUFF

Sheri Burrell, Sallis, MS
*"This is a big hit with my family."*

**1 stick margarine**
**1 can cream of mushroom soup**
**2 cans cream of chicken soup**
**2 soup cans of water**
**1 cup raw rice**
**1½ pounds round steak**

OVEN 325°

Mix the soups, water, and margarine and put half of this mixture in pan. Stir in the rice. Cut the steak into serving portions and layer on top of rice. Cover with remaining soup mixture. Cover with foil and bake at 325° for 2 to 2½ hours.

## BRISKET

Edith Crittenden, Fort Worth, TX

**4–6 pounds brisket**
**Salt and pepper**
**½ cup Coca-Cola brand soda pop**
**½ cup catsup**
**1 package dry onion soup mix**

OVEN 325°

Pour Coke and catsup over brisket; then add onion soup. Seal well. Bake 6 hours at 325°. Serve with rice.

## DELUXE ROAST BEEF

Tamela H. Murray, Manassas, VA

**Editor's Note:** Tamela wrote *Picture of Love* for the Heartsong Presents series.

**3 or more pounds roast beef (I use rump roast, bottom round, eye of round)**
**1 can cream of celery soup**
**1 can cream of mushroom soup**
**½ soup can of water**
**1 or 2 onions**

OVEN 325°

Enough aluminum foil to line the baking dish (I usually use a 9x13-inch dish), with plenty of foil to cover and seal the meat. Heat your oven to 325°. Generously line your pan with the aluminum. I like to cut off as much visible fat as I can from the meat I cook. Place your meat in the center of the foil-lined pan. Slice your onion. Place the pieces on the top and sides of the meat.

In a medium-sized bowl, combine the soups. Add water. Stir soup mixture well. Spoon over the beef, moistening all visible meat. Seal the meat in aluminum foil. Cook at 325° for about 45 minutes a pound. I prefer to cook the meat as long as I can without burning it so that it comes out fork tender.

My family prefers super simple gravies, so I don't add seasoning. Most soups on the market should have enough salt on their own. However, there's no reason why you cannot add thyme, sage, or other herbs and spices to your gravy, suited to your taste.

Creamed potatoes are perfect with this entree since you'll have gravy. I also like to serve either green peas or a triple medley of fresh cauliflower, broccoli, and carrots boiled together as my second vegetable. Don't forget the bread if company's coming!

## CREAMY HAM & BROCCOLI BAKE

Carole Keller, Coopersburg, PA

**1½ pounds fresh broccoli, cooked to almost tender**
**1 can cream soup (any kind)**
**¼ cup milk**
**½ cup shredded cheese**
**1 cup baking mix**
**½ cup ham, cut up into small pieces**
**¼ cup firm margarine**

OVEN 400°

Place cooked broccoli and ham in 1½-quart baking dish. Heat oven to 400°. Beat soup and milk until smooth. Pour over broccoli and ham. Sprinkle with cheese. Mix baking mix with margarine until crumbly; sprinkle over top. Bake until crumbs are light brown, about 20 minutes.

Makes about 6 servings.

## FAMILY DELIGHT HAM LOAF

Roberta Perry, Milton, FL

**2 pounds ground ham, or more according to taste**
**½–1 pound lean ground chuck**
**1–1½ cups dry bread crumbs**
**2 eggs, do not beat**
**½–1 cup brown sugar**
**15- to 16-ounce can crushed pineapple, with juice**
**1–2 tablespoons mustard**

OVEN 350°

Use hand grinder or blender to grind ham. Mix all ingredients together and press into glass or metal oblong baking dish. Bake at 350° (lower if hot oven) for 45 minutes to 1 hour. Cut into cubes. If for a holiday treat, put a piece of maraschino or candied cherry on top.

## PINEAPPLE HAM CORN BREAD BAKE

Barbara Fellows, Sargent, NE

*"This is an unusual recipe that my sister used in The Tea Room in Maryville, TN. Amounts are not definite and are adjustable."*

**1 can crushed pineapple, drained, reserve juice**
**Ham, chopped**
**Favorite corn bread recipe**
**⅓ cup water**
**1 tablespoon cornstarch**
**Dash of salt**
**Sugar to taste**
**1 tablespoon butter**

OVEN 350°

Butter an 8x8- or 9x13-inch baking dish. Add layer of drained pineapple, then ham; top with favorite corn bread. (I like to add ¾ cup, per 8x8-inch pan, of cream style corn to my recipe for buttermilk corn bread. It makes it moist.) Bake at 350° for 30–40 minutes (until corn bread is done). Add about ⅓ cup water to reserved pineapple juice, dash of salt, sugar to taste and thicken with 1 tablespoon cornstarch. Add 1 tablespoon butter. May need extra juice to make enough sauce. Cut casserole into squares. Turn over on plate and pour a little sauce over the top.

## CRUSTLESS GRITS & HAM PIE

LaWanda Andrews, Hazel Green, AL

**1/3 cup quick cooking grits, uncooked**
**1 cup evaporated skim milk**
**1 cup water**
**¾ cup (3 ounces) shredded cheddar cheese**
**¾ cup lean ham cooked, chopped**
**3 eggs, beaten**
**1 tablespoon fresh chopped parsley**
**½ teaspoon dry mustard**
**½ teaspoon hot sauce**
**¼ teaspoon salt**
**Vegetable oil cooking spray**

OVEN 350°

Cook grits in water according to package directions, omitting salt. Combine cooked grits, milk, cheese, ham, eggs, parsley, mustard, hot sauce, and salt; mix well. Pour grits mixture into 9-inch pie plate coated with cooking spray. Bake at 350° for 30–35 minutes or until set. Let stand 5–10 minutes before serving.

## CRANBERRY PORK ROAST

Cheryl Sand, Columbus, OH

**1 lean, boneless pork roast (size can vary)**
**1 can jellied cranberry sauce**
**½ cup cranberry juice**
**½ cup sugar**
**1 teaspoon dry mustard**
**1/8 teaspoon cloves**

Place roast in Crock-Pot. Combine and pour remaining ingredients over roast. Cook on low 6–8 hours. Thicken juice with cornstarch. Makes terrific gravy for mashed potatoes.

## CANDIED PORK CHOPS

B. Ervin, Gooding, ID

**4–6 pork chops**
**2–3 apples, sliced with cores removed**
**Brown sugar**
**1 stick butter or margarine**

OVEN 350°

Brown pork chops on both sides in skillet in small amount of oil. Heat oven to 350°. In 9x13-inch pan place apple slices to line bottom of pan. Sprinkle apple slices generously with brown sugar. Dot with thin pats of butter or margarine. Bake at 350° for 1 hour, turning chops halfway through. Baste chops often with juice from apples and brown sugar.

This dish is good with cheese scalloped potatoes, pork stove top stuffing, and fresh or frozen green peas.

## BARBECUED PORK AND BEEF SANDWICHES

Jeannette Carter, Covington, VA

*"This is something you make in the morning and it is ready to serve in the evening. Great with cole slaw."*

**1½ pounds stew beef**
**1½ pounds pork cubes**
**2 cups chopped onion**
**3 green peppers, chopped**
**6-ounce can tomato paste**
**½ cup brown sugar**
**¼ cup cider vinegar**
**¼ cup chili powder**
**2 teaspoons salt**
**1 teaspoon dry mustard**
**2 teaspoons Worcestershire sauce**

In 3½- to 5-quart slow cooker, combine all ingredients. Cover and cook on high (300°) for 8 hours. With wire whisk, stir mixture until meat is shredded. Begin 8½ hours before serving.

Makes 12 sandwiches

## COUNTRY PORK 'N KRAUT

Darlene Mindrup, Glendale, AZ

**Editor's Note:** Author of four Heartsong Presents romance novels, Darlene is a "radical feminist turned radical Christian."

**2 pounds country style pork ribs**
**1 medium onion, chopped**
**1 tablespoon cooking oil**
**14-ounce can sauerkraut, undrained**
**1 cup applesauce**
**1 teaspoon garlic powder**
**2 tablespoons brown sugar**

Cook ribs and onion in oil until ribs are browned and onion is tender. Place in Crock-Pot. Combine remaining ingredients and pour over ribs. Cook on high 4–6 hours (or until ribs are tender). May also be cooked in a Dutch oven and baked at 350° for 1½–2 hours.

## SAUSAGE GUMBO

Sharon Gilmer, Brookfield, MO

**1 to 1½ pounds sausage, browned and drained well**
**½ stick margarine**
**1 cup diced carrots**
**1 cup diced onion**
**1 cup diced celery**
**1 cup diced green pepper**
**1 cup sliced fresh mushrooms**
**¼ cup soy sauce**
**1 quart tomato juice**
**1 can diced tomatoes**

In large skillet sauté in margarine the carrots, onion, celery, green pepper, and mushrooms. When vegetables start to get tender add soy sauce. Keep vegetables crunchy. In big pot put tomato juice, diced tomatoes, sausage, vegetables, and cooked rice. Heat until hot, do not boil. (Add more juice if necessary.) Good with cornbread.

## AFRICAN CHOW MEIN

Norma Goodoien, Apple Valley, MN

**1 pound ground beef, lean**
**1 chopped onion**
**2 cups chopped fresh celery**
**½ cup raw rice**
**1 can cream of mushroom soup**
**1 can chicken rice soup**
**¼ cup soy sauce**
**2 tablespoons Worcestershire sauce**
**2 cups water**

OVEN 350°

Brown beef and onions. Drain grease. Boil 2 cups water and pour over other ingredients. Bake 1 hour at 350°.

Serves 8.

## AMERICAN STIR-FRY

Carol Johnson, Mobile, AL

*"This is my own original recipe."*

**4 potatoes, peeled, washed, and chunked**
**1 pound Kielbasa or Polish sausage, sliced into bite-size pieces**
**1 large green pepper, diced**
**1 can kernel corn, drained**
**Salt and pepper to taste**

In a skillet place enough oil to fry the potatoes, on high heat. Once the potatoes brown and begin to soften, add the sausage, and brown. Stir often to keep from scorching and for even cooking. After sausage has browned, lower heat to medium and add bell pepper. Stir in thoroughly then add corn, stir thoroughly and leave on heat just long enough for peppers and corn to be heated thoroughly.

## S.I.T.T. (Something I Threw Together)

Amy Clouse, Severn, MD

**1 pound leftover meat**
**2 cups leftover vegetables**
**1 can tomato soup (for spicy dish, try salsa or spaghetti sauce)**
**1 can cheddar cheese soup (for spicy dish, use nacho cheese soup)**
**1 pound cooked macaroni**

OVEN 350°

Mix meat, vegetables, and tomato soup; put in casserole dish. Mix cheddar soup and macaroni; spread on top of meat mixture. Bake at 350° for 20 minutes.

Vary soups to make different flavors. Also works with canned meats, mixed meats, and canned vegetables.

## MOUSAKA

(Greek Eggplant Casserole)

Melanie Panagiotopoulos, Athens, Greece

*"Kali Orexi! Good appetite."*

**Editor's Note:** Melanie was born in Virginia and now lives in Athens with her husband and two children. She is the author of *Odyssey of Love* and *Race of Love* for Heartsong Presents.

**2½ pounds eggplant**
**1½ pounds ground meat (soy may be used instead of or a combination of the two)**
**½ cup grated Parmesan cheese**
**½ cup water, or wine**
**4 tablespoons butter or margarine**
**1 cup bread crumbs**
**2 tablespoons chopped onion**
**2 tablespoons chopped parsley**
**1½ pounds ripe tomatoes (canned tomatoes may be substituted)**
**1 portion white sauce**
**Oil for frying**
**Salt and pepper to taste**

**White Sauce:**
**2 tablespoons butter**
**2 tablespoons flour**
**1 cup milk**
**Salt and pepper to taste**

OVEN 375°

Brown the ground meat and onion in 2 tablespoons of butter. Stir to avoid lumping and pour in water. Add strained tomatoes, parsley, salt, pepper and let simmer until all the liquid is absorbed. Meanwhile, wash, dry, and clean the eggplant. Cut lengthwise, one by one, into thin slices (a little bit less than ½-inch thick) and fry both sides in hot oil. Remove, drain, and sprinkle with salt and pepper.

Prepare white sauce: In small saucepan melt butter. Over low heat add flour and stir until flour vanishes. Slowly stir in milk and stir until sauce thickens. Season with salt and pepper.

Lay half of the eggplant slices in rows on the bottom of a large baking dish. Add half the bread crumbs and half the cheese to the ground meat. Mix and spread mixture on top of the eggplant. Lay the rest of the eggplant over the meat sauce and cover it all with the white sauce. Sprinkle with remainder of the cheese and bread crumbs. Pour 2 tablespoons melted butter over the top and bake for 1 hour, or until the top turns golden brown.

## HAMBURGER RICE AND CHEESE

April Tarket, Lachine, MI

**1½ pounds hamburger**
**1 medium onion, diced**
**2 or so cups brown rice**
**1 cup grated cheddar cheese**

In large fry pan, fry the hamburger and onion. In separate saucepan, boil the rice; drain. Add rice to the hamburger and onion; stir. Sprinkle cheese over top and cover with a lid until cheese melts.

## HOT DOG / SLOPPY JOE SAUCE

Connie Steele, Bellville, WV

**4 pounds ground beef**
**4 cups ketchup**
**2 cups chopped onion**
**2 cups chopped green pepper**
**4 teaspoons salt**
**4 teaspoons pepper**
**4 tablespoons chili powder**
**2 teaspoons mustard**
**1 cup vinegar**
**1 cup sugar**
**1 cup water**

Brown ground beef, onion, and green pepper together; then drain. Add balance of ingredients and bring to slight bubble stage. Reduce to a simmer. Cook on low, stirring intermittently for 1 hour. Can be stored in refrigerator for up to a week.

Makes approximately 1 gallon.

## HAMBURGER SUMMER SAUSAGE

Rickie Lackey, Farmington, NM

**¾ cup water**
**2 pounds lean hamburger**
**¼ teaspoon onion powder**
**1 tablespoon Liquid Hickory Smoke**
**1 tablespoon mustard seed**
**¼ teaspoon pepper**
**¼ teaspoon salt**
**¼ teaspoon garlic powder**
**2 tablespoons Tender Quick Curing Salt (Morton brand)**

OVEN 350°

Mix all ingredients together. Form 2 long rolls, wrap in foil. Refrigerate 24 hours. Poke fork hole on bottom of rolls. Place on rack over a pan to catch liquid. Bake at 350° for 1 hour 15 minutes.

## HEAVENLY HAMBURGER

Sharon Johnston, Independence, KS

**2 tablespoons butter**
**1½ pounds ground beef**
**1 clove garlic**
**1 teaspoon salt**
**Dash of pepper**
**1 teaspoon sugar**
**8-ounce package lasagna noodles**
**8 green onions, chop tops off**
**3-ounce package cream cheese**
**1 cup sour cream**
**½ pound grated cheddar cheese**
**2 small cans tomato sauce**

OVEN 350°

Brown meat, garlic, salt, pepper, and sugar in butter. Drain excess grease. Add tomato sauce and simmer 20 minutes. Cook noodles in salted water and drain. Soften cream cheese. Add to sour cream and onions. Layer in 9x13-inch pan. Layer noodles with sauce and cheese. Bake at 350° for 20 minutes.

## DAD'S FAVORITE SIX-LAYER BAKED DINNER

Birdie L. Etchison, Ocean Park, WA

*"This recipe is for the homemaker to put together early in the afternoon and then dinner is complete. I made it many times for my father; it's still his favorite casserole. Great with salad and rolls! I like it because I consider it historical, and that's what I enjoy writing for Heartsong Presents."*

**Editor's Note:** Birdie has written several books for the Heartsong Presents series, including *The Heart Has Its Reasons* and *Albert's Destiny*.

**1 pound ground beef, lean and uncooked**
**2 medium white potatoes, sliced**
**1 onion, sliced**
**½ cup white rice, uncooked**
**2 medium carrots, sliced thin**
**1 large can tomatoes, or 1 quart canned**

OVEN 350°

Layer the potatoes, onions, rice, hamburger, and carrots in a large oven-safe dish and top with tomatoes. Sprinkle salt and pepper on each layer. Cover and bake in a 350° oven for 3 hours.

Optional: After baked, sprinkle with grated cheddar cheese.

## PIZZA BURGERS

Dorothy Justice, Rofeville, OH

*"Very good. Grandchildren love this!"*

**1 pound ground beef**
**10¾-ounce can tomato soup**
**15-ounce can pizza sauce**
**8 ounces mozzarella cheese**
**12 sandwich buns**

Brown ground beef in skillet; add tomato soup and pizza sauce, mix well. Cover and simmer 10 minutes. Separate buns, place on cookie sheet, put sauce on buns, add mozzarella cheese on top. Place under broiler in oven for 3 minutes or until brown.

## PIZZA / HAMBURGER CRUST

Libby Gastin, Canton, OH

**1 pound ground beef**
**½ cup dry bread crumbs**
**1 teaspoon salt**
**½ teaspoon oregano**
**1 cup tomato sauce**
**1 can kidney beans**
**Cheddar or mozzarella cheese**

OVEN 425°

Mix in large bowl, with spoon, hamburger, bread crumbs, salt, and oregano. Stir in tomato sauce. Spread meat mixture in an ungreased 10-inch pizza pan. Pour ½ cup tomato sauce on top. Add kidney beans. Sprinkle with cheddar cheese or mozzarella cheese. Bake uncovered for 20 minutes.

Serves 4.

## SATTLER FAMILY GOOP

Gail Sattler, Maple Ridge, British Columbia

*"This recipe doesn't have a real name, but my kids call it Goop. It's a kind of 'desperate times call for desperate measures' recipe—kids love it."*

**Editor's Note:** Gail wrote *Walking the Dog* for Heartsong Presents which was inspired by her own Standard Schnauzer. She lives in Canada with her husband and three sons.

**1 pound ground beef**
**1 onion**
**1 can tomato soup**
**1 can cream of mushroom soup**
**1 package macaroni and cheese dinner**
**Grated Parmesan cheese (optional)**

Brown the ground beef with onion, drain fat. Cook macaroni and drain. When the meat is cooked, add soups, cheese sauce package mix (no milk or butter, JUST the powder), and stir well. Heat until bubbly and remove from element. Add the macaroni and serve. Sprinkle with grated Parmesan cheese if desired.

## ITALIAN DELIGHT

Pamela Lance, Cleveland, TN

**1 pound ground beef, browned and drained**
**1 small onion, chopped**
**1 package egg noodles, cooked and drained**
**1 can Italian stewed tomatoes**
**4-ounce can tomato sauce**
**4-ounce can mushroom pieces, drained (optional)**
**1 cup mozzarella cheese**
**1 cup cheddar cheese, grated**

OVEN 350°

Cook beef and onions together, while boiling noodles. Combine beef/onion mixture with noodles, tomatoes, sauce, and mushrooms. Toss until mixed well. Pour into 2½-quart baking dish. Top with cheeses. Bake at 350° for 30 minutes or until heated through and cheese melts.

## GLOOP, GLOP, AND GLEEP

Jean Vandenburg

*"This was a great favorite of my family and my nephews!"*

**1 pound ground beef**
**3 medium potatoes, sliced thin**
**1 large onion, sliced thin**
**15-ounce can creamed corn**
**10-ounce can condensed tomato soup**
**Lawry's Seasoned Salt**
**Pepper**
**Worcestershire sauce**

OVEN 350°

Brown beef, making into small chunks. Season to taste with Lawry's salt, pepper, and Worcestershire sauce, in large skillet. Pour off excess grease. Layer onions, then potatoes, then onion, then potatoes, about 3 layers of each and season each layer. Spread can of creamed corn over that, then the tomato soup (undiluted) over all. Cover and bake in 350° oven for 1 hour or until potatoes are done.

## HAYSTACK DINNER

Sue Ellen Slabach, Sturgis, MI

*"This is an all-time favorite; ingredients can be varied for personal preference."*

**1 pound ground beef**
**1 small can tomato sauce**
**Mustard**
**Brown sugar**
**Sloppy Joe seasoning mix**
**1 cup rice, cooked**
**1 can nacho cheese soup**
**1 soup can of milk**
**1 tablespoon flour**
**12 club-style crackers, crumbled**
**2 cups chopped/shredded of each:**
**lettuce, tomato, green pepper,**
**cheddar cheese, mozzarella cheese**

Brown ground beef, add Sloppy Joe seasoning mix (with onion if you like), brown sugar, and mustard (like a Sloppy Joe mixture). Set aside. Prepare rice following package instructions. (Either cook or minute kind will work.) To prepare cheese sauce: Heat cheese soup and milk. Thicken slightly with a white sauce (flour and milk).

Each person then "builds his or her own stack." Layer as follows: Crumbled club crackers, rice, Sloppy Joe mixture, lettuce, tomato, green peppers, grated cheeses, and hot cheese sauce over top of stack.

This amount serves approximately 6.

## SHEPHERD'S PIE

Veda Boyd Jones, Joplin, MO

*"Every Christmas Eve we have the same meal: Shepherd's Pie. I know the shepherds didn't eat my concoction, but it's the way my family observes the Christmas story. My boys aren't actually fond of the casserole, but tradition is tradition. Enjoy."*

**Editor's Note:** Veda has authored several novels for Heartsong Presents including the award-winning *Callie's Mountain* and *Sense of Place.*

**2 cups chopped cooked roast beef**
**1 can corn**
**3 cups mashed potatoes**
**1½ cups brown gravy**

OVEN 350°

In casserole dish, layer the beef, corn, gravy, then top with the potatoes. Bake for 30 minutes at 350°. I usually make hot rolls to go with it.

## SHEPHERD'S PIE

Eva Pennel, Wenatchee, WA

**1½ pounds hamburger**
**1 medium onion, chopped**
**1 can tomato soup**
**15-ounce can tomato sauce**
**1 can whole sweet corn**
**1 can green beans**
**Cheddar cheese, grated**
**7 or 8 potatoes, cooked and sliced**
**Salt to taste**
**Garlic powder to taste**
**Cheese spread**

Brown hamburger with onion, drain. Add other ingredients. Season with salt and garlic powder. Pour into 9x13-inch baking dish. Sprinkle with cheese spread.

## SUPER SUPPER PIE

Sharon Edwards, Montpelier, ND

**1 pound hamburger**
**½ cup chopped celery**
**¼ cup chopped green pepper**
**1 small onion**
**2 medium grated carrots**
**¼ teaspoon chili powder**
**½ cup uncooked rice**
**1 cup water**
**¼ cup catsup**
**Favorite biscuit dough**
**1 can cream soup (chicken, mushroom, or celery)**
**½ soup can milk**
**½ cup cheese, grated**

OVEN 375°

Brown hamburger, celery, green pepper, and onion. Add carrots, chili powder, uncooked rice, and water. Simmer until rice is tender. Add catsup. Mix favorite biscuit dough and divide in half. Pat ½ into pie pan. Spread meat mixture on dough. Dilute soup with milk. Pour over meat. Sprinkle with grated cheese. Roll out remaining dough and cover pie. Bake at 375° for 25–30 minutes.

Note: Meat mixture alone makes a skillet meal. It can be varied to taste.

## GERMAN SKILLET DINNER

Lillie Colvin, Louisville, KY

**1–1½ pounds ground beef**
**1 medium onion**
**¾ cup quick cooking rice, uncooked**
**2 tablespoons margarine**
**1-pound can sauerkraut, with juice**
**8 ounces tomato sauce**

In a 10-inch skillet (with lid) melt margarine and add sauerkraut (with juice). Spread kraut evenly and add (uncooked) rice. Sprinkle the diced onion over the rice and kraut. Distribute (uncooked) ground beef over mixture. Pour tomato sauce over the (uncooked) ground beef. Cover and cook over medium heat for 20 minutes.

## SHIPWRECK
Sue Bird, Gainesville, TX

**3–4 large potatoes, sliced**
**2 pounds hamburger**
**1 small onion, chopped**
**2 15-ounce cans pork & beans**
**2 10½-ounce cans tomato soup**
**8 ounces grated cheese**

OVEN 350°

Cook hamburger and onion together. Layer all items in order given in a 9x13-inch baking dish (except cheese). Bake at 350° until potatoes are done, about 1½ hours. Put cheese on and resume cooking until cheese is melted.

## OVEN MEATBALLS
Shirley Monday, Knoxville, TN

**2 pounds lean ground beef**
**1 cup cornflake crumbs**
**¼ cup chopped parsley**
**2 eggs**
**2 tablespoons soy sauce**
**¼ teaspoon pepper**
**½ teaspoon garlic powder**
**⅓ cup ketchup**
**2 tablespoons instant minced onion**

Combine ingredients, shape into 30 small balls. Place in a 9x13-inch pan.

**Sauce:**
**1-pound can jellied cranberry sauce**
**12-ounce bottle chili sauce**
**2 tablespoons brown sugar**
**1 tablespoon lemon juice**

OVEN 350°

Combine sauce ingredients. Cook over medium heat, stir until smooth. Pour over meatballs. Bake uncovered 35–45 minutes.

## BARBECUED MEATBALLS
Barbara Ray, Oceola, OH

**3 pounds ground chuck**
**2 cups oatmeal**
**2 eggs**
**13-ounce can evaporated milk**
**1 cup chopped onions**
**2 teaspoons salt**
**½ tablespoon garlic powder**
**2 teaspoons chili powder**
**½ teaspoon pepper**

**Sauce:**
**2 cups catsup**
**1½ cups brown sugar**
**½ teaspoon garlic powder**
**½ cup chopped onion**

OVEN 350°

Mix loaf ingredients and make into balls. Place in flat pan, one layer to each pan. Bake 20 minutes at 350°. Remove from oven and drain grease. Mix sauce ingredients together until sugar dissolves. Pour over balls and bake uncovered about 40 minutes.

## MEATBALLS WITH SAUCE

Pauline Miller, North Manchester, IN

**3 pounds hamburger**
**13-ounce can evaporated milk**
**2 eggs**
**2 cups quick oats**
**2 teaspoons salt**
**½ teaspoon pepper**
**1 chopped onion**
**½ teaspoon garlic powder**
**2 teaspoons chili powder**
**2–3 tablespoons Worcestershire sauce**

**Sauce:**
**2 cups catsup**
**2 teaspoons Liquid Smoke**
**1½ cups brown sugar**
**¾ cup onion**
**½ teaspoon garlic powder**

OVEN 350°

Mix meatball ingredients together and shape into balls about 1½-inches in diameter. Place in single layer in pan. Pour sauce over top and bake for 1 hour.

## GRANDMA LUCY'S MEATBALLS

Lucille Kiel, Milaca, MN

**2 pounds ground beef**
**2 eggs**
**2½ cups bread crumbs**
**1 medium onion, chopped fine**
**1 tablespoon salt**
**1 teaspoon chili powder**

**Sauce:**
**2 cups water**
**1 teaspoon chili powder**
**1 teaspoon salt**
**1 can tomato soup**
**1 onion, chopped fine**
**1 green pepper, chopped fine**

Mix all meat ingredients together and form into balls, size of an egg. Set aside. Sauce: mix all ingredients together in a Dutch oven or electric fry pan. Heat to boiling. Drop in meatballs. Bake 1 hour in moderate oven or cook on top of stove or in electric fry pan. Stir occasionally. Serve with rice, pasta, or potatoes.

## MEXICAN SANDWICHES

Ruby Ann Schlabach, Howe, IN

**3 pounds ground beef**
**1 medium onion, chopped**
**10- to12- ounce package grated cheese (Colby)**
**15-ounce can tomato sauce**
**4-ounce can ripe olives, chopped**
**4-ounce can salsa**
**2 dozen hard rolls**

OVEN 350°

Brown beef and onions, drain. Add remaining ingredients except rolls. Pinch bread out of center of rolls; fill with beef mixture. Wrap each roll in foil. Bake at 350° for 30 minutes.

## CHEESY BARBECUED MEATBALLS

Eileen Horning, Ephrata, PA

**2 cups cornflakes**
**2 eggs**
**⅓ cup milk**
**½ teaspoon salt**
**⅛ teaspoon pepper**
**½ pound ground beef**
**1 cup shredded cheddar or mozzarella cheese**

**Sauce:**
**1 cup catsup**
**¾ cup water**
**2 tablespoons vinegar**
**3 tablespoons brown sugar**
**1 tablespoon minced onion**
**1 teaspoon salt**

OVEN 350°

Crush cornflakes in medium-size bowl. Add eggs, milk, salt, and pepper. Mix well. Let stand 5 minutes. Add ground beef and cheese, mix well. Shape into 1-inch balls. Place in baking dish. Mix ingredients for sauce together. Pour over meatballs. Bake at 350° for 40–50 minutes.

## SWEDISH MEATBALLS

Barbara Sidfried, Blackfoot, ID

*"This is very good to take to church suppers. I've never had any left over."*

**1 can cream of chicken soup**
**½ soup can of water**
**1 envelope dry onion soup mix**
**1 pound ground beef**
**½ cup cracker crumbs**
**1 egg**

OVEN 375°

Mix ground beef, cracker crumbs, egg, and half of the onion soup mix. Shape into balls. Combine chicken soup, water, and the other half of onion soup mix. Pour over meatballs that are in a casserole. Bake at 375° for 35 minutes.

## SWEDISH MEATBALLS

Beverly Jackson, Franklin, NH

**2 pounds ground chuck**
**1 cup bread crumbs**
**½ cup milk**
**Salt and pepper to taste**

Mix together and make small balls.

**Sauce:**
**2 tablespoons Worcestershire sauce**
**1 cup catsup**
**2 tablespoons vinegar**
**Dash Tabasco sauce**
**Dash nutmeg**
**1 onion, chopped finely**
**2 tablespoons horseradish**

OVEN 350°

Mix together and pour over small balls which have been put in an ungreased casserole dish. Bake at 350° for 1 hour.

## SWEDISH MEATBALLS

Shana Henley, El Dorado Springs, MO

**½ cup onion**
**2 tablespoons butter or margarine**
**1 egg, slightly beaten**
**1½ cups bread crumbs**
**½ cup evaporated milk**
**¼ cup fresh parsley**
**¼ teaspoon nutmeg**
**¼ teaspoon ginger**
**1¼ teaspoons salt**
**½ teaspoon pepper**
**1½ pounds ground beef or turkey**

**Sauce:**
**3 tablespoons butter**
**1 teaspoon beef bouillon**
**1 tablespoon soy sauce**
**2 tablespoons flour**
**1¼ cups water**

OVEN 350°

Cook onion in butter until tender, drain (save butter). Combine beaten egg, bread, milk, spices, meat, and onion. Mix well, cover and chill for at least one hour. Shape into balls. Spray pan with cooking spray. Bake at 350° for 10–12 minutes. While baking in saucepan combine butter drippings with remaining sauce ingredients. Mix well. Cook, stirring until thick and bubbly. Drain excess grease off meatballs, then pour sauce over meatballs and bake about 20 minutes longer. Serve with mashed potatoes.

## SAUCY MEATBALLS

Maralyn Williams, West Palm Beach, FL

**2 pounds ground beef (or turkey)**
**¼ teaspoon pepper**
**Dash salt**
**⅓ cup catsup**
**1 cup crushed cornflakes**
**2 tablespoons onion, finely chopped**
**½ teaspoon garlic powder**
**2 tablespoons low-salt soy sauce**
**2 eggs**

Mix all ingredients well. Form into small balls, 1½- to 2-inches.

**Sauce:**
**½ bottle chili sauce**
**1 can jellied cranberry sauce**
**2 tablespoons brown sugar**
**1 teaspoon lemon juice**

OVEN 350°

Mix together and pour over meatballs. Bake at 350° for about 45 minutes in a foil-lined pan. These freeze well. I serve this over noodles or mashed potatoes.

## MUSHROOM MEAT LOAF

Nell Baldwin, Blum, TX

*"My husband loved to cook and created this recipe."*

**2 pounds very lean ground beef**
**1 cup coarse uncooked oatmeal**
**3 large eggs**
**2 cans mushroom soup, no water added**
**Heavy sprinkle garlic powder**
**Black pepper to taste**
**Chopped onion to taste (2–4 tablespoons)**
**No salt (salt in soup)**

OVEN 350°

Measure all, reserving 1 can mushroom soup for topping, into a baking dish; mix well. Smooth out and put a second can of mushroom soup over top and spread around. Cut through the mixture, once, end to end. Cut across 3 times. Bake until well done at 350°, about 1 hour. Freezes well.

## VEGGIE MEAT LOAF

Gertrude Crittendon, Imlay City, MI

*"This is very tasty."*

**1 pound ground beef**
**1 onion**
**1 egg**
**Salt and pepper to taste**
**1 can vegetable soup**
**Enough cracker crumbs to hold loaf together**

OVEN 350°

Mix all ingredients, put into baking dish. Bake at 350° for about 1 hour.

## MEAT LOAF USING TAPIOCA

Betty Faris, Rochester Hills, MI

**2½–3 pounds ground beef**
**1 large onion, chopped**
**4 tablespoons quick-cooking tapioca**
**1 teaspoon salt**
**2 eggs, beaten**
**1½ cups drained, canned tomatoes (diced)**
**4 tablespoons catsup**
**½ teaspoon pepper**
**1 teaspoon Worcestershire sauce**

OVEN 375°

Mix together all ingredients thoroughly. Put into loaf pan. Bake at 375° for 45 minutes.

## MEAT LOAF WITH OATMEAL

Susie Khoury, Jonesboro, AR

**1 pound lean ground beef or ground chuck**
**1 tablespoon minced onion or 2 ounces onion**
**2 tablespoons chopped parsley**
**1 teaspoon seasoned salt**
**½ teaspoon oregano**
**2 tablespoons ketchup**
**¾ cup oatmeal, uncooked**
**1 cup milk**
**1 tablespoon Worcestershire sauce**
**1 tablespoon brown sugar replacement**

OVEN 350°

Combine all ingredients. Place in a loaf pan and press into meat loaf form. Bake, uncovered, at 350° for at least 1 hour until meat is no longer pink.

Optional: After pressing into pan, cover with ketchup. May also cover with cornflake crumbs.

## MEAT LOAF WITH CARROTS

Louise Totten, Cowgill, MO

**1½ pounds ground beef**
**1 tablespoon diced onion**
**½ cup crushed crackers**
**Salt and pepper to taste**
**½ cup grated carrots**
**2 eggs**
**¼ cup milk**

**Topping:**

**¼ cup brown sugar**
**1 tablespoon mustard**
**¼ cup catsup**

OVEN 350°

Combine meat ingredients. Put into loaf pan. Combine topping and pour over top of meat. Bake at 350° for 45 minutes.

## MEAT LOAF WITH SAUCE

Beverly Moorhead, International Falls, MN

**2 pounds ground beef**
**½ cup oatmeal**
**½ cup bread crumbs**
**4 eggs**
**Medium onion, diced**
**¼ cup dill pickle juice**

**Sauce:**

**½ cup ketchup**
**¼ cup water**
**2 teaspoons sugar**
**1 teaspoon Worcestershire sauce**
**½ cup diced dill pickles**

OVEN 350°

Mix meat ingredients together thoroughly and put into greased pan. Mix sauce and pour over shaped loaf. Bake at 350° for 1–1½ hours.

## FLUFFY MEAT LOAF

Ruth Bond, Aurora, IL

**1 pound ground beef**
**½ pound ground pork**
**2 cups bread crumbs**
**1 egg, beaten**
**1½ cups milk**
**4 tablespoons minced onion**
**2 teaspoons salt**
**¼ teaspoon pepper**
**¼ teaspoon mustard**
**⅛ teaspoon sage**

OVEN 350°

Mix thoroughly; pack into greased baking dish. Bake 1½ hours at 350°.

## TAMALE LOAF

Cindie Hantho, La Center, WA

**1 large onion, minced**
**1 large can creamed corn**
**1 large can tomatoes with puree**
**Salt and pepper to taste**
**¾ cup cornmeal**
**1 egg, beaten**
**1 cup raw ground meat**
**Olives**

OVEN 350°

Fry onion in oil until tender. Add corn, tomatoes, salt, and pepper (break up tomatoes). Bring to boil and add cornmeal gradually. Cook about 10 minutes. Remove from heat; add egg, olives, and raw ground meat. Bake about 45 minutes in a moderate oven at 350°.

## MEXICAN MEAT LOAF

Sue Smith, Pampa, TX

**1½ pounds hamburger**
**½ onion**
**1 can tomato paste**
**1 can chopped green chilies**
**1 can chicken rice soup**
**Grated cheese**
**Tortilla chips**

OVEN 350°

Brown hamburger and onion together. Add tomato paste, chilies, and soup to meat mixture. Put half of mixture into casserole. Layer tortilla chips. Add rest of mixture. Grate cheese on top. Bake at 350° for 30 minutes.

## BLACK BEAN BURRITOS

Doreen Sanford, Galesburg, IL

**2 medium carrots, chopped**
**2 cloves garlic, chopped**
**1 medium onion, chopped**
**2 teaspoons vegetable oil**
**1 can black beans, drained**
**1 cup shredded Monterey Jack cheese**
**1 cup corn**
**¾ teaspoon cumin**
**¼ teaspoon salt**
**¼ teaspoon pepper**
**8 flour tortillas**

OVEN 350°

Preheat oven to 350°. In large skillet, sauté carrots, garlic, and onion in oil for 5 minutes, until tender. Partially mash beans. Add to skillet with corn, cumin, salt, and pepper. Cook 2 minutes. Lay tortillas on flat work surface; place ¼ cup bean mixture in center of each tortilla. Roll up and place seam-side down in 9x13-inch pan. Sprinkle with cheese, bake 10 minutes. Serve immediately.

Makes 4 servings.

## FESTIVE FAJITAS

Vickee Widbin, Wever, IA

*"As a mother of 5 children my schedule is busy! This is fast, easy, nutritious, and my kids love it!"*

**3–4 boneless chicken breasts**
**1 tablespoons oil**
**¼ teaspoon garlic powder**
**1 cup green pepper, cut into strips**
**¾ cup sliced onions**
**10-ounce package Mexican-style processed cheese food spread**
**8-inch tortillas**
**Tomatoes, chopped for topping**

Cut chicken breasts and stir-fry in oil and garlic powder. Add green pepper strips and onions. Continue to stir-fry for 5 minutes. Cut cheese into cubes and add to chicken. Stir until cheese is melted, do not allow to boil. Place desired amount of chicken/cheese mixture in center of 8-inch tortilla. Top with chopped tomatoes. Fold.

## MEXICAN ROLL-UPS

Sylvia Buller, Warner Robins, GA

**2½ cups cubed chicken or turkey (leftovers work great!)**
**½ cup sour cream**
**1 cup shredded cheese**
**1½ teaspoons taco seasoning**
**½ can mushroom soup**
**1 small onion, chopped**
**½ cup salsa**
**¼ cup sliced ripe olives**

**Sauce:**

**1 cup sour cream**
**1½ teaspoons taco seasoning**
**½ can mushroom soup**

OVEN 350°

Combine and place ⅓ cup on each of 10 flour tortillas (7-inch); roll up and place in greased 9x13-inch baking dish. Combine sauce ingredients and pour over tortillas and bake at 350° for 30 minutes. Sprinkle with more shredded cheese. Serve with shredded lettuce, chopped tomatoes, and salsa.

## BLACK BEAN & CHEESE TORTILLA PIE

Jill Allison, Knoxville, TN

**1 deep-dish pie crust**
**3 tablespoons vegetable oil**
**½ cup chopped onion**
**½ cup chopped green pepper**
**15-ounce can black beans, drained and rinsed**
**½ cup salsa**
**2 cups shredded cheddar cheese**
**3 flour tortillas**
**Sour cream (optional)**

OVEN 350°

Prepare pie crust by package directions for unfilled crust. Heat oil in skillet, add onion and green pepper. Stir-fry until tender (about 5 minutes). Add beans and salsa, simmer 7–10 minutes. Spoon ½ cup bean mixture into pie crust. Layer with cheese then tortilla. Bake at 350° until cheese is melted. Serve with sour cream if desired.

## MEXICAN BEAN ROLLS

Joyce West, Farmington, KY

**1½ pounds ground chuck (brown & drain)**
**1 package taco seasoning mix**
**1 can Rotel tomatoes with chilies**
**1 can water**
**1 or 2 cans refried beans**
**Monterey Jack cheese for topping**
**Ripe olives for topping**
**Sour cream for topping**

Simmer down until thick. Put meat mix in flour tortillas and roll up. Sprinkle with Monterey Jack cheese. Put in microwave until cheese melts. Top with lettuce, tomatoes, olives, and sour cream.

## TACO PIE

Beth Beck, Villas, NJ

**1 pound ground turkey or beef**
**1 package taco seasoning**
**¾ cup water**
**1 large jar mild salsa**
**8-ounce can kidney beans**
**Cheddar cheese**
**Taco chips**

OVEN 350°

Crumble chips to cover the bottom of 9x13-inch pan. Brown meat and spread on chips. Mix taco seasoning and water; pour over meat. In blender, mix salsa and beans, pour on top. Top with cheese. Bake at 350° for 20 minutes. Top each serving with favorite taco toppings.

## CHICKEN TACO

Dorothy Arnold, Rienzi, MS

*"This is one of our favorites at my home."*

**4 chicken breasts (boiled) torn in pieces**
**8-ounce bag tortilla chips**
**½ pound processed cheese food, cubed**
**1 can mushroom soup**
**1 can Rotel tomatoes, regular or hot**

Mix all ingredients together, except tortilla chips, in baking dish. Top with chips. Heat in microwave until cheese is bubbly. Serve with more chips.

## CHILI RELLENOS CASSEROLE

Rickie Lackey, Farmington, NM

**1 cup half-and-half**
**2 eggs**
**⅓ cup flour**
**3 4-ounce cans whole green chilies or fresh chilies**
**½ pound Monterey Jack cheese, grated**
**½ pound longhorn Colby cheese, grated**
**1 can tomato sauce**

OVEN 350°

In blender, mix together half-and-half, eggs, and flour until smooth. Toss together cheeses and reserve ½ cup. Split chilies, wash seeds out; drain on paper towels. Make layers of cheese, chilies, and egg mixture; repeat until done. Pour tomato sauce over top and sprinkle with cheese. Bake 45 minutes to 1 hour at 350°, until done.

## TACO CASSEROLE

Sheryl Inalls, Texhoma, OK

**1 pound ground beef, browned and drained**
**1 can chili beans, drained**
**1 can Rotel tomatoes**
**1 can cream of mushroom soup**
**1 package taco seasoning mix**
**1 bag tortilla chips**
**Lettuce**
**Chopped tomato**
**Shredded cheddar cheese**

OVEN 350°

In casserole dish, crumble enough of tortilla chips to cover bottom of dish. In large bowl, mix together beef (browned and drained), chili beans (drained), Rotel, and cream of mushroom soup. Add taco seasoning. Pour into casserole dish, top with crushed tortilla chips. Bake for 30 minutes. Top with lettuce, chopped tomatoes, and shredded cheddar cheese.

## POP-OVER TACO

Donna Conklin, Stanwood, MI

**1 pound ground beef**
**1 large onion, diced**
**1 envelope taco seasoning mix**
**15-ounce can tomato sauce**
**½ cup water**
**16 ounces refried beans**
**4 ounces chopped green chilies, divided**
**1 cup grated Monterey Jack cheese**
**1 cup milk**
**2 eggs**
**1 tablespoon oil**
**1 cup flour**

OVEN 400°

Brown beef and onion. Stir in taco seasoning, tomato sauce, and water. Simmer 10 minutes. Spread refried beans in greased 9x13-inch baking pan. Layer ½ chilies over beans, pour meat mixture evenly over chilies, layer remaining chilies over meat. Top with grated cheese. Blend milk, eggs, oil, and flour. Pour evenly over pan. Bake for 30 minutes or until golden brown. Cut into squares.

## NAVAJO TACO

Clarice Watts, Lamar, MO

**2 cups flour**
**1 teaspoon baking powder**
**1 teaspoon salt**
**1 rounded tablespoon shortening**
**¾ cup water**
**¼ cup milk**

Cut shortening into water and milk. Mix and knead until elastic. If top is sticky, add flour sparingly. Let stand 15 minutes or for a few hours (it can rest in refrigerator up to a few hours). Divide dough into 8 equal parts. Roll out as pie dough. Fry in ½-inch hot grease until medium light brown. Turn to the other side and brown. Top with lettuce, tomatoes, and cheddar cheese.

## CHICKEN ENCHILADA CASSEROLE

Ruth McCormick, McCook, NE

*"This is a family favorite from my mother and now includes all four son-in-laws and grandchildren of mine."*

**4 cups chicken, cooked and cubed**
**1 cup chicken broth**
**1 cup cream of mushroom soup**
**1 cup cream of chicken soup**
**1 medium chopped onion**
**2–3 tablespoons margarine**
**1 small can chopped green chilies**
**1 dozen corn tortillas, torn into eighths**
**1 pound grated longhorn cheese**

OVEN 350°

Sauté onion in margarine. Mix all ingredients together in a large bowl. Spray large casserole dish with cooking spray. Layer several times: chicken mixture, tortillas, and cheese. Bake at 350° for 30 minutes.

Serves 8.

## CHICKEN ENCHILADAS

Charlene Ricker, Wichita, KS

**8–10 chicken breasts or turkey, boiled and chopped**
**2 cans of diced green chilies**
**1 medium chopped onion**
**2 dozen corn tortillas**
**2 cans cream of chicken soup**
**1 can broth from boiled chicken**
**¼ teaspoon cumin**
**¼ teaspoon sage**
**½ teaspoon chili powder**
**½ teaspoon oregano**
**Grated cheese**
**Black olives (optional)**

OVEN 300°

Mix chopped chicken with chilies and onion. Set aside. Dip tortillas in hot oil until soft. Place a small amount of chicken mixture in each tortilla and roll. Place tortilla rolls in a deep pan. Combine soup, broth, and spices. Pour over tortilla rolls and cover with cheese and olives. Bake for 30 minutes. Can be served with lettuce, tomatoes, and taco sauce. Reheats well.

## JEAN'S CHICKEN ENCHILADAS

Jean Farmer, Charleston, WV

**8 flour tortillas (large)**
**2 cans cream of chicken soup**
**1 cup sour cream**
**½ teaspoon salt**

**Filling:**

**1 pound grated longhorn cheese**
**1 cup onion, diced**
**1 whole chicken, cooked and diced**

OVEN 350°

Heat sauce until smooth. Mix cheese, onion, and chicken together. Fill each tortilla with cheese mix. Add small amount of sauce to filling, then roll each tortilla. Place in greased 9x13-inch pan or dish. Pour sauce over top and bake 25–30 minutes in 350° oven. This freezes very well.

## CHICKEN ENCHILADAS

Beth Wagner, Shermansdale, PA

**1 medium onion, chopped**
**2 tablespoons margarine**
**½ cup shredded cooked chicken**
**12 ounces picante sauce**
**8 flour tortillas (6-inch)**
**3 ounces cream cheese, cubed**
**8 ounces shredded sharp cheese**

OVEN 350°

Cook and stir onion in margarine in skillet until tender. Stir in chicken, ¼ cup picante, and cream cheese. Cook until thoroughly heated. Stir in 1 cup cheese. Spoon about ⅓ cup mixture in center of each tortilla; roll up. Place seam side down in 7x12-inch baking dish. Top with remaining picante and cheese. Bake for 15 minutes at 350°.

## CHICKEN ENCHILADAS

Carla Moore, Wichita, KS

**Boiled chicken, chopped**
**1 stick butter**
**1 medium onion**
**1 small can green chilies, drained**
**2 cans cream of chicken soup**
**1 can evaporated milk**
**Cheddar cheese, grated**
**Tortilla shells**

OVEN 300°

Cook onions and chilies in butter until onions are clear. Mix soup and milk and add onions/chilies mixture. Roll chopped chicken and cheese in tortilla shells and place in 9x13-inch pan. After enchiladas are in pan ladle sauce over top. Bake at 300° for 30 minutes. Add cheese on top, bake until melted.

## MEXICAN CASSEROLE

Jane Messimer, Weatherford, TX

**1 pound hamburger**
**½ onion**
**8 ounces taco sauce**
**1 can enchilada sauce**
**1 can cream of chicken soup**
**Cheddar cheese, grated**
**Corn tortillas**
**1 can sliced black olives (optional)**

OVEN 350°

Brown meat and onions; drain. Add soup and sauces. In 9x13-inch casserole dish layer tortillas, half of meat mixture, and half of cheese; repeat. Bake at 350° for 20–30 minutes.

## ENCHILADA CASSEROLE

Sandra Peterson, Saint Albans, ME

**1 pound hamburger, browned**
**1 can refried beans**
**1 can mushroom soup**
**1 can enchilada sauce**
**1 can cheddar cheese soup**
**1 pound grated cheese**
**1 can green chilies (optional)**
**1 package corn tortillas, frozen**
**1 onion, chopped**

OVEN 350°

Mix soups, sauce, and beans together to make a pudding. Layer ingredients starting with pudding, then tortillas, pudding, meat, chilies, onion, and cheese. Repeat until all is used. Bake at 350° for 30 minutes to 1 hour.

## CHICKEN ENCHILADAS TEXAS STYLE

Verla Pinkerton, Clute, TX

**3 pounds skinless, boneless chicken breasts, cut in short thin strips**
**3 slices bacon**
**2 cloves garlic, minced**
**1½ cups picante sauce**
**16-ounce can black beans, undrained**
**1 teaspoon ground cumin**
**¼ teaspoon salt**
**½ cup sliced green onions**
**12 flour tortillas (6–7-inch)**
**1½ cups shredded Monterey Jack cheese**

OVEN 350°

Cook bacon in 10-inch skillet until crisp, crumble. Pour off all but 2 tablespoons drippings. Cook and stir chicken and garlic in drippings until chicken is done. Stir in beans, cumin, and salt, and ½ cup picante sauce. Simmer until thickened, 7–9 minutes, stirring occasionally. Sir in onions and bacon. Spoon heaping ¼ cup bean mixture down center of each tortilla; top with 1 tablespoon cheese. Roll up and place seam side down in lightly greased 9x13-inch dish. Spoon remaining picante sauce evenly over enchiladas. Bake at 350° for 15 minutes. Top with remaining cheese; return to oven for about 3 minutes. If desired serve with additional picante sauce and top with lettuce, tomatoes, sour cream, and avocado slices.

Makes 6 servings.

## MEXICAN CHICKEN CASSEROLE

Sharon Gilmer, Brookfield, MO

**3 pounds chicken cooked, boned, and cut up**
**2 cans cream of mushroom soup**
**1 large can Rotel tomatoes, or regular diced tomatoes**
**1 large onion, chopped**
**1 bag tortilla chips, crushed**
**1 pound cheddar or American cheese, grated**

OVEN 350°

Butter a 4-quart dish. Place a layer of chicken, chips, onions, soup, tomatoes and juice, and cheese in that order. Repeat layers using ½ ingredients each time. Top generously with cheese. Bake at 350° for 1 hour.

## MEXICAN CHICKEN CASSEROLE

Evelyn Stiles, Muskogee, OK

**1 chicken, boiled and deboned**
**1 onion, chopped**
**¼ pound butter**
**1 can Rotel tomatoes**
**3 cans cream of chicken soup**
**1 large bag Doritos**
**½ pound shredded cheese**

OVEN 350°

Sauté onion in butter. Mix soups and add to onion mixture. Cook until hot and bubbly. Layer 9x13-inch dish with Doritos. Next layer, chicken pieces. Next layer, soup mixture. Next layer, Doritos. Next layer, shredded cheese. Bake at 350° for 30 minutes.

## EASY ENCHILADA PIE

Jill Stengl, Goldsboro, NC

*"With four children and a hungry husband to feed, I appreciate a fast and nutritious recipe. In* Finally Love, *Darlene Althrop prepared a Mexican casserole for Jake after his return home from Aviano, Italy—this is the recipe I had in mind. Hope you enjoy it as much as Jake Edgewood did!"*

**Editor's Note:** Jill is an author for Heartsong Presents who has *Eagle Pilot, Finally Love*, and *The Promised Child* to her credit. She is a military wife and home school mom.

**1½ pounds lean ground beef or turkey**
**½ cup chopped celery**
**1 small can mild enchilada sauce**
**2 or 3 8-ounce cans tomato sauce**
**1 package corn tortillas**
**½ pound cheddar cheese**
**½ cup chopped onion**

OVEN 350°

Brown meat, celery, and onion together. Add enchilada sauce and tomato sauce to the meat (adding more tomato sauce will tone down the "heat" somewhat). In a 9x13-inch baking pan, put a layer of meat sauce then a layer of torn up corn tortillas. Repeat, ending with sauce on top. Sprinkle olives and grated cheese on top. Bake at 350° for 30 minutes or until hot and bubbly.

This casserole is best served with a cold side dish like tossed or fruit salad.

## EASY ENCHILADA CASSEROLE

Tammy Gosser Egnew, Russell Springs, KY

**1 pound browned ground beef**
**2 cans enchilada sauce**
**Corn tortillas**
**Cheddar cheese, shredded**

OVEN 350°

Mix together beef and sauce, cook until bubbly. Place small amount (⅓) of mixture in bottom of 9x13-inch pan and spread. Place corn tortillas over mixture, then add cheese and repeat layers again. Bake at 350° for 45 minutes. Serve over rice with side dish of fresh or canned tomatoes.

## EASY CASSEROLE

Viola Gersema, New Hardford, IA

**1 pound ground beef**
**1 can undiluted creamed soup (chicken, celery, or mushroom)**
**1 package frozen Tater Tots**

OVEN 350°

Pat ground beef in the bottom of a square cake pan. Spread undiluted soup on top of meat. Sprinkle Tater Tots over top of soup. Bake at 350° for 45 minutes, drain off grease if necessary.

## QUICK CASSEROLE

Lois M. Behm, Alliance, NE

**2 cups cooked elbow macaroni**
**1 can creamed soup (mushroom, chicken, or celery)**
**1 can milk, water, or broth**
**2 cups hamburger, cooked; or raw, cubed chicken or ham**
**Parsley flakes**
**Onion flakes, or diced onion**
**Salt and pepper to taste**
**Mozzarella cheese**

OVEN 325°

Combine macaroni, meat, soup, and liquid. Stir together parsley, onion, salt and pepper; add to meat mixture. Place in 9x13-inch pan. Sprinkle mozzarella cheese on top. Bake at 325° for 40 minutes in conventional oven, or microwave.

## BEEF ENCHILADAS

Sandra Dueck, Chih, Mexico

*"This is a popular Mexican food. I hope you enjoy this Mexican dish."*

**2 cups hamburger meat**
**1 tablespoon vinegar**
**1 teaspoon salt**
**1 teaspoon chili powder**

**Sauce:**

**½ blended onion**
**¼ teaspoon cumin**
**¼ teaspoon oregano**
**1 teaspoon salt**
**2 cups tomato juice**
**2 tablespoons lard**
**1 tablespoon flour**
**2 tablespoons chili powder**

Mix together meat, vinegar, salt, and chili powder; fry until brown. Blend onion with spices together. Put meat on fried tortillas. Combine sauce ingredients and pour over meat and tortillas. Top with shredded cheese if you wish.

## BEEF ENCHILADAS

Jan Ludlow, Biloxi, MS

**1 pound ground beef**
**10 pack of flour tortillas**
**1 cup mozzarella cheese, shredded**
**1 cup cheddar cheese, shredded**
**1 can golden cream of mushroom soup**
**1 can refried beans**
**1 tablespoon salsa (optional)**

Brown meat and drain; mix in refried beans, ½ cheese, ½ soup, and the salsa. Heat on low heat until cheese melts. Spoon meat mixture into tortillas, roll up, and place in casserole dish. Pour remaining soup and cheese over the top and bake until cheese melts.

Note: This recipe can be easily altered for individual taste.

## CASSEROLE FOR A BUSY DAY

Lenza Wright, Towson, MD

*"This is a great meal for a busy day. Quick to prepare and can be cooking while you are busy with other things. Can be kept warm at a lower heat."*

**4 blade steaks or boneless pork chops**
**1 can low-salt tomato sauce**
**2 large onions**
**4 medium potatoes**
**Carrots**

OVEN 350°

Sear meat on each side. Place in baking dish. Halve onions and place on each piece of meat. Place potatoes around meat and then add carrots. Dilute tomato sauce with half water, add tomato sauce. Pour over the meat and vegetables. Place lid on dish and bake at 350° for about 2–2½ hours.

Serves 4.

## TACO CASSEROLE

Cheryl Lord, Orangevale, CA

**1 pound ground meat**
**½ teaspoon garlic salt**
**9½-ounce package corn chips**
**1 cup grated cheese**
**Prepared salsa or use recipe below**

OVEN 350°

Cook meat until browned; drain. Stir in garlic salt. Coarsely crush corn chips and place in bottom of ungreased 8-inch square pan. Spoon hot meat over chips. Top with cheese. Bake at 350° for 10–12 minutes. Serve with salsa, sauce, and lettuce.

**Sauce:**

**16-ounce can stewed tomatoes**
**1 teaspoon sugar**
**¾ teaspoon oregano**
**½ teaspoon Worcestershire sauce**
**¼ teaspoon salt**
**⅛ teaspoon pepper**
**¼ teaspoon hot sauce**
**¼ cup chopped onion**
**¼ cup chopped green pepper**

## CASSEROLE READY IN 45 MINUTES

Elizabeth DeVivo, Waupaca, WI

*"Delicious meal. Quick and easy."*

**Ground beef**
**Onion**
**1 can cream of celery soup**
**Small can sauerkraut**
**Tater Tots**

OVEN 350°

Brown ground beef and onions, drain grease off, and put in casserole dish. Pour soup over top. Drain sauerkraut (usually rinse it to get rid of strong acid taste) and put over ground beef and soup. Cover top with Tater Tots. Bake at 350° for 45 minutes.

## HAMBURGER CASSEROLE

Tracey Allen, Cummings, GA

**2 pounds ground beef**
**1 small package frozen chopped broccoli, thawed**
**4 slices American cheese**
**1 can cream of mushroom soup**
**1 can cream of chicken soup**
**1 package frozen Tater Tots**
**2 medium onions (optional)**

OVEN 350°

Brown beef; drain and place in square pan. Add broccoli after breaking it apart. Place separated onion rings over broccoli. Cover onions with cheese. Mix soup mixture and pour over top. Place Tater Tots on top. Bake at 350° for 45 minutes.

## ZUCCHINI / HAMBURGER CASSEROLE

Lorraine M. Belval, Winooski, VT

**1 to 2 large zucchini**
**2 medium summer yellow squash**
**¾ cup instant rice**
**1 medium onion**
**1 pound hamburger**
**1 (or 2) cans stewed tomatoes**
**1 teaspoon basil leaves**
**¼ teaspoon dill weed**
**Mrs. Dash brand seasoning**
**Salt and pepper to taste**
**Bread crumbs**
**Cheese (optional)**

OVEN 350°

Cook hamburger, onion, and rice in frying pan. In separate pan, in butter, cook squash and zucchini until tender. Combine all ingredients in glass dish, sprinkle bread crumbs on top (with cheese), and bake at 350° for ½ to 1 hour.

## ZUCCHINI-BEEF CASSEROLE

Mrs. Donald Bowling, Charleston, WV

*"This is an original recipe from my mother."*

**1 pound ground beef**
**1 zucchini, diced (medium or large)**
**1 medium onion, chopped**
**Buttered bread crumbs for topping**

OVEN 350°

Brown ground beef, drain off fat. Cook zucchini and onion until tender. Drain water. Salt to taste. Grease 1½- to 2-quart casserole dish. Layer meat and zucchini mixture, starting with ground beef. Pour white sauce over mixture. Top with buttered bread crumbs. Bake at 350° for 25 minutes or until bubbly and bread crumbs have browned.

**Medium white sauce:**

**4 tablespoons margarine**
**4 tablespoons flour**
**Dash of pepper**
**½ teaspoon salt**
**2 cups milk**

Melt margarine. Stir in flour and seasonings. Add cold milk and cook on medium heat until mixture thickens. Stir occasionally.

Note: sometimes I add shredded cheese and stir until cheese melts.

## LAZY LINDA'S CASSEROLE

Linda G. Harleman, Orting, WA

*"This recipe is great for church potluck dinners, at home, or it can be put in the freezer and heated at a later date!"*

**3 cups dry macaroni (cooked and drained)**
**1 can cream of mushroom soup**
**1 can cheddar cheese soup**
**½ cup milk**
**1½ pounds lean hamburger, browned**
**¼ cup dried onion, or fresh**
**Sprinkle of parsley**
**1 cup green peas (optional to suit taste)**
**½ cup IMO (an artificial sour cream), or bouillon or consommé may be substituted**
**1½ tablespoons Worcestershire sauce**

OVEN 350°

Combine all ingredients, mix well. Pour into greased baking dish. Bake for 30 minutes at 350° (or put in heated Crock-Pot and slow cook).

## PORK CHOP AND RICE CASSEROLE

Kathy S. Miller, Belle Glade, FL

**½ stick margarine**
**1 cup uncooked rice**
**Salt**
**4 to 5 pork chops**
**1 envelope dry onion soup mix**
**1 can cream of mushroom soup**
**1½ cans water**

OVEN 350°

Melt margarine in 9x13-inch baking dish; cool slightly. Pour rice over margarine; arrange salted pork chops over rice. Sprinkle this with dry onion soup mix. Mix mushroom soup with water and pour over casserole. Cover tightly. Bake at 350° for 1 hour.

Yields: 6 servings.

Chicken may be substituted, baking 1½ hours for medium fryer.

## BROCCOLI & RICE CASSEROLE

Laura Wilson, McRae, AR

**2 cups rice**
**4 cups water**
**1 onion, chopped, sautéed**
**1 pound frozen broccoli, chopped**
**2 cans water chestnuts, chopped**
**1 pound jalapeno processed cheese food**
**1 can cream of mushroom soup**
**1 can cream of celery soup**

OVEN 350°

Cook rice in water. Add broccoli to onion and let soften over low heat. Melt cheese. Mix all ingredients together. Put in a 9x13-inch pan. Bake uncovered at 350° for 45 minutes.

## BROCCOLI & RICE CASSEROLE

Martha Ball, Palmetto, GA

**3 stalks fresh or 1 box frozen broccoli, steamed**
**1 cup short- or long-cook brown or white rice**
**1 can cream of chicken soup (celery or mushroom is good too)**
**½ cup mayonnaise**
**3 cups grated cheddar, Colby, or other favorite cheese**

OVEN 350°

Mix steamed broccoli, cooked rice, soup, mayonnaise, and 1 cup cheese together. Salt and pepper to taste. Put remaining cheese on top of casserole. Bake at 375° for 20–30 minutes or until cheese on top is how you like it.

# MAIN DISHES

## PIZZA CASSEROLE

Marietta Eash, Utica, OH

*"Our family really enjoys this recipe. Sometimes they serve it at weddings."*

**1 to 2 pounds hamburger**
**½ cup green pepper, chopped**
**1 can cream of mushroom soup**
**1 small can pizza sauce**
**1 can mushrooms with liquid**
**¼ teaspoon garlic powder**
**½ teaspoon oregano**
**½ can Parmesan cheese**
**8-ounce package noodles**
**Pepperoni (optional)**
**Mozzarella cheese for topping**

OVEN 350°

Fry hamburger, add green pepper. Cook noodles separate, then add the rest of the ingredients, except the pepperoni and cheese. Put in a casserole dish and add the pepperoni and cheese on top. Bake at 350° for 30 minutes.

## PIZZA CASSEROLE

Wilma Brouwer, Zephyrhills, FL

**2 pounds hamburger**
**¼ cup green pepper**
**1 small onion, chopped**
**1 can mushrooms**
**12 ounces shredded mozzarella cheese**
**½ teaspoon oregano**
**2 cans cream of mushroom soup**
**2 cans tomato soup**
**½ can water**
**8 ounces pepperoni**
**1 teaspoon garlic salt**
**12 ounces egg noodles**

OVEN 350°

Brown hamburger with green pepper and onion; drain excess grease. Boil noodles. In large mixing bowl mix soup, water, mushrooms, garlic salt, oregano, noodles, and browned meat. Preheat oven to 350°. Layer half in 9x13-inch pan, top with ½ cheese, repeat and put pepperoni on top. Bake uncovered 1 hour or until done. Can cover toward end of baking if needed.

## CHICKEN DELIGHT CASSEROLE

Viola Lowe, Allenwood, PA

**2 chicken breasts, cooked and cut into small pieces**
**1 can chicken broth; or 2 cups broth with grease removed; or 2 cups water and 2 cubes bouillon**
**1 can cream of chicken soup**
**2 small cans mushroom pieces, drained**
**1½ cups diced potatoes (optional)**
**1 large bag bread cubes**

OVEN 350°

Cook potatoes, stirring constantly. Mix all together very well until soup and broth are not lumpy. Put in casserole. Add bread cubes, and cheese (optional). Cook in 350° oven for 30–40 minutes. Don't let top get too brown.

## BISCUIT-TOPPED ITALIAN CASSEROLE

Cindy Wilkinson, New Castle, IN

**1 pound ground beef**
**½ cup chopped onion**
**¾ cup water**
**¼ teaspoon pepper**
**8-ounce can tomato sauce**
**6-ounce can tomato paste**
**9-ounce package mixed vegetables, cooked thoroughly**
**2 cups shredded mozzarella cheese**
**1 can biscuits**
**½ teaspoon oregano**

OVEN 375°

Grease 8x12-inch baking dish. Brown ground beef and onion, drain. Stir in water, pepper, tomato sauce, and tomato paste; simmer for 15 minutes, stirring occasionally. Remove from heat, stir in veggies and 1½ cups cheese. Spoon mixture into baking dish. Separate dough into 10 biscuits. Separate each biscuit into 2 layers. Place biscuits near outer edge of hot meat mixture, overlapping slightly. Sprinkle remaining cheese in center and around edge. Sprinkle with oregano. Bake at 375° for 22–27 minutes or until biscuits are golden brown.

Serves 6–8.

## TATER TOT CASSEROLE

Diana Gentry, Paris, TX

**1 pound ground turkey or beef**
**6 slices of cheese**
**1 can of mushroom soup**
**1 can of celery soup**
**Bag of Tater Tots**

In a 10½x7-inch pan layer the ingredients as listed. Ground turkey or beef, cheese slices, the two cans of soup, and Tater Tots. Put enough Tater Tots on to cover top of casserole. You'll probably have some Tater Tots left. Bake at 350° for 1 hour.

## CHICKEN / BROCCOLI CASSEROLE

Mary Wiles, Somerset, KY

**10-ounce package frozen broccoli**
**1 onion, chopped**
**1 cup Hellman's Reduced Fat Mayonnaise**
**8-ounce can water chestnuts**
**1 cup reduced-fat cream of chicken soup**
**3 cups cooked chicken**
**Reduced-fat Ritz brand crackers**

OVEN 350°

Cook broccoli to directions. Put chicken in large bowl. Add undiluted soup and mayonnaise and stir; add drained water chestnuts, cheese soup, and broccoli. Place mixture in large casserole dish (3-quart). Sprinkle crumbled Ritz crackers on top. Bake at 350° for 30 minutes.

May substitute green beans or 8 ounces artichoke hearts in place of broccoli.

## GRACE'S CHICKEN CASSEROLE

Grace Witt, Lake City, FL

**2 cups cooked, boned chicken**
**1 can cream of chicken soup**
**1 cup milk**
**2 tablespoons onion, chopped**
**1 small package stuffing mix**
**1 stick margarine**
**2 cups chicken broth**
**Celery**

OVEN 350°

Place chicken in 2-quart baking dish. Combine soup and milk and pour over chicken. Top with layer of celery and onion and then cover with stuffing mix. Pour margarine and broth over all ingredients. Bake in 350° oven for 30 minutes.

## CHICKEN CASSEROLE

Joann Kaser, Largo, FL

**3 cups chicken, cooked and chopped**
**3 teaspoons chopped onion**
**2 cups chopped celery**
**1 can cream of chicken soup, do not add water**
**¾ cup Hellman's mayonnaise, do not use any other**
**¼ cup margarine**
**1 small flat can of water chestnuts**
**1 cup croutons or cornflakes**
**1 cup sliced almonds (optional)**

OVEN 350°

Mix all ingredients and put in casserole. Melt margarine and sprinkle over top. Over all this, sprinkle croutons or cornflakes and almonds. Bake at 350° for approximately 1 hour.

Serves 8.

Options: Ingredients—onions and garlic; mushrooms and pimientos. This recipe can be doubled, or more for a crowd.

## CHICKEN CASSEROLE

Louise Barr, Macon, MO

**3–4 pounds chicken, boiled and deboned (reserve 1½ cups liquid)**
**1 can evaporated milk**
**1 can cream of chicken soup**
**1 can cream of mushroom soup**
**8-ounce package Pepperidge Farm dressing mix**
**⅓ cup butter, melted**
**1½ cups chicken broth**

OVEN 350°

Mix well and pour into greased 9x13-inch pan. Mix dressing mix, butter, and chicken broth. Mix well and spread on top of chicken mixture. Bake 45 minutes at 350°. Cover with foil to keep dressing moist.

## PECAN CHICKEN CASSEROLE

Evelyn Lehman, Logan, OH

**2 cups chopped cooked chicken**
**½ cup chopped pecans**
**2 teaspoons dried, minced onions**
**2 cups sliced celery**
**1 cup mayonnaise**
**2 teaspoons lemon juice**
**1 cup potato chips, broken**
**½ cup shredded cheddar cheese**

OVEN 350°

Mix first six ingredients together. Place in a greased 1½-quart casserole. Mix chips and cheese and sprinkle on top. Bake uncovered at 350° for 30 minutes.

## NINA'S CHICKEN CASSEROLE

Nina Wright, Arlington, TX

**1 whole chicken**
**1 can mushroom soup**
**4 ounces sour cream**
**1 stick butter**
**8 ounces Ritz crackers**

OVEN 350°

Boil chicken for 1 hour. Cool and debone. Mix chicken, mushroom soup, and sour cream together. Set aside. Melt butter slightly and mix with crackers. Put half of cracker mixture in pan then put chicken mixture next and the rest of cracker mixture on top. Cook on 350° for 30 minutes until brown.

## HAM & MACARONI CASSEROLE

Shirley Halpain, Kansas City, KS

*"This is a recipe my mother makes and serves as a main dish. It was given to her by a friend several years ago. It's one of our favorite meals, and only needs a salad along with it."*

**1 cup diced cooked ham**
**1 cup diced green onion, tops also**
**1 cup peeled, diced fresh tomatoes**
**1 cup elbow macaroni, cook until ½ done**
**Salt and pepper to taste**
**2 cups American cheese**
**1¾ cups milk**

OVEN 375°

Combine all except American cheese and milk; mix well. In a saucepan put diced American cheese and milk, cook until the cheese is dissolved; add to first mixture. Place in greased baking dish. Bake 1 hour at 375°.

## HAM AND POTATO CASSEROLE

Jo Anne Swift, Osgood, IN

**3 bags (1-pound size) frozen hash browns**
**3 8-ounce bags shredded cheddar cheese**
**2 pounds diced ham**
**2 11-ounce cans cheese soup**
**3 large onions, diced**
**1 quart skim milk**

OVEN 400°

Mix all in a large aluminum roaster pan. Bake at 400° for 1 hour. Stir occasionally (once or twice). Season to taste.

## TURKEY-CHEESE MILITARY CASSEROLE

Mrs. Donald Bowling, Charleston, WV

**1 cup elbow macaroni**
**¼ cup butter or margarine**
**¼ cup finely chopped onion**
**¼ cup flour**
**1 teaspoon salt**
**Dash thyme**
**¼ teaspoon pepper**
**2 cups milk**
**1¼ cups chopped cooked turkey**
**4 slices cheddar cheese**
**½ cup bread crumbs**
**2 tablespoons butter, melted**
**1 teaspoon minced parsley**

OVEN 350°

Cook macaroni as directed. Drain. Melt butter, add onion, and cook over low heat 3–5 minutes. Stir in flour, salt, thyme, and pepper. Gradually add milk and cook, stirring constantly until thickened. Arrange half of macaroni in bottom of lightly greased 2-quart casserole. Put half of turkey over macaroni. Arrange cheese slices over turkey. Repeat. Pour sauce over all. Mix crumbs, butter, and parsley; sprinkle over top. Bake at 350° for 25 minutes.

## CHICKEN, RICE, & CHEESE CASSEROLE

Mary Ann Hall, College Park, GA

**8 chicken breasts, cooked and cut up**
**8 cups cooked rice**
**2 cans cream of mushroom soup**
**½ soup can milk**
**2 cups sliced processed cheese spread**

Combine and bake at 350° for 20–30 minutes.

Can use cooked ham chopped up. It makes a great casserole also.

## HETTIE'S CHICKEN & RICE CASSEROLE

Hettie Powers, Fort Mill, SC

**6–8 large chicken breasts, skinned**
**2 cans cream of chicken soup, or substitute one can other cream soup**
**1 cup raw rice, uncooked**
**1 soup can of water**

OVEN 350°

Lightly spray 9x13-inch pan with PAM cooking spray, or grease. Combine soup and water in bowl. Pour in pan and spread evenly. Sprinkle rice over soups combination. Place chicken on top. Cover tightly with foil. Bake at 350° for 1½ hours. This can be halved.

## CHICKEN-RICE CASSEROLE

Karen Martin, Denver, PA

**½ cup butter**
**½ cup chopped onion**
**1 cup chopped celery**
**2½ cups chicken, cooked and cubed**
**¼ teaspoon pepper**
**1 can cream of chicken soup**
**1 cup milk**
**2½ cups chicken broth**
**1 cup rice**

OVEN 350°

Sauté onion and celery in butter, but do not brown. Mix everything together and bake 2 hours at 350°. Stir after 1 hour.

## SPINACH QUICHE

Katy Williams, Crawfordsville, IA

**1 package frozen chopped spinach, cook and drain well**
**2 cups skim milk**
**4 eggs, beaten**
**¼ cup finely chopped onions**
**4 slices bacon, fried and broken into pieces**
**½ teaspoon salt**
**¼ teaspoon paprika**
**½ teaspoon dry mustard**
**1 cup shredded cheddar cheese**
**9-inch pie shell**
**¼ cup more cheese, for topping**

OVEN 400°

Add all ingredients and put in unbaked shell. Sprinkle ¼ cup cheese on top. Bake at 400° for 40 minutes or until set.

Serves 6.

## KATHY'S KASSEROLE

Kathy Hunka, Uhrichsville, OH

**Editor's Note:** Kathy has worked as a Heartsong Presents customer service representative, and she also works with customers through the American Adventure book club.

**1 box chicken stuffing mix**
**1 can of cream of chicken soup**
**1 small can of diced chicken (do not drain)**
**1 cup shredded cheddar cheese**

OVEN 350°

Make the stuffing according to the box directions. Empty soup and chicken in the bottom of a medium-size casserole dish and stir to mix. Sprinkle cheese over the soup and chicken. Spoon cooked stuffing on top. Bake at 350° for 30 minutes.

## CHICKEN STUFFING CASSEROLE

Nancy Collier, Russellville, AR

**1 chicken, boiled**
**8 ounces sour cream**
**1 can cream of mushroom soup**
**1 box Stove Top stuffing mix (chicken)**

OVEN 350°

Mix sour cream and soup together in baking dish. Cut chicken in chunks. Mix stuffing mix according to directions on package. Spread stuffing mix over chicken. Bake at 350° for 45 minutes or until stuffing is crisp.

## HAMBURGER QUICHE

Carolyn Anne Taylor, Gaffney, SC

**1 pound hamburger**
**½ block sharp cheese, grated**
**2 tablespoons cornstarch**
**2 eggs**
**½ cup mayonnaise**
**½ cup milk**
**Onion, chopped**
**2 pie shells**

OVEN 350°

Brown hamburger and onion. Drain. Combine above ingredients. Add hamburger. Pour into 2 unbaked pie shells. Bake at 350° for 30 minutes.

## ASPARAGUS HAM QUICHE

Marie Pipes, Grandview, TX

**1 package (10 ounces) frozen cut asparagus**
**½ pound cooked ham, chopped**
**1 cup shredded cheese**
**¼ cup chopped onion**
**3 eggs**
**1 cup milk**
**¾ cup quick-baking mix**
**¼ teaspoon pepper**

OVEN 375°

In a greased 9-inch pie pan layer asparagus, ham, cheese, and onion. Beat egg and milk. Add baking mix to black pepper. Pour in pie pan. Bake at 375°, 30 minutes or until done.

## VEGETABLE PIZZA

Debra Jackson, Matheson, CO

**2 cans crescent rolls**
**1 cup mayonnaise**
**2 8-ounce packages cream cheese**
**1 package Ranch dressing (dry mix)**
**Assorted vegetables, chopped: broccoli, tomatoes, cauliflower, green peppers, olives, or your favorites (even cooked meat).**
**Shredded cheese**

OVEN 375°

Spread rolls and press in 12x18-inch cookie sheet, joining seams for crust. Bake at 375° for 10–15 minutes or until golden brown. Mix mayonnaise, cream cheese, and dressing. Spread over cooled crust. Top with raw, chopped vegetables. Top with shredded cheese. After assembling, pizza can be covered with wax paper and refrigerated overnight. Next day top with shredded cheese before serving. Cut with pizza cutter. Recipe can be halved.

## BUBBLE-UP PIZZA

Gina Myers, Anna, IL

**3 7-ounce cans refrigerator biscuits, quartered**
**8 ounces shredded mozzarella cheese**
**4-ounce can mushrooms, drained**
**15-ounce can pizza sauce**
**Cooked sausage, ham, veggies, or anything else you like on your pizza**

OVEN 350°

In a medium bowl mix the quartered biscuits, mozzarella cheese, mushrooms, pizza sauce, and the other items you've chosen. Pour into a greased 9x13-inch baking dish. Sprinkle remaining cheese on top. Bake at 350° for 30–40 minutes or until biscuits are golden.

## VEGETABLE STIR-FRY

Annalu Pagano, Spring Hill, FL

**¼ cup vegetable oil**
**2 stalks celery, sliced**
**3 green onions or 1 medium onion**
**1 small bunch Chinese cabbage, or Chinese celery**
**1 cup sliced fresh mushrooms**
**16 ounces frozen pea pods, thawed**
**2 cloves garlic, crushed**
**1 can stir-fry vegetables (Hokan); contains small corn, water chestnuts, bean sprouts, bamboo shoots**
**1 cup cooked cubed chicken (can be canned) optional**
**2 cups chicken broth**
**1 teaspoon brown gravy sauce**
**1 tablespoon soy sauce**
**¼ cup dry white wine, if desired**

Cook liquid and all ingredients, except vegetables, until thick and clear; add white wine if desired. Stir in vegetables. Serve over cooked rice.

## POOR MAN'S GOULASH

Phyllis Denison, Greensburg, IN

*"Kids love this. Quick, easy, and tasty."*

**1 pound ground beef**
**1 tall can spaghetti**
**1 tall can pork & beans**
**1½ cups ketchup**
**¾ cup regular barbeque sauce**
**Shredded cheddar cheese**

OVEN 350°

Brown beef and pour off fat. Add rest of ingredients and simmer. You can also pour into a large casserole, top with shredded cheddar cheese and crumbs. Bake 1 hour at 350°.

Serve with tossed salad and garlic bread sticks.

## TEXAS HASH

JoAnn Phillips, Morton, MI

*"My family thinks this is a must for all family get-togethers and also many church potluck dinners."*

**1 pound ground chuck**
**1 onion, chopped**
**½ cup chopped bell pepper**
**Hot pepper, chopped (to taste)**
**8-ounce can tomato sauce**
**Salt and pepper to taste**
**¼ cup uncooked rice**
**1 tablespoon sugar**
**16-ounce can diced tomatoes**

Brown meat with onion, peppers, salt, and pepper. Drain off grease. Then add rice, sauce, tomatoes, and sugar. Add enough water to cook rice. Simmer until rice is done.

## RED FLANNEL HASH

B. Geesaman, Knoxville, TN

*"This is one of my yummiest skillet meals!"*

**3 tablespoons cooking oil**
**15-ounce can sliced beets, drained and chopped**
**2 cups chopped cooked corned beef**
**2½ cups diced cooked potatoes**
**1 medium onion, chopped**
**¼ cup half-and-half cream**
**2 tablespoons butter, melted (or margarine)**
**2 teaspoons dried parsley flakes**
**1 teaspoon Worcestershire sauce**
**¼ teaspoon salt**
**⅛ teaspoon pepper**

Heat oil in a 12-inch skillet. Add remaining ingredients. Cook and stir over low heat for 20 minutes or until lightly browned, and heated through.

Yield: 4 servings.

## BARBECUED HAMBURGER MUFFINS

Janet Sartain, Brownwood, TX

**1 pound hamburger**
**½ cup barbecue sauce**
**½ cup onion**
**1 can biscuits (10)**
**Cheese**
**Garlic powder**

OVEN 375°

Brown hamburger meat and onions. Add barbecue sauce and garlic powder. Put rolled out biscuits in muffin pan. Put meat mixture on top of biscuits. Cook 15–20 minutes in 375° oven. Put grated cheese on top of each muffin and bake 5 minutes more.

Makes 10 muffins.

## BUNSTEAKS

Norene Morris, Ashtabula, OH

*"Had to get our family favorite in so everyone else can enjoy it."*

**Editor's Note:** Norene is a grandmother who has penned four successful romances for Heartsong Presents.

**¼ pound melting type cheese (Velveeta brand, for example), 1 cup cubed**
**3 hard-cooked eggs, chopped**
**7-ounce can tuna fish or 2 cups diced chicken**
**2 tablespoons chopped onion**
**2 tablespoons sweet pickle relish**
**½ cup mayonnaise or salad dressing**
**8 wiener buns**
**½ cup margarine, melted (optional)**

OVEN 350°

Combine all except buns. Mix lightly. Fill sliced buns. Place, filling side up, in a rectangular baking pan. Cover with aluminum foil, tightly. Bake at 350° for 20 minutes until filling is heated and cheese melts. Serve hot.

Fills 8 buns.

## BUNSTEAKS

Marjorie Garner, Carthage, NC

**¼ pound cheese, diced**
**3 hard-cooked eggs, chopped**
**1 small can tuna**
**2 tablespoons chopped onion**
**2 tablespoons sweet pickle, chopped**
**½ cup margarine, melted**
**12 hot dog buns**

OVEN 350°

Mix together and put into buns. Wrap each in foil. Bake at 350°, 20 minutes.

Makes 12.

## ITALIAN SUBS

Reba Dennis, Freeport, FL

**3 pounds Italian link sausage**
**1 onion, diced**
**1 teaspoon oregano**
**1 bell pepper, diced**
**2 cans tomato sauce**
**6 sub sandwich buns**

Combine onion, bell pepper, oregano, and tomato sauce in slow cooker. Add Italian sausage links. Cook on medium heat about 4 hours. On each sub put one link sausage, add sauce to season.

This is a good meal served with tossed salad.

## CRABMEAT CASSEROLE

Joanna Burinski, Camillus, NY

**1 can cream of celery soup**
**⅓ cup milk**
**4-ounce can mushrooms, drained**
**1 can crabmeat, drained**
**Parsley to taste**

OVEN 350°

Mix in casserole. Sprinkle with buttered bread crumbs. Bake in preheated 350° oven for 30 minutes.

## "SEAFOOD" LUNCH

D. Meyer, Crockett, TX

*"Great for preschoolers!"*

**1 package hot dogs (octopus)**
**1 package goldfish crackers (fish)**
**1 package apple-biscuits (rocks)**
**Applesauce (sand)**

Cut hot dogs in half. Cut each half lengthwise (do not cut completely) to make 8 legs for an octopus. Boil water, remove from heat, add hot dogs and cover. Let sit for 10 minutes.

## MOCK SHRIMP CASSEROLE

Winona Peters, Fairfield, ME

**1 pound sea legs**
**1 can cream of shrimp soup**
**2 cups water**
**1 cup Ritz brand cracker crumbs**

OVEN 350°

Combine and bake at 350° for 30–45 minutes. Be sure it is thoroughly warmed.

## HEAVENLY BROILED FISH

Barbara Williams, Lawrenceville, GA

**2 pounds fish fillets, fresh or frozen (I use Orange Roughy)**
**½ cup grated Parmesan cheese**
**1 tablespoon margarine, softened**
**3 tablespoons reduced-calorie mayonnaise**
**3 tablespoons chopped green onions, with tops**
**Dash Tabasco sauce**

Thaw fish if frozen. Place fillets in a single layer on a well-oiled baking pan. Combine remaining ingredients and spread evenly over fish. Broil 6 inches from source of heat for approximately 10 minutes, or until top is lightly browned and fish flakes easily when tested with fork.

Makes 6 to 8 servings.

## BUTTERMILK BAKED COD

Gloria Brandt, Viroqua, WI

*"I won a recipe contest with this in the Wisconsin State Journal for the fish/poultry category."*

**Editor's Note:** Gloria is the author of *Behind the Scene* and *The Mountain's Son* for Heartsong Presents. She is the mother of four girls and the wife of a farmer.

**1½ pounds cod fillets**
**1 teaspoon salt**
**2 cups herbal stuffing mix**
**½ cup melted butter**
**1 teaspoon paprika**
**1 teaspoon garlic powder**
**1 teaspoon lemon juice**
**1 cup buttermilk**

OVEN 450°

Rinse and dry cod fillets, cut into serving pieces. Melt butter; add paprika, garlic powder, and lemon juice. Dip fish in buttermilk; roll in stuffing. Place in foil-lined 9x13 baking pan. Drizzle butter mixture over fish. Bake at 450° degrees for 10–15 minutes.

## TUNA SURPRISE!

Susan Newcomb, Fishkill, NY

*"My children are older now but we still laugh over this name. Great do-ahead recipe."*

**3½ cups egg noodles (I like wide)**
**13 ounces tuna (any type)**
**½ cup mayonnaise**
**1 cup chopped celery (optional)**
**⅓ cup chopped onion**
**¼ cup diced green pepper**
**1 teaspoon salt**
**1 can cream of mushroom or celery soup (your preference)**
**½ cup milk**
**1 cup sharp or extra sharp cheese, grated**

OVEN 425°

Prepare egg noodles; set aside. Chop tuna into small pieces in mixing bowl. Add and mix well all ingredients but soup, milk, and cheese. Mix milk into soup, add grated cheese and mix until blended, heat until cheese is melted. Mix into tuna mixture, pour in casserole dish. Bake 20 minutes at 425°.

## RICE AND TUNA PIE

Cheryl A. Bardaville, St. Louis, MI

**2 cups cooked rice**
**1 tablespoon chopped onion**
**2 tablespoons butter**
**¼ teaspoon dried marjoram, crushed**
**1 slightly beaten egg**
**9¼-ounce can tuna, drained**
**3 beaten eggs**
**4 ounces shredded Swiss cheese**
**1 cup milk**
**¼ teaspoon salt**
**Dash pepper**
**¼ teaspoon dried marjoram, crushed**
**1 tablespoon onion, chopped**

OVEN 350°

For rice shell, combine first 5 ingredients; press onto bottom and sides of lightly buttered 10-inch pie plate or 10x6-inch baking dish. Sprinkle tuna evenly over rice shell. Combine remaining ingredients; pour over tuna. Bake for 50–55 minutes, or until knife inserted off center comes out clean.

Makes 6 servings.

## SALMON PATTIES

A. Adelle Hoppe, Burnsville, MN

**1 can salmon, drained; save liquid**
**1 egg**
**⅓ cup minced onion**
**½ cup flour**
**1½ teaspoons baking powder**

Combine baking powder with 2 tablespoons reserved salmon liquid. Mix all ingredients together and make into small balls. Deep fry until golden brown.

Variation:
Pam Cameron, New Baltimore, MI

**4 cans pink salmon**
**1½ packages plain crackers, to taste**
**4 eggs (1 per can of salmon)**

Crush crackers in a plastic baggie. Drain salmon and put in bowl. Add eggs and crushed crackers. Mix together with hands. Form patties. Set in stir-fry pan with boiling grease. Fry until browned.

## CRAWFISH ETOUFFEE

Shirley Williams, Newllamo, PA

**1 cup large, chopped bell pepper**
**1 cup large, chopped onion**
**Pinch of parsley**
**Salt and red pepper to taste**
**½ teaspoon chopped garlic**
**¼ cup Worcestershire sauce**
**2 bay leaves**
**1 stick butter**
**½ cup all-purpose flour**
**1 pound cooked crawfish tails**

Sauté onion and bell pepper until tender; set aside. Add flour to melted butter, stirring until roux looks like peanut butter, add Worcestershire sauce and enough hot water to make heavy gravy; add garlic, parsley, bay leaves, salt, and pepper (to taste). Should be on the hot side; add onion, bell pepper, and crawfish tails. Heat thoroughly. Serve over rice or cornbread to the side. Top etouffee with fresh green onions.

Serves 4 to 6.

## MY FAVORITE SPAGHETTI

Beth Joy Fowler, Monroe, NC

**6 pork chops, trimmed of fat and cubed**
**30 ounces of your favorite spaghetti sauce**
**½ cup brown sugar**
**8-ounce can crushed pineapple**
**4-ounce can mushroom pieces (optional)**

Fry pork chops until light brown on all sides. Add brown sugar, pineapple, and mushrooms (optional) to pork chops and simmer together until ready to serve over cooked spaghetti.

## MAMA PATTON'S SPAGHETTI

Sherry Tatman, Brooklyn Center, MN

**5 pounds hamburger meat**
**10 large cans tomatoes**
**3 large cans tomato paste**
**3 large cans tomato sauce**
**4 bell peppers, diced**
**4 big onions, diced**
**1 bunch celery, diced**
**4 tablespoons to ½ bottle Worcestershire sauce**
**1 tablespoon sugar**
**2 heaping tablespoons chili powder**
**Salt and pepper to taste**
**1 teaspoon celery salt**
**Tabasco sauce; or 2–3 hot peppers**
**1 tablespoon garlic powder**

Fry meat, drain off grease. Sauté pepper, onions, and celery. Put tomatoes in big saucepan. Rinse cans with water, adding to tomatoes. Put sautéed veggies and meat in tomatoes. Add Worcestershire sauce, sugar, seasonings, Tabasco sauce, or hot peppers. Cook six hours.

## SPAGHETTI PIZZA-STYLE

Margaret Wade, Bellville, OH

*"This is the most often asked for dish at pot-luck and carry-in dinners. My son James loves it!"*

**1 pound spaghetti**
**1 cup milk**
**2 eggs**
**32-ounce jar spaghetti sauce**
**½ pound ground beef**
**½ to 1 cup sliced pepperoni**
**3 cups shredded mozzarella cheese**
**½ teaspoon garlic powder**

OVEN 350°

Prepare spaghetti as directed, drain. Beat milk, eggs, garlic powder, and 1 cup cheese together and toss with noodles. Spread mixture in a greased jelly roll pan, 11x18-inches. Pour spaghetti sauce over noodles. Crumble ground beef over sauce and then arrange pepperoni slices evenly over beef. Sprinkle with remaining cheese. Bake at 350° for 30 minutes. Let stand for 5 minutes before cutting into squares.

## DAVE'S SPAGHETTI

Carol Ford, Lavonia, GA

**1½ pounds ground beef**
**Onion**
**Seasoning**
**1 can cream of mushroom soup**
**32-ounce jar Ragu Old Style sauce**
**8 ounces mozzarella cheese, grated**
**7 to 10 ounces spaghetti, cooked and drained**

OVEN 350°

Brown meat and cook until done. Add seasonings to taste. Add soup and sauce to hamburger and cook slightly. In either a baking dish or Crock-Pot, layer spaghetti, sauce, and cheese; repeat layers until all used up. Heat in oven until cheese is melted.

This is great to take to a friend's because after layering it is finished and can be kept covered in the refrigerator overnight or for a day or two; then heated in the oven at 350° until bubbly. It can sit overnight in the Crock-Pot and be plugged in the morning and be ready for lunch!

## BAKED SPAGHETTI

Carolyn Anne Taylor, Gaffney, SC

**8-ounce box spaghetti, cooked and drained**
**1 pound hamburger, browned and drained**
**1 cup grated cheese**
**1 jar Ragu sauce, traditional or original**

OVEN 350°

Mix together spaghetti, hamburger, and cheese. Add sauce. Spray dish with cooking spray. Put mixture in dish and cover with grated cheese. Bake for 35–40 minutes.

## SPAGHETTI SAUCE

Margaret Huffer, Bellevue, OH

*"This was given to me by my mother-in-law when I got married to her son."*

**1 family-size can of tomato sauce**
**2 small cans of tomato paste (fill each can 3 times with water)**
**1 small onion, chopped (½ in sauce and ½ in meatballs)**
**½ teaspoon garlic salt**
**½ teaspoon sugar**
**4 tablespoons grated cheese**
**½ teaspoon oregano**
**¼ teaspoon sweet basil**
**Salt and pepper to taste**

**Meatballs:**

**1½ pounds hamburger**
**3 slices bread, soak in water then squeeze out the water**
**½ chopped onion**
**Garlic salt**
**Salt and pepper to taste**

Put meatballs in sauce, cook over low heat for about 2 hours.

## NIGHT-BEFORE LASAGNA

Carol Cox, Ash Fork, AZ

**Editor's Note:** Carol debuted in the Heartsong Presents series with *Journey toward Home.*

**2 pounds lean ground beef (ground turkey works well, too)**
**¼ teaspoon garlic powder**
**1 teaspoon salt**
**1 teaspoon basil**
**1 tablespoon parsley flakes**
**½ cup Parmesan cheese**
**2 small cans tomato paste**
**2 cups hot water**
**1 package lasagna noodles**
**12-ounce carton low-fat cottage cheese**
**1½ cups grated low-fat mozzarella cheese**

OVEN 350°

Brown meat and drain fat off. Mix in garlic powder, salt, basil, parsley, Parmesan cheese, and tomato paste, and blend with hot water. Simmer uncovered for 30 minutes. In 9x13 baking pan, layer half the uncooked noodles, half the cottage cheese, half the meat sauce, and half the mozzarella cheese. Repeat layers. Chill in refrigerator overnight. Bake for 55 minutes at 350°.

(Not having to cook and drain the noodles makes this a super-simple recipe to make a day ahead of time.)

## SEMI-EASY LASAGNA

Marguerita Bates, Joplin, MO

**9 strips of ribbed lasagna (1 package)**
**32 ounces spaghetti sauce, best homemade with a pound of meat**
**15 ounces drained cottage cheese**
**12 ounces grated mozzarella cheese**
**¼ cup grated Parmesan cheese**

OVEN 375°

Grease 9x13-inch pan. Place small amount of spaghetti sauce. Place three strips of cooked lasagna noodles lengthwise, spread ⅓ spaghetti sauce, ½ dry cottage cheese, and ⅓ cheese; repeat. Add last three strips, rest of sauce, mozzarella cheese, and sprinkle Parmesan cheese over dish. Cover, bake at 375° for 30 minutes, remove cover, cook 30 minutes more. Let stand 10 minutes before eating.

## ONE DISH LASAGNA

Cheryl Boxeth, Rochester, MN

**32 ounces Prego spaghetti sauce**
**12 ounces lasagna noodles, not cooked**
**1 pound raw hamburger**
**¼ cup onion**
**8 ounces cottage cheese**
**8 ounces American cheese**
**8 ounces mozzarella cheese**
**Parmesan cheese**
**1½ cups hot water**

OVEN 375°

Cover bottom of pan with ⅓ jar sauce; layer noodles, ½ raw meat, onion, cottage cheese, ⅓ sauce, noodles, American cheese, rest of raw meat, rest of sauce, mozzarella cheese. Press down with spoon, add hot water, press down again. Sprinkle with Parmesan cheese and cover with foil. Bake at 375° for 1 hour. Remove foil, bake at 375° for 45 minutes, or less, until thick or set.

## SPAGHETTI-PIZZA LASAGNA

Garnet Nekuinda, Emily, MN

**12 ounces spaghetti (can use up to 16 ounces)**
**1 cup milk**
**2 eggs**
**1 pound hamburger**
**Onion**
**32 ounces Ragu (or sauce of your choice)**
**Green pepper (optional)**
**Pepperoni (optional)**
**2 to 3 cups mozzarella cheese**

OVEN 350°

Cook spaghetti according to package directions, drain, and pour into cake pan or glass cake pan. Mix spaghetti with milk, beat slightly, add eggs. Brown hamburger and onions, drain; add Ragu, and green pepper if desired. Pour sauce mixture over spaghetti in pan and mix all together. Top with pepperoni if you like. Top with mozzarella cheese. Bake at 350° for 35 minutes (cover with foil the first 30 minutes then uncover for 5 minutes).

## PIZZA-SPAGHETTI BAKE

Lawana Keister, Beaver Springs, PA

**1 pound spaghetti noodles, cooked and drained**
**½ cup milk**
**2 eggs**
**1 cup shredded mozzarella cheese**
**½ teaspoon salt**
**¾ teaspoon garlic powder**
**1½ teaspoons oregano**
**32-ounce jar spaghetti sauce**
**12 ounces pepperoni (1 package)**
**2 cups mozzarella cheese**

OVEN 400°

Put in greased 9x13-inch cake pan. Bake at 400° for 13 minutes. Take out and turn oven back to 350°, add spaghetti sauce, mozzarella cheese, and pepperoni. Bake ½ hour.

## LASAGNA

Betty Birky, Middleburg, IN

**1½ pounds ground beef**
**2 cloves garlic (minced)**
**6-ounce can tomato paste**
**½ teaspoon oregano**
**12-ounce carton cottage cheese**
**¼ teaspoon marjoram**
**1 bay leaf**
**8-ounce package lasagna noodles**
**Enough grated Muenster and mozzarella cheeses to equal 1½ cups**
**1 can tomatoes (29 ounces or larger)**
**1 teaspoon salt**
**¾ teaspoon pepper**
**¼ cup onion (optional)**

OVEN 350°

Brown beef and garlic. Add tomatoes, tomato paste, salt, pepper, oregano, marjoram, and bay leaf. Cover and simmer 20 minutes. Cook noodles as directed on package. In 8x12-inch glass baking dish, alternate layers of meat sauce then noodles and cheeses. Sprinkle with Parmesan cheese. Bake for 20–30 minutes.

## FELICIA'S LASAGNA

Lois E. Lynn, Connersville, IN

**1 to 2 pounds ground beef, browned and drained**
**12–16 lasagna noodles (kind you don't have to cook first)**
**28- to 32-ounce jar of your favorite spaghetti sauce**
**24 ounces mozzarella cheese**
**Parmesan cheese**

OVEN 350°

Brown ground beef, drain; mix with spaghetti sauce. Rinse noodles. Alternate noodles, sauce, cheese, to top of casserole dish. Sprinkle Parmesan cheese until it is covered. Cover with aluminum foil. Bake at 350° for 50 minutes. Remove foil and bake for another 10 minutes to brown.

## FETTUCCINI ALFREDO

Lana Gilder, Colorado Springs, CO

**6 ounces (½ package) fettuccini, uncooked, or whole package fresh**
**¼ cup butter or margarine**
**½ cup heavy whipping cream**
**¾ cup grated Parmesan cheese**
**2 tablespoons chopped parsley (optional)**

Cook fettuccini according to package directions; drain. Meanwhile in small saucepan, melt butter over medium heat; gradually stir in cheese then cream until well blended. Continue heating sauce, stirring constantly, just to boiling point. Remove from heat, stir in parsley. Pour over noodles.

Can also add chicken, shrimp, bacon bits, or whatever you like.

## SPINACH AND MUSHROOM CHICKEN ALFREDO

DiAnn Mills, Houston, TX

**Editor's Note:** DiAnn debuted in the Heartsong Presents series with *Rehoboth.* This mother of four young men wrote since the time she could hold a pencil.

**10-ounce box frozen creamed spinach**
**1 to 2 tablespoons cornstarch**
**1½ cups milk**
**4 boneless, skinless chicken breasts**
**1 to 2 tablespoons olive oil**
**1 small jar or can sliced mushrooms, drained**
**1–2 cloves garlic**
**2 tablespoons butter**
**½ cup Parmesan cheese**
**8 ounces spiral-shaped pasta, cooked**

Prepare spinach according to package directions. Set aside. In a small bowl, mix 1 tablespoon cornstarch with ½ cup of milk to make a paste. Set aside. Slice chicken into thin strips.

Alfredo sauce: In same frying pan, melt butter. Stir bowl of cornstarch paste. Add to melted butter substitute along with the Parmesan cheese and the remaining milk. Cook and stir until thick.

Return chicken-mushroom mixture to pan. Open bag of prepared spinach and add to pan. Heat and stir alfredo until bubbly. Serve over hot, cooked spiral pasta. Heat olive oil in large frying pan over medium-high heat. Add mushrooms, garlic, and chicken to pan. Stir-fry until chicken browns. Remove chicken-mushroom mixture to a separate plate and keep warm.

## WESTERN MACARONI

Virginia Smith, Malden, MA

**1 pound ground beef**
**¼ cup chopped onion**
**½ cup chopped green bell pepper**
**2 cups frozen kernel corn, thawed and drained**
**8-ounce can whole tomatoes, cut up (undrained)**
**1 teaspoon salt**
**7¼-ounce package macaroni and cheese dinner**
**Dash of pepper**

In small skillet, combine ground beef, green pepper, and onion. Cook until meat is browned; drain, add corn, tomatoes, salt, and pepper. Simmer 10 minutes. Prepare macaroni and cheese dinner as directed. Stir in meat mixture. Heat through. Refrigerate leftovers.

Serves 4 to 6.

## LO-CAL PASTA

Mary Sutley, Franklin, PA

**½ pound spaghetti**
**2 cups chicken, cut up**
**1 can chicken broth**
**Broccoli, cauliflower, celery, and carrots; cut up**
**Onion, green pepper, cut into strips**
**Mushrooms, water chestnuts**
**Cornstarch for thickening**
**1 can peas**
**3 tablespoons soy sauce**
**2 tablespoons lemon juice**
**Salt and pepper to taste**
**2 packages Ramen Seasoning**

Cook and drain spaghetti, keep hot. In a wok or a chicken fryer, cook cut-up chicken until pink is gone. Put in chicken broth. Put in broccoli, cauliflower, carrots, and celery; cook about 10 minutes and then add onion and green pepper, mushrooms, and water chestnuts. Mix small amount of cornstarch with water, add to mixture to thicken (not too thick). Then add peas, soy sauce, lemon juice, salt, and pepper. Do not overcook vegetables. Put spaghetti in low flat dish and put vegetables over and mix in Ramen Seasoning.

## MACARONI BAKE

Velma E. Rodgers, Springfield, IL

**1½ cups dry elbow macaroni (cook and drain)**
**1 can cream of mushroom soup, undiluted**
**1 small can mushrooms, include juice**
**¼ cup chopped green pepper**
**¼ cup chopped onion**
**2-ounce can pimiento**
**1 cup mayonnaise**
**1½ cups grated cheddar cheese**
**Bread crumbs**

OVEN 350°

Mix all together, cover with buttered bread crumbs. Bake at 350° for 30–35 minutes.

## NOODLES AND GLUE

Penny M. Kelley, Stewartsville, MO

*"Definitely a kids' favorite!"*

**1 pound hamburger**
**⅓ cup milk**
**1 box Kraft elbow macaroni**
**8 ounces mozzarella cheese**

Cook hamburger in skillet. Prepare macaroni as directed on box. Combine macaroni, hamburger, and milk. Mix well. Mix a little cheese in and then let the rest melt on the top.

## MEATLESS NOODLE MAIN DISH

Miriam Hammond, Lincoln, ND

*"My husband cannot eat meat, so I'm used to cooking meatless meals. I know there are a lot of people who can't eat meat and I'd like to share this with you."*

**8 ounces flat noodles**
**1 cup sour cream**
**2 eggs**
**$1/3$ cup buttermilk**
**1 teaspoon chives**
**8 ounces cottage cheese**

OVEN 350°

Boil noodles in salted water until tender. Drain. Mix sour cream, eggs, cottage cheese, buttermilk, and chives in a mixing bowl; blend thoroughly. Add noodles and mix again. Place in a greased baking dish (9x13-inch or larger), dot with butter or grated cheese. If more moisture is needed, add more buttermilk. Bake at 350° for 1 hour until crusty brown.

## CAVATINI

Claudia Elliott, Belle Rive, IL

**1 pound ground beef**
**$1/8$ teaspoon garlic powder**
**1 chopped onion**
**1 chopped green pepper**
**1 package pepperoni**
**1 small can mushrooms**
**32 ounces spaghetti sauce**
**½ pound curly noodles, cooked and drained**
**½ pound mozzarella cheese, grated**

OVEN 375°

Brown ground beef; add garlic powder, onion, and green pepper. Cook until tender and drain. Stir in pepperoni, mushrooms, and add spaghetti sauce. Grease 9x13-inch pan. Layer cooked noodles and cheese. Add ground beef mixture. Top with cheese. Bake at 375° for 35–40 minutes. Let stand 5–10 minutes before serving.

## MOSTACCIOLI

Karla Kolle, Red Wing, MN

**1 pound package Creamette brand mostaccioli**
**1 pound lean ground beef, turkey, or pork**
**2 26-ounce jars Classico brand pasta sauce (tomato & basil)**
**4 cups (1 pound) shredded mozzarella cheese**

OVEN 350°

Preheat oven to 350°. Prepare pasta as package directs. In large bowl, combine pasta, meat, and 2 cups cheese. Mix well. Turn into greased 9x13-inch baking dish; cover and bake 45 minutes or until hot and bubbly. Uncover, top with remaining 2 cups cheese. Bake 10 minutes or longer until cheese melts.

Makes 12–15 servings.

## CHICKEN WILD RICE CASSEROLE

Elizabeth Hunt, Ithaca, MI

**3 cups cooked chicken or turkey, cut up**
**2½ cups cooked wild or regular rice**
**1 cup cream of chicken or celery soup**
**1 cup mushroom soup**
**1 soup can of milk**
**6-ounce can sliced mushrooms, drained**
**½ cup chopped green pepper**
**4-ounce jar pimientos, drained and sliced**
**½ cup slivered almonds**
**½ cup minced onions**

OVEN 350°

Pour into 9x13-inch casserole dish and bake at 350° for 40–45 minutes. Garnish with pimiento strips.

## WILD RICE HOT DISH

Lorraine Anderson, Cambridge, MN

**½ cup raw wild rice (wash and pre-cook)**
**½ cup raw white rice (do not pre-cook)**
**2 cups celery, diced small**
**1½ pounds hamburger**
**1 large onion, diced**
**½ cup cashew nuts**
**2 cans cream of mushroom soup**
**2 cans cream of chicken soup**
**1 can mushroom pieces, drained**
**1½ cups milk**
**2 tablespoons soy sauce**
**2 tablespoons brown sugar**

OVEN 350°

Brown meat lightly. Add onion, do not brown. Combine all ingredients and put into a greased 3-quart casserole. Bake 2 hours, or more, until rice is done. Bake at 350°.

Serves 12.

## GREEN RICE

Louise Barr, Macon, MO

*"My family expects this dish on holidays. I have made this often."*

**1 onion, chopped fine**
**1 stick butter or margarine**
**2 boxes chopped broccoli**
**1 can cheddar cheese soup**
**1 can cream of mushroom soup**
**¼ can water**
**½ cup milk**
**1 cup quick-cooking rice**

OVEN 350°

Cook broccoli until tender, drain. In large skillet combine rest of ingredients, stirring until completely mixed. Pour into baking dish. Bake at 350° for 40–45 minutes until lightly browned.

## SPANISH CHICKEN AND RICE

Melinda Chemin, Gainesville, FL

**Olive oil, enough to cover bottom of skillet**
**4 green onions, diced**
**2 cloves garlic, minced**
**1 large Spanish yellow onion, chopped**
**1 cup Spanish green olives with pimentos, chopped**
**½ cup juice from green olives**
**1 teaspoon chili powder**
**1 teaspoon crushed red pepper**
**2 tablespoons Morton's seasoned salt**
**6 boneless skinless chicken thighs, cubed**
**16-ounce package Spanish yellow rice**
**Water**

Set electric skillet at 200º to 250º. Saute in olive oil both onions, garlic, olives, and juice. Saute until onions are tender. Add seasonings and chicken. Continue to saute until chicken is cooked through. Add rice with its seasoning and enough water to cover. Remember to stir in seasoning thoroughly. Cover and simmer until rice is desired texture, adding more water if needed.

## RICE 'N MUSHROOMS

Luanne Ogg, McCutchenville, OH

**1 cup rice (not instant)**
**1 can mushrooms, drained**
**1 can French onion soup**
**1 can beef broth**
**¼ cup margarine**
**2 tablespoons Worcestershire sauce**

OVEN 350°

Combine ingredients in 2-quart casserole dish. Bake 1 hour at 350°, uncovered.

## DAVE'S TEXAS SPANISH RICE

Vaneita Null, Wellington, TX

*"This is hot and spicy. My son's recipe!"*

**2 tablespoons cooking oil**
**1 cup converted rice**
**1 large bell pepper, chopped**
**2 jalapeno peppers, chopped**
**1 large onion, or 2 bunches green onions, chopped**
**¾ cup water**
**3 cans whole canned tomatoes, blended**
**1 teaspoon cumin**
**1 teaspoon black pepper**
**1 dash crushed red pepper**
**1 tablespoon salt**
**3 teaspoons chili powder**

Heat oil in a 9-inch non-stick skillet. Add raw rice and cook until lightly browned. Add pepper and onions; then sauté until translucent. Add tomatoes, water, and seasonings to rice mixture. Stir well and cook over low heat for about 20–25 minutes or until rice absorbs the moisture. Stir frequently.

## FRANCES'S STEW

Frances Callaway, Rincon, GA

*"My kids and grandkids love this one."*

**1 pound hamburger or ground chuck**
**2 cans tomato sauce**
**2 cans mixed vegetables or frozen ones**
**1 large onion, chopped**
**1 tablespoon curry, taco, or chili powder (any flavor you want)**
**Salt and pepper to taste**

Brown meat with onion and drain. Add sauce and veggies to meat and simmer for 1 hour or less. Cook in Dutch oven or Crock-Pot. Serve with cornbread or over rice.

Serves 6.

## OVEN STEW

Marjorie Gammon, Bradenton, FL

**1½ pounds stew meat**
**1 envelope onion soup**
**1 can cream of celery soup**
**1 can cream of mushroom soup**
**2 stalks celery, cut up**
**6 carrots, cut up**
**5 potatoes, cut up**
**⅔ can water**

OVEN 300°

Spread stew beef in large casserole dish. Sprinkle with onion soup mix. Add soups and sprinkle with celery. Add layer of veggies. Pour water over all. Cover with foil. Bake 4 hours in 300° oven. Don't peek!

## SALSA STEW

Bettie Sutton, Macy, IN

**1 to 2 pound steak**
**Salsa (amount used depends on your taste)**
**Kitchen Bouquet (optional)**
**1 or 2 cans mixed vegetables**

On trivet in pressure cooker place one steak. Cover with salsa (be sure there is water under the trivet), cook 15 minutes. Remove from heat, when pressure is down remove steak. Scrap any salsa from the trivet, if any, into the liquid in cooker. Mix 1 heaping tablespoon with water and Kitchen Bouquet, if desired; stir into boiling liquid until mixed well. Add vegetables, depending on amount needed to feed your "group." Add the cut-up steak. Cook slowly for about 15 minutes.

## BEEF STEW

Rosey Dow, Grenada, West Indies

*"Beef stew was a staple in the areas where cattle was king. In* Megan's Choice, *it is served at least twice a week. It filled the house with a comforting aroma. A Crock-Pot achieves the same delicious results."*

**Editor's Note:** Rosey is the author of *Megan's Choice* and *Em's Only Chance* in the Heartsong Presents series. She, her husband, and seven children work as missionaries in Grenada.

**1 pound beef**
**4 potatoes, peeled and quartered**
**1 carrot, scrubbed and cut into 1-inch lengths**
**1 medium onion, halved**
**2-inch wedge of cabbage**
**1 rib celery, whole with leaves left on**
**½ teaspoon seasoned salt**
**⅛ teaspoon pepper**
**1 beef bouillon cube**
**1 tablespoon flour**
**¼ cup water**

The night before, place beef (can be frozen), onion, celery, cabbage, seasoned salt, pepper, and bouillon cube in Crock-Pot with 1 quart of water. Cook on low overnight. The next morning, remove onion, celery, and cabbage and discard them. Break beef into bite-size pieces, removing any fat or bone. Add potatoes and carrots to Crock-Pot. Cook until vegetables are tender but not mushy. Twenty minutes before serving, mix flour with water and stir into pot. Cover. Serve with hot bread.

Serves 4.

Hint: If the Crock-Pot must simmer all day, cut potatoes in larger pieces to keep them from becoming overdone.

## OVEN STEW

Rose Yoder, Shipshewana, IN

*"Great for Sunday noon."*

**2 pounds stew meat (do not brown)**
**8 potatoes, cubed**
**4 carrots, coined**
**2 cans cream of mushroom soup, undiluted**
**1 can tomato soup, undiluted**
**2 cans onion soup, undiluted**

OVEN 300°

Combine but do not stir. Bake at 300° for 3 hours.

## OVEN BEEF STEW

Linda Larson, Hawthorne, NV

**1 pound beef stew meat, cut up**
**1 package dried onion soup mix**
**1 can beef broth**
**1 can cream of mushroom soup**
**1 soup can of water**

Add desired amounts of:

**Carrots, peeled and chopped**
**Potatoes, peeled and cut into chunks**
**Onions, peeled and cut into chunks.**

OVEN 300°

Cook 3 hours in 300° oven, or in 4- or 6-quart Nesco Roaster. I serve this with bread made in a bread machine.

## BOLOGNA STEW

Lauri Baranski, Indster, MI

**8 to 10 potatoes, cubed (8 pieces to medium one)**
**1 ring bologna, cut in pieces**
**2 16-ounce cans pork 'n beans**
**½ cup ketchup (to taste)**
**1 can tomato soup**
**1 can tomato juice**
**2 medium onions, cubed (optional)**
**Salt and pepper to taste**
**¼ teaspoon meat tenderizer**
**Any other seasoning you'd like to add**

Fry bologna and onions in fry pan to brown; then season with meat tenderizer. Boil potatoes until done. Add both to a big pot. Add the rest of ingredients. Simmer to hot. The longer you cook it the better it is. Mix often so beans do not stick to pot.

## SKILLET CHICKEN STEW

Carol Buker, Salem, OR

**⅓ cup flour**
**½ teaspoon salt**
**Dash of pepper**
**1½ pounds boneless chicken breasts, cut into 1-inch pieces**
**3 tablespoons butter or margarine**
**1 medium onion, sliced**
**2 medium potatoes, peeled and cut into ¾-inch cubes**
**3 celery ribs, sliced**
**3 medium carrots, sliced ¼-inch thick**
**1 cup chicken broth**
**½ teaspoon dried thyme**
**1 tablespoon ketchup**
**1 tablespoon cornstarch**

Combine flour, salt, and pepper in a shallow bowl; coat chicken. In large skillet melt butter, brown chicken. Add onion and celery; cook for 3 minutes. Stir into skillet: potatoes, broth, thyme, ketchup, and cornstarch. Bring to a boil, reduce heat; cover and simmer for 15–20 minutes or until the vegetables are tender.

## CABBAGE PATCH STEW

Linda Lackey, Vicksburg, MS

**½ large cabbage head**
**2 pounds hamburger**
**3 tablespoons oil**
**1 large onion**
**1 large bell pepper**
**2 stems celery**
**5 or more cups water**
**2 cans chopped tomatoes**
**1 can tomato sauce**
**1 can chili beans**
**2 teaspoons garlic salt**
**2 teaspoons mustard seed**
**1 teaspoon crushed red pepper**
**½ teaspoon celery seed**
**4 teaspoons parsley flakes**
**1 tablespoon sugar**
**4 teaspoons salt**
**1 teaspoon oregano**
**½ teaspoon marjoram**
**1 teaspoon onion salt**
**1 teaspoon thyme**

In large skillet cook hamburger in cooking oil until gray. Add onion, pepper, cabbage, and celery, after chopping them. Add water also. Cover and simmer 15 minutes. Stir often. Transfer from skillet to Dutch oven or large pot. Add tomato sauce, chopped tomatoes, and all other seasonings. Cover and simmer over medium heat for 45 minutes, stirring often. May serve "as is" or over rice or creamed potatoes, or with Mexican or regular cornbread.

## CROCK-POT CHILI CON CARNE

Phyllis Mitton, Yarmouth, ME

**½ pound hamburger**
**1 medium onion**
**½ green pepper**
**1 clove garlic**
**1 can Italian stewed tomatoes**
**1 can drained kidney beans**
**1 teaspoon soy sauce**
**1 teaspoon parsley**
**1 teaspoon McCormick garlic and herb seasoning**
**2 to 3 partially cooked potatoes**
**1 teaspoon brown sugar (optional)**

Sauté hamburger, add onion, green pepper, and garlic. Put in Crock-Pot, add tomatoes, beans, soy sauce, parsley, seasonings, and potatoes. Cook 4–8 hours on low.

Note: Potatoes help to reduce acid from mixture. Partially cook potatoes if cooking time is less than 5–6 hours.

## HOT DOG CHILI

Mrs. Frances Bowling, Charleston, WV

**1 pound hamburger**
**1 medium onion, diced fine**
**1 small can tomato paste**
**3 cans water**
**½ cup catsup**
**1 teaspoon vinegar**
**1½ teaspoons chili powder**
**1 teaspoon salt**

Combine all ingredients, adding water a can at a time, mixing well each can. Simmer 1½ hours. Freeze in small containers. Serve hot over hot dogs.

## SWEET & SOUR VENISON STEW

Joyce Goss, Warsaw, IN

**¼ cup flour**
**1 teaspoon salt**
**Dash of pepper**
**2 pounds venison round steak, cut into 1-inch cubes**
**¼ cup cooking oil**
**1 cup water**
**½ cup catsup**
**¼ cup brown sugar**
**¼ cup cider vinegar**
**1 tablespoon Worcestershire sauce**
**1 teaspoon salt**
**1 chopped onion**
**3 carrots, cut into ¾-inch pieces**

Combine flour, the first teaspoon salt, and the pepper; coat meat with flour mixture. In large skillet or Dutch oven, brown meat on all sides in hot oil. Combine water, catsup, brown sugar, vinegar, Worcestershire sauce, and the second teaspoon salt. Stir into browned meat; add onion. Cover and cook over low heat for 45 minutes to 1 hour, stirring once or twice. Add carrots and cook until meat and carrots are done (about 1 hour). Serve hot over cooked rice. You may substitute beef in this recipe.

Serves 4–6.

## CHILI

Mary Ratliff, Mt. Sterling, KY

**1 can Bush chili beans**
**1 can Franco-American Spaghetti with Cheese**
**1 package Lipton Onion Soup (dried)**
**1 small jar Green Giant Mushrooms**
**½ can Red Gold Tomato Juice (about 18–20 ounces)**
**1 heaping tablespoon chili powder**
**1½ pounds hamburger, browned and drained**

Add all together in 4-quart kettle. Simmer 30 minutes after start of boiling. Add 2 slices of Kraft sandwich cheese before serving.

## HOMEMADE CHILI SAUCE

Dorothy M. Moore, South Gate, CA

*"This is very good with any meat dish."*

**6 to 8 cups ripe tomatoes, peeled and cut into quarters**
**2½ cups sugar (to taste)**
**¼ cup vinegar**
**1 solid head of cabbage, cut as if for coleslaw**
**1 large white onion, cut into small pieces**
**1 stalk celery, cut into small pieces**
**½ green bell pepper, cut into small pieces**

Place tomatoes in large kettle. Take potato masher and mash the tomatoes to bring up the juice. Add sugar to taste and then vinegar. Add cabbage and onion. Add salt and small amount of pepper to season. Add a small cloth bag with pickling spices and let it cook with all ingredients until it is quite thick. Remove the bag with pickling spices and put in jars when very hot, and seal.

## WHITE CHILI

Karen Johnson, Calpine, CA

**2 tablespoons vegetable oil**
**4 boneless chicken breasts, cooked, cut into small cubes**
**1 medium onion, finely chopped**
**4-ounce can chopped green chilies**
**2 teaspoons garlic powder**
**2 teaspoons salt**
**2 teaspoons ground cumin**
**2 teaspoons ground oregano**
**2 teaspoons ground coriander**
**½ teaspoon cayenne pepper**
**6 15- or 16-ounce cans Great Northern beans (do not drain)**
**2 10½-ounce cans chicken broth**

In a large stock pot heat oil, cook chicken and onions. Add next 7 ingredients; stir until well blended. Stir in remaining ingredients. Bring to a boil, reduce heat to low. Simmer 15–20 minutes.

## WHITE CHICKEN CHILI

Peggy McDaniel, Adel, GA

**1 2- or 3-pound chicken**
**½ pound Great Northern beans**
**1 large onion, chopped**
**1 cup celery, chopped**
**1 cup carrots, chopped**
**1 can mushrooms**
**1 can chili style tomatoes**
**1 can cream of chicken soup**
**Dash of cayenne pepper**
**Dash of celery salt**
**Dash of Season-All salt**
**Dash of garlic**
**Sour cream and green onions, for topping**

Boil, debone, and cut chicken into small pieces. Cook beans in broth until tender. Add onions, celery, and carrots. Simmer for a while. Add seasoning, tomatoes, and soup. Add chicken and cook until done. To serve, put chili in bowls, top with a spoonful of sour cream and green onions.

# DESSERTS

## EMMA'S AMBROSIA

Jacquelyn Cook, DeSoto, GA

*"Ambrosia, a traditional dessert of the Old South, is served in all of my books."*

**Editor's Note:** Jacquelyn's books include *Rivers Rushing to the Sea* and *Beyond the Searching River* for Heartsong Presents.

**12 large navel oranges**
**Freshly grated or ½ can coconut**
**¾ cup sugar**

Working over a large bowl to save juice, peel oranges and cut across sections to form bite-size pieces. Remove any tough membranes. Stir in sugar (to taste) and coconut. Cover and refrigerate for 4 hours until very juicy. (Dessert will keep in refrigeration for a week. It may be made 3 to 4 weeks in advance and frozen.) Serve in compote dishes plain or garnished with whipped cream and cherry. Good alone or with cake and cookies. One serving per orange used.

## STRAWBERRY DELIGHT

Penny Combs, Castlewood, VA

**1 angel food cake**
**1 cup cold milk**
**2 small or 1 large vanilla instant pudding**
**1 quart vanilla ice cream, softened**
**1 small box strawberry gelatin**
**1 cup boiling water**
**2 10-ounce packages frozen strawberries**

Slice angel food cake and arrange in 9x13-inch pan. Mix together milk and pudding until mixture starts to thicken. Add ice cream. Mix and pour over cake slices. Place in refrigerator. Mix together gelatin and boiling water until gelatin is dissolved. Add frozen strawberries and stir until berries are separated. Pour over ice cream mixture and chill.

## CHERRIES IN THE SNOW

Janice Lowrey, Anacoco, LA

*"Makes a large amount, enough for a party. Good for Christmas. To halve recipe, use only half of each ingredient."*

**1 angel food cake**
**2 cans cherry pie filling**
**2 cups confectioners' sugar**
**2 8-ounce packages cream cheese, softened**
**4 packages Dream Whip (powdered whipped topping)**

Combine sugar and softened cream cheese until smooth. Prepare Dream Whip according to package directions; add to creamed mixture. Butter 11x13-inch pan, or large platter. Put half of the mixture in pan with crumbled cake. Add remaining mixture. Cover top with cherry pie filling. Refrigerate before serving.

Variations: Blueberry or apple pie filling may be substituted. Sprinkle apple with cinnamon.

## ANY FRUIT COBBLER

Ann Geier, Girard, KS

**½ cup butter, softened**
**1 cup sugar**
**2 cups flour**
**4 teaspoons baking powder**
**4 teaspoons salt**
**1 cup milk**
**½–¾ cup sugar**
**32 ounces of canned fruit**

OVEN 375°

Cream together butter and 1 cup sugar. Sift together flour, baking powder, and salt. Add to other mixture, alternately with milk. Beat until smooth. Pour into greased 8x10-inch pan. Spoon drained fruit over batter: Sprinkle sugar over top. Pour juice over this. Bake 45–50 minutes or until top springs back. Batter will rise to top.

## PEACH COBBLER

Mrs. Wanda Reed, Loman, MN

**3 cups sliced fresh peaches**
**¾ cup sugar**
**3 tablespoons flour**
**2 tablespoons lemon juice**
**2 tablespoons butter**

**Topping:**

**2 cups flour**
**½ teaspoon salt**
**4 teaspoons baking powder**
**1 tablespoon sugar**
**⅓ cup butter**
**1 egg, well beaten**
**¾ cup milk**

OVEN 425°

Put peaches in a greased baking dish. Mix sugar and flour. Sprinkle over the peaches. Sprinkle the lemon juice, dot with butter. Sift dry ingredients and mix in butter until mixture is like coarse crumbs. Add combined egg and milk, and mix until just moistened. Drop dough in mounds over peaches. Bake for 30 minutes.

## QUICK COBBLER

Laura Baker, Bernalillo, NM

**½ cup margarine**
**1 cup flour**
**1 cup sugar**
**1 cup milk**
**1 teaspoon baking powder**
**2 cans fruit**

OVEN 375°

Melt margarine in 9x13-inch pan. Mix other ingredients, except fruit, together. Pour mixture over margarine. Pour fruit on top and bake 30 minutes.

## PUMPKIN PIE DESSERT SQUARES

Sonja Barnwell, Morral, OH

**1 box yellow cake mix, divided**
**½ cup butter or margarine, melted**
**1 egg**

**Filling:**
**3 cups (1 pound 14-ounce can) pumpkin pie mix**
**2 eggs**
**⅔ cup milk**

**Topping:**
**1 cup reserved cake mix**
**¼ cup sugar**
**1 tablespoon cinnamon**
**¼ cup butter or margarine, room temperature**

OVEN 350°

Grease bottom only of 9x13-inch pan. Reserve 1 cup of the cake mix for topping. Combine cake mix, melted butter or margarine, and egg. Press in bottom of pan. Mix filling ingredients until smooth and pour over bottom layer. Mix topping ingredients and sprinkle over the top of filling. Bake for 40–45 minutes or until knife inserted in the middle comes out clean. If desired, serve with whipped topping.

Variation: Increase sugar and cinnamon in the topping, for more cinnamon flavor.

## EASY COBBLER DESSERT

Louise Bishop, Pineland, TX

**2 cans cherry, apple, or peach pie filling**
**1 box white or yellow cake mix**
**1¼ sticks margarine, melted**
**1 cup pecans or walnuts**

OVEN 350°

Place both cans of pie filling in a 9x13-inch pan. Spread dry cake mix over it. Pour margarine evenly over cake mix. Top with nuts. Bake for 35–45 minutes. Serve hot with ice cream or top with whipped cream.

## FRUIT COBBLER

Martha Boyd, Opp, AL

**1 stick butter**
**1½ cups self-rising flour**
**1¼ cups milk**
**1 cup sugar**
**1 can fruit pie filling**

OVEN 350°

Melt butter in 9x9-inch baking pan. Mix flour, milk, and sugar well (should be soupy) and pour into baking pan. Divide pie filling into 6–8 globs that the flour mixture comes around. Bake for about 1 hour and serve with vanilla ice cream.

## GRANDMA'S CANDIED APPLES

Rebecca Germany, Scio, OH

*"My brother won't sit down to a holiday meal without these on the table, so he has learned to make them for his own children."*

**Editor's Note:** Rebecca is the author of two novellas and is the managing editor for the Heartsong Presents series.

**Approximately 4 cups granulated sugar and 4 cups water**
**Approximately ¾ cup cinnamon candies**
**10–12 Golden Delicious apples, peeled, halved, and cored**

Combine equal parts sugar and water, enough to cover 2 inches in the bottom of a large pan. Cook over low heat, dissolving candies in the sugar water. Cook one layer of apples at a time. Turn halfway through. Cook until soft but solid enough to use a fork to lift out. Arrange on a plate or platter. This dish makes a very attractive addition to a holiday table. Best served on the same day they are cooked. After cooking the apples, boil the syrup until it is thick enough to cling to the tines of a fork. The syrup makes a wonderful, tasty, and colorful jelly that keeps well in the refrigerator.

## FLUFFY RUFFLES

Leslie Sheldon, Gaston, OR

**20 graham crackers or cookies, crushed**
**¼ cup butter**
**¼ cup sugar (optional)**
**3 3-ounce packages gelatin**
**8-ounce container Cool Whip**

OVEN 375°

Crust: In 9x13-inch pan combine graham crackers or cookies, butter, and sugar (optional). Mix well and pat into pan. Bake 8 minutes.

Filling: Dissolve gelatin according to quick-set instructions. When thickened add Cool Whip. Mix well, pour over crust. Chill until set.

## LIGHT DANISH PASTRY

Joyce Todd, Pasco, WA

**1 tablespoon cake yeast**
**½ cup milk**
**⅔ cup shortening, melted**
**2 eggs**
**3 tablespoons sugar**
**1 teaspoon salt**
**2¼ cups flour**

OVEN 375°

Soften cake yeast in milk. To softened yeast mixture add flour and refrigerate for 2 hours. Roll into 6x18-inch rectangle. Fold dough into thirds. Combine shortening, beaten eggs, sugar, and salt. After spreading with 1½ tablespoons of shortening, roll out after each fold. Make large coil. Let rise until doubled. Bake for 15–20 minutes.

## CHOCOLATE-PEANUT BUTTER PIZZA

Jerri Willman, Pasco, WA

**½ cup sugar**
**½ cup packed brown sugar**
**½ cup soft margarine**
**½ cup peanut butter**
**½ teaspoon vanilla**
**1 egg**
**1½ cups flour**
**2 cups miniature marshmallows**
**1 cup (6 ounces) semisweet chocolate chips**

OVEN 375°

In large bowl, combine sugar, brown sugar, margarine, peanut butter, vanilla, and egg. Blend well. Stir in flour. Press dough evenly over bottom of 12- or 14-inch pizza pan, forming a ridge along edge. Bake for 10 minutes. Sprinkle with marshmallows and chocolate chips. Bake 5–8 minutes more, or until marshmallows are lightly browned. Cool. Cut into wedges. Store tightly covered.

Makes 2 dozen wedges.

## BANANA SPLIT BROWNIE PIZZA

Kim Mace, Kotzebue, AK

**1 box brownie mix (or your own mix, for an 8x8 pan)**
**12-ounce package cream cheese**
**⅓ cup sugar**
**3 bananas**
**6-ounce can crushed pineapple, drained**
**1 pint fresh strawberries**
**Caramel ice cream topping**
**Chopped nuts**

Mix brownie mix according to directions and bake on round pizza pan. Cool. Blend cream cheese and sugar. Spread on cooled crust. Cut into bite-size squares. Layer sliced fruit and pineapple on cream cheese. Drizzle caramel topping over fruit and top with chopped nuts.

## LEMON DESSERT

Deborah LeBrun, Saint Cloud, MN

**1 package Jiffy yellow cake mix**
**8 ounces cream cheese**
**½ cup milk**
**1 small package instant vanilla pudding**
**1 can lemon pie filling**
**1½ cups milk**
**Cool Whip whipped topping**
**Walnuts (optional)**

OVEN 350°

Prepare cake mix according to package directions and pour into 9x13-inch pan. Bake for 10–15 minutes. Let cool. Beat cream cheese in milk until smooth; then add vanilla pudding and milk. Spread on cooked cake. Top with lemon pie filling. Follow with layer of Cool Whip, add chopped walnuts if desired.

Variation: For a chocolate layered dessert use cherry or blueberry pie filling and chopped chocolate chips on top of Cool Whip. Chocolate cake may be used instead of yellow cake.

## SNICKER FRUIT SALAD

Mrs. Leland Park, Albert Lea, MN

**1 can fruit cocktail**
**3 bananas cut up**
**3 apples cut up**
**8-ounce container Cool Whip**
**6 full-size Snicker candy bars, cut up**
**1½ cups miniature marshmallows**

Mix all together and serve.

## RONZINI

Florence N. Fonser, Dallas, WV

*"Makes a lot! I sometimes halve it. Nice for church dinners or reunions."*

**2 cans crushed pineapple**
**½ teaspoon salt**
**2 eggs**
**2 tablespoons flour**
**¾ cup sugar**
**1 pound orzo macaroni**
**1 large jar maraschino cherries, halved**
**12-ounce can mandarin oranges**
**1 bag miniature marshmallows**
**1 cup chopped nuts**
**1 large or 2 small containers Cool Whip**

Drain pineapple, save juice and pulp, and set pineapple aside in refrigerator. Bring juice, salt, eggs, flour, and sugar to boil. Cool and then add to cooked, well-drained macaroni. Let stand overnight in refrigerator. Next day fold in pineapple, cherries, oranges, marshmallows, nuts, and Cool Whip.

## APPLE CHEESE CASSEROLE

Sue M. Allen, Vernon, AL

**2 cans sliced apples**
**1 stick margarine**
**1 cup sugar**
**¾ cup self-rising flour**
**8 ounces Velveeta cheese, cut up**

OVEN 350°

Spray medium to large casserole dish with cooking spray. Place apples in casserole dish. In separate bowl add margarine, sugar, flour, and Velveeta cheese. Put cheese mixture in microwave on high for 30 seconds at a time, stirring after each time until mixed well. (Usually takes less than 2 minutes.) Pour over apples and bake until golden. Delicious reheated in microwave.

# DESSERTS

## ORANGE FLUFF JELL-O

Ruby Bell, Wichita, KS

**2 small boxes orange Jell-O**
**2 cups boiling water**
**2 cups cold water**
**Several heaping tablespoons orange sherbet**
**1 can crushed pineapple, drained**
**Cool Whip whipped topping**

Combine all ingredients and pour into small glass dish to jell. When completely jelled pour into a large dish to beat whipped topping in. Pour back into smaller dish and keep in refrigerator to stay cool.

## YUM YUM

Linda Etheredge, Needham, AL

**1 cup flour**
**1 cup pecans**
**½ cup margarine, melted**

Mix together and press into 2-quart casserole dish to make crust. Bake until light brown.

**10-ounce package cream cheese**
**1 cup confectioners' sugar**
**1 cup Cool Whip whipped topping**

Combine above ingredients. Beat until smooth and spread on cooled crust.

**1 small box instant chocolate pudding mix**
**1 small box instant vanilla pudding mix**
**3 cups milk**

Mix together above ingredients, beat until thick enough for pudding. Place on top of other mixture in casserole dish. Top with the rest of the Cool Whip. Sprinkle with pecans.

## CHERRY CRUNCH

Mary R. Dean, Kosciusko, MS

**1 large can crushed pineapple**
**1 can cherry pie filling**
**1 box Duncan Hines butter cake mix**
**2 sticks butter**
**1 cup pecans, chopped**

OVEN 325°

Spread pineapple in bottom of a 9x13-inch pan. Spread cherry pie filling on top of pineapple. Sprinkle dry cake mix over top. Melt 2 sticks butter and pour over mixture. When mixture starts to rise, sprinkle pecans on top. Bake 20–30 minutes, or until done.

## WALNUT WALKAWAYS

Rose Adams, Washington, MI

**1 package dry yeast**
**¼ cup warm water**
**2 8-ounce packages cream cheese**
**1½ cups sugar**
**2 teaspoons lemon juice**
**¾ cup margarine**
**2 cups sifted flour**
**¼ teaspoon salt**
**1 egg**
**1 cup chopped nuts**

OVEN 375°

Soften yeast in water. Beat cream cheese, sugar, and lemon until smooth. Set aside. Cut margarine into flour and salt. Add yeast and egg. Mix well. Roll dough half at a time on floured surface. Spread cheese mixture on both pieces of dough. Sprinkle with nuts. Roll up like a jelly roll and seal ends. Place seam down on greased cookie sheet. Cut both cakes halfway lengthwise. Bake for 25 minutes. Cool and slice.

## CREAM TORTE

Bernadine Cook, Golden Valley, MN

*"My husband pastored four churches over a 30-year span. I collected recipes at each place. Not only do I enjoy making and serving various dishes but I have wonderful memories of the places we lived and the women who shared their best recipes with me."*

**4 egg whites**
**½ cup sugar**
**4 tablespoons cold water**
**4 egg yolks**
**½ cup sugar**
**1 cup flour**
**2 teaspoons baking powder**

OVEN 350°

Beat egg whites until stiff. Gradually add ½ cup sugar, beat, and set aside. Add cold water to egg yolks, beat. Add ½ cup sugar, flour, and baking powder. Fold egg whites into this mixture. Bake in two greased and floured 9-inch layer-cake pans for 25 minutes. Remove from pans and cool on rack. Split layers with a thin knife.

**Filling:**

**1 package instant vanilla pudding**
**1½ cups milk**
**4 ounces Cool Whip**

Mix pudding mix and milk. Fold in Cool Whip. Put this mixture between the layers (1/3 each) and push powdered sugar through a strainer (or sprinkle over a doily) to decorate the top. Refrigerate several hours.

Serves at least 12.

## FOUR-LAYERED DESSERT

Barbara Ray, Ray City, GA

**1 stick butter**
**1 cup flour**
**1 cup pecans**

OVEN 350°

Melt butter and mix with flour and pecans. Press in bottom of 9x13-inch pan and bake for 25 minutes. Let cool.

**8-ounce package cream cheese**
**1 cup powdered sugar**
**½ large package Cool Whip**

Mix all and pour over first layer.

**2 small packages chocolate instant pudding**
**3 cups milk**

Mix and pour over second layer.

**½ large Cool Whip**

Put over third layer. Refrigerate at least 6 hours.

Variations:
Charlene Ricker, Wichita, KS
You may put a layer of butterscotch pudding on top of chocolate pudding and then add the whipped topping. It's very good with both flavors and nuts on top!

## HEAVENLY HASH

Pam Sluder, Columbus, GA

**1 bag miniature marshmallows**
**½ cup chopped pecans**
**1 large can chunk pineapple, drained**
**1 Washington State and 1 Granny Smith apple, diced**
**Small bottle of red or green cherries, chopped and drained**
**1 carton sour cream**

Mix all of the above; let stand at least overnight in refrigerator. Serve as a salad or dessert.

## OREO DELIGHT

April Tarket, Lachine, MI

**16-ounce bag Oreo cookies, crushed**
**1 stick margarine, melted**
**3 cups milk**
**2 small packages vanilla instant pudding**
**1 tablespoon vanilla**
**8 ounces softened cream cheese**
**8 ounces Cool Whip whipped topping**

Crush Oreo cookies with rolling pin; then mix together with margarine. Pat into a 9x13-inch pan, reserving some cookies for topping. Mix together milk, vanilla pudding, and vanilla; set aside. Mix together cream cheese and Cool Whip; then add to pudding mixture. Pour over top of Oreo crust, sprinkle with remaining Oreo cookies; chill for 2 hours or more.

## CINNAMON CRUSTED BAKED APPLES

Eleu Braddock, Charleston, SC

*"Great side dish, or after-school snack."*

**Butter-flavored cooking spray**
**⅓ cup water**
**5 medium cooking apples**
**⅓ cup firmly packed brown sugar**
**¼ cup all-purpose flour**
**½ teaspoon ground cinnamon**
**¼ teaspoon ground nutmeg**
**2 tablespoons reduced-calorie margarine, softened**

OVEN 350°

Coat a 9x9-inch baking dish with spray. Pour water into dish. Peel, core, and slice apples. Arrange apple slices in prepared dish; coat apple slices lightly with vegetable spray. Combine brown sugar, flour, cinnamon, and nutmeg; cut in margarine with a pastry blender until mixture resembles coarse meal. Sprinkle mixture evenly over apples. Bake, uncovered, for 30 minutes or until apple is tender.

## RAISIN PUFFS

Patricia Strakal, Morgantown, WV

**1 cup raisins**
**1 cup water**
**1 cup shortening**
**1½ cups sugar**
**2 eggs**
**1 teaspoon vanilla**
**3½ cups flour**
**1 teaspoon soda**
**½ teaspoon salt**

OVEN 350°

Cook raisins in water until dry. Mix shortening, sugar, eggs, and vanilla. Add raisins, then dry ingredients. Roll into balls. Dip in sugar. Put on cookie sheet. Bake for 12–15 minutes.

## BUTTER PECAN DESSERT

Kathy Rice, Pomeroy, OH

**1 stick margarine**
**1 cup flour**
**1 cup chopped pecans**
**8 ounces cream cheese**
**½ cup confectioners' sugar**
**1 large tub Cool Whip**
**3 small boxes butter pecan instant pudding**
**4 cups milk**

OVEN 350°

Melt margarine, mix in flour, put in a 9x13-inch pan, and pat it down; add pecans; bake for 10 minutes. Cool. Mix together cream cheese and confectioners' sugar; when creamy add ½ container of Cool Whip and spread on crust. Mix 3 boxes of butter pecan instant pudding with milk and spread on Cool Whip. Spread on the rest of the Cool Whip. Refrigerate.

# DESSERTS

## CHERRY-CREAM CHEESE TURNOVERS

Kathleen Baker, Davisville, MO

**8-ounce package cream cheese**
**1 cup butter**
**1 teaspoon vanilla**
**2 cups sifted flour**
**Pinch of salt**
**1 can cherry pie filling**
**Powdered sugar**

OVEN 350°

Blend the cream cheese and butter in a bowl; then stir in vanilla. Add the flour and salt; mix well. Place in refrigerator for 1 hour. Roll out thin on a floured surface and cut into 2-inch squares. Place 2 cherries from cherry pie filling in center of each square. Fold over and seal edges. Place on a baking sheet. Bake for about 25 minutes. Cool and dust with powdered sugar. Makes 50 turnovers.

## SWEET POTATO DELIGHT

Judith Fillingim, Columbus, GA

**1 large can sweet potatoes or 1 medium can of mashed**
**½ stick margarine**
**2 eggs**
**½ cup evaporated milk**
**¾ cup sugar (more or less, to suit taste)**

Mix all together and put in glass casserole dish.

**Topping:**
**¾ stick margarine**
**¾ cup light brown sugar**
**½ cup flour**
**1 cup chopped nuts**

OVEN 325°

Mix topping ingredients and spread on top of potato mixture. Bake about 45 minutes.

## SHEEN ISLAND

Goldye Blomgren, Medway, MA

*"Can be a salad or dessert."*

**1 large lime Jell-O**
**1 small bag of marshmallows**
**1 large can pineapple rings**
**1 large package cream cheese**
**Chopped nuts (optional)**

Fix Jell-O with hot water, stir to let it all dissolve. Let gelatin partly set in refrigerator. In a separate bowl, chop pineapple rings, saving juice. Blend juice with cream cheese. Add pineapple and cheese, then marshmallows, to Jell-O.

Variations: Strawberry-banana Jell-O can be used. Finely chopped nuts can be added to cream cheese mixture.

## ANGEL FOOD DESSERT

Jean Brouwer, Lansing, IL

*"Make a week ahead!"*

**1 large angel food cake**
**½ gallon vanilla ice cream**
**1 small package each strawberry, lime, and orange Jell-O**
**16-ounce package strawberries**
**10-ounce can crushed pineapple**
**10-ounce can mandarin oranges**

Divide cake into thirds and crumble. In large tube pan, place ⅓ crumbled cake over bottom, pour strawberries mixed with dry strawberry Jell-O, cover with ⅓ of ice cream. Then add ⅓ cake, slightly drained pineapple mixed with dry lime Jell-O, cover with ⅓ ice cream. Add last ⅓ cake, mandarin oranges mixed with dry orange Jell-O. Top with last of ice cream. Freeze cake until ready to serve. Unmold and serve.

## STRAWBERRY SHORTCAKE

Amy Fisher, Longmont, CO

**Cake:**

**Sugar**
**1 package Duncan Hines Deluxe French Vanilla cake mix**
**3 eggs**
**1¼ cups water**
**½ cup of butter**

OVEN 350°

Grease two 9-inch round cake pans with butter or margarine. Sprinkle bottom and sides with sugar. Combine cake mix, eggs, water, and butter in large bowl. Beat at medium speed with electric mixer for 2 minutes. Pour into pans. Bake for 30–35 minutes. Cool in pans for 10 minutes. Invert onto cooling rack. Cool completely.

**Filling and Topping:**

**2 cups whipping cream, chilled**
**⅓ cup sugar**
**½ teaspoon vanilla extract**
**1 quart fresh strawberries, sliced**
**Mint leaves (optional)**

In large bowl, beat whipping cream, sugar, and vanilla extract until stiff. Reserve ⅓ cup for garnish. Place one cake layer on serving plate. Spread with half of remaining whipped cream and sliced strawberries. Repeat with remaining layer and whipping cream. Garnish with reserved whipped cream and mint leaves. Refrigerate until ready to serve.

# DESSERTS

## CHERRY ANGEL DESSERT
Darlene Tipper, Castle Rock, CO

**1 angel food cake**
**1 small box vanilla instant pudding**
**2 cups milk**
**1 20-ounce can cherry pie filling**

Pull apart one angel food cake into bite-size pieces. Prepare pudding according to box directions. Pour pudding over angel food cake pieces and stir until cake is moistened well. Pour into 2- or 3-quart glass dish. Spread mixture to cover bottom of dish. Pour cherry pie filling over cake and pudding mixture. Spread to cover. Refrigerate until ready to serve.

Makes 6–8 servings.

## APPLE PIZZA
Diane Wiggers, LaPine, OR

**Pie dough:**
**1 egg, separated**
**1 cup water**
**5 cups flour**
**$^5/3$ cup shortening**
**1 teaspoon salt**

OVEN 350°

Add egg yolk to water, set aside egg white. Mix all ingredients except egg white, and roll out half of the crust to fit a cookie sheet. Roll other half out the same size and save for top layer.

**Filling:**
**8–10 apples, sliced**
**1½ cups sugar**
**2 teaspoons cinnamon**
**4–5 teaspoons butter**

Toss apples in sugar and cinnamon. Sprinkle cornflakes on crust. Layer with apples and place butter on top. Seal top crust. Spread on egg white. Cut slits in crust. Bake for 1 hour. Cool completely; add frosting.

**Frosting:**
**2 teaspoons cream**
**2 tablespoons butter**
**1 teaspoon vanilla**
**Enough powdered sugar to make glaze**

Mix frosting ingredients. Drizzle over top of pizza. Cut into squares.

## PUNCH BOWL DESSERT
Mrs. Walter Cloud, Morrow, LA

**1 box or package vanilla wafers**
**3–4 bananas**
**1 large can crushed pineapple, drained**
**3⅔ cups milk**
**2 small boxes instant vanilla pudding**
**12-ounce whipped topping**

Mix pudding with milk and half of whipped topping. Put layer of wafers in bowl, spread with half of pineapples, bananas, and pudding; repeat. Put rest of whipped topping on top. Garnish with nuts, cherries, and coconut if desired.

## HEMMELS FLUTTER

(HEAVENLY FOOD)

Ora M. Berhow, Osceola, WI

*"My mother got this recipe over sixty years ago from a Scottish lady."*

- **1 teaspoon vanilla**
- **1 cup sugar**
- **2 eggs**
- **6 tablespoons flour**
- **2 teaspoons baking powder**
- **1 cup dates, chopped fine**
- **1 cup chopped nutmeats (not too finely chopped)**

OVEN 325°

Mix a little of the flour with the dates to keep them separated. Mix remaining ingredients in order given. Pour and spread out in ungreased 9x13-inch cake pan. Bake in slow oven 30–40 minutes. After baking, cut into squares and break up into bite-size pieces in dessert dishes. Spoon a couple tablespoons of pineapple over and some slices of bananas; top with whipped cream.

## FRUIT PIZZA

Candi Swift, Taylor, MI

- **1 box Duncan Hines Golden Sugar Cookies, or 1 box (1 lb. 1-ounce size) Pillsbury sugar cookies**
- **8-ounce cream cheese**
- **½ cup sugar**
- **1 teaspoon vanilla**
- **Fresh fruit**

OVEN 350°

Follow directions on the Duncan Hines Golden Sugar Cookies for rolled sugar cookies. Spread on an ungreased large pizza pan or jelly roll pan. Bake for 8 10 minutes. Cool. Mix cream cheese, sugar, and vanilla together. Spread over cooled cookie crust. Place fruit on top of cream cheese mixture. Arrange fruit on top. Pour fruit glaze on top of fruit.

**Fruit Glaze:**

- **1 cup water**
- **¾ cup sugar**
- **2 tablespoons cornstarch**
- **2 tablespoons strawberry Jell-O**

Cook water, sugar, and cornstarch until thickened. Add Jell-O. Let cool. The Jell-O is for color and a little flavoring.

Note: I like to use strawberries, blueberries, raspberries, and blackberries. If you want to use bananas, dip them first in pineapple juice to prevent them from turning brown.

## APPLE PIE PIZZA

Bonnie A. Johnson, Wahpeton, ND

*"I had this at a friend's house when I was fifteen, and brought the recipe home. I made it for my family and it was an instant hit. It became a family favorite. I always knew when Dad wanted me to make it, because he'd start peeling apples!"*

**Pastry for 2-crust pie**
**7–8 medium apples, pared, cored, sliced**
**1½ tablespoons lemon juice**
**½ cup sugar**
**1 teaspoon cinnamon**
**½ teaspoon nutmeg**
**¾ cup all-purpose flour**
**½ cup sugar**
**½ cup butter, softened**

OVEN 350°

Line a 12x14-inch pizza pan with pastry dough. Place dough carefully to avoid tears in bottom. Arrange apples in an attractive pattern in pastry shell. Sprinkle apple slices with lemon juice. Combine ½ cup sugar with the spices; sprinkle over apple slices. Combine flour with other ½ cup sugar; cut in butter until crumbly, sprinkle over apple slices. Bake 20–25 minutes, until crust is golden brown and apples are tender. Serve warm or cold.

## PRUNE WHIP

Roberta Lindstrom, Chandler, AZ

**2 packages lemon Jell-O (or more to taste)**
**5 jars baby food prunes**
**4 ounces Cool Whip**

Prepare Jell-O according to package directions, set until semi-solid. Using mixer, mix Jell-O, prunes, and Cool Whip (don't over-mix). Chill in refrigerator until set to pudding consistency.

## SUGAR-FREE FRUIT CRISP

Julie Hunter, West Rockport, ME

**2½ cups fruit (blueberries, peaches, apples, your favorite fruit or a combination); cut into bite-size pieces**
**2 tablespoons all-purpose flour**
**⅛ teaspoon cinnamon**
**1 cup organic muesli (or mix your own oatmeal, raisins, and sunflower seeds to equal 1 cup)**
**3 tablespoons all-purpose flour**
**¼–½ teaspoon fresh lemon zest**
**⅛ teaspoon cinnamon**
**3 tablespoons canola/corn oil blend**
**½ cup 100% pear juice**

OVEN 375°

In a 9-inch glass pie plate, combine fruit, 2 tablespoons flour, and ⅛ teaspoon cinnamon. In separate bowl, mix together muesli, 3 tablespoons flour, lemon zest, ⅛ teaspoon cinnamon, and oil. Pour fruit juice over all. Bake for 45 minutes. Serve warm or cold. Flavor mellows and becomes sweeter if you refrigerate for 2–3 days.

## ZUCCHINI-APPLE CRISP

Caroline Strain, Mason, OH

**½ cup packed brown sugar**
**2 teaspoons lemon juice**
**¼ cup water**
**1 teaspoon salt (optional)**
**1 teaspoon cinnamon**
**3 cups zucchini, peeled, quartered, seeded, and sliced to look like apples**
**3 cups apples, peeled and sliced**
**1 cup raisins (optional)**

**Topping:**
**½ cup flour**
**½ cup oatmeal**
**½ cup brown sugar**
**1 teaspoon cinnamon**
**2–4 tablespoons oil**

OVEN 375°

Mix first 8 ingredients in large saucepan. Boil 10 minutes, stirring so zucchini is thoroughly mixed with apples. Pour into 9x13-inch ungreased baking dish. Mix topping with fork and sprinkle on top. Bake for 45 minutes.

If desired this can be served with Cool Whip or ice cream. It is delicious hot or cold!

Variation: Substitute apple juice for lemon juice and water.

## RHUBARB CRISP

Ruth Gregory, Shoreline, WA

**3 cups rhubarb**
**1 egg**
**¾ cup sugar**
**2 tablespoons flour**
**¼ teaspoon mace**

**Topping:**
**¼ cup margarine**
**⅓ cup white or brown sugar**
**⅔ cup flour**

OVEN 375°

Mix rhubarb, egg, sugar, 2 tablespoons flour, and mace; put in deep glass dish. Combine topping ingredients and cover rhubarb with with topping. Bake 30 minutes.

## CINNAMON APPLE CRISP

Ruth Hagemeier, Hillsdale, WY

**6 medium apples**
**1 cup water**
**1 package white cake mix**
**1 cup firmly packed brown sugar**
**½ cup margarine, melted**
**1 teaspoon cinnamon**
**Whipped topping or ice cream**

OVEN 350°

Arrange apple slices in ungreased 9x13-inch pan. Pour water over top. Combine cake mix, brown sugar, melted margarine, and cinnamon. Stir until thoroughly blended. (Mixture will be crumbly.) Sprinkle crumb mixture over apple slices. Bake for 50–55 minutes or until lightly browned and bubbly.

Variations: To reduce sweetness, use ½ cup brown sugar. You can substitute 2 21-ounce cans apple pie filling for fresh apples. Omit water.

## CHOCOLATE-CHERRY DELICIOUS

Teresa Pridmore

**2 cans cherry pie filling**
**¾ cup butter, melted**
**1 box chocolate cake mix**

OVEN 350°

Spread pie filling in a 9x13-inch pan. Sprinkle dry cake mix evenly over pie filling. Drizzle butter evenly over cake mix. The butter will leave some dry spots, but don't worry about them. Bake for 45 minutes until done. Serve warm or cold.

## ICE CREAM DESSERT

Bernadine Cook, Golden Valley, MN

**Crust:**
**½ package low-fat Hydrox Cookies (approximately 26 cookies)**
**¼ cup margarine, melted**

**Filling:**
**½ gallon low-fat or fat-free ice cream**

**Topping:**
**16-ounce jar fat-free hot fudge sauce.**
**8-ounce low-fat Cool Whip**

Crush cookies and combine with margarine. Press in bottom of 9x13-inch pan and chill in freezer. Cut ice cream into thick slabs and cover crust. Heat topping for one minute in microwave. Spoon over ice cream and spread as much as possible. Cover with Cool Whip and freeze. Cut into squares and top with a cherry, chocolate curls, or chopped pecans.

## EASY CHOCOLATE MINT CHIP DESSERT

Joan Funk, Waterford, WI

*"This is a hit whenever I serve it."*

**16 frozen waffles**
**½ gallon chocolate mint chip ice cream**
**Chocolate syrup**
**12-ounce container Cool Whip**

Separate waffles and put 8 in a 9x13-inch pan (or put in a plastic bag or wrapped in aluminum foil when done). Cut ice cream into ½-inch slices and cut each slice in two, to fit waffles. Put slices on the waffles and top each with another waffle. Put in your freezer until ready to use. When ready to serve, remove from freezer, top with a couple of tablespoons of chocolate syrup (or however much you prefer). Top this with a large tablespoon of Cool Whip.

## CRANBERRY NUT LOAF

Robin L. Woods, Norcross, GA

**8-ounce package cream cheese**
**1/3 cup margarine**
**1¼ cups sugar**
**1 teaspoon vanilla**
**3 eggs**
**2 tablespoons lemon juice**
**1 teaspoon lemon peel**
**2¼ cups flour**
**2 teaspoons baking powder**
**½ teaspoon baking soda**
**1½ cups chopped cranberries**
**1 cup chopped walnuts or pecans**

OVEN 325°

Beat cream cheese, margarine, sugar, and vanilla until well blended; add eggs one at a time. Mix in lemon juice and lemon peel, then flour, baking powder, and baking soda. Add cranberries and nuts. Bake for 1 hour 15 minutes.

## FRUIT LOAF

Pauline R. Herr, Minburn, IA

**2 cups sugar**
**1 cup water**
**Lump of butter**
**1 teaspoon vinegar**
**Honey**
**1 pound (2 cups) mixed nuts**
**1 pound coconut**
**1 pound dates**
**½ pound figs**
**1 pound (2 2/3 cups) powdered sugar**

Syrup: Boil sugar, water, butter, and vinegar, adding honey for flavor, until it threads. Chop or grind nuts and fruit until fine. Mix well with syrup in large mixing bowl. Turn out onto board and mix with powdered sugar. Mix well with hands; form into a loaf. Roll into several long rolls and put away to cool. When cooled, cut into thin slices for serving. Keeps long while in refrigerator or may be frozen.

## CHOCOLATE ECLAIR DESSERT

Bette Smee, San Luis Obispo, CA

**1 large package French vanilla instant pudding mix**
**3 cups milk**
**8-ounce carton Cool Whip**
**1-pound box graham crackers**

**Frosting:**

**3 ounces margarine, melted**
**2 ounces unsweetened baking chocolate, melted**
**2 tablespoons light corn syrup**
**3 tablespoons milk**
**1 teaspoon vanilla**
**1½ cups powdered sugar**

Mix pudding mix and milk as package directs; fold in Cool Whip. In 9x13-inch pan place one layer of graham crackers. Cover with ½ pudding mixture. Repeat once again. Beat together frosting ingredients; spread over top layer of graham crackers.

Makes 15 servings.

## PINEAPPLE SURPRISE

Karen Drwal, Flushing, NY

**16-ounce can undrained cubed pineapple**
**Yellow cake mix**
**½ cup walnuts**
**6 pats of butter**

OVEN 350°

Butter glass or metal pan, put in pineapple with juice. Spread half of cake mix evenly over pineapple, do not mix. Put 6 pats of butter on top. Sprinkle walnuts on top. Bake 30 minutes for glass pan, 50 minutes for metal pan.

Note: Use other half of cake mix to repeat the recipe. Freeze this dessert for later.

## PINEAPPLE AU GRATIN

Sarah Martin, Aiken, SC

*"Great for potlucks. Even my 5-year-old enjoys this dish."*

**3 cans crushed pineapple, drained**
**6 tablespoons self-rising flour**
**2 cups shredded cheddar cheese**
**1 sleeve of butter crackers (Ritz or Townhouse), crushed**
**1 stick of margarine or butter, melted**

OVEN 350°

Mix pineapple and flour in 9x13-inch baking dish. Stir in cheese. Spread crushed crackers on top and drizzle with melted butter. Bake until cheese melted on top is light brown (about 20 minutes).

## BAKED PINEAPPLE

Gladys Harris, Red Cloud, NE

**½ cup flour**
**⅓ cup sugar**
**1 egg**
**2 tablespoons butter**
**20-ounce can pineapple chunks, reserve juice**
**½ pound American cheese, chopped (Velveeta works well)**
**Small marshmallows**

OVEN 350°

Combine flour, sugar, egg, butter, and pineapple juice in pan. Cook until thick. Add cheese. Stir in pineapple chunks. Pour in buttered baking dish. Top with marshmallows. Bake for 15–20 minutes.

## ANYTIME TREATS

Menga Castle, Alhambra, CA

**1–2 packages graham crackers**
**Miniature marshmallows**
**Chocolate chips**

OVEN 350°

Line a cookie sheet with one package of graham crackers. Sprinkle graham crackers generously with marshmallows and chocolate chips. Put in oven for 5 minutes or until chocolate chips start to melt. Remove from oven and cool.

Note: to put in lunch boxes or wrap for gift giving, place another package of graham crackers on top of chocolate chips when you remove from oven.

## OREO COOKIE DESSERT

Mary Dunlap, Peebles, OH

**1-pound package Oreo cookies**
**1 stick butter, melted**
**1 large box vanilla instant pudding**
**2½ cups milk**
**8-ounce package cream cheese, softened**
**1 cup powdered sugar**
**12-ounce container Cool Whip**

Crush cookies (set aside ½ cup crushed cookies), add melted butter and press into bottom of 9x13-inch pan. Beat pudding mix and milk together until thickened. Pour over crumb mixture and refrigerate. Beat softened cream cheese and sugar together. Fold in ½ container Cool Whip. Remove mixture from refrigerator and spread cream cheese mixture on top of pudding. Spread remaining Cool Whip on top and sprinkle with remaining ½ cup crushed Oreos.

Variations: Use vanilla or peanut butter cookies with chocolate pudding.

## APPLE ROLL

Ollie Woodworth, Rochester, PA

**1½ cups sugar**
**2 cups water**
**2 cups flour**
**½ teaspoon salt**
**2 tablespoons sugar**
**4 teaspoons baking powder**
**3 tablespoons shortening**
**¾ cup milk**
**4 medium apples, chopped fine**

OVEN 350°

Combine sugar and water, cook to dissolve sugar, and pour into 9x11-inch cake pan. Combine next six ingredients. Roll flour mixture ½-inch thick. Spread apples over flour mixture. Roll up like a jelly roll and cut slices 1-inch thick. Place in the sugar water. Put small pieces of butter on top and sprinkle with cinnamon. Bake for 30 minutes.

Variation: Use peaches instead of apples.

## BLACKBERRY GRUNT
LaVeta Williams, Aberdeen, WA

**4 cups blackberries**
**1 cup sugar**
**½ cup water**
**1½ tablespoons butter**
**1 cup flour**
**1½ teaspoons baking powder**
**Dash of salt**
**2 tablespoons sugar**
**½ cup milk**
**2 tablespoons butter, melted**

Combine berries, 1 cup sugar, water, and 1½ tablespoons butter in a heat-proof casserole dish to be used on top of range. Bring to a boil. In a separate bowl, mix the flour, baking powder, salt, remaining sugar, milk, and melted butter. Spoon the dough over the berry mixture and cover tightly. Simmer 12 minutes. When cooked, a knife inserted in center will come out clean.

## BLUEBERRY DELIGHT
Mary Kinder, Columbus, GA

**Crust:**
**1 cup walnuts, chopped fine**
**2 cups graham cracker crumbs or vanilla wafer crumbs**
**½ cup butter or margarine**

OVEN 350°

Mix well and press into casserole dish. Bake until slightly brown. Cool.

**Filling:**
**2 8-ounce packages cream cheese**
**2 cups powdered sugar**
**1 package Dream Whip, prepared as directed**
**1 can blueberry pie filling**

Soften cream cheese and add sugar, then Dream Whip. Mix well using mixer. Pour filling into crust. Top with pie filling. Chill 2 to 3 hours.

## FOUR-LAYER BLUEBERRY DELIGHT
Sybil H. Beasley, Gatesville, TX

**1½ cups flour**
**1½ sticks margarine, melted**
**1 cup chopped nuts**

OVEN 350°

Mix and press crust into 9x13-inch pan. Bake 15 minutes.

**2 8-ounce cream cheese**
**2 14-ounce cans condensed milk**
**⅔ cup lemon juice**
**2 teaspoons vanilla**

Beat cream cheese until creamy, add other ingredients in order listed. Pour over cooled crust.

**1–2 cans blueberry pie filling**

Top cream cheese layer with filling, to taste.

**8-ounce Cool Whip**

Top pie filling with Cool Whip. Refrigerate.

## BLUEBERRY BUCKLE

Barbara Peters, West Buxton, ME

**2 cups sifted flour**
**3 teaspoons baking powder**
**½ teaspoon salt**
**½ cup soft butter or margarine**
**½ cup sugar**
**2 eggs**
**¾ cup milk**
**2 cups blueberries, washed and drained**

**Topping:**
**⅓ cup flour**
**¼ cup butter**
**¾ cup brown sugar**
**2 teaspoons cinnamon**

OVEN 375°

Grease and flour square 9-inch pan (or equivalent). Sift flour and baking powder with salt, in large bowl. In another bowl, combine butter, sugar, and eggs; beat at high speed until fluffy. At low speed, add the dry ingredients alternately with milk. Fold in the berries last. Turn into prepared pan. Mix topping ingredients to consistency of peas and sprinkle on top of batter. Bake 35 minutes or until done. Can be frozen for later use.

## SPRING TEMPTATION

Sandra Phillips, Interlaken, NY

**1 small package orange Jell-O**
**1 cup hot water**
**1½ cups orange sherbet**
**1 small can crushed pineapple**
**1 small can mandarin oranges**
**1 cup small marshmallows**

Mix together Jell-O, hot water, and sherbet. Mix until sherbet is melted. Refrigerate until almost set. Stir in pineapple, mandarin oranges, and marshmallows. Refrigerate.

## COOL FRUIT

Ruth Winch, Cincinnati, OH

*"Great as appetizer or dessert! We served this at a sweetheart banquet as an appetizer and folks came back for more after dessert!"*

**1 cup Cool Whip whipped topping**
**1 cup condensed milk**
**1 cup tidbit pineapple, drained**
**2 small cans mandarin oranges**
**1 cup small marshmallows**
**½ cup chopped walnuts**
**1 cup cherry pie filling**

Mix all together and chill.

## STRAWBERRY-NUT JELL-O

Elizabeth Hinkley, Mechanicstown, OH

**2 packages strawberry Jell-O**
**1 cup boiling water**
**2 10-ounce packages sliced strawberries, thawed**
**1 large can crushed pineapple**
**3 bananas, mashed**
**1 cup coarsely chopped walnuts**
**1 pint sour cream**

Dissolve Jell-O in water. Fold in strawberries with juice, pineapple, bananas, walnuts. Put ½ in pan, for first layer. Set 1½ hours, spoon sour cream on top evenly. Put on balance of Jell-O mixture and let set.

## SUGAR-FREE JELL-O DESSERT

Clara B. Roberts, Albemarle, NC

**2 3-ounce or 1 6-ounce orange sugar-free Jell-O**
**20-ounce can crushed pineapple**
**2 cups buttermilk**
**8-ounce Cool Whip Lite**

Heat Jell-O and pineapple. Mix well until Jell-O is dissolved. Let cool. Add buttermilk and Cool Whip. Mix well. Put in refrigerator until Jell-O sets up.

Makes 4–6 servings.

## PEACHES AND CREAM

Shelley Dee Jackson, Deweyville, TX

**1 can peaches**
**1 can evaporated milk**
**1 cup sugar**

Open can of peaches and set aside. Put milk in metal or glass bowl (not plastic). Put bowl and beaters in freezer for 20 minutes. Remove and beat milk on high speed. Then add sugar. Beat until smooth and frothy. Put peaches in individual bowls. Spoon on cream. Eat immediately. Will not keep.

## CREAMY MOCHA FROZEN DESSERT

Karen E. Douglas, Buffalo, SD

**2 teaspoons instant coffee granules**
**1 tablespoon hot water**
**1 cup cream-filled chocolate cookie crumbs (about 7 cookies)**
**¾ cup chopped pecans, divided**
**¼ cup butter or margarine, melted**
**2 8-ounce packages cream cheese, softened**
**14-ounce can condensed milk**
**½ cup chocolate-flavored syrup**
**8-ounce frozen whipped topping, thawed**

In a small bowl dissolve coffee granules in hot water, set aside. In another bowl, combine cookie crumbs, ½ cup pecans, and butter. Pat into the bottom of a 9x13-inch baking pan. In a mixing bowl, beat cream cheese until light and fluffy. Blend in coffee mixture, milk, and chocolate syrup. Fold in whipped topping; spread over crust. Sprinkle the remaining pecans on top. Freeze.

## MILLION-DOLLAR PUDDING

Amy Dean, Fort Gay, WV

**1 small box instant sugar-free pudding (vanilla or butterscotch)**
**1 cup Whipping cream**
**Half of 8-ounce tub Cool Whip**
**3-ounce cream cheese**
**1 cup unsweetened pineapple**
**1 package Equal sweetener**
**½ cup walnuts**

Blend pudding and whipping cream, add rest of ingredients and chill.

## "LIL'S" CREAMY RICE PUDDING

Sarah M. Harvey, Harveys Lake, PA

*"Very, very tasty. Will disappear quickly. You can cut recipe by ½ or ¼ and it still works very well."*

**1⅓ cup uncooked rice**
**2⅔ cups sugar**
**2 teaspoons salt**
**14 cups milk**
**4 eggs**
**4 teaspoons vanilla**
**Nutmeg or cinnamon to taste**

Heat rice, sugar, salt, and milk in top of double boiler over direct heat until milk is scalded. Occasionally stir rice from bottom of pan with fork. Place over boiling water in bottom of double boiler. Cover and cook for 2½ to 3 hours, stirring occasionally. Beat eggs, add a small amount of hot pudding to eggs first, so not to scramble eggs. Then add remaining egg mixture a small amount at a time. Add flavorings. Serve hot or cold.

# DESSERTS

## CARAMEL PUDDING

Jan Willman, Noblesville, IN

**3 cups hot water**
**2 cups brown sugar**
**1 tablespoon butter**
**1½ teaspoons vanilla**
**½ cup milk**
**½ cup sugar**
**1 tablespoon margarine**
**1½ cups flour**
**1½ teaspoons baking powder**
**Pinch of salt**
**Vanilla**

Combine first four ingredients and boil for 10 minutes. Mix rest of ingredients. Drop by spoonfuls into other mixture and boil ½ hour, covered.

## LEMON DELIGHT

Brinda Hines, Ft. Wayne, IN

**Crust:**
**2 cups flour**
**2 sticks margarine, softened or melted**
**1 cup pecans, chopped**

OVEN 375°

Mix crust ingredients, may be crumbly. Press into 9x13-inch pan. Bake for 15–20 minutes. Cool.

**Filling:**
**2 cups powdered sugar**
**1 8-ounce package cream cheese**
**2 small packages lemon instant pudding mix**
**3 cups milk**
**1 carton Cool Whip**

Combine powdered sugar and cream cheese. Chill 15 minutes and spread over cooled crust. Whisk together pudding and milk. Let set a few minutes after thickens. Spread over cream cheese mixture. Cover with Cool Whip. Place twist of lemon in center for garnish.

## CHERRY ICE BOX DESSERT

Alice E. Jones, Maize, KS

**24 large marshmallows**
**½ cup hot milk**
**20 graham crackers**
**3 tablespoons powdered sugar**
**1 stick butter or margarine**
**½ pint whipping cream or 1 pint Cool Whip**
**1 can prepared cherry pie filling**

Melt marshmallows in hot milk on top of double boiler. Cool. Crush graham crackers very fine. Add sugar and melted butter to cracker crumbs; press into bottom of 8x12-inch dish. Whip cream, sweetened to taste, and fold into cooled marshmallow mixture. Spread ½ whipped cream mixture on top of crust. Spoon on entire can of cherry pie filling. Top with remaining whipped cream mixture. Chill at least 6 hours, overnight is best.

## MY PISTACHIO DELIGHT

Mary Jane Blazer, Apache Junction, AZ

*"A friend had this when I was at her house, and it was so delicious that I asked for the ingredients. I don't know the name so I call it My Pistachio Delight. It's so easy for something so delicious!"*

**16- or 20-ounce can crushed pineapple**
**1 small package pistachio instant pudding**
**8-ounce tub Cool Whip**
**½ 10-ounce package mini marshmallows**

Put crushed pineapple in bottom of large mixing bowl. Add pudding and mix well. Add marshmallows and mix well. Place in small bowl, refrigerate until firm.

## HOT FUDGE PUDDING

Madeline Carter, Brooklin, ME

**1 cup flour**
**¼ teaspoon salt**
**2 tablespoons cocoa**
**2 teaspoons baking powder**
**¾ cup sugar**
**½ cup milk**
**2 tablespoons shortening**
**1 cup nuts**
**4 tablespoons brown sugar**
**2 tablespoons cocoa**

OVEN 350°

Mix first 5 ingredients in a bowl. Stir in milk, shortening, and nuts. Spread in a 9-inch pan. Mix brown sugar and additional cocoa and sprinkle over mixture. Pour 2 cups of hot water on top and bake for 40 minutes. Serve with ice cream, whipped cream, or Cool Whip.

## APPLE PUDDING

Darleen Christianson, Viroqua, WI

*"My family always like this dish very much. It's very simple to make. If you need a larger amount, just double the recipe!"*

**Apples, peeled and sliced**
**¼–½ cup sugar**
**Cinnamon**
**Butter**
**½ cup sugar**
**2 eggs**
**⅓ cup flour**
**¼ teaspoon baking powder**

OVEN 350°

Butter 1- or 1½-quart casserole dish. Fill a baking dish half full of apples. Put ¼–½ cup sugar over apples. Sprinkle with cinnamon and dot with butter. Make a batter of ¼–½ cup sugar, eggs, flour, and baking powder; pour over apples, do not stir. Bake for ½ hour or until apples are tender.

## MY ORIGINAL BANANA PUDDING

Judy K. Archibald, Durango, CO

*"This is a dessert my family loves to see me make and I enjoy making it for them."*

**¾ cup sugar**
**½ cup flour**
**Dash of salt**
**4 eggs, separated**
**2 cups milk**
**½ teaspoon vanilla**
**Vanilla wafers**
**5 to 6 medium bananas**

OVEN 425°

Combine ½ cup sugar, flour, and salt in a double boiler. Stir in 4 egg yolks and milk. Cook, uncovered, over boiling water. Stir constantly until mixture thickens. Reduce heat and cook 5 more minutes. Remove from heat and add vanilla. Spread on bottom of dish and layer with wafers and bananas. Repeat this process several times.

Beat egg whites until stiff peaks form. Add remaining sugar and beat until dissolved. Cover entire top of banana pudding and seal sides. Bake for 5 minutes or until brown on top. Add cookie crumbs on top for garnish.

## BIG-AS-TEXAS BANANA PUDDING

Pat Cauthen, Pasadena, TX

**2 packages vanilla instant pudding**
**4 cups milk**
**1 can Eagle brand fat-free milk**
**8-ounce package cream cheese**
**8 bananas**
**1 container fat-free Cool Whip**
**1 box vanilla wafers**

Beat together pudding and milk, set aside. Mix cream cheese and fat-free milk. Mix together cream cheese and pudding mixtures. Fold in Cool Whip and bananas. Layer in dish with wafers.

## PEACH PUDDING

Pamela Hunsicker, Lehighton, PA

**¼ cup sugar**
**1 tablespoon cornstarch**
**2 eggs**
**¼ cup water**
**1 large can peaches**
**1 tablespoon vanilla**
**½ pint whipped cream or small container of Cool Whip**

Mix sugar, cornstarch, and eggs with water. Heat juice from peaches and sugar mixture. Cook until thick, cool. Cut peaches in dish and add cooled mixture; add vanilla and whipped cream.

## WALNUT PUDDING

Dorothy Cessna, Cherry Tree, PA

**1 cup sugar**
**1 cup milk**
**½ cup raisins**
**1 teaspoon cloves**
**1 teaspoon nutmeg**
**2 tablespoons butter**
**1 teaspoon baking powder**
**1 cup walnuts**
**1 teaspoon cinnamon**
**2 cups flour**

OVEN 350°

Combine all ingredients except flour. Add flour until stiff.

**Sauce:**

**2 tablespoons butter**
**3 cups brown sugar**
**5 cups boiling water**

Combine sauce ingredients in deep pan, drop batter into sauce by spoonfuls. Bake for 1 hour.

## GRAHAM CRACKER PUDDING

Janet Mast, Baltic, OH

**½ cup margarine**
**1 cup brown sugar**
**1½ cups water**
**2 rounded tablespoons flour**
**2 rounded tablespoons cornstarch**
**½ cup sugar**
**2 egg yolks**
**1 cup milk**
**8- or 12-ounce whipped topping**

**Crumbs:**

**12 graham crackers, crushed**
**2 tablespoons melted butter**
**¼ cup white sugar**

Melt margarine, add brown sugar, and let come to a boil. Add water and let almost come to a boil again. Combine flour, cornstarch, sugar, egg yolks, and milk. Stir into hot mixture. On low heat, stir and cook until it thickens. Cool. Mix cracker crumbs, butter, and sugar. Layer crumbs, chilled pudding, and whipping cream in a clear bowl. Refrigerate.

## S'MORE PUDDING DESSERT

Sherrill Swartz, Fairview, MI

**9 full-size graham crackers, crushed**
**3¼ cups milk**
**3 1¼-ounce chocolate candy bars**
**5-ounce box vanilla pudding**
**2 cups miniature marshmallows**

Line bottom of 1½-quart baking dish with ⅓ of graham cracker crumbs. Using 3¼ cups milk, cook pudding as directed on package; cool 5 minutes. Spread half of pudding over crackers. Top with second layer of ⅓ of crackers. Place candy bars on crackers. Spread remaining pudding over candy. Top with ⅓ layer of crackers. Sprinkle with marshmallows. Broil until golden brown. Serve warm or chilled in refrigerator.

## FRUIT AND NUT BREAD PUDDING

Catherine Kramer, Greenwood, DE

**16 slices day-old bread, torn into 1-inch pieces**
**2 cups sugar**
**4 eggs**
**3 cups milk**
**2 teaspoons ground cinnamon**
**½ teaspoon salt**
**2 tablespoons vanilla extract**
**21-ounce can apple pie filling, slices cut in half**
**2 cups coarsely chopped pecans**
**1 cup golden raisins**
**¾ cup butter or margarine, melted**
**Whipped cream (optional)**

OVEN 350°

In a large bowl, combine bread and sugar. Set aside. In another bowl, beat eggs, milk, cinnamon, salt, and vanilla until foamy. Pour over bread and sugar, mix well. Cover and refrigerate for 2 hours. Stir in remaining ingredients except cream. Pour into a greased 9x13-inch baking pan. Bake for 45–50 minutes or until firm. Cut into squares. Serve warm or cold, with whipped cream, if desired.

Makes 12–15 servings.

## MOUSSE IN MINUTES

Shirley M. Deemer, Baltmore, MD

**1½ cups cold skim milk**
**1 package (4 servings) Jell-O chocolate flavored fat-free, sugar-free, instant reduced calorie pudding**
**2 cups Cool Whip Lite, thawed**

Beat skim milk and pudding in large bowl, whisk one minute. Stir in Cool Whip. Garnish as desired.

Makes 6 servings.

## CUSTARD RAISIN BREAD PUDDING

Margie McDowell, Elkhart, IN

**4 or 5 slices raisin bread**
**2 cups milk, scalded**
**1 tablespoon butter**
**¼ teaspoon salt**
**½ cup sugar**
**2 eggs, lightly beaten**
**1 teaspoon vanilla**
**Ground cinnamon**

OVEN 350°

Soak bread in scalded milk for five minutes. Add butter, salt, sugar, eggs, and vanilla. Mix well. Pour into greased 1-quart casserole dish. Sprinkle lightly with cinnamon. Place casserole in pan of hot water in middle of oven. Bake for 45–50 minutes or until center is firm.

## ORANGE BREAD PUDDING

Geri Hunt, Lutz, FL

**3 eggs, beaten**
**1⅓ cups sugar**
**¼ teaspoon salt**
**1½ cups orange juice**
**4 cups bread cubes, cut from day-old bread with crusts removed**
**¼ cup coconut**
**2 tablespoons raisins**

OVEN 350°

Grease 1-quart casserole. In medium bowl combine beaten eggs, sugar, salt, and orange juice. Add bread cubes, coconut, and raisins; mix, place in buttered casserole, and bake 40–45 minutes or until set. Increase heat to 450° for 2–3 minutes to brown peaks. Spoon into dessert dishes and serve with orange sauce.

Serves 6.

**Orange sauce:**

**1 tablespoon cornstarch**
**½ cup sugar**
**1 teaspoon grated orange peel**
**1 cup orange juice**
**1 teaspoon lemon juice**
**2 tablespoons butter or margarine**

In pan combine cornstarch, sugar, orange peel, and orange juice. Bring to boil and cook over medium heat for 5 minutes, stirring constantly. Remove from heat; stir in lemon juice and butter until butter is melted and sauce is smooth.

## RAISIN-NUT PUDDING

Clara Carlson, Edmonton, Alberta

**2 tablespoons butter**
**2 teaspoons sugar**
**1 cup flour**
**2 teaspoons baking powder**
**⅛ teaspoon salt**
**½ teaspoon cinnamon**
**1 cup raisins**
**½ cup chopped nuts**
**½ cup milk**
**1 cup brown sugar**
**1 tablespoon butter**
**1¾ cups boiling water**

OVEN 375°

Cream butter and sugar. Sift flour, baking powder, salt, and cinnamon; add to creamed mixture. Blend until mealy. Add raisins and nuts. Stir in the milk. Stir only until blended. Put in a greased casserole. Mix together brown sugar, butter, and boiling water and pour over batter. Bake for 35–40 minutes.

# DESSERTS

## TAPIOCA DESSERT
Crystal A. Bailey, Berne, IN

**5 cups boiling water**
**1 cup small ball tapioca**
**3-ounce box gelatin, any flavor**
**1 scant cup sugar**
**20-ounce can crushed pineapple, undrained**
**Cool Whip whipped topping**
**Miniature marshmallows**

Combine boiling water and tapioca; boil 10 minutes. Remove from heat. Keep covered 10 minutes. Add gelatin, sugar, and pineapple. Add Cool Whip and miniature marshmallows to your desired taste.

You can use any kind of canned or frozen fruit. Nuts can be added also.

## EASY CUSTARD
Glena M. McIntyre, Dublin, TX

**6 eggs**
**1 can condensed milk**
**2½ cans warm water**
**¼ teaspoon salt**
**1 teaspoon vanilla**
**Nutmeg**
**Cool Whip whipped topping**

OVEN 325°

Beat eggs until frothy. Add condensed milk, water, salt, and vanilla; beat well. Pour into cooking-spray coated 9-inch baking dish. Sprinkle with nutmeg. Bake approximately 1 hour or until your knife comes out clean. (The warmer the water the faster it bakes.) It will finish cooking after you take it out. Cool. Top with Cool Whip.

## EASY JELLY ROLL
Carol Mackinder, Northville, MI

**1 cup margarine**
**1½ cups sugar**
**4 eggs**
**2 cups flour**
**1 teaspoon vanilla**
**8-ounce can prepared pie filling**
**Confectioners' sugar**

OVEN 350°

Cream margarine and gradually add sugar; add one egg at a time and beat after each addition, add flour and vanilla. Spread on an 11x14-inch jelly roll pan. Drop pie filling into batter, making 4x5-inch pattern. Bake for 35 minutes. Cool on rack. After 15 minutes sprinkle confectioners' sugar on top. When using blueberry filling, substitute lemon juice for vanilla.

## HAWAIIAN DELIGHT

Nancy Clark, Everett, PA

**2 cups crushed cinnamon graham crackers**
**½ cup margarine, melted**

Mix and press into 9x13-inch pan, set aside.

**2 small packages instant banana pudding**
**3 cups milk**
**¾ cup coconut**

Mix pudding and milk; then add coconut and spread onto first layer.

**2 large bananas, sliced and quartered**

Spread onto second layer.

**20-ounce can of crushed pineapple, drained**
**8-ounce Cool Whip**

Mix together pineapple and Cool Whip and spread on top of other layers. Chill.

## HAWAIIAN DELIGHT

Sharon Kerr, Janesville, WI

**18¼-ounce box yellow cake mix**
**3 small packages instant vanilla pudding mix**
**4 cups cold milk**
**1½ teaspoons coconut extract**
**8-ounce package cream cheese, softened**
**20-ounce can crushed pineapple, well drained**
**2 cups heavy cream, whipped and sweetened**
**2 cups flaked coconut, toasted**

OVEN 350°

Mix cake batter according to box directions. Pour into two greased 9x13-inch baking pans. Bake for 15 minutes or until done. Cool completely. In large mixing bowl, combine pudding mixes, milk, and coconut extract; beat for 2 minutes. Add the cream cheese and beat well. Stir in pineapple. Spread over the cooled cakes. Top with whipped cream. Sprinkle with coconut. Chill at least 2 hours.

Makes 24 servings.

## MY MOTHER'S SNOW ICE CREAM

Janet Gortsema, Pleasantville, NY

*"This is not the ice cream we are accustomed to buying from the store, but it is fun all the same."*

**Editor's Note:** Janet has written *Design for Love* and *Mockingbird's Song* for Heartsong Presents.

**2 cups milk**
**2 eggs**
**½ teaspoon salt**
**1½ cups sugar**
**½ teaspoon salt**

Mix all ingredients and gently fold in clean, fresh snow until the mix is at saturation. Should yield about one gallon. You can halve the recipe.

## PAVLOVA

Mary Hawkins, New South Wales, Australia

**Editor's Note:** Mary is the author of many Heartsong Presents romances. They include *Search for Tomorrow* and *Damaged Dreams*.

**6 egg whites**
**1½ cups granulated sugar**
**1 tablespoon vinegar**
**1 tablespoon vanilla**
**2 tablespoons cornmeal**
**Whipped cream**
**Fruit (bananas, kiwi, strawberries, with passion fruit juice squeezed over all or just fresh fruit salad)**

OVEN 300°

Beat egg whites until stiff meringue consistency, then slowly add sugar until you cannot see sugar grains. One at a time fold in the vinegar, vanilla, and then the cornmeal. Spread onto a piece of aluminum foil that has been lightly greased and place on baking tray. Cook for 1½ hours. Allow to cool in oven—preferably overnight. When ready to serve, top with whipped cream and your choice of fruit.

## LAMINGTONS

Mary Hawkins, New South Wales, Australia

Cook your favorite 2-egg sponge cake in a 12x10-inch cake tin and when cool, freeze. (Or if in a hurry, buy your sponge slab cake from the nearest bakery and pop it straight into the freezer!)

**Chocolate Icing:**
**1 large tablespoon butter**
**½ cup water (approximately)**
**3 cups confectioners' sugar**
**⅓ cup cocoa**
**½ teaspoon vanilla**
**2 cups coconut (approximate—have more on hand)**

Place all ingredients except coconut into a small saucepan. Bring almost to boil on low heat. Make sure butter is melted but do not boil, as icing will become too hard when cool. The icing must be thin enough so that squares of cake can be readily and rapidly coated, but not so thin that it soaks into cake too much—add more sugar or less water as required. While mixture is heating, cut frozen cake into approximately 30 small squares. Using a long, two-pronged carving fork to hold each square, plunge one at a time into the hot icing and drop onto a pile of coconut, quickly roll until coated, and leave to dry on a plate. Before serving, cut in half and put whipped cream in center or leave it uncut and pipe on whipped cream top, placing a strawberry or cherry on it.

Note: Using frozen cake prevents it from crumbling into icing. Cut a few squares at a time to prevent pieces from thawing out too much before being iced. It is much easier for 2 (or 3!) people to roll squares. When cooking alone, make up half of icing at a time so it is not cooled too quickly by frozen cake.

## ENGLISH TRIFLE

Ruth Richert Jones, Omaha, NE

*"Trifle was a dessert which likely appeared on the Stonehurst table in* A Rose Is a Rose. *It is a showpiece usually served in a crystal bowl."*

**Editor's Note:** *A Rose Is a Rose* was Ruth's first book published by Heartsong Presents.

**4 sponge dessert shells (often featured in the produce department in markets)**
**⅓ cup raspberry jam**
**1 small package raspberry gelatin dessert**
**2 cups fresh fruit**
**1 envelope Bird's Custard Style Dessert Mix (found in markets featuring imported products)**
**3 tablespoons sugar**
**1½ cups milk**
**½ cup heavy cream, whipped**

Slice dessert shells horizontally and spread four halves with jam. Replace tops and arrange shells in the bottom of a glass serving dish. Prepare gelatin dessert according to package directions and pour half over dessert shells. Reserve remaining gelatin for other use. When the gelatin is set, arrange fruit over the gelatin.

Combine dessert mix and sugar in a saucepan. Add 2 tablespoons of the milk and mix until smooth. Add remaining milk. Bring the mixture to a full boil over medium heat, stirring constantly. Remove from heat and cool a few minutes, stirring occasionally. Pour over layers in the glass bowl. Chill. Top with whipped cream and decorate top with fruit and nuts.

Serves 6.

## CHEESECAKE DESSERT

**Crust:**

**2 cups graham cracker crumbs**
**6 tablespoons sugar**
**½ cup butter or margarine, melted**

Mix well and press into bottom of 9x13-inch pan.

**Filling:**

**2 cups powdered sugar**
**2 8-ounce packages cream cheese**
**1 teaspoon vanilla**
**8-ounce tub Cool Whip**
**1 large can cherry pie filling**

Combine sugar, cream cheese, and vanilla; mix well. Add Cool Whip. Pour over crust. When set, pour cherry pie filling on top.

## CREAMY FRUIT AND CAKE DELIGHT

Mrs. Annalu Pagano, Spring Hill, FL

**1 cup Entenmann's Fat-Free Golden Loaf Cake cubes (½ inch)**
**½ cup diced banana**
**½ cup sliced strawberries (fresh or frozen unsweetened)**
**¾ cup boiling water**
**1 package (4-serving size) sugar-free gelatin, any red flavor**
**½ cup cold water**
**Ice cubes**
**1 cup thawed whipped topping**

Divide cake cubes and fruit evenly among 6 dessert glasses, reserving several strawberry slices for garnish, if desired. Stir boiling water into gelatin in large bowl 2 minutes or until completely dissolved. Mix cold water and ice cubes to make 1¼ cups. Add to gelatin, stirring until slightly thickened. Remove any remaining ice. Stir whipped topping into gelatin with wire whisk until well blended. Let stand 5 minutes or until thickened. Spoon into dessert glasses. Refrigerate 1 hour or until firm. Garnish with reserved strawberry slices.

## CHERRY CHEESECAKE

Rhonda Lowery, Greensburg, IN

**1 package Dream Whip powder mix**
**1 package cream cheese**
**2 cups powdered sugar**
**1 premade graham cracker crust**
**Cherries**

Follow instructions on package of Dream Whip. Mix in one bowl until the mixture forms peaks when beaters are removed. In separate bowl mix cream cheese and sugar. This must peak also. Add Dream Whip to cream cheese mixture. Make sure it peaks when you remove beaters. Place into graham cracker crust. Top with cherries. Chill in refrigerator for 2 hours before serving.

## FROZEN PEPPERMINT CHEESECAKE

Jenni Hannan, Milwaukie, OR

*"Christmas and New Year's favorite!"*

**1 9-inch premade chocolate pie crust**
**8-ounce package cream cheese, softened**
**14-ounce can condensed milk**
**1 cup crushed hard peppermint candy**
**2 cups whipping cream, whipped**

In large mixer bowl, beat cheese until fluffy. Gradually beat in condensed milk. Stir in crushed candy. Fold in whipping cream. Pour into crust. Garnish as desired. Freeze 6 hours or until firm. Return leftovers to freezer.

Ideas for garnishes: crushed peppermint candies. Milk chocolate shavings (use a peeler).

## CHOCOLATE CHIP CHEESECAKE

Beth Kissell, Cheyenne, WY

**3 8-ounce packages cream cheese, softened**
**3 eggs**
**¾ cup sugar**
**1 teaspoon vanilla**
**3 rolls refrigerator chocolate chip cookie dough**

OVEN 350°

Beat together cream cheese, eggs, sugar, and vanilla until well mixed. Set aside. Slice the cookie dough into 1/3-inch slices. Arrange the slices from 1½ rolls on bottom of greased 9x13-inch glass baking dish. Press together so there are no holes. Spoon cream cheese mixture evenly over the top. Top with the remaining dough. Bake for 45–50 minutes or until golden and the center is slightly firm. Remove from oven. Let cool, then refrigerate. Cut when well chilled.

## CHEESECAKE

Gwen Schafer, Freemont, MI

*"This recipe is submitted in loving memory of my mother Joan Pekel, who passed away July 19, 1996."*

**3-ounce package any flavor Jell-O**
**1 cup boiling water**
**12-ounce can evaporated skim milk (refrigerated for 24 hours)**
**8-ounce package cream cheese, softened to room temperature**
**1 cup sugar**

**Crust:**

**3 cups graham crackers, crushed**
**½ cup sugar**
**1 teaspoon cinnamon (optional)**
**1 cup margarine, melted**

Mix Jell-O and water. Set aside to cool. Prepare graham cracker crust by mixing crust ingredients together; press into greased 9x13-inch pan. Whip milk until peaks form. Mix cream cheese and sugar, add to whipped milk. Mix Jell-O with cream cheese and milk. Pour mixture over crust. Refrigerate until set.

## PEACH CHEESECAKE

Brenda Thompson, Rogers, AR

**1 envelope unflavored gelatin**
**¼ cup cold water**
**16-ounce can lite peaches, drained (reserve juice)**
**8-ounce lite cream cheese, softened**
**6 packets Equal Sweetener**
**8-inch prepared graham cracker crust**

In blender sprinkle gelatin over cold water, let stand 2 minutes. In small saucepan, bring reserved juice to a boil. Add hot juice to blender and process at low speed until gelatin is completely dissolved, about 2 minutes. Add peaches, cream cheese, and Equal. Process at high speed until blended, pour into prepared crust. Chill until firm, about 3 hours. Garnish if desired.

## PINEAPPLE CHEESECAKE
Wanda Stubblefield, Chattanooga, TN

**Filling:**
- **2 8-ounce cream cheese, softened**
- **1/3 cup lemon juice**
- **16-ounce tub of Cool Whip**
- **2 large cans chilled, crushed pineapple, drained**

**Crust:**
- **3 tablespoons melted butter**
- **4 tablespoons brown sugar**
- **3 cups graham cracker crumbs**
- **1 cup finely chopped pecans**

OVEN 325°

Beat cream cheese until smooth and creamy, beat in lemon juice. Fold ½ Cool Whip into cheese mixture. Stir in 1 can pineapple until mixed well.

Crust: Mix butter, sugar, graham cracker crumbs, and ¾ cup pecans; press in bottom of 9x13-inch dish. Bake 15 minutes, let cool. When crust is cool, spread ½ filling over crust, then spread remaining can pineapple over mix. Then spread remaining cheese mixture over pineapple. Top with remaining Cool Whip. Sprinkle remaining pecans on top. Chill and eat.

## IMPOSSIBLE CHEESECAKE
Caroline Strain, Mason, OH

- **¾ cup milk**
- **2 teaspoons vanilla**
- **2 eggs**
- **1 cup sugar**
- **½ cup Bisquick mix**
- **2 8-ounce packages cream cheese, softened**

OVEN 350°

Place milk, vanilla, eggs, sugar, and Bisquick in blender. Cover and blend on high for 15 seconds. Add cream cheese. Cover, blend on high for 2 minutes. Pour into greased 9- or 10x14-inch pan. Bake until center is firm, about 40–45 minutes.

## PEACHES & CREAM CHEESECAKE
Ruth M. Benner, Northfield, NJ

- **¾ cup flour**
- **1 teaspoon baking powder**
- **3 tablespoons butter, softened**
- **1 egg**
- **½ cup milk**
- **1 package vanilla pudding mix (not instant)**
- **1 large can drained sliced peaches, reserve juice**
- **¾ cup sugar**
- **1½ 8-ounce packages cream cheese**
- **1 tablespoon sugar**
- **½ teaspoon cinnamon**

OVEN 350°

Combine flour, baking powder, butter, egg, milk, and vanilla pudding; pour into a greased, deep-dish pie plate. Arrange drained peach slices over batter. Combine sugar and cream cheese and 5 tablespoons juice; spoon within 1 inch of edge. Mix cinnamon and sugar and sprinkle on top. Bake for 30–35 minutes.

## LOW-FAT CHEESECAKE

Gale R. Jones, Creston, NC

**1/3 cup graham cracker crumbs**
**2 8-ounce cartons non-fat cream cheese**
**2/3 cup sugar**
**3 eggs (or ¾ cup egg substitute)**
**2 tablespoons almond extract**

OVEN 350°

Spray 9-inch pan with cooking spray. Sprinkle crumbs in pan (optional). Mix together cream cheese, sugar, eggs, and almond extract. Spread over crumbs. Bake for 30–35 minutes.

**Topping:**

**8 ounces non-fat sour cream**
**3 tablespoons sugar**
**1 teaspoon vanilla**

Combine topping ingredients and spread over baked cake. Return to oven for additional 10 minutes. Let cool.

Makes about 8–9 servings.

## VERY LOW-FAT CHEESECAKE

Tricia Kibbe, Grayling, MI

**1¼ cups crushed low-fat graham crackers**
**2 tablespoons sugar**
**3 tablespoons fat-free spread**
**2½ 8-ounce packages fat-free cream cheese**
**1 cup sugar**
**1 teaspoon lemon juice**
**¼ teaspoon vanilla**
**¾ cup egg substitute**
**1 can favorite fruit topping**

OVEN 350°

Mix crumbs, 2 tablespoons sugar, and fat-free spread. Spray 9-inch springform pan with cooking spray and press crumb mixture into bottom. Bake 10 minutes. Cool. Reheat oven to 300°. Beat cream cheese in large bowl. Gradually add sugar, beating until fluffy. Add lemon juice and vanilla. Beat in egg substitute, ¼ cup at a time. Pour over crumb mixture. Bake until center is firm, about 1 hour. Cool to room temperature. Loosen edges of cake from pan with knife before removing side of pan. Refrigerate at least 3 hours but no longer than 10 days. Top with favorite fruit topping!

## LOW-FAT, SUGAR-FREE CHEESECAKE

Paula Crocker, Cleburne, TX

**8-ounce package fat-free cream cheese**
**3 packages of Sweet-N-Low sweetener**
**1/3 cup lemon juice**
**½ teaspoon vanilla**
**8-ounce container fat-free Cool Whip**
**9-ounce fat-free graham cracker crust**

Mix softened cream cheese with Sweet-N-Low. Add lemon juice, mix, then add vanilla, mix well. Mix with Cool Whip and pour into graham cracker crust. Let set 45 minutes to 1 hour.

## MINIATURE CHEESECAKES

Julie Christenson, Fayetteville, NC

**2 eggs**
**2 8-ounce packages cream cheese**
**½ cup sugar**
**1 teaspoon vanilla extract**
**1 can cherry pie filling**

OVEN 350°

Beat first four ingredients until smooth. Line small muffin pans with paper liners. Fill each cup ¾ full with mixture. Bake for 15 minutes. When cool, top each with one cherry from can of cherry pie filling.

Makes approximately 48 servings.

# CAKES

## CRUMB CAKE

Carol J. Fisher, West Bend, WI

**2 cups brown sugar**
**¾ cup shortening**
**2½ cups flour**
**1 egg, beaten**
**1 cup sour milk or buttermilk**
**1 teaspoon baking soda**
**1 cup nuts**
**1 cup raisins**
**½ teaspoon ginger**
**½ teaspoon cinnamon**

OVEN 350°

Blend sugar, shortening, and flour until crumb consistency; set aside ½ cup for topping. Add remaining ingredients. Pour into 9x13-inch greased and floured pan. Put the ½ cup of dry mix on top. Bake 30 to 40 minutes.

## DONNA'S CRUMB CAKE

Donna Sunberg, Hudson, FL

**3 cups flour**
**1 cup shortening**
**1 cup sugar**

Mix into crumbs. Take out 1 cup crumbs and set aside for top.

**1 cup white sugar**
**2 whole eggs**
**1 teaspoon cloves**
**1 teaspoon cinnamon**
**1 teaspoon allspice**
**1 teaspoon nutmeg**
**½ teaspoon salt**
**1 teaspoon baking soda**
**1 pint buttermilk**

OVEN 350°

In another pan dissolve baking soda in buttermilk, add remaining ingredients. Stir well by hand. Pour into 9x13-inch dish. Sprinkle reserved cup of crumbs on top. Bake 45 minutes. Freezes well.

## LEMON CRUMB CAKE

Ida Mae Shown, Knoxville, TN

**1 package lemon cake mix**
**1 can sweetened condensed milk**
**9-ounce container frozen whipped topping**
**6-ounce can frozen lemonade, undiluted**
**7-ounce bag coconut**

Mix and bake cake, according to package directions, in a 9x13-inch pan; let cool. Crumble half of cake into a 9x13-inch pan. Blend together lemonade and condensed milk. Pour over crumbs in pan. Crumble remaining cake. Sprinkle and press down rest of crumbs over milk mixture. Spread whipped topping over all; sprinkle coconut on top. Keep in a cool place.

## APPLE CAKE

Jo Anne Swift, Osgood, IN

*"This recipe, as you can tell, is very simple to make, but my retarded 34-year-old son wanted me to send it in because he and his dad make it frequently. It is very good!"*

**1 box white cake mix**
**1 can prepared apple pie filling**

OVEN 350°

Prepare cake batter according to box instructions. Spread half of batter in bottom of 9x11-inch pan. Spoon pie filling over layer in pan. Cover filling with remainder of cake batter. Bake at 350° until knife comes out clean.

## EASY AND DELICIOUS APPLE CAKE

Judith Newton, Brazil, IN

**2 cups diced apples**
**1 cup sugar**
**1 egg**
**1 cup flour**
**1 teaspoon baking soda**
**Dash of salt**
**1½ teaspoons cinnamon**
**½ cup nuts**

OVEN 350°

Mix together apples and sugar, let stand. Add egg to apple mixture. Mix together dry ingredients and add to apple mixture. Add nuts. Bake 40 minutes at 350° in greased and floured 9-inch square pan.

## APPLE CAKE

Donna S. Brown, Murray, KY

**2 eggs**
**¼ cup shortening**
**1 teaspoon vanilla**
**1 cup sugar**
**1 cup flour**
**1 teaspoon baking soda**
**1 teaspoon cinnamon**
**4 diced apples**

OVEN 350°

Cream together eggs, shortening, vanilla, and flour. Sift three times, flour, soda, and cinnamon. Mix all ingredients together; add apples. Bake in moderate 350° oven until brown. May top with light powdered sugar icing. Nuts or raisins may be added to batter if desired.

## FRESH APPLE CAKE

Jennifer Forrester, Westville, OK
Doris Hilmer, Columbus, NE
Virginia Davis, Ooltewah, TN

**3 eggs, beaten**
**½ teaspoon salt**
**2 cups sugar**
**2 teaspoons vanilla**
**3 cups flour**
**1 teaspoon cinnamon**
**1½ cups oil**
**3–4 cups raw apples, diced fine**
**1 cup pecans**
**1 cup raisins (optional)**

**Topping:**
**¾ cup butter**
**1 cup sugar**
**1 cup evaporated milk**
**½ cup coconut**
**½ cup pecans**

OVEN 350°

Mix all ingredients except for topping in a large bowl. Bake for 30–45 minutes. Mix topping ingredients together. Boil milk and butter 8–10 minutes, add sugar and boil 8–10 minutes. Add coconut and pecans. Spread over warm cake.

## APPLE KUCHEN

Inona L. Coburn, Phoenix, AZ

**1 box yellow cake mix**
**½ cup butter or margarine**
**½ cup coconut**
**20-ounce can apple pie filling**
**¼ cup sugar**
**1 teaspoon cinnamon**
**1 cup sour cream**
**1 egg**

OVEN 350°

Cut butter into the cake mix. Add coconut. Mix. Pat lightly in ungreased 9x13-inch pan. Bake 10 minutes at 350°. Add apple slices, one slice at a time, onto the warm crust. Spread any remaining contents of the apple filling onto the crust top. Mix sugar and cinnamon; sprinkle on the apples. Bake 25 minutes more at 350°. Serve warm or cold.

## FRESH APPLE CAKE

Sharon Dunlap, Sumerco, WV

**2 cups sugar**
**1½ cups oil**
**3 eggs**
**3 cups self-rising flour**
**1 cup nuts**
**1 cup coconut**
**1 cup raisins**
**3 cups diced apples**

**Topping:**
**½ cup buttermilk**
**½ stick margarine**
**½ cup sugar**

OVEN 325°

Dust apples, coconut, raisins, and nuts with one cup flour, set aside. Blend oil, sugar, and eggs. Sift remaining flour and add to egg mixture, fold in apple mixture. Turn into 10-inch tube pan. Bake at 325° for 1 hour and 15 minutes. Topping: Boil ingredients rapidly for 2 minutes, stirring constantly. Pour over cake.

## RAW APPLE CAKE

Amy Armstrong, Pateros, WA
Christine Davis, Waterford, OH
Melodie Raposa, Santa Clara, CA

**1½ cups flour**
**½ teaspoon salt**
**1 teaspoon baking soda**
**1 teaspoon baking powder**
**1 teaspoon cinnamon**
**1 cup sugar**
**½ cup oil**
**½ cup milk**
**2 eggs**
**1 teaspoon vanilla**
**3 cups chopped raw apples**
**½ cup walnuts**

OVEN 350°

Sift dry ingredients. Mix with remaining ingredients until crumbly. Pat into a 9x13-inch pan. Bake at 350° for 40–45 minutes. Great for freezing. No icing necessary.

**Topping: (optional)**

**4 teaspoons oleo**
**½ cup brown sugar**
**1 teaspoon Crisco**
**2 teaspoons flour**
**½ cup nuts, chopped fine**

Mix together well. Spread over cake before baking.

Note: This recipe is for ripe apples. For tart apples use 2 teaspoons baking soda and no baking powder.

## BANANA CUPCAKES

Phyllis Johnson, Billings, MT

**1⅓ cups sugar**
**3 very ripe bananas**
**½ cup shortening**
**2 eggs**
**2 cups + 2 tablespoons flour**
**1 teaspoon baking soda**
**1 cup milk**
**1 teaspoon baking powder**
**1 teaspoon vanilla**

OVEN 350°

Cream sugar, bananas, shortening, and eggs until smooth. Add flour, baking powder, and baking soda, then milk. Beat 5 minutes. Fill paper muffin cups half full. Bake at 350° for 30 minutes until done.

## BLUSHING APPLE CAKE

Rosa Dietzler, Santa Rosa, CA

*"I got this from a Good Shepherd Craft Stitches Club and it has been one of my favorites ever since! Can eat as is, or top with ice cream or whipped topping."*

**1¼ cups flour**
**2 tablespoons sugar**
**1 teaspoon baking powder**
**1 egg, beaten**
**3-ounce package strawberry-flavored gelatin**
**1 tablespoon milk**
**½ teaspoon salt**
**½ cup shortening or butter**
**4 cups sliced apples**

**Topping:**
**1 cup flour**
**1 cup sugar**
**½ cup margarine**

OVEN 350°

Mix flour and 1 tablespoon sugar with baking powder and salt. Cream shortening or butter. Mix in dry ingredients. Combine beaten egg, milk, and add to shortening mixture. Press into greased 9x13-inch pan. Add sliced apples. Mix remaining tablespoon of sugar in gelatin, sprinkle over apples in pan. Topping: Mix topping ingredients until crumbs form. Sprinkle over cake.

## STRAWBERRY POP (SODA) CAKE

Orvella Suit, McAlester, OK

**1 yellow cake mix**
**1 can strawberry pop (soda)**
**1 small package strawberry gelatin**
**1 package vanilla instant pudding mix**
**1½ cups milk**
**1 large tub whipped topping**
**1 large container strawberries**

Prepare cake mix according to package directions. Punch holes in top of cake with meat fork, dissolve gelatin in pop and pour over cake. Pour strawberries and juice over cake. Mix pudding with milk. When pudding is firm mix with whipped topping and spread over cake.

## PINEAPPLE CAKE

Melody Walker, Maywood, NE
Louise Harman, Kenosha, WI
Arlene L. Wardwell, Calis, ME
Alice Seebart, Burns, OR
Maxine Weaver, Home, PA

**2 eggs, beaten**
**2 cups sugar**
**½ teaspoon salt**
**½ cup chopped nuts (pecans, walnuts)**
**2 tablespoons oil, optional**
**1 teaspoon vanilla**
**2 teaspoons baking soda**
**2 cups flour**
**20-ounce can crushed pineapple, with juice**

OVEN 350°

Beat eggs. Add sugar and oil. Sift flour and baking soda. Add alternately with pineapple. Stir in vanilla and nuts. Bake 30–45 minutes at 350° in 9x13-inch pan. Cool and frost.

**Frosting:**

**8-ounce cream cheese**
**½ cup shortening or butter**
**1 teaspoon vanilla**
**2 cups powdered sugar**
**½ cup chopped nuts, optional**

Beat all ingredients well; adding additional sugar if necessary to get proper spreading consistency.

**Topping variation:**

**½ cup butter**
**½ cup milk**
**1 cup sugar**
**1 teaspoon vanilla**

Boil five minutes and pour over cake while still hot.

## STRAWBERRY CAKE

Aretha Yates, Durant, FL

**1 box white cake mix**
**½ cup oil**
**3 eggs**
**1 small box strawberry gelatin**
**½ cup water, minus 2 tablespoons**
**½ cup mashed berries**

OVEN 350°

Mix together all ingredients, pour into greased 9x13-inch pan and bake at 350° for 25–30 minutes.

**Icing:**

**1 box confectioners' sugar**
**1 stick butter, softened**
**½ cup mashed berries**

Beat together all ingredients and frost cooled cake.

## FROSTED APPLE SHEET CAKE

Marietta Eash, Utica, OH

*"It's our family's favorite cake recipe!"*

**2 cups sugar**
**2 eggs**
**3 cups unsifted flour**
**1 cup vegetable oil**
**4 cups finely chopped apples**
**1 teaspoon salt**
**2 teaspoons vanilla**
**2 teaspoons cinnamon**
**2 teaspoons baking soda**
**½ cup nuts (optional)**
**½ cup raisins (optional)**

OVEN 350°

Combine sugar and eggs with mixer; add vegetable oil, mix well. Add dry ingredients, apples, nuts, and raisins (optional). Bake in large greased and floured cookie sheet at 350° for 35–45 minutes.

**Cream Cheese Frosting:**

**8 ounces cream cheese, room temperature**
**½ cup shortening, softened**
**1 pound powdered sugar**
**1 teaspoon vanilla**

Mix cream cheese, shortening, and vanilla together; then add powdered sugar. Spread on cooled cake.

## LEMON CAKE PIE

Maxine Weaver, Home, PA

*"I used to bake this pie in a baking dish without the crust and took it for our dessert when we were delivering dressed chickens at Pittsburgh stores in the 1950s."*

**1 cup sugar**
**3 tablespoons flour**
**3 tablespoons butter**
**2 eggs, separated**
**Juice and rind of 1 lemon**
**1 cup milk**
**1 unbaked pie shell**

OVEN 350°

Cream sugar, flour, and butter, stir in beaten egg yolks. Add lemon juice, rind, and milk slowly. Beat egg whites and fold into mixture. Pour into unbaked pie shell and bake in 350° oven for 30 minutes or until firm.

## LEMON NUT CAKE

Alma Williamson, Randleman, NC

**1 pound butter**
**2 cups sugar**
**6 eggs, separated**
**1 teaspoon baking powder dissolved in 1 tablespoon water**
**3 cups flour**
**1 quart pecans**
**1 pound white raisins**
**2 ounces lemon extract**

OVEN 250°

Cream butter and sugar, add egg yolks and dissolved baking powder. Combine flour, nuts, and raisins. Add this mixture to creamed mixture; then add lemon extract. Beat egg whites until stiff. Fold into mixture. Bake in large tube pan lined with wax paper for 2 hours and 45 minutes at 250° in a pan of water under the tube pan.

## BANANA SPLIT CAKE

Virginia James, Lexington, NC
Betty Crawford, Fort Gay, WV

**2 cups graham cracker crumbs**
**1 stick butter, softened**
**1/4 cup sugar**
**2 egg whites**
**2 cups powdered sugar**
**1 stick butter, melted**
**3 bananas, sliced**
**20-ounce can crushed pineapple, reserve juice**
**12 ounces whipped topping**
**1 small jar sliced cherries, drained and halved**
**Nuts (optional)**

Use stand mixer to beat egg whites, powdered sugar, and softened butter for 18 minutes. In the meantime, mix crumbs, melted butter, and sugar. Place this crumb mixture in a deep casserole dish. When 18 minutes are completed, put on top of crumb mixture. Arrange bananas for the next layer. Place pineapple on top of bananas and whipped topping on top of pineapple. Sprinkle with nuts and top with halved cherries.

Note: Soak bananas in pineapple juice to keep them from turning brown.

# CAKES

## CHERRY NUT CAKE
Leota Henderson, El Cajon, CA

**⅔ cup shortening**
**2 cups sugar**
**3 cups cake flour**
**3 teaspoons baking powder**
**½ teaspoon salt**
**1 teaspoon vanilla**
**½ teaspoon almond extract**
**5 egg whites, beaten**
**½ cup chopped maraschino cherries, with juice**
**½ cup chopped nut meats**
**½ cup milk**

OVEN 350°

Cream together shortening and sugar. Sift together flour, baking powder, and salt; add alternately with ½ cup maraschino cherry juice and milk. Add vanilla and almond extract. Fold in beaten egg whites. Add chopped cherries and nuts. Pour into three 9-inch layer pans. Bake at 350° for 35 minutes. Very good with fluffy white frosting.

## CHERRY SPICE CAKE
Kathy McKinney, El Dorado, AR

**2 cups sugar**
**3 cups flour**
**1 cup butter or oil**
**1 teaspoon baking soda**
**2 eggs**
**1 cup dried apples (cooked and sweetened)**
**1 cup nuts**
**1 cup cherries**
**1 teaspoon allspice**
**1 teaspoon cloves**
**1 teaspoon vanilla**
**1 teaspoon cinnamon**
**1 teaspoon baking powder**
**1 cup buttermilk**

OVEN 325°

Cream sugar and butter. Add eggs and beat together. Add apples. Sift dry ingredients together and add alternately with buttermilk. Flour cherries and nuts and fold in. Cook about 1 hour.

## BLUEBERRY BUCKLE CAKE
Crystal Shaffer, Middleburg, PA

**½ cup butter**
**1 cup sugar**
**2 eggs**
**4 cups sifted flour**
**4 teaspoons baking powder**
**1 teaspoon salt**
**1 cup milk**
**4 cups washed fresh blueberries**

Mix all together. Add topping:

**½ cup soft butter**
**¾ cup sugar**
**⅔ cup flour**
**1 teaspoon cinnamon**

OVEN 375°

Mix together and sprinkle over top of cake. Bake at 375° for 50 minutes.

## WEARY WILLIE BLUEBERRY CAKE

Kristin Powell, Canton, MA

**1½ cups flour**
**1 cup sugar**
**2 teaspoons baking powder**
**½ teaspoon salt**
**1 cup blueberries**
**⅓ cup shortening, melted**
**1 egg**
**Milk**
**1 teaspoon vanilla extract**
**2 tablespoons sugar**
**Cinnamon**

OVEN 350°

Sift together flour, sugar, baking powder, and salt. Put blueberries in flour mixture and stir. Put shortening in a one-cup measure and add egg, fill cup to top with milk. Add to flour and blueberries. Mix well, gently. Add vanilla. Pour into greased and floured 8x8-inch square pan, sprinkle top with sugar and cinnamon mixture. Bake at 350° for about 35 minutes.

## PEACH CAKE

Betty L Faris, Rochester Hill, MI

**1 stick margarine**
**2 cups sugar**
**2 eggs**
**2 cups flour**
**1 teaspoon baking soda**
**1 teaspoon baking powder**
**1 teaspoon cinnamon**
**1 large can peaches, drained and cut small**

OVEN 350°

Cream shortening, sugar, and eggs. In another bowl mix flour, baking soda, baking powder, and cinnamon. Mix with creamed ingredients, add peaches. Bake at 350° for 35 minutes.

**Icing:**

**½ cup sugar**
**½ cup evaporated milk**
**1 stick shortening**
**1 teaspoon vanilla**

Cook until thick, cool down a little, and spread on cool cake.

## EASY PEACH CAKE

Lana Yerkes, West Grove, PA

**29-ounce can peaches, cut up, with juice**
**1 yellow cake mix**
**1 small bag of walnuts (1 cup chopped)**
**1 stick butter or margarine, melted**

OVEN 350°

Place peaches in ungreased 8x12-inch baking pan or long oven-safe glass dish, juice and all. Sprinkle cake mix on top of peaches and juice in the pan. Sprinkle nuts on top of mixture. Melt butter or margarine and dribble on top. Bake at 350° for 1 hour.

## MANDARIN ORANGE CAKE

Lisa J. Vice, Fremont, IN

*"It is one of the best cakes you'll ever eat!"*

**1 butter cake mix**
**11-ounce can mandarin oranges, with juice**
**4 eggs**
**½ cup corn oil**

OVEN 325°

Mix together cake mix, mandarin oranges with juice, eggs, and shortening. Pour into two 9-inch round cake pans, floured and greased. Bake in 325° oven for 30 minutes or longer if necessary.

**Topping:**

**12 ounces whipped topping**
**1 small instant vanilla pudding mix**
**20-ounce can crushed pineapple, with juice**

Whip together, spread on bottom layer then place other round cake on top and finish putting topping on top and sides.

## ORANGE SLICE CAKE

Birdie Etchison, Ocean Park, WA

*"This is good! This recipe is great for Christmas substitutes for fruitcake which my family does not enjoy."*

**Editor's Note:** Birdie has written several books for the Heartsong Presents series, including *The Heart Has Its Reasons* and *Albert's Destiny.* She loves to research family history and her findings are often part of her stories.

Celeste Harper, Cadiz, KY

*"This cake recipe has been in my family for a very long time. This is a good holiday cake so I hope you'll enjoy it as much as I do."*

**3½ cups flour**
**½ teaspoon salt**
**1 pound orange slice candy, cut up**
**2 cups pecans**
**8-ounce package chopped dates (optional)**
**1 cup flaked coconut**
**1 cup butter**
**2 cups sugar**
**4 eggs**
**1 teaspoon baking soda**
**½ cup buttermilk**

**Topping:**

**1 cup orange juice**
**2 cups powdered sugar, sifted**

OVEN 300°

Mix together orange juice and powdered sugar. Set aside. Use ½ cup of flour to toss and coat evenly the orange slices, nuts, and coconut. Set aside. Cream butter and sugar together. Add eggs, one at a time, beating well after each addition. Combine baking soda and buttermilk. Add alternately with flour and salt. Add floured candy mixture. Mix well. Spoon into greased and floured 10-inch tube pan. Bake until inserted toothpick comes out clean. When done, remove from oven and immediately pour the topping over hot cake. Let stand overnight before removing from pan.

## SUNNY ORANGE CAKE

Joan Waldron, Sand Creek, MI

**1 package yellow cake mix**
**1 package lemon instant pudding**
**¾ cup water**
**¾ cup oil**
**4 eggs**

**Icing:**

**2 cups powdered sugar**
**⅓ cup orange juice**
**2 tablespoons warm water**
**2 tablespoons melted butter**

OVEN 325°

Blend dry cake mix and pudding mix. Add water slowly. Then add shortening. Add eggs, one at a time. Mix on high speed. Pour into 8x12-inch pan. Bake at 325° for 35–40 minutes. Prick hot cake with fork in many places. Mix together the four icing ingredients. Drizzle icing over warm cake.

## FIG CAKE

Virginia Lear, London, Ky

**1½ cups sugar**
**1 cup vegetable oil**
**1 teaspoon baking soda**
**½ teaspoon cloves**
**1 cup fig preserves**
**1 cup pecans, chopped**
**3 eggs, beaten**
**2 cups flour**
**1 cup buttermilk**
**1 tablespoon vanilla**

OVEN 325°

Add sugar to eggs and mix well. Add oil. Sift dry ingredients. Combine sugar and egg mixtures. Add preserves, pecans and vanilla. Bake in greased tube pan for 1 hour at 325°. May use whipped cream or plain.

## APRICOT PRESERVE CAKE

Mauree Moore, Pampa, TX

**2 cups sugar**
**2 sticks margarine, softened**
**4 eggs**
**1 cup apricot preserves**
**1 cup buttermilk**
**1 teaspoon baking soda**
**1 teaspoon cinnamon**
**3 cups flour**
**1 cup chopped pecans**
**8-ounce package chopped dried apricots**

OVEN 325°

Cream sugar and margarine, add eggs one at a time, beat thoroughly after each addition. Add preserves and blend. Dissolve baking soda in buttermilk. Sift flour and cinnamon and add to creamed mixture alternately with buttermilk. Stir in pecans and apricots. Pour into a greased and floured bundt pan. Bake at 325° for 1 to 1¼ hours. Cool only a few minutes before removing from pan.

## BLACKBERRY SPICE CAKE

Glenna Keisler, Huntington, WV

*"I don't like to cook or bake, but this cake is so simple, even I can do it! It's a favorite at our church luncheons and dinners."*

**1 can blackberry pie filling (I prefer Thank You or Lucky Leaf brand)**
**1 box spice cake mix (I prefer Duncan Hines mixes)**
**4 eggs**

OVEN 350°

Grease and flour 9x13-inch cake pan. Mix ingredients until well mixed. Pour into cake pan. Bake for 40–45 minutes. Top with vanilla or sour cream icing if so desired.

## DARK FRUITCAKE

Madeline Carter, Brooklin, ME

**½ cup molasses**
**½ cup raisins**
**½ cup prepared coffee**
**2 cups flour**
**½ cup butter or shortening**
**3 eggs**
**1 cup brown sugar**
**¼ teaspoon allspice**
**¼ teaspoon cinnamon**
**¼ teaspoon cloves**
**1 teaspoon baking soda**
**½ teaspoon nutmeg**
**1 cup fruit flavored nuts**

OVEN 350°

Beat eggs, brown sugar, butter or shortening, molasses, and cool coffee. Sift dry ingredients. Add to mixture. Fold in fruit last. Beat 3 minutes. Flour and grease pan (size your preference). Bake at 350° for 1 hour or until done.

## CRANBERRY SAUCE CAKE

Virginia Chaffin, Huntington, WV

*"I use a tube or bundt pan and arrange pecan halves on the top."*

**1½ cups whole cranberry sauce**
**1 cup mayonnaise**
**Grated rind of 1 orange**
**⅓ cup orange juice**
**1 cup chopped nuts**
**3 cups sifted flour**
**1½ cups sugar**
**1 teaspoon baking soda**
**1 teaspoon salt**

OVEN 350°

Mix together and bake at 350° until cake is done, about 1 hour 15 minutes. Cool, frost.

**Frosting:**

**2 tablespoons margarine**
**2 cups confectioners' sugar**
**¼ cup whole cranberry sauce**

Cream together margarine and sugar, add cranberry sauce. Beat until very creamy.

## GUMDROP FRUITCAKE

Carol J. Fisher, West Bend, WI

*"This recipe is nice for those who don't like the usual sweet fruits and rinds used in fruit-cake. It looks like a stained glass window!"*

**1 cup shortening**
**2 eggs, beaten**
**½ teaspoon salt**
**1 pound gum drops, no black**
**1 pound white raisins**
**2½ to 3 cups flour**
**1½ cups sugar**
**1 cup applesauce**
**1½ teaspoons baking soda**
**1 cup walnuts, broken**
**1 teaspoon vanilla**

OVEN 350°

Cream shortening; add sugar and beaten eggs. Add baking soda to applesauce and salt, add to mixture. Add gum drops, raisins, broken walnuts, vanilla, and flour. Mix well. Put in 2 medium bread tins or 3 small greased pans, line bottom with wax paper. Bake at 350° for 1 hour.

## FRUIT COCKTAIL CAKE

Bernice Libby, Elsworth, ME

*"This was a favorite recipe from the Farm Bureau in Aroostook County, Maine, many years ago, but is still popular wherever it is used, both for ease of preparation and for taste. It is yummy!"*

**1 beaten egg**
**1 #2-can fruit cocktail, and juice**
**1¼ cups flour**
**1 cup sugar**
**1 teaspoon baking soda**
**½ teaspoon salt**
**½ cup brown sugar**
**½ cup nut meats**

OVEN 350°

Combine cake ingredients. Combine brown sugar and nut meats; sprinkle on top of cake ingredients before baking. Bake in a 9x9-inch pan at 350° for 40 minutes. Serve warm or cold with whipped cream or ice cream.

## EASY FRUITCAKE

Ruth Ann Yaun, Oregon, WI

**1 egg**
**1 cup warm water**
**1 package of (Pillsbury) bread mix, date, nut, cranberry, or your choice**
**1 cup chopped walnuts**
**1 cup raisins**
**1 package fruitcake mix**

OVEN 350°

Stir all together. Stir until mixture is well blended. Put into 9x5-inch greased loaf pans. Bake at 350° for 65 to 70 minutes.

Makes 2 loaves.

## FESTIVE FRUITCAKE

Barbara League, Fremont, NE

*"If you don't like citrus peel in fruitcake. . ."*

**2 eggs**
**2 cups water**
**¼ cup oil**
**2 packages date bread mix (Pillsbury)**
**2 cups pecans, finely chopped**
**2 cups raisins**
**2 cups (1 red, 1 green) candied cherries**
**1 cup bananas**
**1 can of fruit cocktail, drained**

OVEN 350°

Combine eggs, water, and oil. Combine date bread mix, pecans, raisins, cherries, fruit cocktail, and bananas; add to egg mixture. Bake at 350° in greased and floured bundt pan for 75 to 85 minutes, until tests done. Cool in pan 30 minutes, loosen edges and remove from pan. Cool completely, wrap in plastic wrap or foil. Refrigerate 2 weeks or freeze for up to 3 months. Glaze with warm corn syrup before serving. Decorate with frosting, candied cherries, and nuts.

## HOLLYDAY CAKE

Maxine J. Peters, Merlin, OR

**2 cups sifted flour**
**2 teaspoons baking soda**
**½ teaspoon salt**
**½ teaspoon cinnamon**
**¼ teaspoon cloves**
**1½ cups applesauce**
**1 egg**
**1 teaspoon vanilla**
**1 cup seedless raisins**
**1 cup mixed candied fruit**
**½ cup butter or margarine**
**1 cup sugar**

OVEN 325°

Sift together flour, baking soda, salt, and spices. Combine ½ cup of this with fruits and nuts. Cream butter and sugar. Stir in egg, vanilla, and applesauce. Add dry ingredients gradually, mix well. Stir in fruit and nuts. Pour into a greased cake pan or loaf pan. Bake in a slow oven at 325° for 1½ hours. Cool and decorate.

## EASY-TO-PLEASE FRUITCAKE

Margaret Tackett, Fayetteville, AR

*"A friend got this recipe from her uncle and gave it to me about four years ago. It has become our favorite cake for the holidays. It is so easy to make and people that don't usually like fruitcake love this one!"*

**1 pound pitted dates, cut in small pieces and softened**
**8 ounces candied pineapple, chopped**
**8 ounces candied cherries, chopped**
**3 cups pecans, chopped**
**1 cup sifted flour**
**1 cup sugar**
**1 teaspoon baking powder**
**¼ teaspoon salt**
**4 well-beaten eggs**
**1 teaspoon vanilla**

OVEN 325°

Mix all ingredients well. Place in paper-lined angel food cake pan. Bake at 325° approximately 1½ hours, or until done.

## RHUBARB CAKE

Carolyn Taylor, Grimes, IA

**3 tablespoons butter, melted**
**½ cup sugar**
**Few drops red food coloring**
**1 pound rhubarb, finely diced**
**1 package (1 layer size) white cake mix**

OVEN 375°

Combine butter, sugar, and food coloring. Add rhubarb, toss lightly; spread in 8x12-inch pan. Prepare cake mix using package directions; pour over fruit. Bake at 375° for about 35 minutes or until done. Immediately run spatula around edge of pan and invert onto serving plate. Before lifting off pan, let syrup drain onto cake for 3 to 5 minutes. Cut warm. Top with whipped cream.

## RHUBARB UPSIDE-DOWN CAKE

Julia A. Crowder, Gaffney, SC

**5 cups diced rhubarb**
**1 to 1½ cups sugar**
**1 small package raspberry or strawberry gelatin**
**3 cups miniature marshmallows**
**1 package yellow, strawberry, or cherry cake mix**

OVEN 350°

Cut rhubarb and put in greased 9x13-inch cake pan. Sprinkle sugar and dry gelatin on rhubarb. Top with marshmallows. Prepare cake mix as directed on package; spread evenly over rhubarb mix. Bakc at 350° for 50 minutes or until done. Cool 10 to 15 minutes then turn out upside down onto tray. Serve warm with whipped cream.

## CARROT CAKE

Irene A. Martin, Ely, MN

*"This recipe is 35 years old!"*

**1¾ cups plain flour**
**¼ teaspoon salt**
**½ teaspoon baking soda**
**1½ cups sugar**
**1 teaspoon cinnamon**
**½ teaspoon nutmeg**
**3 eggs**
**1 cup corn oil**
**1 cup grated carrots**
**1 cup grated pecans**

OVEN 350°

Sift all dry ingredients. Add eggs and oil, mix well and add carrots and pecans. Mix well and bake in tube pan at 350° for 55 minutes.

## PINEAPPLE-COCONUT CARROT CAKE

Diane Baxter, Ely, MN
Ruth Kowalewski, Nichols, NY
Carol Catledge, Glennallen, AK

**1 cup oil**
**1½–2 cups sugar**
**3 eggs (4 if small)**
**2 cups flour**
**2 teaspoons baking soda**
**½ teaspoon salt**
**2 teaspoons cinnamon**
**1 cup crushed pineapple**
**2 cups shredded carrots**
**1 cup flaked coconut**
**1 cup chopped nuts**
**1 teaspoon vanilla**
**1 cup raisins (optional)**

OVEN 350°

Mix oil, sugar, and eggs. Add remaining ingredients. Pour into 9x13-inch pan and bake for 50 minutes at 350°.

**Frosting:**

**½ cup soft butter or margarine**
**8-ounce package cream cheese**
**2 cups powdered sugar**
**2 teaspoons vanilla**
**1 cup chopped nuts**

Cream first four ingredients with electric mixer. Fold in nuts. Spread on cooled cake.

## PUMPKIN CAKE

Ruth McDonald, Front Royal, VA

**1 package yellow cake mix**
**½ cup salad oil**
**¼ to ½ cup water**
**4 eggs, beaten**
**1 can pumpkin**
**Dash of nutmeg**
**1 teaspoon cinnamon**
**½ to ¾ cup sugar**

OVEN 350°

Mix ingredients in order given; beat with mixer for about 3 minutes. Pour into greased tube pan. Bake at 350° for 1 hour and 10 minutes.

## PUMPKIN BUNDT CAKE

Barbara Fox, Hampton, SC

**3 cups flour**
**½ teaspoon salt**
**2 teaspoons baking powder**
**¼ teaspoon baking soda**
**2 teaspoons allspice**
**1 teaspoon cinnamon**
**1 cup salad oil**
**3 cups sugar**
**3 large eggs**
**16-ounce can pumpkin**

OVEN 350°

In a mixer bowl blend salad oil and sugar thoroughly. Add eggs, one at a time, beating well after each addition. Add pumpkin and mix thoroughly. Turn mixer to lowest speed and blend in dry ingredients. Pour into greased and floured 10-inch tube pan. Bake for 1 hour. Make a glaze or frosting of confectioners' sugar and water; drizzle over cake.

## PUMPKIN PIE CAKE

Doris Thomas, Festus, MO

- **4 eggs, beaten**
- **1½ cups sugar**
- **1 box yellow cake mix**
- **15-ounce can pumpkin**
- **12-ounce Milnot non-dairy canned milk**
- **1 cup chopped pecans**
- **2 teaspoons pumpkin pie spice**
- **1 teaspoon salt**
- **2 sticks shortening, melted**
- **Pecans**

OVEN 350°

Mix pumpkin, eggs, sugar, salt, spice, and Milnot. Pour into ungreased 9x13-inch pan. Sprinkle cake mix over filling. Pour melted shortening over top of cake mix. Sprinkle with pecans. Bake at 350° for 1 to 1½ hours or until knife comes out clean when inserted in center. Cut into squares. Serve warm or cold with or without topping (whipped topping, or whipped cream).

## PUMPKIN CAKE

Darlene Jackson, Utica, KY

*"Excellent for fall and holiday baking!"*

- **2 cups sugar**
- **1-pound can pumpkin**
- **1 cup vegetable oil**
- **4 eggs, beaten**
- **2 cups all-purpose flour**
- **1 teaspoon salt**
- **2 teaspoons baking soda**
- **2 teaspoons baking powder**
- **2 teaspoons cinnamon**
- **½ cup coconut**
- **½ cup pecans**

OVEN 350°

Combine sugar, pumpkin, oil, and eggs; beat 1 minute. Separately combine next 5 ingredients. Add to pumpkin mixture. Beat until smooth and creamy. Stir in coconut and pecans. Pour into three 8-inch greased pans. Bake at 350° for 25–30 minutes.

**Frosting:**

- **½ cup softened butter**
- **8 ounces cream cheese**
- **1 pound powdered sugar**
- **2 teaspoons vanilla**
- **½ cup coconut**
- **½ cup pecans**

Combine butter and cream cheese. Beat until light and fluffy. Add sugar and vanilla, mix well. Stir in coconut and pecans. Stack and frost cooled layers.

## PUMPKIN PIE CAKE

Addie Davis, East Millinicket, ME
Jean McRae, Cut Bank, MT

**1 box yellow cake mix (remove 1 cup for topping)**
**1 stick melted shortening or ½ cup oil**
**2 eggs, beaten**

OVEN 350°

To cake mix add melted shortening or oil and beaten eggs. Mix well and press into pan, as a pie crust.

**Filling:**
**1 large can pumpkin**
**3 eggs**
**½ cup light brown sugar & ¼ cup white sugar (or 1 cup white sugar)**
**⅔ cup milk**
**1½ teaspoons cinnamon**
**½ teaspoon nutmeg**

Mix and spread over crust.

**Topping:**
**1 cup reserved cake mix**
**½ cup sugar**
**½ cup nuts**
**½ stick shortening**

Mix ingredients together and drop on top. Bake at 350° for 55 minutes or longer.

## SWEET POTATO CRISP

Janet Adkins, Greensboro, NC

**2 cups sweet potatoes**
**1 can evaporated milk**
**1 cup sugar**
**½ teaspoon cinnamon**
**3 eggs**
**1 box yellow cake mix**
**1 cup chopped nuts**
**2 sticks butter (melted)**

OVEN 325°

Line 9x13 pan with wax paper. Mix potatoes, milk, sugar, eggs, and cinnamon. Pour on wax paper. Spread dry cake mix evenly over mixture. Put nuts over mix. Pour melted butter on top. Bake 50–60 minutes. Turn cake onto plate or board. Peel off wax paper, completely cool. Frost.

**Frosting:**
**8 ounces cream cheese**
**¾ cup whipped topping**
**2 cups powdered sugar**

## NANNY'S POUND CAKE

JoAnn Klutts, Groves, TX

**2 cups sugar**
**2 cups flour**
**6 eggs, large**
**2 sticks butter, softened**
**1 teaspoon vanilla**
**½ teaspoon lemon juice (optional)**
**Nuts (optional)**

OVEN 325°

Add sugar and flour into butter. Beat with electric mixer, add one egg at a time, beating about 2 minutes each. Batter is thick. Add nuts if desired. Spray tube pan with non-stick spray, sprinkle with sugar. Put batter in tube pan. Bake at 325° for 1 hour. Can be served with lemon sauce or ice cream.

## BLACKBERRY WINE POUND CAKE

Irene A. Martin, Greensboro, NC

**1 white cake mix**
**4 eggs**
**1 cup corn oil**
**1 box blackberry gelatin**
**1 cup blackberry wine**

OVEN 325°

Mix cake and dry gelatin, add eggs, oil, and wine; beat mixture until smooth. Bake in bundt pan at 325° for 40–50 minutes. Let set 5–8 minutes then turn out onto plate and glaze. (Mixture very thin and runny!)

**Glaze:**

**1½ cups powdered sugar**
**4 to 5 tablespoons blackberry wine**

Stir together until smooth. Spoon over hot cake.

## BLACK WALNUT POUND CAKE

Gail Hobelman, Easley, SC

**½ pound butter**
**½ cup shortening**
**3 cups sugar**
**5 eggs**
**2½ teaspoons vanilla flavoring**
**3 cups cake flour**
**1 teaspoon baking powder**
**1 cup milk**
**1 cup chopped black walnuts**

OVEN 325°

Cream together butter, shortening, sugar, and eggs. Flour nuts and add them and rest of ingredients to creamed mixture; mix well. Bake at 325° for 1 hour and 20 minutes.

## MILLIE'S POUND CAKE

Dorothy Abshier, Gentry, AR

*"I was given this recipe by my friend, Mildred. Because I frequently forget to preheat the oven, this was the perfect recipe for me. Also, it is delicious."*

**3 sticks margarine**
**3 cups sugar**
**3 cups flour**
**6 eggs**
**12 ounces cream cheese**
**1 teaspoon vanilla flavoring**
**½ teaspoon almond flavoring**
**½ teaspoon anise flavoring**

OVEN 300°

Cream margarine, sugar, and cheese until fluffy. Add eggs one at a time; then flavorings and flour. Beat well after adding each ingredient. Place in cold oven and bake 1½ hours at 300°.

## BANANA POUND CAKE

Esther W. Fearins, Preston, MD

**1 box yellow cake mix, any brand**
**1 package instant vanilla pudding**
**1 teaspoon cinnamon**
**½ teaspoon nutmeg**
**4 eggs**
**⅓ cup oil**
**½ cup water**
**1⅓ cups very ripe, mashed bananas**

OVEN 350°

Beat well the egg, oil, and water; then add dry ingredients. Last add mashed bananas. Bake in a large bundt pan or five mini pans at 350° until tests done. Freezes very well and is moist.

## 7-UP® POUND CAKE

Billie Chisholm, West Lake, LA

**2 sticks margarine**
**½ cup yellow shortening**
**3 cups sugar**
**5 eggs**
**1 teaspoon vanilla**
**3 cups all-purpose flour**
**1 teaspoon salt**
**1 cup 7-Up**

OVEN 325°

Cream margarine and shortening, add sugar and cream. Add eggs, one at a time, and vanilla. Add flour slowly and salt. Add 7-Up. Bake in greased and floured angel food cake pan at 325° for 1 hour until tests done. Will stay fresh for at least one week or longer if covered.

## BLUEBERRY POUND CAKE

Charlene Wilson, Mathiston, MS

**1 butter flavor cake mix**
**3 eggs**
**½ cup oil**
**8 ounces cream cheese**
**2 cups fresh or frozen blueberries**

OVEN 350°

Cream the cheese. Add other ingredients except blueberries and mix well. Fold in the berries. Bake in a sprayed bundt or tube pan at 350° until done. Cool in pan 5 minutes. Turn out onto plate. You may glaze with powdered sugar glaze, or not, as you prefer.

## BROWNIE CAKE

**1 cup water**
**4 tablespoons cocoa**
**2 cubes margarine**
**2 cups sugar**
**2 cups flour**
**1 teaspoon baking soda**
**Dash of salt**
**2 eggs, beaten**
**½ cup buttermilk**

OVEN 350°

Bring water, cocoa, and margarine to a boil. Mix remaining ingredients into margarine mixture. Beat 2 minutes. Pour into greased and floured 9x13-inch pan. Bake for 40–45 minutes.

**Frosting:**

**½ cup margarine**
**3 tablespoons cocoa**
**3 tablespoons milk**
**1 pound powdered sugar (approx.)**

Bring ingredients to a boil. Add sugar.

## MUDSLIDE CAKE

Julie Darby, Kansas City, MO

**1 chocolate cake mix**
**1 can Eagle brand milk**
**6 ounces SKOR baking pieces**
**1 jar hot fudge ice cream topping**
**1 small container Cool Whip**

Prepare and bake chocolate cake per cake instructions, in 9x13-inch pan. While cake is still hot, poke holes all over it with wooden spoon handle. Drizzle entire can of milk into holes. Sprinkle with SKOR cooking pieces. Spread jar of hot fudge topping over entire cake. Cool cake in refrigerator. One to four hours before serving spread small container of Cool Whip on top.

## HEATH BAR CAKE

Becky Orten, Dawson Springs, KY
Vera Villinger, Newark, OH

*"This recipe was given to me by my niece. It is so sweet and so rich. It costs around $10.00 to make."*

**1 box German chocolate cake mix**
**1 can sweetened condensed milk**
**1 jar caramel ice cream topping**
**8-ounce tub of whipped topping**
**3–6 Heath bars, crushed**

Bake cake according to package directions. While cake is still hot, poke holes in cake about one inch apart, using the handle of a wooden spoon. Pour sweetened condensed milk and ice cream topping mixture over cake, making sure cake is completely covered. Refrigerate overnight. When serving, garnish with whipped topping and sprinkle with Heath bar crumbs.

Note: You can easily crush the candy bars by freezing them first, then breaking them with a hammer.

## MISSISSIPPI MUD CAKE

Johnnie Beck, Stillwater, OK

**2 cups sugar**
**4 eggs**
**⅓ cup cocoa**
**1 cup pecans**
**1 cup Crisco**
**1½ cups flour**
**3 teaspoons vanilla**
**¼ teaspoon salt**
**7 ounces marshmallow cream**

OVEN 350°

Cream sugar and Crisco, add eggs one at a time. Sift flour, salt, cocoa, and add to creamed mixture. Mix and add nuts, and vanilla. Bake at 350° for 30 minutes in 9x13-inch pan. Put marshmallow cream on as soon as it comes out of the oven. Cool. Ice.

**Frosting:**

**2 sticks oleo (not melted)**
**⅓ cup cocoa**
**1 box powdered sugar**
**1 teaspoon vanilla**
**½ cup nuts**
**¼ cup canned milk**

Mix and put on cake. Keep refrigerated.

## CHOCOLATE FUDGE UPSIDE-DOWN CAKE

Brenda Thompson, Rogers, AR

**2 tablespoons shortening**
**1 cup milk**
**1 teaspoon salt**
**2 teaspoons baking powder**
**1½ cup sugar**
**2 cups flour**
**1 teaspoon vanilla**
**3 tablespoons cocoa**

**Topping:**
**2 cups sugar**
**½ cup cocoa**
**2½ cups boiling water**

OVEN 375°

Mix together all ingredients and place in cake pan; sprinkle with nuts if desired. Set aside. Topping: Mix sugar with cocoa and spread over batter in the pan. Then pour boiling water over top. Bake 30 minutes at 375°.

## OATMEAL CHOCOLATE CHIP CAKE

Diane Flicker, The Woodlands, TX
Donna Lea Magner, Peoria, IL

**1¾ cups boiling water**
**1 cup uncooked oatmeal**
**1 cup brown sugar**
**1 cup sugar**
**½ cup margarine**
**2 eggs or 3 small eggs**
**¾ cup walnuts, chopped**
**1¾ cups flour**
**1 teaspoon baking soda**
**½ teaspoon salt**
**1 tablespoon cocoa**
**1 cup chocolate chips**
**¾ cup nuts (optional)**

OVEN 350°

Pour boiling water over oatmeal; let stand at room temperature for 10 minutes. Add both sugars and margarine to oatmeal. Stir with spoon until margarine melts. Add eggs and mix well. Add flour, baking soda, salt, and cocoa stirring until well blended. Add half of chocolate chips. Pour batter into greased 9x13-inch pan. Sprinkle chopped nuts and rest of chocolate chips on top. Bake at 350° for 40 minutes. Needs no other frosting.

## NO-FAT CHOCOLATE CAKE

Deborah Gallaway, Belen, NM

**3 cups flour**
**2 cups sugar**
**6 tablespoons cocoa**
**2 teaspoons baking soda**
**2 teaspoons vanilla**
**2 tablespoons vinegar**
**2 cups water**
**1 teaspoon salt**
**¾ cup applesauce or no-fat mayonnaise**

OVEN 350°

Preheat oven to 350°. Mix all ingredients together well. Beat for 10 minutes. Pour into a 9x13-inch greased and floured pan. Bake for 30 minutes or until done. Frost as desired.

## OATMEAL CAKE

Marlene Young, McMinnville, TN
Diana Tourtillott, Canton, IL
Mary Jo Biers, Somerset, KY

*"This was my grandmother's. I have to make it for all of my family gatherings."*

**1 cup oats**
**1¼ cups boiling water**
**½ cup butter**
**1 cup brown sugar**
**1 cup white sugar**
**2 eggs (can use 1 egg and 2 whites)**
**1 teaspoon baking soda**
**1⅓ cups flour**
**½ teaspoon cinnamon**
**½ teaspoon salt**
**½ teaspoon nutmeg**

OVEN 350°

Combine rolled oats and boiling water; let cool. Beat the butter into oatmeal and water mixture. Combine both sugars, and add to oatmeal mixture, beating well. Add eggs and beat well. Sift flour, baking soda, salt, nutmeg, and cinnamon; add to oatmeal mixture, beating well. Pour and bake at 350° for 35–40 minutes. When done, add topping.

**Topping:**

**6 tablespoons margarine or butter**
**¾ cup brown sugar**
**¼ cup milk (can use ⅓ cup cream or evaporated milk)**
**1 teaspoon vanilla**
**1 cup nuts**
**1 cup coconut (optional)**

Mix topping ingredients well over stove allowing margarine or butter to melt. Remove from stove and add nuts and coconut. Spread over cake after cake is done. Put under broiler and leave cake in pan to brown topping.

## CHOCOLATE CHIP CAKE

Dosha Thompson, Hurricane, WV

**1 yellow cake mix**
**1 instant chocolate pudding mix**
**1 cup sour cream**
**4 eggs**
**½ cup water**
**½ cup oil**
**6-ounce package chocolate chips**

OVEN 350°

Mix all ingredients, use floured bundt pan. Bake 350° for 45–55 minutes. Glaze while warm.

**Glaze:**

**½ stick butter or margarine**
**3 tablespoons milk**
**2 tablespoons cocoa**
**½ box confectioners' sugar**
**½ teaspoon vanilla**

Bring butter or margarine, milk, and cocoa to a boil. Add sugar and vanilla. Drizzle on cake.

## DAN'S CHOCOLATE CAKE

Rachel Norton, Tipton, IA

**2 sticks margarine, melted**
**1 cup water**
**4 tablespoons cocoa**
**2 cups flour**
**2 cups sugar**
**2 eggs**
**½ teaspoon baking soda**
**⅛ teaspoon baking powder**
**½ cup buttermilk***
**1 teaspoon vanilla**

OVEN 350°

Melt margarine, add water and cocoa; bring mixture to a boil then cool. Add flour and sugar, sifted together. Beat in eggs, one at a time. Add baking soda and baking powder dissolved in buttermilk. Add vanilla. Bake at 350° for at least 30 minutes.

*I use dry buttermilk adding the required water to my water and the buttermilk powder to my dry ingredients.

## CHOCOLATE CHIFFON CAKE

Jo Waldner, Winnipeg, Manitoba

**2 cups hot water**
**⅔ cup cocoa**
**2 cups flour**
**4 teaspoons baking powder**
**1 teaspoon salt**
**½ teaspoon baking soda**
**2 cups white sugar**
**½ cup corn oil**
**6 eggs, separated**
**1 teaspoon vanilla**
**½ teaspoon cream of tartar**

OVEN 350°

Combine hot water and cocoa. Boil 1 minute. Cool. Sift flour, baking powder, baking soda, salt, and sugar in bowl. Add cooled cocoa syrup, corn oil, vanilla, and egg yolks. Blend until smooth. Beat egg whites and cream of tartar until very stiff. Fold egg whites into first mixture carefully. Bake in ungreased tube pan at 350° for about 50 minutes.

**Cocoa Frosting:**

**1½ cups cold milk**
**1 envelope whipped topping mix**
**1 package (4 serving) chocolate fudge pudding mix**

Pour cold milk in mixing bowl; add whipped topping and pudding mix. Beat on low for 1 minute. Slowly increase speed and beat for 4–6 minutes.

## HERSHEY CAKE

Doris Conley, Morganton, NC

**12 ounces cream cheese**
**2 sticks butter**
**2 boxes powdered sugar**
**8-ounce bar German sweet chocolate**
**¼ cup water**
**¼ cup shortening**
**3 whole eggs**
**2¾ cups plain flour**
**1 teaspoon baking soda**
**1 teaspoon vanilla**
**1 teaspoon salt**
**1 cup buttermilk**

OVEN 350°

Cream together cream cheese and butter. Add powdered sugar. Melt German chocolate in water and add to creamed mixture. Reserve half of this mixture for icing. To other half of this mixture add shortening, eggs, flour, baking soda, vanilla, salt, and buttermilk. Bake at 350° for about 45 minutes.

## REESE'S CUP CAKE

Penny Combs, Castlewood, VA

**1 box chocolate or yellow cake mix**
**1 small box chocolate instant pudding**
**1 to 3 cups crumbled Reese's cups (according to how many you want)**
**¼ cup water**

OVEN 325°

Preheat oven to 325°. Mix cake according to directions on box. Add dry pudding. Add crumbled Reese's cups. Add water. Bake for about 45 minutes. Ice.

**Icing:**
**8 ounces cream cheese, softened**
**3 to 4 tablespoons peanut butter**
**8-ounce tub whipped topping**
**1 box powdered sugar**

Mix together and top with crumbled Reese's cups.

## HERSHEY SYRUP CAKE

Juanita J. Brown, Elkton, MD

**1 cup sugar**
**4 eggs**
**1 cup flour**
**1 teaspoon baking powder**
**1 stick butter**
**½ teaspoon salt**
**16-ounce can Hershey Syrup**
**1 cups nuts (optional)**

OVEN 350°

Cream sugar and butter; add eggs. Combine flour, baking powder, and salt; add to creamed mixture, add syrup. Mix 2 minutes. Use greased 9x13-inch pan. Bake until done.

**Frosting:**
**⅓ cup evaporated milk**
**½ stick butter**
**1 cup sugar**
**1 cup milk chocolate chips**

Add milk, butter, and sugar in saucepan. Bring to a boil over medium heat. Cook for 2 minutes, do not let it stick. Remove from heat, add chocolate chips, stir until melted. Spread.

## OREO COOKIE CAKE

Laurie Gordon, Hudsonville, MI

*"My family insists I make this when I have to bring dessert!"*

**1 pound Oreo-brand cookies**
**1 cup melted margarine**
**2 8-ounce containers whipped topping**
**8 ounces cream cheese, softened to room temperature**
**1 cup powdered sugar**
**1 large instant chocolate pudding**

Crush cookies, set aside ½ cup. Combine the rest of the cookie crumbs and melted margarine. Mix and press into 9x13-inch pan. Refrigerate for one hour. Mix softened cream cheese, powdered sugar, and 8 ounces whipped topping together and spread on cookie layer. Refrigerate 1 hour. Make pudding as package directs, spread on white layer and refrigerate 1 hour. Spread on other 8 ounces of whipped topping on top of pudding layer, sprinkle with extra cookie crumbs.

## GERMAN CHOCOLATE CAKE

Nancy Jane Fankell, Grayson, KY

**2 cups flour**
**2 cups sugar**
**½ teaspoon salt**
**2 sticks margarine**
**3 tablespoons cocoa**
**1 cup water**
**2 eggs**
**1 teaspoon baking soda**
**½ cup buttermilk**
**1 teaspoon vanilla**

OVEN 350°

Sift together twice, flour, sugar, and salt. In saucepan place margarine, cocoa, and water. Bring to a boil; stir until butter is melted. Beat this mixture slowly into flour mixture. Beat together eggs, baking soda, buttermilk, and vanilla. Add to other mixture and mix well. Bake in 10x13-inch pan at 350° for 30–45 minutes.

**Frosting:**

**1 cup canned cream**
**1 cup sugar**
**3 egg yolks**
**¼ pound margarine**
**1 teaspoon vanilla**
**1 cup coconut**
**1 cup pecans**

Combine in saucepan. Cook, stirring, over medium heat for 12 minutes or until mixture thickens. Remove from heat. Add coconut and pecans. Beat until cool. Spread on cake in pan.

## GRANDMOTHER YUTZ'S ONE EGG, ONE BOWL CHOCOLATE CAKE

Kay Cornelius, Huntsville, AL

*"This was my husband's great-grandmother's recipe. All the brides in the family get this recipe and use it for birthday cakes and other special occasions. It is as easy as a mix and sooooo good!"*

**Editor's Note:** Kay has written several Heartsong Presents titles which include *Sign of the Bow* and *Politically Correct.*

OVEN 350°

Prepare 2 8-inch cake pans (I cut out waxed paper liners if I am going to ice the cake, or spray on cooking spray). This will also make a sheet cake or about 19 cupcakes.

In a large bowl, sift together:

**1½ cups flour**
**1 cup sugar**
**1 teaspoon baking soda**
**2 heaping tablespoons cocoa**
**1 generous pinch of salt**

Make a hole in the center and drop in:

**1 egg**
**1 cup sour milk (add 1 teaspoon vinegar to milk and let it set a short time)**
**½ cup cooking oil**
**1 heaping teaspoon vanilla flavoring**

Mix well and beat for 3 minutes. Bake cupcakes at 350° about 20 minutes and cake layers about 30 minutes.

## DIRT CAKE

Jennifer Arthur, Creston, WV

**16-ounce package Oreo cookies**
**8-ounce package cream cheese**
**1 stick butter**
**1 cup confectioners' sugar**
**8-ounce tub Cool Whip**
**3 cups milk**
**2 3-ounce packages vanilla instant pudding**
**1 teaspoon vanilla**

Crush cookies and put half of crumbs in a 9x13-inch pan. Mix cream cheese and butter until smooth. Mix in confectioners' sugar. Fold in Cool Whip. In separate bowl mix pudding, milk, and vanilla. Fold in cream cheese mixture. Stir both batters together well. Pour batter on top of crumbs. Sprinkle remaining crumbs on top. Refrigerate.

## APPLE DUMP CAKE

Bernice Thomas, Tucson, AZ

**1 large can pineapple, crushed but not drained**
**1 cup apple pie filling**
**¼ teaspoon cinnamon**
**¼ pound margarine**
**1 package yellow cake mix**
**1 cup coconut**
**½ cup chopped walnuts**

OVEN 350°

Pour pineapple with juice and apple filling in a 9x13-inch pan. Sprinkle with cinnamon. In a bowl mix margarine, cake mix, and nuts. Spread over fruit in pan. Sprinkle top with coconut. Cover and bake 30 minutes at 350°. Uncover and bake another 15 minutes.

## CHOCOLATE SHEET CAKE

Nina Law, Morgantown, IL

**2 cups flour**
**1½ teaspoons baking soda**
**2 cups sugar**
**½ teaspoon salt**
**2 sticks butter**
**4 tablespoons cocoa**
**1 cup water**
**½ cup buttermilk**
**2 eggs**
**1 teaspoon vanilla**

OVEN 350°

Sift together flour, soda, sugar, and salt. Melt butter, add cocoa and water, bring to boil, and pour over dry ingredients. Add buttermilk, eggs, and vanilla. Mix and pour into a greased 10x16-inch sheet cake pan. Bake at 350° for 15–20 minutes. Ice.

**Icing:**

**1 stick butter**
**4 tablespoons cocoa**
**6 tablespoons buttermilk**
**1 box powdered sugar**
**1 cup nuts**
**1 teaspoon vanilla**

Melt butter, cocoa, and buttermilk; bring to boil and add powdered sugar, nuts, and vanilla. Pour over cake while hot.

## ZUCCHINI CHOCOLATE CAKE

Stephanie Turner, Taylorsville, MS

*"Zucchini chocolate cake is my favorite zucchini disguise! Cream cheese frosting is particularly nice on this cake."*

**4 ounces unsweetened chocolate**
**½ cup vegetable oil**
**½ cup butter, at room temperature**
**2 cups sugar**
**3 eggs, beaten**
**1 tablespoon vanilla extract**
**2 cups sifted all-purpose unbleached flour**
**⅓ cup cocoa**
**2 teaspoons baking soda**
**2 teaspoons baking powder**
**1 teaspoon salt**
**⅓ cup buttermilk or sour cream**
**3 cups coarsely grated zucchini or summer squash**
**½ cup chopped nuts**

OVEN 350°

Melt the chocolate and oil in small saucepan over very low heat. Cream butter until light; add the sugar, eggs, and vanilla. Beat well. Add the melted chocolate and mix well. Sift together the dry ingredients and stir them into the batter with the buttermilk. Mix the zucchini and nuts into the batter. Divide the batter between two greased and floured 9-inch cake pans. Bake on middle shelf of oven for 40 minutes until tests done. Cool the cake completely before frosting with whipped cream or your favorite frosting.

## DUMP CAKE

Carla Hinkle, Upland, PA

**1 can chunky pineapple**
**1 can cherry pie filling**
**Yellow cake mix**
**Coconut (optional)**

OVEN 350°

Combine pineapple and cherry pie filling, dump dry cake mix on top (do not mix). Add coconut if desired. Bake in greased and floured pan for 45 minutes. It's best if you use glass baking dish. You can eat it right out of the oven. Serve with ice cream.

Variations:
Hallie M. Cook, Carrollton, IL

Add 2 sticks shortening and chopped nuts.

Juanita Fulton, Eden, NC

Substitute 1 can cherries for cherry pie filling and 1 can pineapple bits for chunky pineapple. Add 1½ sticks butter, ¾ cup chopped nuts (pecans or walnuts), ½ bag frozen coconut.

## STIR CRAZY CAKE

Mrs. S. J. Patrick, Iowa Falls, IA

**2½ cups flour**
**1½ cups sugar**
**½ cup cocoa**
**2 teaspoons baking soda**
**½ teaspoon salt**
**⅔ cup oil**
**2 tablespoons vinegar**
**1 tablespoon vanilla**
**2 cups cold coffee**
**¼ cup sugar**
**½ teaspoon cinnamon or nutmeg**

OVEN 350°

Put all ingredients in 9x13-inch pan. Stir with fork to mix. Form 3 wells. Pour oil in one well; vinegar in another well, and vanilla in another. Pour cold coffee over all. Stir with fork until well mixed. Do not beat. Combine sugar, cinnamon, or nutmeg. Sprinkle over batter in pan. Bake at 350° for 35–40 minutes.

Note: Batter will be thin. May look like it is ready to boil. Not to worry—comes out fine.

## CRAZY CAKE

Jan Zeck, Prairie Du Sac, WI

**3 cups flour**
**2 cups sugar**
**⅓ cup cocoa**
**2 teaspoons baking soda**
**1 teaspoon salt**
**2 tablespoons vinegar**
**1 teaspoon vanilla**
**¾ cup salad oil**
**2 cups cold water**

OVEN 350°

Stir together ingredients. In ungreased 9x13-inch pan bake at 350° for 45–50 minutes or when cake springs back when you touch the middle. No need to grease your pan. Or makes 30–36 cupcakes. Delicious with a cream cheese frosting!

## WACKY CAKE

Frances Burns, Gouldsboro, PA

**1½ cups flour**
**½ teaspoon salt**
**3 tablespoons cocoa**
**1 teaspoon baking soda**
**1 cup sugar**
**1 teaspoon vanilla**
**1 teaspoon vinegar**
**5 tablespoons salad oil**
**1 cup water**

OVEN 350°

Stir together in ungreased 8x8-inch pan: flour, salt, cocoa, baking soda, and sugar. Make 3 holes in ingredients. In first hole put vanilla; in second put vinegar; in third salad oil. Pour water over all and mix well. Bake at 350° for 25–30 minutes.

# CAKES

## WACKY CAKE

Connie Manry, Colorado Springs, CO

*"This is very moist. No need to frost. My kids and grandkids all love it. I started making this for group picnics. There are never any leftovers. My 5-year-old grandson loves to help."*

**3 cups flour**
**2 cups sugar**
**½ teaspoon salt**
**10 tablespoons cocoa**
**½ cup oil**
**3 tablespoons vanilla**
**2 tablespoons white vinegar**
**2 cups cold water**
**1 cup water**

OVEN 350°

In 9x13-inch pan mix together flour, sugar, salt, and cocoa. Make three holes. Put oil in first hole. In second hole put vanilla, and in third hole put white vinegar and baking soda. Add water. Stir until mixed completely. Bake at 350° for 25 minutes.

## JEWISH COFFEE CAKE

Alice Kennedy, Granite City, IL

**1 package yellow cake mix**
**1 package instant vanilla pudding**
**½ cup vegetable oil**
**4 eggs**
**1 cup sour cream**
**½ teaspoon vanilla**
**½ cup sugar**
**1 teaspoon cocoa**
**1 teaspoon cinnamon**
**½ cup chopped pecans**

OVEN 350°

Mix cake mix, pudding, oil, eggs, sour cream, and vanilla; set aside. Mix together sugar, cocoa, cinnamon, and pecans. Pour part of the cake mixture into greased tube pan or two loaf pans. Sprinkle on top by teaspoon part of the sugar mixture, add more cake batter. Sprinkle remaining sugar mixture on top. Take a knife and make zigzag lines through the batter. Bake at 350° for 50–55 minutes.

## GRANNY'S CRAZY CAKE

Josephine Priebe, Orlando, FL

**1 egg**
**1 cup sugar**
**½ cup milk**
**½ cup cocoa**
**½ cup shortening**
**½ teaspoon salt**
**1 teaspoon baking powder**
**1½ cups flour**
**½ cup boiling water**

OVEN 325°

Put all ingredients in order in bowl; after adding boiling water stir and mix. Pour into greased and floured pan and bake at 325° for 30 minutes. Makes 9-inch square or round layer pan. Double the recipe for 9x13-inch pan.

## RED VELVET CAKE

Amy Dollins, Valier, IL

**2 ounces red food coloring**
**3 tablespoons milk chocolate cocoa**
**½ cup shortening**
**1½ cups granulated sugar**
**2 eggs**
**1 cup buttermilk**
**1 teaspoon baking soda**
**1 tablespoon vinegar**
**½ teaspoon salt**
**2½ cups flour**
**1 teaspoon vanilla**

OVEN 350°

Mix food coloring with cocoa. Cream shortening with sugar; add eggs and coloring. Mix and beat well. Add buttermilk, flour, salt, and vanilla. Beat again. Remove from mixer and add vinegar and baking soda. Mix by hand. Pour into two greased and floured 8-inch pans. Bake at 350° for 30–35 minutes. Cut each layer in half while still warm. Ice.

**American Beauty Icing:**

**4 tablespoons flour**
**1 cup milk**
**Pinch of salt**
**1 cup granulated sugar**
**½ cup margarine**
**½ cup shortening**
**2 teaspoons vanilla**

Cook flour, milk, and salt until thick and put in refrigerator to cool. When cooled, add sugar, margarine, shortening, and vanilla; mix at high speed with electric mixer.

## JELLY ROLL COFFEE CAKE

Lindy Halberda, Lake, MI

**2½ cups flour**
**½ teaspoon salt**
**½ teaspoon cinnamon**
**¾ cup sugar**
**1 cup brown sugar**
**¾ cup salad oil**
**1 cup buttermilk**
**1 egg**
**1 teaspoon baking soda**
**1 teaspoon baking powder**

OVEN 350°

Mix first six ingredients to a fine crumb mixture, then divide equally into two bowls. Add to one mixture, ½ cup buttermilk, egg, baking soda, and baking powder. Beat for 2 minutes then add another ½ cup buttermilk and beat for 2 more minutes. Pour into greased 12x18-inch jelly roll pan. Put leftover crumb mixture on top. Bake at 350° for approximately 20 minutes.

## COWBOY COFFEE CAKE
Dolores R. King, Torrington, WY

**2½ cups flour**
**1½ cups brown sugar**
**½ teaspoon salt**
**⅔ cup shortening**
**2 teaspoons baking powder**
**½ teaspoon cinnamon**
**½ teaspoon nutmeg**
**½ teaspoon allspice**
**2 eggs**
**½ teaspoon baking soda**
**1 cup sour milk**

OVEN 375°

Combine flour, brown sugar, and salt. Cut in shortening until very fine. Take out 1½ cups of crumbs to be put on top of cake. To remaining crumbs add baking powder, baking soda, and spices. Mix well. Add eggs and milk to dry mixture, mix well (batter will be thin). Pour into well-greased and floured 9x11-inch pan. Sprinkle with reserved crumbs. Bake at 375° for 45 minutes.

## BUBBLE COFFEE CAKE
Becky Sailer, Independence, IA

**1 loaf frozen bread dough, thawed**
**1 small package instant butterscotch pudding**
**1 teaspoon cinnamon**
**½ cup brown sugar**
**½ cup shortening**
**1 cup pecans**

OVEN 350°

Mix the pudding and cinnamon together in a bowl. Pinch off small balls of bread dough and roll in pudding and cinnamon mixture. Place in a greased bundt pan with the nuts in the bottom. Pour any remaining mixture over the top. Bring the brown sugar and shortening just to a boil and pour over. Cover and allow to rise until doubled. Bake uncovered 30–40 minutes at 350°. Invert immediately after removing from the oven.

## EARTHQUAKE CAKE
Fern Anderson, Carlton, MN
*"It's rich but very delicious. You have to try it to believe how special it is!"*

**1 cup chopped nuts**
**1 cup fine chopped coconut**
**1 package German chocolate cake mix**
**8 ounces cream cheese**
**1 stick shortening (¼ pound)**
**1 pound powdered sugar**

OVEN 350°

Grease 9x13-inch cake pan and put nuts and coconut in pan. Mix cake according to directions on package and add on top of nuts and coconut. Then beat together cream cheese, shortening, and powdered sugar until fluffy. Put in blobs all around on top of cake mix in pan. Bake at 350° for 40 minutes or until done when tested.

## ECLAIR CAKE

Evelyn Lenora Scowden, Orange Park, FL
Ann McKinney, Ft. Worth, TX

*"My husband cannot have chocolate, so I use french vanilla pudding and lemon icing. Makes a wonderful light dessert and is even better the second day."*

Cake:

**16-ounce box graham crackers**
**2 (4 serving size) packages instant vanilla pudding**
**3 cups milk**
**1 large tub of non-dairy whipped topping, thawed**

Sauce:

**1 cup sugar**
**¼ cup cocoa**
**¼ cup milk**
**½ stick butter**

Butter bottom of 9x13-inch pan. Line pan with crackers; do not crush. Prepare pudding with milk, beating at medium speed until well blended (approximately 2 minutes). Carefully fold in whipped topping. Pour ½ of mixture over crackers. Cover with another layer of crackers; pour remaining pudding mixture over crackers. Cover with more crackers. Refrigerate at least 2 hours.

Sauce: Mix sugar, cocoa, and milk in saucepan; boil for 1 minute stirring occasionally. Take off heat; add butter, beat with spoon until thickened. Pour on top of crackers.

Variation: carefully spread a can of chocolate or lemon frosting on top.

Note: the recipe can easily be halved.

## SOUR CREAM COCONUT CAKE

Earlene Chapman, Keota, OK

**1 yellow cake mix**
**1 pound powdered sugar**
**8 ounces sour cream**
**1 small package flaked coconut**
**Whipped topping**

Prepare cake mix according to package directions. Cook in two round cake pans. Split layers. Filling: Mix together sugar, sour cream, and coconut. Ice between layers. Save some filling. Mix whipped topping with remains. Ice cake. This cake is more moist the longer it sits.

## TWINKIE CAKE

Wilma Brown, Brownsburg, IN

**1 yellow cake mix**
**3 tablespoons cornstarch**
**1 cup water**
**1 cup margarine**
**1 cup sugar**
**1 teaspoon vanilla**

Prepare cake mix according to package directions. Bake in oblong cake pan or 2 square pans. Let cool and cut into two layers, lay top aside. Cook cornstarch, water, margarine, sugar, and vanilla until clear; cool. (I usually cook this mixture while the cake bakes. It gets a crust and I mix it by hand then with an electric mixer until it is light and fluffy, about 5–10 minutes.) Spread on bottom of cake and lay top back on. It keeps well for a week and I freeze one for later use. Any kind of cake mix can be used.

## REESE'S PEANUT BUTTER CAKE

Ginny Dix,Virginia Beach, VA
(thanks to Sue Langen)

**2 sticks margarine**
**1 cup water**
**2 well beaten eggs**
**¼ cup cocoa (unsweetened)**
**½ cup buttermilk**
**2 cups sugar**
**2 cups flour**
**1 teaspoon baking soda**
**1 teaspoon vanilla**
**1 cup peanut butter**
**1 tablespoon oil**

OVEN 350°

Heat margarine, water, beaten eggs, cocoa, and buttermilk until bubbly. Add sugar, flour, baking soda, and vanilla. Bake at 350° for 25–30 minutes in greased and floured 9x13-inch pan. Mix 1 cup peanut butter with 1 tablespoon of oil, spread over cooled cake. Ice.

**Icing:**

**½ cup margarine**
**¼ cup cocoa (unsweetened)**
**6 tablespoons buttermilk**
**1 box confectioners' sugar (4 cups)**
**1 teaspoon vanilla**

Heat margarine, cocoa, and buttermilk until bubbly. Add sugar and vanilla; beat until smooth and spreading consistency. Spread on top of peanut butter layer.

## LEMON TWIST COFFEE CAKE

Mrs. Myra L. Jensen, Downers Grove, IL

**¾ cup milk**
**1 package dry yeast**
**¼ cup lukewarm water**
**1 tablespoon & ½ cup sugar**
**¼ pound (one stick) margarine**
**3 eggs**
**4½ cups flour**
**¾ teaspoon lemon extract**
**1 tablespoon grated lemon peel**
**White frosting mix**
**Red (or red and green) candied cherries**
**Nuts (optional)**

OVEN 375°

Scald milk; let cool. Dissolve dry yeast in lukewarm water. Put 1 tablespoon sugar in the water/yeast mixture and let stand for 5 minutes. Cream margarine and ½ cup sugar. Add eggs; mix in milk mixture and yeast mixture. Add 2 cups flour and lemon extract. Beat with beaters and add 2½ cups more flour and grated lemon peel. Knead one minute. Let stand in greased bowl overnight, preferably in warm area. In the morning, divide the dough into 2 sections. Take one section and divide it again into two sections. Roll out like a tube and braid it. Place on cookie sheet in 2 circles or a horseshoe shape. Place in warm spot to raise for about 1½ hours until double in size. Bake at 375° for 12–15 minutes. Frost when cool. Add cherries and nuts.

## UNBAKE CAKE

George Clanton, Weldon, CA

**2 cups pecans, chopped fine**
**1 cup walnuts, chopped fine**
**1 cup Brazil nuts, chopped fine**
**2 packages vanilla wafers (or 1 pound), crushed**
**1 can condensed milk (NOT evaporated milk)**

Mix thoroughly. Shape in a loaf; wrap in foil and put in the refrigerator for four days.

## CRUNCH CAKE

Robbie Sauvie, Columbus, GA

**2 cups flour**
**2 cups sugar**
**1 cup cooking oil**
**7 large eggs**
**1 tablespoon vanilla flavoring**

OVEN 275°

Sift 1 cup flour and 1 cup sugar into mixing bowl. Sift the other cup of flour and sugar and repeat. Add other ingredients and beat 12 minutes on high speed. Pour batter in tube pan lined with wax paper. Bake 1 hour and 30 minutes at 275°. Do not open oven door until time for it to be done, because it will fall. Take out of oven, turn over, and let it sit for about 30 minutes. Sit it up and cut loose from side of pan and turn out onto a cloth until it cools.

## COFFEE CAKE SWIRL

Cynthia Quaintance, Edgerton, KS

**Cake:**

**1 cup flour**
**¼ cup sugar**
**¼ cup brown sugar**
**½ teaspoon baking soda**
**½ teaspoon baking powder**
**¼ teaspoon salt**
**½ teaspoon cinnamon**
*** ½ cup buttermilk**
**⅓ cup shortening**
**1 egg**

**Topping:**

**¼ cup brown sugar**
**½ teaspoon cinnamon**
**¼ teaspoon nutmeg**

**Glaze:**

**½ cup powdered sugar**
**3 to 4 teaspoons milk**
**¼ teaspoon vanilla**

OVEN 350°

Grease and flour bottom of 9-inch round pan. Combine all cake ingredients. Blend at low speed until moistened. Beat 3 minutes at medium speed. Spread in pan. Blend topping ingredients. Sprinkle over batter, cover, refrigerate overnight (or bake immediately). Heat oven to 350°; uncover and bake for 20–25 minutes or until toothpick comes out clean. Blend glaze ingredients until smooth. Drizzle over cake.

Or you can make muffins instead of cake; bake about 15 minutes.

* To make your own buttermilk, in measuring cup add 2 teaspoons lemon juice or vinegar then milk to make ½ cup total.

## PEANUT BUTTER TANDY CAKE

Crystal Shaffer, Middleburg, PA

**1½ cups sugar**
**2 cups flour**
**2 teaspoons baking powder**
**¼ teaspoon salt**
**2 teaspoons shortening**
**4 eggs**
**1 cup milk**
**1 tablespoon vanilla**
**1 small jar peanut butter**
**1 8-ounce chocolate bar**

OVEN 350°

Combine first 5 ingredients; mix thoroughly. Beat eggs, add milk and vanilla. Add liquid to dry batter. Pour into greased pan. Bake at 350° for 25 minutes. While hot, spread peanut butter on top. Cool. Spread melted chocolate bar over peanut butter. Put cake in refrigerator. Serve when chocolate is firm.

## 7-UP® CAKE

Annie Ladehoff, Houston, TX

*"My friends request this cake for their birthdays. I've made it for weddings and dinners at church. Very special friends ask me to make it without icing and they put it in the freezer. It's like a pound cake."*

**1½ cups butter (3 sticks)**
**3 cups sugar**
**5 eggs**
**3 cups all-purpose flour**
**2 tablespoons lemon extract**
**¾ cup 7-Up**

OVEN 325°

Cream sugar and butter together and beat until light and fluffy. Add eggs, one at a time; beat well. Add flour and beat well. Beat in lemon extract and 7-Up. Pour batter into well-greased and floured jumbo fluted tube pan or big bundt pan. Bake at 325° for 1¼ hours. Remove from oven, let cool for 15 minutes; turn upside down on cake rack. Ice with your favorite icing.

## SOUR CREAM COFFEE CAKE

Lois Buehler, Glendora, CA
Sandra Foster, Paulsboro, NJ

*"Great for breakfast or anytime!"*

**½ cup butter**
**1 cup sugar**
**2 eggs**
**1 teaspoon vanilla**
**1 cup sour cream**
**2 cups flour**
**1 teaspoon baking soda**
**1 teaspoon baking powder**
**1 teaspoon salt**

**Topping:**
**½ cup chopped walnuts**
**1 teaspoon cinnamon**
**½ cup sugar**

OVEN 350°

Cream butter and sugar. Add eggs to creamed mixture. Add vanilla and sour cream. Sift dry ingredients and add to creamed mixture. Mix walnuts, cinnamon, and sugar together. Pour half of batter into a greased and floured tube pan, sprinkle with half of nut mixture. Pour balance of batter in pan and top with remaining nut mixture. Bake 45 minutes at 350°.

Variation:
Jacqueline Jelley, Toms River, NJ

*"This recipe is one my mother-in-law gave me. She would always make it for covered dish suppers at our church and everyone would always rave about it. She went home to be with the Lord last year. She wasn't only my mother-in-law but my friend and sister in Christ. Her name was Elizabeth Jelley. A more loving person you couldn't have met."*

Add ¼ cup brown sugar, being sure to double batter ingredients except salt.

## SPECIAL COCONUT CAKE

Lena Nelson Dooley, Hurst, TX

**Editor's Note:** Lena is the author of *Home to Her Heart* for Heartsong Presents but her writing extends to curriculum, scripts, articles, software manuals, international business reports, and much more.

**1 yellow cake mix**
**14-ounce package coconut**
**1 can Coco Lopez Cream of Coconut**
**Small package whipped topping**

Mix cake according to directions. Then stir in ½ package of coconut. Bake in 9x13 pan according to directions. While cake is baking, put can of Coco Lopez in pan and cover with hot water. Immediately after removing from oven, poke holes one inch apart all over the cake using an instrument about the size of a pencil. (I use the handle of one of my spatulas.) Pour Coco Lopez over the top of the hot cake making sure some liquid goes into each hole. When cake is cool, top with whipped topping. Then add the rest of the coconut.

Variations:

Jean Exley, Wichita, KS

Use white cake mix. Add 1 can sweetened condensed milk, and use one cup pina colada instead of Coco Lopez

## HORNET'S NEST CAKE

Shelvy Harrison, Bandy, VA

**4¾-ounce package vanilla pudding**
**$2^2/_3$ cups milk**
**1 teaspoon vanilla**
**18-ounce box yellow or French vanilla cake mix**
**6-ounce package butterscotch chips**
**1 cup chopped nuts**

OVEN 350°

Cook pudding, milk, and vanilla until thick. Pour over cake mix. Stir with mixer. Will be like whipped cream. Pour into greased 9x13-inch pan. Sprinkle with butterscotch chips and nuts. Bake at 350° for 25–30 minutes or until done. Serve plain or with whipped topping.

## ELEGANT ANGEL FOOD CAKE

Laura Wilson, Desert Hot Springs, CA

**Blueberry or cherry pie filling**
**1 angel food cake cut in thirds lengthwise**
**8 ounces cream cheese, softened**
**8 ounces powdered sugar**
**8 ounces whipped topping**

Blend cream cheese and sugar together. Add whipped topping. Stir until well blended. Frost between layers of cake, top and sides. Top with cherry or blueberry pie filling. Refrigerate until ready to serve.

## EGGLESS CAKE

Dorothy Thuston, Kingman, AZ

*"This recipe was used during World War I, when eggs and milk were scarce. This was handed down to me by my grandmother."*

**2 cups sugar**
**2 cups water**
**½ cup butter**
**2 teaspoons cloves**
**2 cups raisins**
**2 teaspoons baking soda**
**1 teaspoon baking powder**
**4 scant cups of flour**

OVEN 350°

Cook all ingredients (except flour and baking powder) until boiling. Remove from stove and let cool. Add flour and baking powder. Bake at 350° until cake springs back when pressed. Do not overbake.

## COCA COLA® CAKE

Stephanie Johnson, Pensacola, FL

**2 cups flour**
**2 cups sugar**
**2 sticks butter**
**3 tablespoons cocoa**
**1 cup Coca Cola**
**½ cup buttermilk**
**2 eggs**
**1 teaspoon baking soda**
**1 teaspoon vanilla**
**1½ cups mini-marshmallows**

OVEN 350°

Combine flour and sugar in mixing bowl. Heat butter, cocoa, and Coca Cola to boiling and pour over flour and sugar. Mix well. Add buttermilk, eggs, baking soda, vanilla, and marshmallows. Mix well. The batter will be thin. Bake in greased and floured 9x13-inch pan for 30–35 minutes at 350°. When you turn the cake out, the top should be up. Very moist! Ice while hot.

**Icing:**

**½ cup butter**
**3 tablespoons cocoa**
**6 tablespoons Coca Cola**
**1 pound powdered sugar**
**1 cup roasted pecans, chopped**

Combine and heat to boiling butter, cocoa, and Coca Cola. Pour over powdered sugar. Beat well. Add pecans. Spread over hot cake.

# CAKES

## JELL-O CAKE

Mary Whisler, Vashon, WA

**¾ cup oil**
**¾ cup water**
**4 eggs**
**1 package lemon gelatin (dry)**
**1 package white or lemon cake mix**
**1½ cups powdered sugar**
**⅓ cup concentrated lemon juice**

OVEN 350°

Mix first five ingredients together. Beat 4 minutes. Bake in lightly greased 9x13-inch pan at 350° for 30 minutes. Remove from oven, wait a few minutes; prick top of cake with fork. Mix sugar and lemon juice. Pour over cake while warm.

## CREAM PUFF CAKE

Melissa Barefoot, Alum Bank, PA

**1 cup water**
**1 stick butter**
**¾ cup flour**
**4 eggs**
**3 (small) boxes instant vanilla pudding**
**3¼ cups milk**
**8 ounces cream cheese, softened**
**8 ounces whipped topping**

OVEN 350°

Heat water and butter together until butter melts. Add flour and eggs, one at a time, beat. Grease pan, pour in batter and smooth out. Bake at 350° for 45 minutes. Cake will be lumpy and bumpy. Make sure cake is cooled, then beat pudding and milk; add cream cheese. Put pudding mix on cake. Spread whipped topping on the top. Keep refrigerated.

## OLD-FASHIONED TEACAKES

Marie Waters, Rome, GA

**2 cups sugar**
**3 eggs**
**1 cup butter (no substitute)**
**3 teaspoons baking powder**
**⅛ teaspoon salt**
**Enough plain flour to make a stiff dough**

OVEN 375°

Combine ingredients, mix well. Roll to ½-inch thickness and cut with 2½-inch round cutter and place on baking sheet. Bake at 375° for 7–12 minutes or until set.

## UPSIDE-DOWN RAISIN CAKE

Carlene Bennett, Wichita, KS

**1⅓ cups sugar**
**4 teaspoons baking powder**
**¼ teaspoon salt**
**1 teaspoon vanilla**
**½ cup melted shortening**
**1 cup raisins**
**⅔ cup milk**
**2 eggs**
**2 cups flour**
**2 cups boiling water**
**1 cup brown sugar**

OVEN 350°

Mix all ingredients together in 9x13-inch pan except for water and brown sugar. Mix together boiling water and brown sugar, pour over cake. Do not stir in! Bake at 350° for 30 minutes.

## PLUM CAKE

Susan Nightingale, Catoosa, OK

**2 cups sugar**
**3 eggs**
**1 cup oil**
**2 small jars plums, baby food**
**1 teaspoon vanilla**
**1 teaspoon red food coloring**
**2 cups flour**
**½ teaspoon baking soda**
**Pinch of salt**
**1 teaspoon cloves**
**1 teaspoon cinnamon**
**1 cup nuts**

OVEN 350°

Mix together sugar, eggs, oil, plums, vanilla, and coloring. Sift together dry ingredients. Combine flour mixture with plum mixture and stir in nuts. Bake 1 hour at 350° in a greased bundt pan. Drizzle with glaze when cooled.

**Glaze:**

**2½ cups powdered sugar**
**3 tablespoons lemon juice**
**1 teaspoon melted margarine**

## WAFER CAKE

Doris Dew, Vicksburg, MS

**2 sticks margarine**
**2 cups sugar**
**12-ounce box vanilla wafers crushed**
**6 whole eggs**
**7-ounce can flaked coconut**
**½ cup sweet milk**
**1 cup pecans, chopped**

OVEN 325°

Cream margarine, add sugar and eggs, one at a time, mixing well after each addition. Crush wafers; add milk and crushed wafers alternately to creamed mixture while beating. Add coconut and pecans; mix well. Bake in greased tube pan 1 hour, 15 minutes at 325°.

## ALMOND POPPY SEED CAKE
Cherie Rivera, Port Charlotte, FL

**3 cups all-purpose flour**
**2 cups sugar**
**1½ teaspoons baking powder**
**1½ teaspoons salt**
**2 tablespoons poppy seed**
**¼ teaspoon baking soda**
**1½ cups milk**
**1 cup cooking oil**
**3 eggs**
**1½ teaspoons vanilla**
**1½ teaspoons almond extract**

OVEN 350°

Combine flour, sugar, baking powder, salt, poppy seed, and baking soda in a large mixer bowl. Add milk, oil, eggs, vanilla, and almond extract. Beat on low speed just until moistened. Beat on high speed for 2 more minutes. Pour into greased and floured 10-inch tube pan. Bake at 350° for 1–1¼ hours. Cool in pan on a rack for 15 minutes. Turn out into a pan.

## CHEESECAKE
Elizabeth Moyer, Buffalo, KY

**Cake:**
**1 stick butter, melted**
**1 egg, beaten**
**1 white cake mix**

**Topping:**
**8 ounces cream cheese, softened**
**2 eggs, beaten**
**1 box powdered sugar**

OVEN 350°

Melt butter in 9x13-inch pan. Beat egg and add to butter; mix together cake mix, press in pan (batter will be stiff). Topping: beat together cream cheese and eggs, add sugar, and pour on top of batter and bake in 350° oven for 40–45 minutes.

## ICE BOX CAKE
Susanne Johnson, Vaccaville, CA

**1 box graham crackers**
**1 large package chocolate pudding (not instant)**
**1 large package vanilla pudding (not instant)**
**½ cup walnuts**

Following package directions, prepare both puddings separately. Let cool 15 minutes, stirring often. In a 9x13-inch glass dish, layer following: Cover bottom with grahams setting side by side; with spoon spread a layer of vanilla pudding; sprinkle nuts; layer of grahams, chocolate pudding, nuts; repeat all layers. Place in refrigerator until chilled.

## CHECKERBOARD CAKE

Joann Willis, Orlando, FL

**2½ cups all-purpose flour**
**2 teaspoons baking powder**
**½ teaspoon baking soda**
**½ teaspoon salt**
**¾ cup shortening**
**2 cups sugar**
**1 tablespoon vanilla**
**5 egg whites, at room temperature**
**1⅓ cups buttermilk or sour milk**
**⅓ cup unsweetened cocoa powder**
**1 tablespoon milk**
**Chocolate frosting**

OVEN 350°

No special pan is needed. Grease and flour three 8½-inch round baking pans. In a bowl combine flour, baking powder, baking soda, and ½ teaspoon salt. In a very large bowl beat shortening with an electric mixer on medium speed for 30 seconds, add 1⅔ cups of sugar, and vanilla; beat until combined. Alternately add flour mixture and buttermilk, beating after each addition just until combined. Thoroughly wash beaters. Beat egg whites on medium speed until soft peaks form (tips curl). Gradually add remaining sugar, beating on medium to high until stiff peaks form (tips stand straight). Gently fold half of egg white mixture into beaten mixture. Fold in the remaining egg white mixture. Spoon half the batter (about 3¼ cups) in a bowl. Sift cocoa powder over remaining batter. Stir in 1 tablespoon of milk.

Set ¾ cup of white batter aside. Spoon 1¼ cups of remaining white batter around the outer edge of each of 2 of the prepared pans. Spoon ¾ cup of chocolate batter in a ring right next to the inner edge of white batter in each of the pans. Spoon half the remaining white batter into center of each pan. In the third pan, using 1¼ cups of chocolate batter, make outer ring, using the reserved ¾ cup white batter make inner ring. Fill center with remaining chocolate batter.

Bake in a 350° oven about 25 minutes or until cakes test done. Cool in pan for 10 minutes. Remove and cool. Place a cake layer with a white outer ring on serving plate. Frost top with ½ cup frosting. Place cake layer with chocolate outer ring on top. Frost sides and top with remaining frosting.

Serves 16.

**Frosting:**

**¼ cup margarine**
**2 cups sifted powdered sugar**
**3 squares (3 ounces) unsweetened chocolate**
**½ cup milk**
**1 teaspoon vanilla**
**2½–3 cups sifted powdered sugar**

Beat together margarine and 2 cups powdered sugar. Beat in chocolate, melted and cooled; add milk and vanilla. Beat in rest of powdered sugar to reach desired consistency.

Makes 4 cups.

## FUNNEL CAKE
Rena Goss, Booneville, MS

**1 cup self-rising flour**
**½ teaspoon ground cinnamon**
**1 egg**
**½ cup milk**

Mix ingredients with fork until smooth, pancake batter consistency. Holding finger under funnel opening, pour about ¼ cup of batter into funnel. Allow batter to pour from funnel into 1-inch of hot oil, moving funnel in a circle to form a spiral shape. Fry 1 minute, turn cake, and fry until golden brown. Remove to paper towel and drain. Sprinkle with confectioners' sugar.

## PLAIN CAKE
Mrs. Mark W. Roberts, Jacksboro, TX
*"This recipe is from Jack County, Texas Sesquicentennial Cookbook."*

**2 cups all-purpose flour**
**1 cup sugar**
**2 teaspoons baking powder**
**2 eggs**
**½ cup cooking oil or 1 stick shortening (melted)**
**1 teaspoon vanilla**
**1 cup milk (enough milk to thin dough)**
**1 cup coconut (optional)**

OVEN 350°

Combine ingredients and hand beat until well mixed. Pour into greased and floured sheet pan or loaf pan. Bake at 350° for 35 minutes or until cake is light brown and tests done.

## DATE CAKE DESSERT
Lorraine Smith, Goshen, IN
*"This was my father's favorite cake."*

**1⅛ cups flour**
**1 teaspoon soda**
**½ teaspoon salt**
**1 tablespoon butter**
**1 cup sugar**
**1 egg, beaten**
**½ pound dates, chopped**
**1 cup boiling water**

OVEN 375°

Sift dry ingredients together. Blend butter and sugar and add egg. Cover chopped dates with the boiling water. Add to the creamed mixture alternately with the flour mixture. Pour into a greased 7x7-inch pan. Bake for 25 minutes or until it springs back to the touch.

## LANE CAKE

Betty Booth, Doyline, LA

**1 cup butter**
**1 cup milk**
**3 teaspoons baking powder**
**8 egg whites**
**Vanilla flavoring**
**3 cups sugar**
**3 cups flour**

OVEN 350°

Cream butter and sugar. Add milk and flour. Then add vanilla. Beat egg whites until stiff, fold into creamed mixture. Pour into 3 cake pans. Bake at 350° for 30 minutes.

**Cake Filling:**

**1½ cups sugar**
**½ cup butter**
**11 egg yolks**
**1 cup pecans**
**1 teaspoon vanilla**

Melt butter in double boiler. Add sugar, egg yolks, and pecans. Cook until thick, stirring continuously, about 10 minutes. Add vanilla flavoring. Put on each layer of cake before the frosting.

**Icing:**

**½ cup sugar**
**1 cup white corn syrup**
**3 egg whites**

Beat egg whites. Cook sugar and corn syrup until it starts thickening, approximately 5 minutes. Add to beaten egg whites, beating as you pour the sugar and corn syrup into the mixing bowl. Mix until it becomes thick enough to ice cake. After each layer, put cake filling and then cake icing. After third layer ice the sides also.

## MOM'S GUESS CAKE

Becky Pallone, Shelocta, PA

*"This was my grandmother's recipe."*

**4 cups flour**
**¼ cup cocoa**
**2 teaspoons cinnamon**
**3⅔ teaspoons baking soda**
**1 teaspoon salt**
**1 cup shortening**
**1 box raisins**
**1 box dates, cut up**
**1 cup walnuts**
**2 cups sugar**
**Buttermilk or sour milk for thinning**

OVEN 350°

Sift dry ingredients into bowl; add enough sour milk or buttermilk to make batter thin enough for baking. Cream sugar and shortening; add to preceding mixture. Add raisins, dates, and nuts. Bake at 350° for 45 minutes, then at 375° until done. Frost with chocolate fudge frosting.

## PEA PICKIN' CAKE

Marge Porter, Gulf Breeze, FL

**1 box butter cake mix**
**4 eggs**
**1 cup corn oil**
**1 can mandarin oranges, with juice**

OVEN 350°

Mix together cake mix, eggs, oil, and mandarin oranges with juice. Bake in 3 layers for 15–20 minutes.

**Topping:**

**1 large can crushed pineapple, with juice**
**1 large carton whipped topping**
**1 small package instant vanilla pudding mix**

Mix carefully, do not beat. Put between layers and on top. Keep refrigerated.

## PIG PICKING CAKE

Jackie Rhoden, Jasper, FL

**1 yellow cake mix**
**3 eggs**
**¾ cup applesauce**
**12-ounce can mandarin oranges (do not drain)**

OVEN 350°

Mix all together, add water if needed in cake mix. Bake at 350° for 35–45 minutes.

**Icing:**

**1 large whipped topping**
**12-ounce can crushed pineapple (drained)**
**1 small box instant vanilla pudding**

Mix together in above order. Refrigerate for 45 minutes.

## SCRIPTURE CAKE

Laura Shepherd, Happy, KY

*"Ingredients are found entirely in the Old Testament."*

**4½ cups I Kings 4:22**
**1 cup Judges 5:25b**
**2 cups Jeremiah 6:20**
**2 cups I Samuel 30:12**
**2 cups Nahum 3:12**
**2 cups Numbers 17:8**
**1 tablespoon I Samuel 14:25**
**1 teaspoon Leviticus 2:13**
**6 Jeremiah 17:11**
**½ cup Judges 4:19b**
**2 teaspoons Amos 4:5**
**2 teaspoons II Chronicles 9:9**

OVEN 325°

Follow mixing direction for any basic fruitcake. Bake slowly in moderate oven.

## PUNCH BOWL CAKE

Martha Williams, Mabank, TX

**1 box cake mix**
**Cherry pie mix**
**Vanilla instant pudding**
**Crushed pineapple (drained)**
**Whipped topping**
**Pecans, chopped (for garnish)**
**Maraschino cherries (for garnish)**

Prepare cake mix as directed on package. Pour into 2 cake pans. Bake and cool. In punch bowl put one layer of cake on the bottom. Cover with layers of cherry pie mix, pudding, pineapple, and whipped topping. Put second layer of cakc on top and laycr with cherry pie filling, pudding, pineapple, and whipped topping. Garnish with pecans and maraschino cherries. Cool before serving. Makes 30 servings.

## ITALIAN LOVE CAKE

Flo Abel, Greenbelt, MD

**1 box chocolate cake mix**
**2 16-ounce containers ricotta cheese**
**¾ cup sugar**
**4 eggs**
**1 teaspoon vanilla**
**1 large box instant chocolate pudding**
**1 cup milk**
**8 ounces whipped topping**

OVEN 350°

Mix cake as directed on box. Pour into greased and floured 9x13-inch pan. In a separate bowl combine ricotta cheese, eggs, vanilla, and sugar. Mix well and spoon over top of unbaked cake. Bake at 350° for one hour. Cake will rise to the top. Cool. Mix pudding with milk, fold in whipped topping. Spread over cooled cake and refrigerate.

## SALLY LUNN (QUICK VERSION)

Birdie Etchison, Ocean Park, WA

*"The original Sally Lunn recipe originated in Bath, England, where Sally was an 18th-century English baker. That recipe calls for yeast as the leavening."*

**Editor's Note:** Birdie has written several books for the Heartsong Presents series, including *Anna's Hope* in which Anna makes Sally Lunn for Dr. Wesley Snow.

**1 cup flour**
**½ cup sugar**
**3 tablespoons baking powder**
**1 teaspoon salt**
**1 egg**
**1 cup milk**
**¼ cup oil**

OVEN 400°

Blend dry ingredients. Add egg, milk, and oil. Mix slightly, do not overmix. Pour into round, or square greased 9-inch pan. Bake for 20–25 minutes. Frost with butter. Cut into wedges.

## AMISH CAKE
Naomi Muncy, Gallipolis Ferry, WV

**1 stick shortening, room temperature**
**2 cups buttermilk**
**3 cups self-rising flour, sifted**
**3 cups brown sugar**
**2 teaspoons baking soda**
**2 teaspoons vanilla flavoring**

**Topping:**
**⅔ cup brown sugar**
**1 cup chopped walnuts**
**1 cup shredded coconut**
**2 tablespoons shortening, melted**
**½ cup canned milk**
**1 tablespoon vanilla flavoring**

OVEN 370°

Cream together sugar and shortening. Add baking soda to buttermilk; add milk, flour, and vanilla. Mix well. Bake at 370° for 40–45 minutes or until done. Remove from oven.

Topping: Mix together topping ingredients. Spread on cake. Place back in oven for 10 minutes or until topping is bubbly.

## SAUERKRAUT CAKE
Adele C. Benjamin, Bradenton, FL

**½ cup butter or shortening**
**1¼ cups sugar**
**3 eggs**
**2 teaspoons vanilla**
**¼ teaspoon salt**
**2 cups flour**
**1 teaspoon baking soda**
**½ cup quick cocoa mix**
**½ cup sour cream**
**½ cup water**
**1 cup sauerkraut, rinsed, drained, and chopped**

OVEN 350°

Grease and flour 9x13-inch cake pan. In a large bowl, cream butter, or shortening, and sugar until light. Beat in eggs and vanilla. Sift dry ingredients together. Mix sour cream and water together, add to creamed mixture alternately with dry ingredients. Fold in sauerkraut and pour into pan. Bake at 350° for 40 minutes. Frost with favorite chocolate frosting.

**Frosting:**
**½ box powdered sugar**
**3–4 tablespoons vanilla**
**3–4 tablespoons cocoa, not too dark**
**¼ stick shortening, softened**
**3 ounces cream cheese**

Mix and frost.

## MAGIC CAKE
Lois Windon, Jamestown, OH

**2 teaspoons baking soda**
**2 cups sugar**
**2 cups flour**
**2 eggs**
**1 teaspoon vanilla**
**20-ounce can crushed pineapple, with juice**

OVEN 350°

Stir and pour into greased and floured 9x13-inch pan. Bake at 350° for 45 minutes. Top with cream cheese icing.

## POPCORN CAKE

Louise Orf, Killdeer, ND

**4 quarts popped corn**
**1 pound gum drops**
**½ package M&M's candy**
**½ cup butter or margarine**
**1 pound marshmallows**
**½ pound salted peanuts**
**½ cup oil**

Mix corn, gum drops, M&M's, and nuts in a large bowl. Melt butter, marshmallows, and oil. Pour over the corn mixture and stir. Press firmly into greased cake pan and cool.

## QUICK EASY FROSTING

Sandy Hagonbeck, Sturgeon Lake, MN

**1 small container frozen whipped topping**
**1 fruit-flavored yogurt**

Mix together and frost cake. Refrigerate cake after frosting.

## TOMATO SOUP CAKE

Wilma Storey, Ankeny, IA

**1 cup sugar**
**½ stick shortening**
**1 cup walnuts**
**1 can tomato soup**
**½ cup boiling water**
**2 cups flour**
**1 teaspoon nutmeg**
**1 teaspoon baking soda**
**1 teaspoon cinnamon**
**2 teaspoons baking powder**
**½ cup sour milk**

OVEN 350°

Cream together sugar and shortening. Add walnuts, soup, and boiling water. Add flour, nutmeg, baking soda, cinnamon, and baking powder. Then add sour milk. Bake in 9x13-inch pan at 350° for 40 minutes.

**Easy Caramel Frosting:**

**1½ cups brown sugar**
**¼ cup & 2 tablespoons milk**
**1 teaspoon vanilla**

Bring ingredients to a boil and boil 3 minutes, stirring constantly. Remove from heat, add vanilla. Cool until lukewarm. Beat until creamy and thick enough to spread. Add more milk if necessary for spreading.

## POOR MAN'S CAKE

Jennifer Tabor, Medina, NY

**2½ cups flour**
**1½ cups sugar**
**2 eggs**
**5 teaspoons baking powder**
**1½ cups milk**
**2 teaspoons vanilla**
**⅔ cup shortening**
**¼ teaspoon salt**

OVEN 350°

Cream shortening and sugar; then add milk and eggs. Add dry ingredients, add vanilla. Pour into greased 9x13-inch pan. Bake at 350° for 25–30 minutes.

## MOM'S GINGERBREAD
Betty Ann Ward, Marshall, VA

**1 stick butter or margarine**
**1 cup sugar**
**1 cup molasses**
**2/3 cup milk**
**2 eggs**
**½ teaspoon salt**
**3 cups flour**
**2 teaspoons baking soda**
**2 teaspoons cinnamon**
**2 teaspoons ginger**

OVEN 325°

Mix together. Put in loaf pan. Bake at 325° until springs back when lightly touched. Serve plain, or topped with lemon sauce, or whipped topping.

**Easy Lemon Sauce:**
**1 package lemon pudding and pie filling**
**½ cup sugar**
**3 cups water**
**1 egg**

Combine gelatin mix and sugar, 1/4 cup of the water in saucepan. Add egg, blend well. Add remaining 2¾ cups water. Cook and stir over medium heat until it comes to full boil. Serve warm over gingerbread.

## PEPPERMINT STICK CAKE
Nola Haney, Deersville, OH

**2 2/3 cup flour**
**3 teaspoons baking powder**
**1 teaspoon salt**
**½ cup shortening**
**1 ½ cup sugar**
**1 ¼ cup milk**
**1 egg yolk**
**1 teaspoon vanilla**
**3 egg whites**
**½ cup peppermint stick candy, finely ground**
**½ cup peppermint stick candy, coarsely ground**

375° oven

Sift flour and measure. Sift again with baking powder and salt. Cream shortening. Continue creaming while gradually adding 4/5 cup of sugar and 3 tablespoons milk. Add egg yolk and vanilla to remaining milk. Add sifted dry ingredients alternately with milk to creamed mixture. Beat egg whites stiff but not dry. Beat in remaining sugar. Fold in cake batter. Pour into two 9-inch pans or one 9x13 pan and sprinkle with finely ground candy. Bake for 25 minutes. Ice with white icing when cooled and sprinkle with the coarsely ground candy.

BAKER'S NOTE:
Cakes "test done" when a wooden toothpick that is inserted into the center of the cake and removed is clean.

# PIES

## BEST PASTRY

Arlene L. Warnwell

**5 cups flour**
**2 teaspoons baking powder**
**2 teaspoons salt**
**1 pound lard or shortening**
**1 egg, beaten well**
**1 tablespoon vinegar with enough water to equal 1 cup**

Makes pastry for 5 single shells or 4 double shells.

## NANNY'S PIECRUST

Donna Mixon, Farmington, AR

*"It is such a large job to mix piecrusts and then the filling and last the meringue for cream pies. I needed a quicker way. My mother, Nanny, an excellent pie maker, came up with this recipe. I mix it all in a large bowl and take out enough for one piecrust. I then place this ball in a plastic bag and flatten. I do this until all dough is used. I freeze the bags and when I want a pie I take out of the freezer what I need. I let the crust thaw for a few hours but if I am in a hurry, I defrost it in the microwave until pliable to work with."*

**5 pounds flour plus 2 cups**
**3 pounds shortening**
**3 teaspoons light salt or 2 teaspoons salt**
**2½ cups water**

Mix flour, salt, and shortening until mixture is coarse as cornmeal. Add water and mix. Follow directions above.

Yields: 15–20 crusts.

## NEVER FAIL PIECRUST

Elizabeth Hunt, Ithaca, MI

*"I make it all up into crusts on foil pans. I freeze pans in zip-lock bags. It's ready when I want to bake a pie."*

**4 cups flour**
**2 cups shortening**
**1 egg**
**2 tablespoons vinegar**
**Water to blend**

Break egg into measuring cup. Beat egg. Add vinegar and fill up with water; add flour and shortening. Blend with piecrust blender; shape into a ball. Refrigerate for one-half hour. Cut off and roll into crusts.

## SUMMER COOL & EASY PIE

Wanda Stubblefield, Chattanooga, TN

**$\frac{2}{3}$ cup boiling water**
**4 serving-size gelatin packages**
**8-inch crumb crust**
**10 ice cubes**
**8 ounces whipped topping**

Stir gelatin into boiling water until dissolved. Stir in ice cubes until it begins to thicken, dip out remaining cubes. Whisk whipped topping in until smooth. Pour into crust. Chill 6 hours. Top with thin layer of whipped topping or fruit, or both. Add nuts and fruit to inside of pie to stretch to 9-inch pie.

## JELL-O PIE

Mary Hill, Friendsville, TN

**1 carton whipped topping**
**12-ounce carton cottage cheese**
**1 cup coconut**
**4-ounce can fruit cocktail, drained**
**1 package orange gelatin (dry)**
**Graham cracker pie crust**

Combine whipped topping, cottage cheese, coconut, and fruit cocktail. Sprinkle gelatin over all, stir to mix well and pour into crust.

## CHESS PIE

Linda S. Gibbs, Edwardsburg, MI

**1 cup sugar**
**1 cup walnut meats**
**1 cup raisins, currents, or dates**
**2 or 3 eggs (depending on size)**
**Pinch of salt**
**$\frac{1}{2}$ teaspoon flavoring**
**$\frac{1}{2}$ cup butter or margarine, softened**

OVEN 350°

Cream butter or margarine and sugar; add beaten eggs, then other ingredients. Fill pastry-lined cupcake tins. Bake at 350° for 20–30 minutes until browned.

## FROZEN COCONUT PIE
Joyce West, Farmington, KY

**2 deep-dish pie shells**
**½ stick margarine**
**1 cup pecans**
**7 ounces coconut**
**16 ounces whipped topping**
**8 ounces cream cheese**
**1 can condensed milk**
**Caramel topping**

Brown margarine, pecans, and coconut in skillet; let cool. Mix together whipped topping, cream cheese, and milk until smooth and creamy. Layer pie shell with half whipped topping mixture and half pecan mixture. Drizzle caramel topping over. Repeat. Put in freezer. Keep frozen. Will keep up to 3 months in freezer.

## TROPICAL PIE
Helen Steele, Madison, FL

**6 egg whites**
**1 teaspoon baking powder**
**2 cups white sugar**
**34 Ritz crackers**
**2 cups pecans, chopped**
**1 teaspoon vanilla**

OVEN 350°

Beat egg whites until foamy. Beat in baking powder until stiff. Add sugar and beat until well mixed. Roll Ritz crackers until fine, fold in with chopped pecans and vanilla. Put into a well-greased 9x13-inch pan. Smooth out and bake at 350° for 25 minutes.

Optional: After it is cooled, cover top with 2 envelopes of whipped topping mix. Store in refrigerator overnight.

## BROWN SUGAR PIE
Vicki Cunningham, Tazewell, TN

**3 cups brown sugar**
**½ cup butter or margarine**
**3 eggs**
**4 tablespoons flour**
**1 cup milk**
**2 unbaked pie shells**
**Black walnut, hickory nuts (optional)**

OVEN 350°

Combine brown sugar, butter or margarine, eggs, and flour. Mix well with milk and pour into pie shells. Bake at 350° until brown on top. Let cool. Garnish with nuts.

## CREEPING CRUST PIE

Janet Fielder, Williamstown, UT

**½ cup margarine or butter**
**1 cup flour**
**1 cup sugar**
**1 teaspoon baking powder**
**½ cup milk**
**2 cups berries**
**1 cup, or less, sugar for berries**

OVEN 350°

Melt butter or margarine in 10-inch baking dish. Mix together well flour, baking powder, and sugar; add milk and mix, pour, or spoon over melted butter. Heat berries with sugar; let cool and pour over batter. Bake in 350° oven until golden brown, for approximately 30 minutes.

## HOSPITALITY PIE

Nelda M. Thornton, Prosperity, SC

*"These pies can be frozen for weeks and are so good to have on hand for unexpected company or to share with sick friends."*

**2 cups coconut (7–8 ounces)**
**1½ cups pecans, chopped**
**1 stick margarine, melted**
**14-ounce can condensed milk**
**8 ounces cream cheese**
**16 ounces whipped topping**
**1 small jar caramel or butterscotch ice cream topping**
**3 graham cracker crusts**

OVEN 350°

Melt margarine in 9x13-inch pan at 350°. Stir in nuts and coconut. Stir every 5 minutes until brown. Cool. Mix milk and cream cheese with electric mixer on low speed until smooth. Fold in whipped topping. Layer in pie shells half of the cream cheese mixture, coconut, and nuts. Drizzle with caramel topping. Repeat once and freeze.

## VINEGAR PIE

Emily Morgan, Warren, IN

**1 baked pie crust**
**1 or 2 beaten eggs**
**3 tablespoons vinegar**
**1 teaspoon lemon extract**
**4 tablespoons flour**
**1 cup sugar**
**1 cup boiling water**

Mix flour and sugar together. Add boiling water and cook for 5 minutes stirring constantly. Add beaten eggs and cook 2 minutes longer. Add vinegar and lemon extract, cook 2 minutes more. Pour into baked crust and let cool.

Low cholesterol variation: Use ½ cup egg substitute. (Also for more lemony flavor use 1 tablespoon real lemon and 2 tablespoons vinegar.)

## MY FAVORITE CREAM PIE

Opal Jenewein, Powhatan Point, OH

**1 cup water, plus 2–3 tablespoons**
**½ stick margarine**
**1 can evaporated milk**
**½ cup sugar**
**3 tablespoons cornstarch**
**Salt**
**3 egg yolks**
**1 cup coconut**
**1 baked pie crust**

Heat water and margarine together, bring to boil. Add milk. Separately, mix sugar, cornstarch, salt, egg yolks, and 2–3 tablespoons water. Add to milk mixture. Cook until thick, stirring constantly. Boil 2 minutes. Add coconut. Pour in a prepared baked pie crust.

## BUTTERNUT BROWNIE PIE

Jennifer Chamblee, Doddridge, AR

*"This recipe came from Luby's Cafeteria and is my favorite dessert when eating there!"*

**1 packet graham crackers, crushed**
**1 cup chopped pecans**
**3 egg whites**
**⅛ teaspoon baking powder**
**1 cup sugar**
**½ pint whipping cream**
**¼ cup sugar**
**1 teaspoon vanilla**

OVEN 350°

Beat egg whites to stiff peaks with baking powder. Gradually add 1 cup sugar. Fold in crushed graham crackers and pecans. Bake in a buttered pie plate for 20–25 minutes at 350°. Topping: Beat whipping cream and fold in sugar and vanilla. Top with whipping cream.

## THREE-MINUTE PIE

Bea Williams, Sebring, FL

**½ stick margarine, melted**
**1 cup sugar**
**3 eggs**
**1 teaspoon vanilla**
**¼ cup buttermilk**
**1 cup coconut**
**1 unbaked pie shell**

OVEN 325°

Combine melted margarine, sugar, coconut, eggs, vanilla, and buttermilk. Mix well. Pour into unbaked pie shell. Bake at 325° for 35–45 minutes. Stick knife in center to test for doneness.

## MILLION DOLLAR PIE

Linda Osborne, Bristol, TN

*"This is very easy and delicious too!"*

**2 graham cracker pie crusts**
**1 can sweetened condensed milk**
**7-ounce bag coconut**
**1 large can crushed pineapple**
**12 ounces whipped topping**
**¼ cup concentrated lemon juice**
**Chopped pecans (optional)**

Mix lemon juice and condensed milk. Drain pineapple and add to milk and all other ingredients. Mix well and pour into pie crust. Refrigerate for several hours or overnight.

## CRUMB PIE

Melanie Fischer, Spokane, WA

*"This recipe was given to me by my step-grandmother who received it from her mother-in-law, many years ago. It is written as it was given to her. Great at Christmas."*

**1 cup warm water**
**1 cup brown sugar (½ molasses and ½ dark corn syrup)**
**1 teaspoon baking soda**
**3 cups flour**
**1 cup sugar**
**1 cup shortening**
**2 pie shells**

OVEN 350°

Mix water, syrup, and baking soda in saucepan. Separately, mix flour, sugar, and shortening until fine like flour. Put liquid in shell and add crumbs on top. This will make two pies. Bake at 350° for 20–30 minutes, until the crumb mixture starts to brown. This will burn quite easily so do not get too hot. Heat until boiling. Put liquid on to cook first and then prepare crumbs.

## FOOLPROOF MERINGUE

Barbara Wren, Batesville, AR

*"This really works! No more weeping pies!"*

**3 egg whites**
**1 cup (½ of 7-ounce jar) Kraft Marshmallow Creme**
**Dash of salt**

OVEN 350°

Beat egg whites and salt until soft peaks form. Gradually add marshmallow creme, beating until stiff peaks form. Spread over pie filling, sealing to edge of crust. Bake at 350° for 12–15 minutes or until lightly browned. Cool.

## RHUBARB CUSTARD PIE

Mary E. Metz, Seymour, IN

**2 cups uncooked rhubarb**
**1 cup brown sugar**
**2 tablespoons flour or cornstarch**
**2 egg yolks, beaten**
**1 tablespoon water**
**Lump of butter**

OVEN 375°

Combine rhubarb, brown sugar, and flour or cornstarch. Add water to beaten egg yolks, pour over rhubarb mixture, add lump of butter. Bake for 35 minutes. Whip meringue, add to top of pie and brown.

## MERINGUE

Wanda Royer, Scio, OH

**3 egg whites**
**teaspoon vanilla**
**teaspoon cream of tartar**
**6 tablespoons sugar**

OVEN 350°

Beat egg whites with vanilla and cream of tartar until soft peaks form. Gradually add sugar, beating until stiff and glossy peaks form and all sugar is dissolved. Spread meringue over hot filling in a 9-inch pie shell, sealing to the edge of pastry. Bake at 350° for 12 to 15 minutes, or until meringue is golden. Cool.

Variation: For an 8-inch pie use only 2 egg whites and 4 tablespoons of sugar with the same amount of vanilla and cream of tartar.

Note: Wet knife before cutting a meringue-topped pie.

## KENTUCKY DERBY PIE

Phyllis Lance, McMinnville, TN

**4 eggs**
**¾ cup brown sugar**
**1 cup white corn syrup**
**1 stick butter**
**1 cup chocolate chips**
**1 cup chopped pecans**
**1 teaspoon vanilla**
**1 teaspoon flour**
**1 unbaked pie shell**

OVEN 350°

Beat eggs. Melt butter. Mix all ingredients and pour into a pie shell. Bake at 350° for 40–45 minutes.

Variation:
Betty J. Warren, Trenton, OH

Use 2 eggs and substitute 1 cup sugar for brown sugar.

## BLACK FOREST PIE (LOW-FAT)

Joanne Bidlen, Broadview Heights, OH

**1½ cups water**
**1 small package sugar-free black cherry gelatin**
**1 small package sugar-free vanilla pudding mix (cook style)**
**1 pound dark sweet pitted fresh/ frozen cherries**
**½ teaspoon almond extract**
**Chocolate pie crust**

Cook gelatin and pudding in water until thick and clear, about 1½ minutes in microwave. Add cherries, cook just about to boil. Add almond extract; pour into chocolate pie crust and refrigerate.

**Topping:**

**8 ounces fat-free softened cream cheese**
**1 cup fat-free whipped topping**
**1 teaspoon vanilla**
**2 teaspoons sugar or sweetener**
**Chopped nuts (optional)**

Blend together and pour over firm pie filling, sprinkle with chopped nuts if desired.

## EGG CUSTARD PIE

Juanita Curry, Westville, FL

**5 eggs, well beaten**
**¾ cup sugar**
**1 cup sweet milk**
**1 teaspoon vanilla**
**1 tablespoon butter or cooking oil**
**1 unbaked pie shell**

OVEN 350°

Mix first five ingredients well and pour into unbaked pie shell. Bake for 45 minutes or until filling is firm.

Note: Mix all ingredients in blender for faster mixing, then pour into pie shell and bake.

## SHOO-FLY PIE

Wanda E. Brunstetter, Wapato, WA

*"A great breakfast pie!"*

**One unbaked pie shell**
**1 cup flour**
**⅔ cup brown sugar**
**1 tablespoon butter**
**1 cup dark molasses**
**¾ cup boiling water**
**1 teaspoon baking soda**
**1 beaten egg**

OVEN 375°

Mix flour, brown sugar, and butter until crumbly. In separate bowl mix molasses, boiling water, baking soda, and beaten egg. Mix molasses mixture with half of crumb mixture, but do not beat. Put combined mixture into a pie shell and cover with the remaining crumbs. Bake for 11 minutes at 375° and then 30 minutes longer at 350°.

## BUTTERMILK PIE

Betty Glover, Carbondale, IL
Sherrie Alexander, Brookhaven, MS

**9-inch unbaked pie shell**
**½ cup butter, softened**
**1½–2 cups sugar**
**2–3 rounded tablespoons flour**
**3 eggs, unbeaten**
**½–1 cup buttermilk**
**1 teaspoon vanilla**
**Dash of nutmeg (optional)**

OVEN 350°

Cream together butter and sugar, mixing well. Add flour and eggs, beat well. Stir in buttermilk, vanilla, and nutmeg. Pour into unbaked pie shell. Bake for 45–50 minutes at 350° or until firm. Place on wire rack to cool completely before serving.

## IMPOSSIBLE BUTTERMILK PIE "ON THE RUN"

Bonnie Watkins, Greensboro, AL

*"It is real easy to make and in very short time. It is a great dessert for working moms and wives."*

**1½ cups sugar**
**1 cup buttermilk**
**½ cup quick-baking mix**
**⅓ cup butter**
**1 teaspoon vanilla**
**3 eggs**

OVEN 350°

Heat oven to 350°. Grease pie plate. Beat all ingredients until smooth. Pour into pie pan. Bake 30 minutes or until knife inserted in center comes out clean. Cool 5 minutes. Serve with mixed fruit if desired.

## CHOCOLATE CHIP ROCKY ROAD PIE

Elizabeth Allen, Lebanon, MO

**1 cup sifted flour**
**½ teaspoon baking powder**
**¼ teaspoon salt**
**⅛ teaspoon baking soda**
**½ cup butter**
**1 cup dark brown sugar, packed**
**1 egg, slightly beaten**
**2 tablespoons hot water**
**1 teaspoon vanilla**
**½ cup chopped nuts**
**1 cup mini semi-sweet chocolate chips**
**1 cup miniature marshmallows**

OVEN 350°

Melt butter over low heat; then mix brown sugar until well blended. Add egg, hot water, and vanilla. Stir together the flour, baking powder, salt, and baking soda. Add to sugar mixture, mix well. Mix in nuts, ½ of the chocolate chips, and ½ of marshmallows. Spread mixture into two 9-inch pie plates, sprinkle with remaining chips and marshmallows. Bake for 20 minutes. Cool.
Makes 2 pies.

## FOUR-LAYER CHOCOLATE/MUD PIE

Marilyn Crowe, Milano, TX

**2 sticks of margarine**
**1 cup nuts**
**2 cups flour**

OVEN 350°

Stir together and press into bottom and sides of 10-inch pie pan. Bake for 10–15 minutes at 350°. Cool.

**8-ounce package cream cheese**
**1 cup confectioners' sugar**
**½ large tub (1 cup) whipped topping**

Beat together until creamy smooth; spread half of mixture into crust.

**1 cup sugar**
**6 tablespoons cocoa**
**4 tablespoons flour**
**¼ teaspoon salt**
**2 cups milk**
**2 slightly beaten egg yolks**
**4 tablespoons butter or margarine**
**1 teaspoon vanilla**

In saucepan, blend sugar, flour, cocoa, and salt; add milk. Cook and stir over medium heat. Stir small amount of mixture into egg yolk; return to hot mixture; cook. Add butter and vanilla. Let cool; then spread on top of second layer.

Spread remaining whipped topping on top of third layer. Sprinkle with nuts. Refrigerate until ready to serve.

Variation:
I usually substitute Layer #1 (the crust) with a vanilla wafer crust (see below). I think it tastes better.

**Vanilla Wafer Crust:**
Mix together 1½ cups finely chopped vanilla wafer crumbs (36 wafers) and 6 tablespoons of melted butter or margarine. Press into 9-inch pie plate. Chill until set.

Variation:
Wanda Salusbury, DeRidder, LA

For layer 3 use: 1 small box instant vanilla pudding, 1 small box instant chocolate pudding, and 3 cups milk. Combine pudding mixes and milk. Pour over cream cheese mixture.

## CHOCOLATE ALMOND PIE

Pauline Batdorf, Minneapolis, MN

*"A 'must have' recipe for all of us chocolate lovers!"*

**½ cup milk**
**16 large marshmallows**
**6 chocolate almond candy bars**
**½ pint whipping cream, whipped**

Heat milk in saucepan until hot, dissolve the marshmallows in the hot milk. Break and add the candy bars. Stir until melted. Remove from heat and cool. Fold in whipped cream. Pour into baked 9-inch pie shell. Refrigerate until set. Serve with sweetened whipped cream and chocolate curl.

## TURTLE PIE

Gail Knoll, Whitefish, MT

**24 Oreo cookies, crushed**
**¼ cup melted butter**
**1 cup chocolate fudge sauce**
**6 cups pecan praline ice cream**
**½ cup caramel sauce**
**½ cup pecans**

Mix butter and cookie crumbs. Press into 9-inch deep pie plate and freeze for 30 minutes. Spread chocolate sauce over bottom. Spread on softened ice cream. Freeze 3–4 hours, drizzle on caramel sauce and chopped nuts. Freeze covered until ready to serve.

## SMEARCASE PIE

Ollie Woodworth, Rochester, PA

**3 eggs**
**½ teaspoon nutmeg**
**½ cup sugar**
**Pinch of salt (about ¼ teaspoon)**
**1 tablespoon flour**
**1 cup canned milk (undiluted)**
**16 ounces cottage cheese (large or small curd)**
**Unbaked pie shell**

OVEN 375°

Combine above ingredients and beat until blended (use fork). Pour into prepared unbaked pie shell. Sprinkle cinnamon on top. Bake at 375° for 50–60 minutes or until knife inserted in center comes out clean. Cool before serving.

## LEMONADE PIE

Wanda Cheek, Live Oak, FL
Anna M. Martin, Fairfield, IA
Naomi McLane, Urbana, MO
Crystle Scutt, Lake Wales, FL

**1 graham cracker or shortbread baked piecrust**
**6-ounce can frozen lemonade, partially thawed (can be pink)**
**1 can sweetened condensed milk (I use Eagle brand) (NOT evaporated milk)**
**8-ounce carton whipped topping**
**1 teaspoon grated lemon rind (optional)**

Mix lemonade and sweetened condensed milk together. Stir in whipped topping. Pour into pie shell. Refrigerate overnight.

Option: Add green or yellow food coloring for effect.

## GLAZED STRAWBERRY PIE

June Ferguson, Fairborn, OH

**1 quart strawberries**
**1¼ cups cold water**
**¼ cups cornstarch**
**1⅓ cup sugar**
**⅛ teaspoon salt**
**1 tablespoon lemon juice**
**Few drops red food coloring**
**Whipped cream**
**2 baked pie shells**

Wash, drain, and hull berries. Dissolve cornstarch in water. Add sugar and salt. Place these ingredients in pot and cook over low heat, stirring constantly until thickened and clear. Remove from heat and add lemon juice and color to make a bright red shade. Pour hot mixture over berries. Mix gently, pour into two baked pie shells. Garnish with whipped cream.

Variations: Peaches, blueberries, etc.

## OUT OF THIS WORLD PIE

Emma Holland, Newport, OH

**1 can cherry pie filling**
**¾ cup sugar**
**20-ounce can crushed pineapple, with juice**
**1 tablespoon cornstarch**
**1 teaspoon red food coloring**
**3-ounce box cherry gelatin**
**4 bananas, sliced**
**1 cup chopped pecans**
**2 baked pie shells**
**Whipped topping**

In saucepan combine cherry pie filling, sugar, pineapple with juice, cornstarch, and food coloring. Cook until thick. Remove from heat and add dry gelatin. Allow to cool. Add bananas and pecans. Pour into 2 baked pie shells. Top with whipped topping. Chill.

## FRESH STRAWBERRY PIE

Rosemond J. Snell, St. Croix Falls, WI
Donnie Mae Corbitt, Brunswick, GA
Elaine Kohl, Brookings, SD
Carolyn Hoffman, Middleburg, PA

**Fresh strawberries, washed and sliced (about 4 cups)**
**1 cup sugar**
**1 cup water**
**2 tablespoons cornstarch**
**⅛ teaspoon salt**
**3 tablespoons corn syrup**
**3 tablespoons strawberry-flavored gelatin**
**1 baked pie shell**

Spread strawberries in pie shell. Cook all other ingredients slowly for 5 minutes. Add strawberry gelatin. Cool. Pour over fresh berries in pie shell.

Two variations:

1. Use raspberries with raspberry gelatin.
2. Add one tablespoon cornstarch, slowly add 1 cup 7-Up®.

## LEMON SPONGE PIE

Carol Macfarlane, Troy, MI

**1 unbaked pie shell**
**1 cup sugar**
**1 tablespoon margarine or butter, softened**
**1 tablespoon flour**
**3 eggs, separated**
**1 cup milk**
**1 lemon, for juice and zest**
**¼ teaspoon salt**

OVEN 425°

Cream sugar, margarine, flour, salt, and 3 egg yolks (save whites); slowly add milk and zest and juice of lemon. Fold in well-beaten egg whites, pour into piecrust. Bake at 425° for 10 minutes then at 350° for 20 minutes more until light brown on top and knife drawn through pie comes out clean. Cool.

## FRESH PEACH PIE

Cathryn Stallings, Maben, MS

**¾ cup sugar**
**3 tablespoons flour (heaping)**
**3 tablespoons butter**
**2 eggs**
**2 cups fresh peaches, sliced**
**9-inch piecrust**

OVEN 400°

Mix together; fold in peaches. Pour into 9-inch pie shell. Bake at 400° for 35 minutes.

## HUSBAND'S PEACH PIE

Christine Sayles, Davison, MI

**Crust:**

**$2^2/_3$ cups all-purpose flour**
**1 teaspoon salt**
**1 cup shortening**
**7 to 8 tablespoons cold water**

**Filling:**

**29-ounce can peaches in heavy syrup**
**3 tablespoons reserved peach syrup**
**3 tablespoons cornstarch**
**1 cup sugar, divided**
**3 eggs**
**$^1/_3$ cup buttermilk**
**½ cup butter, melted**
**1 teaspoon vanilla**

**Glaze:**

**2 tablespoons butter, melted**
**Sugar**

OVEN 400°

Crust: Spoon flour into measuring cup and level. Combine flour and salt in medium bowl. Cut in shortening using pastry blender (or 2 knives) until flour is blended to form pea-size chunks, sprinkle with water, 1 tablespoon at a time. Toss lightly with fork until dough forms a ball. Roll out ½ on floured surface and press into bottom of 10-inch pie plate. Do not bake. Heat oven to 400°.

Filling: Drain peaches, reserve 3 tablespoons of syrup; set aside. Cut peaches into small pieces and place in large bowl. Combine cornstarch and 2 to 3 tablespoons sugar. Add reserved peach syrup. Add remaining sugar, eggs, and buttermilk. Mix well. Stir in ½ cup melted butter and vanilla. Pour over peaches. Stir until peaches are coated. Pour filling into unbaked piecrust. Moisten pastry edge with water. Cover pie with top crust. Cut slits or designs in top crust to allow steam to escape.

Glaze: Brush with 2 tablespoons melted butter. Sprinkle with sugar. Bake for 45 minutes or until filling in center is bubbly and crust is golden brown. Cool. Refrigerate leftover pie.

## CHERRY CHEESECAKE PIE

Terry Mason, Haysville, KS

*"This is a rich dessert, so the initial mixture can be used to fill two piecrusts, and one can of pie filling divided to top the two pies. And they still think they're getting an elegant and delicious dessert. Whipped topping can be added if desired."*

**8-ounce package cream cheese, softened**
**½ cup sugar**
**1 tub whipped topping**
**9-inch unbaked graham cracker crust**
**1 can cherry pie filling**

Beat together cream cheese and sugar until creamy. Blend in whipped topping. Pour into unbaked pie shell. Top with cherry pie filling. Chill 3 hours before serving.

Variations: Fat-free/cholesterol-free ingredients may be used. Regular baked piecrust may be substituted for graham cracker crust.

## CHERRY CREAM CHEESE PIE

Wanda (Ruth) Debury, Marietta, MN

*"I made this for a hospital benefit last year. It brought $625.00! I couldn't believe it but it is a pretty pie!"*

**1 graham cracker crust (9- or 10-inch)**
**8-ounce package cream cheese (regular, low-fat, or fat-free, all work)**
**1 can sweetened condensed milk (also regular, low-fat, or fat-free)**
**⅓ cup lemon juice**
**1 teaspoon vanilla**
**1 can cherries, blueberries, or pineapple**

Whip together cream cheese, and milk until light; add juice and vanilla, blend. Pour into crust and top with canned fruit. Chill.

## COCONUT PIE

Alma Vernon, Lynchburg, VA

**2 cups sugar**
**⅔ cup cornstarch**
**4 eggs, separated**
**12-ounce can milk**
**3 cups water**
**½ stick margarine**
**1 tablespoon vanilla**
**1 large package coconut**
**2 baked piecrusts**
**½ cup sugar**

Cook 2 cups sugar, cornstarch, egg yolks, milk, water, margarine, vanilla, and ½ package coconut. Pour into baked pie crusts. Beat egg whites. Add ½ cup sugar. Beat until stiff. Spread on pies. Add remaining coconut. Brown in oven.

## KEY LIME PIE

Mrs. Eugene Warren, Cincinnati, OH

**14-ounce sweetened condensed milk (can be non-fat)**
**½ cup key lime or regular lime juice**
**8-ounce container whipped topping**
**1 graham cracker crust**

Beat milk and lime juice at medium speed until smooth and thick. Fold in whipped topping. Cover and refrigerate at least one hour.

## KEY LIME PIE

Paula Shea, Corinth, MS

**4 egg yolks**
**6 egg whites**
**1 can sweetened condensed milk**
**½ cup lime juice**
**¾ cup sugar**
**½ teaspoon cream of tartar**

OVEN 330°

Beat egg yolks until lemon colored. Blend in condensed milk slowly. Add lime juice and mix well. Add cream of tartar to egg whites and beat until foamy. Continue beating adding sugar, 1 tablespoon at a time, until egg whites peak, to make meringue. Fold 6 tablespoons of the meringue into the filling mixture. Pour into a 9-inch baked pie shell. Top with meringue and bake in a slow oven at 330° until golden brown.

## WALNUT PIE

Sandy Gellinger, Canby, OR

**8-inch unbaked pie shell**
**½ cup brown sugar**
**½ cup butter**
**¾ cup sugar**
**3 eggs**
**¼ teaspoon salt**
**¼ cup white corn syrup**
**½ cup light cream**
**1½ cups walnuts**
**½ teaspoon vanilla**
**Whipped topping**

OVEN 350°

In double boiler cream together brown sugar and butter. Stir in sugar, eggs, salt, corn syrup, and cream; cook over hot water for 5 minutes, stir constantly. Remove from heat. Stir in nuts and vanilla. Pour into pie shell. Bake at 350° for 50 minutes. Cool. Top with whipped topping and serve.

## SOUTHERN PECAN PIE

Anna Lee Williams, Aurora, MO
L. Dill, Hot Springs, AR

**1 cup white corn syrup**
**⅔ cup sugar**
**3 eggs, slightly beaten**
**1 teaspoon vanilla**
**⅓ cup butter, or margarine**
**¾–1 cup pecans**
**Dash of salt**
**1 unbaked pie shell**
**6 pecan halves**

OVEN 350°

Mix all ingredients together, adding pecans last. Pour mixture into pie shell. Top with pecan halves. Bake at 350° for approximately 50 minutes.

Serves 6–8.

## CHOCOLATE PECAN PIE
Maytie L. Cherry, Riverside, CA

**9-inch one-crust pie shell**
**2 squares unsweetened chocolate**
**2 tablespoons butter**
**3 eggs**
**½ cup sugar**
**¾ cup dark corn syrup (may use ½ amount of light syrup)**
**1 cup pecan halves**

OVEN 375°

Melt chocolate and butter together. Beat eggs, sugar, chocolate mixture, and syrup together. Mix in pecans. Pour into pastry-lined pie pan. Bake 40–50 minutes, just until set. Serve slightly warm, or cold, with ice cream or whipped cream.

## JELL-O PUDDING PECAN PIE
Mrs. Earldeen Pryor, Arma, KS

**1 large package vanilla pudding**
**1½ cups corn syrup**
**1 cup plus 1 tablespoon evaporated milk**
**2 eggs, slightly beaten**
**1½ cups chopped pecans**
**9-inch unbaked pie shell**

OVEN 375°

Blend pudding with corn syrup; add milk and eggs, mix well; add pecans, and pour into pie shell. Bake at 375° until top is firm and begins to crack, about 45–50 minutes. Cool about 3 hours. Garnish with whipped topping.

## PECAN PIE
Mrs. Charlie Hughes, Gardendale, AL
Ora Maddox, Orlando, FL

**¼ cup butter**
**¾ cup sugar**
**1 tablespoon flour**
**1 cup white corn syrup**
**¼ cup dark corn syrup**
**Dash salt**
**4 eggs**
**1 cup broken pecans**
**1 teaspoon vanilla**
**1 unbaked pie shell**

OVEN 450°

Cream butter, add sugar and flour gradually. Cream until fluffy. Add salt and eggs. Beat thoroughly, add syrups, beat well. Spread pecans over bottom of unbaked pie shell. Bake ten minutes at 450°. Add filling. Lower heat to 350° and bake 50 minutes until set.

## PEANUT BUTTER PUDDING PIE

Dawn Ambrose, Tyner, NC

**1 (small) box instant vanilla pudding**
**1 graham cracker crust**
**1 cup confectioners' sugar**
**½ cup peanut butter, creamy**
**1 small tub whipped topping**

Mix confectioners' sugar and peanut butter until they become like crumbs. Mix the instant pudding as directed on package for pie filling. Sprinkle ⅓ cup of peanut butter crumbs on bottom of piecrust. Empty pudding on top. Sprinkle ⅓ cup of peanut butter crumbs on top of pudding. Put whipped topping on top and put remaining crumbs on top of whipped topping. Chill in refrigerator.

## CHOCOLATE PEANUT BUTTER PIE

Louise Sisk, Ridgecrest, NC

**2 cups peanut butter, extra crunchy**
**8 ounces cream cheese (fat-free), softened**
**2 cups powdered sugar**
**1 cup milk, skim**
**3 8-ounce containers whipped topping**
**3 chocolate piecrusts**

Mix peanut butter and cream cheese until smooth. Add powdered sugar, milk, and 12 ounces of whipped topping (1½ containers). Blend thoroughly and pour into piecrusts, spreading evenly. Top each pie with 4 ounces whipped topping. These pies freeze and keep well. For added freshness, store pies in one-gallon freezer bags.

## LOW-FAT, SUGAR-FREE PEANUT BUTTER PIE

Jane Jackson, Russellville, AL

*"Always serve partially frozen. Super for diabetics!"*

**2 graham cracker crusts**
**8 ounces fat-free cream cheese**
**½ to ¾ cup low-fat peanut butter**
**24 packages of artificial sweetener**
**½ cup skim milk**
**12 ounces low-fat whipped topping**

Beat cream cheese and peanut butter at room temperature until smooth. Add Equal. Add milk slowly and continue beating, fold in whipped topping. Keep in freezer. Remove from freezer 30–40 minutes before serving.

## PEANUT BUTTER PIE

Ruth Woodard, De Ridder, LA
*"It does sound nasty, but I promise it is very good!"*

Laurajean Zauner, Vineland, NJ
*"This is real easy and delicious."*

**8 ounces cream cheese**
**1 cup powdered sugar**
**1 cup peanut butter**
**12 ounces whipped topping**
**1 graham cracker crust**

Mix and reserve small amount of whipped topping for topping, if desired. Pour into graham cracker crust.

## SOUR CREAM RAISIN PIE

Connie Sprague, Berthoud, CO

**10-inch baked pie shell**
**(I use wheat flour)**
**2 cups no-fat sour cream**
**1½ cups sugar**
**1 cup golden raisins**
**6 egg yolks (or egg substitute)**
**6 egg whites**
**1 to 2 tablespoons cinnamon**
**¼ teaspoon vanilla extract**
**2 teaspoons baking soda**
**Cream of tartar**

Mix all ingredients and cook over medium heat until it thickens and browns. Stir occasionally. If you stir too much it will not brown. Remove from heat and stir in baking soda; it will bubble up. Pour into pie shell and top with meringue. Meringue: Beat egg whites, adding sugar very slowly. Should be a lot of meringue. Center should be close to 1½-inches deep. Toast the top almost dark brown and serve. Best if hot.

## PEANUT BUTTER CREAM PIE

Glenna Riddle, Tallmadge, OH

**2 egg yolks**
**4 tablespoons cornstarch**
**¾ cup sugar**
**3 tablespoons warm water**
**2½ cups milk**
**⅔ cup peanut butter**
**1 teaspoon vanilla**
**2 tablespoons butter**
**9-inch baked pie shell**

Combine egg yolks, cornstarch, sugar, and water. Mix into a paste and add milk. Cook over medium heat, stirring constantly, until mixture begins to thicken. Remove from heat and beat in peanut butter, butter, and vanilla. Pour into pie shell; top with meringue.

## CRUNCHY PEANUT BUTTER PIE

Elizabeth Rowland, Norfolk, VA

**3 eggs, separated**
**1 cup sugar**
**2 heaping tablespoons crunchy peanut butter**
**2 tablespoons cornstarch**
**2 cups milk**
**1/8 teaspoon salt (optional)**
**1 baked pie shell or graham cracker shell**

OVEN 350°

Beat egg yolks until creamy. Mix sugar and cornstarch. Add to egg yolks. Add milk, peanut butter, and salt. Cook until thick. Pour batter into a pie shell. Beat egg whites and place on top of pie. Bake in 350° oven until top is brown.

## RAISIN CREAM SMOOTHIE PIE

Irene Houck, Branson, MO

*"A dear little German lady gave me this recipe when I was first learning to cook (about 10 years old). It has been our family favorite all through the years, and won my daughter (and me) a trip to New York in 1951 for the Pillsbury Bake Off Contest."*

**Crust:**

**1 cup flour**
**1/3 teaspoon salt**
**1/3 cup shortening**
**2–3 tablespoons cold water**

Cut together until crumbly. Sprinkle with cold water. Toss lightly with fork until dough is moist enough to hold together. Form in ball. Roll out on floured board to 11-inch circle. Fit loosely into 9-inch pie pan. Fold edge to form standing rim, flute.

**Filling:**

**3 eggs, slightly beaten**
**1¼ cups sugar**
**1/3 teaspoon salt**
**1 teaspoon cinnamon**
**¼ teaspoon cloves**
**1¼ cups sour cream**
**1½ cups raisins**

OVEN 400°

Mix eggs, sugar, salt, cinnamon, and cloves thoroughly. Blend in sour cream and raisins. Pour into pastry-lined pan. Bake at 400° for 10 minutes, then at 325° for 30–35 minutes, until tests done.

## RAISIN CREAM PIE

Grace Handrich, Mio, MI

**1 cup raisins, with enough water to cover them**
**1 cup sugar**
**1 heaping tablespoon flour**
**1 cup milk**
**2 eggs, separated**
**8-inch piecrust**

Cook raisins in water until tender. Mix sugar, flour, milk, and egg yolks. Pour in with cooked raisins. Continue cooking until thickened. Pour in piecrust. Cover with beaten egg whites or meringue. Brown in oven.

## ZUCCHINI "APPLE" PIE

Jane Scott, Greenville, SC

**4 cups zucchini, peeled, quartered, sliced**
**2 tablespoons lemon juice**
**Dash of salt**
**1¼ cups sugar**
**1½ teaspoons cinnamon**
**1½ teaspoons cream of tartar**
**Dash of nutmeg**
**3 tablespoons flour**

OVEN 400°

Combine zucchini, lemon juice, and salt; cook until zucchini is tender. Mix together sugar, cinnamon, cream of tartar, nutmeg, and flour. Add dry mixture to cooked zucchini and pour into prepared piecrust; dot with butter and bake at 400° for 40 minutes.

## QUICK AND CHEESY ZUCCHINI PIE

Traci Lange, Idaho Falls, ID

**3 cups zucchini, shredded**
**1 cup quick-baking mix**
**½ cup oil**
**1 cup sharp cheddar cheese, grated**
**1 tablespoon parsley**
**4 eggs, beaten**

OVEN 325°

Stir ingredients with fork. Add beaten eggs. Pour into a lightly greased 9-inch pan and bake at 325° for 35–40 minutes or until tests done. Should be lightly browned on outside.

## JIFFY ZUCCHINI PIE

Phyllis Metton, Yarmouth, ME

*"Tastes like an apple pie."*

**1 box Jiffy piecrust Mix (2 crusts)**
**1 zucchini, peeled and sliced like apple pie-size pieces**
**2/3 cup sugar**
**Cinnamon to taste**
**Nutmeg to taste**
**Salt to taste**
**2 tablespoons flour**
**2 to 3 tablespoons margarine**
**Juice of 1 lemon (optional)**

OVEN 350°

Mix and roll out dough for bottom crust for 8- or 9-inch pie plate. Sprinkle zucchini with cinnamon, nutmeg, and salt. Add flour and lemon juice, if desired. Roll out top crust, spread margarine over crust, press on top of zucchini. Run water over top. Sprinkle sugar over top crust. Make cuts throughout top crust. Bake at 350° for 1 hour, leave in warm oven ½ hour.

## BEST-EVER SWEET POTATO PIE

Belle S. Tawney, Martinsville, VA

**1 cup cooked mashed sweet potatoes**
**1/3 cup butter, melted**
**2 eggs, beaten**
**1/3 cup milk or half-and-half**
**½ teaspoon baking powder**
**Pinch of salt**
**1 teaspoon ground nutmeg**
**1 teaspoon pure vanilla extract**
**1 cup sugar, or less if desired**
**1 unbaked pie shell**

OVEN 400°

Blend all ingredients with electric mixer or by hand with wooden spoon. Pour into unbaked pie shell. Bake at 400° for about 30 minutes or until golden brown and puffy.

## SUGAR-FREE PUMPKIN PIE

Virginia Hadley, Bartlesville, OK

**3 ounces light cream cheese**
**1 cup, plus 1 tablespoon, skim or low-fat milk**
**1 graham cracker piecrust**
**6-ounce package vanilla instant sugar-free pudding mix**
**1 teaspoon cinnamon**
**¼ teaspoon cloves**
**½ teaspoon nutmeg**
**16-ounce can pumpkin**
**1½ cups whipped topping**

Mix cream cheese and 1 tablespoon milk with wire whisk until smooth. Gently stir in whipped topping. Spread on bottom of crust. Add pudding to 1 cup of milk and beat until smooth. Add remaining ingredients and mix well. Spread on cheese layer and refrigerate at least 2 hours. Garnish with whipped cream or nuts.

## IMPOSSIBLE PUMPKIN PIE

I. Grace Howe, Lansdale, PA

**¾ cup sugar**
**½ cup quick-baking mix**
**2 tablespoons margarine or butter**
**13-ounce can evaporated milk**
**2 eggs**
**16-ounce can pumpkin**
**2½ teaspoons pumpkin pie spice, or any spice you like**
**2 teaspoons vanilla**

OVEN 350°

Lightly grease 10-inch pie plate. Beat all ingredients well until smooth, 1 minute in blender on high speed, or 2 minutes by hand beater. Pour into pie plate. Bake until golden brown and tests done, 50–55 minutes. Refrigerate leftovers.

## HONEY PUMPKIN PIE

Clarice Logan, Bryant, SD

**2 cups pumpkin**
**1 cup honey, plus ¼ cup brown sugar**
**3 eggs**
**1 can evaporated milk, plus 1 can milk**
**½ teaspoon salt**
**½ teaspoon ginger**
**1 teaspoon cinnamon**
**½ teaspoon nutmeg (optional)**
**⅛ teaspoon cloves (optional)**
**1 cup pecans**

OVEN 450°

Mix together and pour into unbaked pie shell, add pecans. Bake at 450° for 10 minutes, then at 325° for 45 minutes.

## MOCK APPLE PIE

Mrs. Paul E. Nester, Meadows Dan, VA
Carol M. Coleman, Cherryville, MO

**2 cups water**
**1½ cups sugar**
**2 teaspoons cream of tartar**
**24 Ritz crackers**
**¼ stick margarine**
**1 teaspoon cinnamon**
**9-inch unbaked piecrust**

OVEN 425°

Combine water, sugar, and cream of tartar in saucepan. Bring to a boil. Add Ritz crackers and boil for 2 minutes. Do Not Stir! Let cool and pour into unbaked piecrust. Dot with butter, or margarine, over top. Sprinkle with cinnamon. Bake at 425° until crust is browned. Let cool completely. Serve with a scoop of ice cream on each slice of pie, if desired.

## SWEDISH APPLE PIE

Debra A. Brouillard, Lowell, MA

**Enough apples peeled and sliced to fill pie pan 2/3 full**
**1 tablespoon sugar**
**1 teaspoon cinnamon**
**¾ cup melted butter**
**1 cup sugar**
**1 cup flour**
**1 egg**
**½ cup nuts**
**Pinch of salt**

OVEN 350°

Fill pie pan 2/3 full with apples. Combine 1 tablespoon sugar with cinnamon; sprinkle over apples. In small bowl combine butter, 1 cup sugar, flour, egg, nuts, and salt; mix thoroughly and spoon over apples. Bake in 350° oven for 35 minutes or until golden brown.

## APPLE CREAM PIE

Pamela Goff, Salem, IL

*"Because my pastor always used the illustration 'as good as apple cream pie,' I asked him if he knew of a recipe for it. He said he never knew that apple cream pie even existed; it just sounded like something very good. One day I was searching my old cookbooks for something to make for a bake sale and was surprised to find a recipe for apple cream pie. I made the first pie and gave it to my pastor. When he assured me that it was very good, I teased him that now he really knew what he was talking about!"*

**2 cups finely chopped tart apples**
**¾ cup sugar**
**2 tablespoons flour**
**1 cup sour cream**
**1 well-beaten egg**
**½ teaspoon vanilla**
**1/8 teaspoon salt**
**Unbaked pastry shell**

OVEN 450°

Combine sugar and flour. Add cream, egg, vanilla, and salt; beat until smooth. Add apples. Mix thoroughly. Pour into pastry lined pan. Bake in hot oven at 450° for 15 minutes. Reduce heat to 325° and bake for 30 more minutes. Remove from oven.

**Topping:**

**1/3 cup sugar**
**1 teaspoon cinnamon**
**1/3 cup flour**
**¼ cup butter, softened**

Combine all ingredients and mix thoroughly. Sprinkle over pie. Return to oven. Bake in slow oven at 325° for additional 20 minutes.

## CARAMEL CRUNCH APPLE PIE

Dorothy Frost, Buchanan, GA

**9-inch piecrust**
**36 caramels**
**2 tablespoons water**
**4 cups apples sliced, peeled**

OVEN 375°

Roll piecrust out to 12 inches, place in pie pan and flute edge. Melt caramels in 2 tablespoons water until smooth. Place apple slices in pie plate, pour caramel over.

**Topping:**

**¾ cup flour**
**⅓ cup sugar**
**½ teaspoon cinnamon**
**⅓ cup margarine**
**½ cup chopped walnuts**

Mix together flour, sugar, and cinnamon; cut in margarine, then add nuts. Sprinkle over top of caramel and bake for 40–45 minutes.

Serves 8.

## ENGLISH APPLE PIE

Lois James, Houma, LA

**½ cup margarine**
**3 tablespoons water**
**½ cup packed brown sugar**
**½ cup chopped pecans**
**1 cup all-purpose flour**
**4 large cooking apples, peeled and sliced (about 6 cups)**
**2 teaspoons cinnamon**
**½ cup granulated sugar**
**Heavy cream or half-and-half (optional)**

OVEN 370°

Mix and beat cream (optional), margarine, and brown sugar until fluffy. Stir in flour, 1 teaspoon cinnamon, and water until smooth and thick. Stir in pecans. Mound apples in 9-inch pie plate. Mix granulated sugar with remaining teaspoon cinnamon. Sprinkle over apples. Spoon pecan topping over apples in dollops. Bake on lowest rack for 45–50 minutes until apples are tender when pierced. Top with favorite topping and serve in bowls if desired.

## CRUSTLESS APPLE PIE

June C. Gestiehr, El Cajon, CA

**¼ cup butter**
**1 cup sugar**
**1 egg**
**2 cups apples, thinly sliced**
**½ cup nuts**
**1 cup flour**
**½ teaspoon baking powder**
**½ teaspoon baking soda**
**½ teaspoon nutmeg**
**¼ teaspoon salt**
**1 teaspoon cinnamon**

OVEN 350°

Cream together butter, sugar, and egg. Sift together in another bowl the flour, baking powder, soda, nutmeg, salt, and cinnamon. Add to creamed mixture. Fold in apples and nuts. Put in greased pie plate. Bake 40–45 minutes at 350°. Serve warm with vanilla ice cream or whipped topping.

## DIABETIC SPICED PUMPKIN PIE

Edith Beavers, Bandy, VA

**Pastry for 9-inch shell**
**16-ounce can pumpkin**
**12-ounce can evaporated skim milk**
**3 eggs**
**5½ teaspoons liquid artificial sweetener, or 18 packets artificial sweetener**
**¼ teaspoon salt**
**1 teaspoon ground cinnamon**
**½ teaspoon ground ginger**
**¼ teaspoon ground nutmeg**
**⅛ teaspoon ground cloves**

OVEN 425°

Roll pastry on floured surface to circle 1-inch larger than inverted pie dish. Ease pastry into dish; trim and flute edge. Beat pumpkin, evaporated milk, and eggs in medium bowl; beat in remaining ingredients. Pour mixture into pastry shell. Bake in preheated oven for 15 minutes. Reduce heat to 350°. Bake about 40 minutes.

## SUGARLESS APPLE PIE

Marjorie Sheeke, Odon, IN

**1 tablespoon cornstarch**
**12-ounce can apple juice concentrate**
**4 cups sliced Golden Delicious apples**
**1 teaspoon apple pie spice**
**1 unbaked pie shell**
**Dash salt**
**½ tablespoon butter**
**3 packets artificial sweetener**

OVEN 400°

Mix cornstarch and apple juice. Cook over medium heat, stirring until mixture begins to clear. Stir in apples, butter, salt, and pie spice. Pour into unbaked crust. Sprinkle sweetener on top. Bake at 400° for 15 minutes, then at 350° for 30 minutes.

## SPRING TEMPTATION PIE

Cheryl Ringley, Monticello, KY

**1 cup boiling water**
**1 (4-serving size) package lemon flavor gelatin**
**1 cup orange or lemon sherbet**
**2 cups thawed whipped topping**
**2 cups miniature marshmallows**
**8-ounce can crushed pineapple, drained (optional)**
**9-inch prepared graham cracker crust**

Stir boiling water into gelatin in medium bowl 2 minutes or until completely dissolved. Stir in sherbet; mix well until melted. Refrigerate 25 minutes or until gelatin mixture is slightly thickened. Fold in whipped topping, marshmallows, and pineapple. Pour into crust. Freeze until firm (overnight is best).

Makes 6–8 servings.

Sugar-free: Use sugar-free gelatin and unsweetened pineapple.

## MARYANZ SUGAR-FREE PIE

Mary Ann Eitelgeorge, Tenino, WA
*"This is a favorite dessert. My whole family enjoys it!"*

**2 pie shells (I use graham cracker crust which do have some sugar)**
**12- or 16-ounce package frozen unsweetened berries (Marionberry is my favorite)**
**1 large package sugar-free gelatin (I use the triple berry)**
**Sugar-free whipped topping**

Mix gelatin with 2 cups boiling water (do not add any more water). In blender, put frozen berries, add hot gelatin and mix thoroughly, then pour into pie shells and chill in refrigerator. When solid add whipped topping.

## DIABETIC FRUIT OR BERRY PIE

Ruth A. Davis, Harrisonville, MO

**3 to 4 cups fruit or berries**
**6 ounces frozen apple juice (do not dilute)**
**1 teaspoon cinnamon**
**1 tablespoon lemon juice (for mild fruits or berries)**
**2 tablespoons cornstarch**
**2 tablespoons margarine**
**2 piecrusts**

OVEN 350°

In saucepan cook fruit or berries, apple juice, and cinnamon until boiling. Remove from heat. Add cornstarch that has been mixed with a little cool water. Stir while adding cornstarch. Pour into piecrust. Top with 2 tablespoons margarine. Add top crust. Bake at 350° for 40–45 minutes or until crust is done.

## NO SUGAR-ADDED PINEAPPLE CREAM PIE

D. Linda Petrey, Lebanon, OH
*"Makes a refreshing lower calorie pie."*

**1 can crushed pineapple, in own juice**
**8 ounces fat-free sour cream**
**1 small box instant sugar-free vanilla pudding**
**1 graham cracker crust, can be low-fat**

Pour pineapple with juice into bowl. Mix in the sour cream. Slowly mix in the pudding mix (dry). Pour into graham cracker crust and chill at least 2 hours.

# COOKIES

## EASTER STORY COOKIES

Birdie L. Etchison, Ocean Park, WA

*"To be made the evening before Easter."*

**Editor's Note:** Birdie is the author of several Heartsong Presents titles including *Anna's Hope* and *Albert's Destiny*.

**1 cup whole pecans**
**1 teaspoon vinegar**
**3 egg whites**
**Pinch of salt**
**1 cup sugar**
**Zipper baggie**
**Wooden spoon**
**Tape**
**Bible**

OVEN 300°

Place pecans in zipper baggie and let children beat them with the wooden spoon to break into small pieces. Explain that after Jesus was arrested He was beaten by the Roman soldiers. Read John 19:1–3.

Let each child smell the vinegar. Put 1 teaspoon vinegar into mixing bowl. Explain that when Jesus was thirsty on the cross he was given vinegar to drink. Read John 19:28–30.

Add egg whites to vinegar. Eggs represent life. Explain that Jesus gave His life to give us life. Read John 10:10–11.

Sprinkle a little salt into each child's hand. Let each taste it, then brush the rest into the bowl. Explain that this represents the salty tears shed by Jesus' followers, and the bitterness of our own sin. Read Luke 23:27.

So far the ingredients are not very appetizing. Add 1 cup sugar. Explain that the sweetest part of the story is that Jesus died because He loves us. He wants us to know and belong to Him. Read Ps. 34:8 and John 3:16.

Beat with a mixer on high speed for 12 to 15 minutes until stiff peaks are formed. Explain that the color white represents the purity in God's eyes of those whose sins have been cleansed by Jesus. Read Isaiah 1:18 and John 3:1–3.

Fold in broken nuts. Drop dough by teaspoons onto waxed-paper-covered cookie sheet. Explain that each mound represents the rocky tomb where Jesus' body was laid. Read Matt. 27:57–60.

Put cookie sheet in oven, close the door and turn the oven off. Give each child a piece of tape and seal the oven door. Explain that Jesus' tomb was sealed. Read Matt. 27:65–66.

Go to bed! Explain that they may feel sad to leave the cookies in the oven overnight. Jesus' followers were in despair when the tomb was sealed. Read John 16:20, 22.

On Easter morning, open the oven and give everyone a cookie. Notice the cracked surface and take a bite. The cookies are hollow! On the first Easter Jesus' followers were amazed to find the tomb open and empty. Read Matt. 28:1–9.

"HE HAS RISEN"—you can be a victor from the dark domain because He arose!

## PECAN SANDIES

Lynn Toman, Rapid City, SD

**1 cup butter or margarine**
**⅓ cup sugar**
**2 teaspoons water**
**2 teaspoons vanilla**
**1 cup flour**
**1 cup chopped pecans**
**Powdered sugar**

OVEN 325°

Cream butter and sugar; add water and vanilla; mix well. Add flour and pecans. Chill 3–4 hours. Shape into balls or fingers. Bake for 20 minutes at 325°. Cool and roll in powdered sugar.

Makes up to 5 dozen.

## PECAN PIE COOKIES

Irene May Van Doren, Wenatchee, WA

*"My mother gave me this recipe, and it's delicious. These cookies freeze well, too."*

**1 cup flour**
**½ cup oats**
**½ cup butter, softened**
**¾ cup brown sugar**
**3 eggs**
**¾ cup light corn syrup**
**1 cup broken pecans**
**1 teaspoon vanilla**
**¼ teaspoon salt**
**1 tablespoon flour**

OVEN 350°

Mix together flour, oats, butter, and brown sugar until they resemble fine crumbs. Press into bottom of well-greased 9x9-inch pan. Bake 15 minutes. While crust bakes, beat together eggs, corn syrup, pecans, vanilla, salt, and flour. Pour over hot crust. Bake 25–30 minutes. Cool and cut.

Makes 16 cookies.

## SMORBAKELSER

(Swedish Butter Cookies)

Tracie Peterson, Topeka, KS

**Editor's Note:** Tracie has been voted favorite Heartsong Presents author for three years in a row. She has written over thirty books, including some under the pen name of Janelle Jamison. This recipe appeared in *An Old-Fashioned Christmas* with Tracie's novella, "God Jul."

**1 cup butter**
**2 egg yolks**
**½ cup sugar**
**1 teaspoon almond extract**
**1 teaspoon vanilla extract**
**2 cups flour**

OVEN 400°

Cream butter, egg yolks, sugar, and extracts together until light and fluffy. Add flour and mix well. Dough will be soft, but not sticky. Roll out (do not overflour surface) and cut with cookie cutter or use in cookie press. Bake for 8–10 minutes. They burn easily, so be careful.

## FORGOTTEN KISSES

Carol Buker, Salem, OR

**2 egg whites**
**¼ teaspoon cream of tartar**
**1 cup sugar**
**1 teaspoon vanilla**
**16-ounce package chocolate chips**

OVEN 375°

Beat egg whites until foamy, add cream of tartar, and beat until stiff peaks are formed. Beat in sugar and vanilla, fold in chocolate chips. Drop by teaspoonsful onto ungreased cookie sheet. Place in oven and shut off heat; leave in oven 5 hours or overnight, without opening the door and peeking.

You can substitute crushed peppermint sticks or cinnamon imperials for chocolate chips.

Makes 40 cookies.

## CHEWY CHOCOLATE COOKIES

Peggy L. Self, Sedalia, MO

**1 package (2-layer size) chocolate cake mix**
**2 eggs**
**1 cup Miracle Whip**
**1 cup chocolate chips**
**½ cup chopped walnuts (optional)**

OVEN 350°

Mix cake mix, eggs, and dressing in large bowl with an electric mixer on medium speed, until blended. Stir in remaining ingredients. Drop rounded teaspoonfuls onto greased cookie sheet. Bake 10–12 minutes or until edges are lightly browned.

Makes 4 dozen.

## CHOCOLATE BUTTERFINGER BALLS

Peggy L. Self, Sedalia, MO

Mix together and roll into balls:

**2 cups crunchy peanut butter**
**3 cups Rice Krispies**
**1 stick margarine**
**1 pound powdered sugar**

Melt in double boiler:

**1 large Hershey bar**
**16-ounce package chocolate chips**
**1 teaspoon vanilla**
**1 slab of paraffin wax**

Dip balls into chocolate mixture. Place on sheets of waxed paper and chill.

## THIN CHOCOLATE CHIP COOKIES

Hazel Soules, Norwich, NY

*"These are thin and crisp and loved by everyone."*

**1½ cups sugar**
**2 sticks (1 cup) margarine**
**2 eggs**
**2 teaspoons vanilla**
**2½ cups Grape Nut Flakes cereal**
**1 cup chocolate chips**
**⅛ teaspoon salt**
**1 teaspoon baking soda**
**2 cups flour**

OVEN 350°

Cream sugar and margarine together; add eggs and stir, add vanilla and stir, add cereal and chocolate chips, stir together. Put salt and baking soda into flour and add to mixture, a small amount at a time. Stir well. Drop by teaspoon on tins and bake for 20 minutes or until golden brown. Bake less time for smaller cookie.

## KRISPIE CHOCOLATE CHIP COOKIES

Kimberly Day, Lynchburg, VA

**1 cup butter**
**1 cup granulated sugar**
**1 cup brown sugar**
**2 eggs**
**1 teaspoon vanilla**
**1 teaspoon salt**
**1 teaspoon baking soda**
**2½ cups flour**
**1½ cups oats**
**1½ cups Rice Krispies cereal**
**2 cups chocolate chips**

OVEN 350°

Cream together butter and sugars. Beat in eggs and vanilla. In separate bowl, combine salt, baking soda, and flour. Mix into first bowl with previous ingredients. Stir in oats and Rice Krispies cereal, then chocolate chips. Drop by spoonfuls onto cookie sheets and bake 10 minutes.

## BIG CHOCOLATE CHIP COOKIES

Kathie Baldwin, Syracuse, NY

**1 cup margarine**
**1 cup brown sugar**
**1 egg**
**1 teaspoon vanilla**
**2 cups flour**
**1 teaspoon baking soda**
**½ teaspoon salt**
**1 cup rolled oats**
**12-ounce package chocolate chips**
**½ cup nuts (optional)**
**½ cup raisins (optional)**

OVEN 350°

Combine margarine, brown sugar, egg, and vanilla. Add flour, baking soda, and salt. Add oats, chocolate chips, nuts, and raisins; mix well. Measure ¼ cup of dough for each cookie, making each cookie 3 inches around and ½ inch thick. Bake on lightly greased pan for 15 minutes. Let cool 5 minutes before removing from tray.

# COOKIES

## CHOCOLATE CHIP COCONUT COOKIES

Andrea Jesse, Cortez, CO

**⅓ cup shortening**
**⅓ cup butter**
**½ cup granulated sugar**
**½ cup brown sugar**
**1 egg**
**1 teaspoon vanilla**
**1½ cups flour**
**½ teaspoon baking soda**
**½ teaspoon salt**
**6-ounce package chocolate chips**
**¼ package coconut**
**1–2 cups oatmeal**

OVEN 375°

Mix shortening, butter, sugar, brown sugar, egg, and vanilla. Blend in flour, baking soda, and salt. Mix in chocolate chips, coconut, and oatmeal. Drop rounded teaspoonfuls 2 inches apart onto ungreased baking sheet. Bake 8–10 minutes. Cool slightly before removing from baking sheet.

## WORLD'S GREATEST CHOCOLATE CHIP COOKIES

Buffy Stuart, The Colony, TX

**1 cup oil**
**1 cup margarine, softened**
**1 cup brown sugar**
**1 cup granulated sugar**
**1 egg**
**1 teaspoon vanilla**
**3½ cups flour**
**1 teaspoon salt**
**1 teaspoon cream of tartar**
**1 teaspoon baking soda**
**1 cup quick oats**
**1 cup Rice Krispies**
**6 ounces butterscotch or peanut butter chips**
**12-ounce package chocolate chips**

OVEN 350°

Blend oil and margarine. Cream with sugars, egg, and vanilla. Sift together dry ingredients. Mix with oats, Rice Krispies, and chips. Bake on greased cookie sheet for 12 minutes or until lightly browned.

## CHOCOLATE CHIP COOKIE BALLS

Melissa Wilds, Selmer, TN

**1 box Duncan Hines Devil's Food Cake Mix**
**1 egg**
**¾ cup vegetable oil**
**1½ cups chocolate chips**
**½ cup pecans, chopped**

OVEN 350°

Mix all ingredients together. Roll in 1-inch balls. Place on ungreased cookie sheet. Bake 5 to 7 minutes. Cool on rack. Store in airtight container.

Makes about 2 dozen.

## CHOCOLATE CHIP CREAM CHEESE COOKIES

Judy Piper, Oasplurg, WI

*"Delicious during the holidays."*

**4 egg yolks**
**2 cups butter (do not substitute)**
**2 cups sugar**
**4 cups flour**
**Pinch of salt**
**2 8-ounce packages cream cheese**
**2 tablespoons almond extract**

OVEN 375°

Combine eggs, butter, and sugar. Add cream cheese and almond extract. Combine flour and salt and add to butter mixture. Drop by spoonfuls onto cookie sheets and bake until edges turn light brown, about 10 minutes.

## DOUBLE CHOCOLATE MINT CHIP COOKIES

Jenni Hannan, Milwaukie, OR

**10-ounce package Nestle Toll House mint-flavored semisweet chocolate morsels, divided**
**1¼ cups all-purpose flour**
**¾ teaspoon baking soda**
**½ cup butter, softened**
**½ cup firmly packed brown sugar**
**¼ cup granulated sugar**
**½ teaspoon vanilla extract**
**1 egg**
**½ cup chopped nuts (optional)**

OVEN 375°

Melt ¾ cup mint chips over boiling water (or in microwave: melt on high 1 minute, stir; repeat). Stir until smooth. Cool to room temperature. In bowl, combine flour, baking soda; set aside. In bowl beat butter, brown sugar, sugar, and vanilla extract until creamy. Add melted morsels and egg; beat well. Gradually blend in flour mixture. Stir in remaining morsels and nuts, if desired. Drop by rounded measuring tablespoonfuls onto ungreased cookie sheets. Bake for 8–9 minutes. Allow to stand 2–3 minutes before removing from cookie sheets, cool completely.

Makes about 1½ dozen cookies.

## PUDDING 'N CHOCOLATE CHIP COOKIES

Anna Dubble, Myerstown, PA

**2 packages vanilla pudding (instant or regular)**
**2 cups Bisquick**
**½ cup vegetable oil or applesauce**
**2 eggs**
**6 tablespoons milk**
**1 cup chocolate chips**

OVEN 350°

Mix ingredients as they come in order. Drop on ungreased cookie sheet by teaspoonfuls. Bake for 8–10 minutes.

# COOKIES

## VERY BEST OATMEAL PAN COOKIES

Iris Kidder, Mason, MI

**1 stick margarine**
**1 cup brown sugar**
**1 egg**
**2¼ cups oatmeal (uncooked)**
**2 teaspoons baking powder**
**½ teaspoon salt**
**1 teaspoon vanilla**

OVEN 425°

Mix ingredients and press into greased pan, about ½-inch thick. Bake until brown, about 10 minutes. Cut while still warm.

## CHOCOLATE CHIP TREASURE COOKIES

Monika Mendoza, Urbana, IL

**14-ounce can sweetened condensed milk**
**½ cup butter, softened**
**1½ cups graham cracker crumbs**
**½ cup flour**
**2 teaspoons baking powder**
**1½ cups flaked coconut**
**2 cups mini semisweet chocolate chips**
**1 cup chopped pecans**
**1 cup raisins**

OVEN 375°

Beat condensed milk and butter. Add mixture of graham cracker crumbs, flour, and baking powder. Mix well. Add other ingredients. Drop by spoonfuls on greased cookie sheets. Bake 9–10 minutes until lightly brown.

Makes 48 or more cookies, depending on size.

## OATMEAL CHOCOLATE CHIP COCONUT COOKIES

Sally Abramat, Belvidere, IL

**1 cup margarine or butter**
**¾ cup brown sugar**
**¾ cup granulated sugar**
**2 eggs, beaten**
**1½ cups flour**
**3 cups oatmeal**
**1 teaspoon vanilla**
**1 teaspoon salt**
**2 tablespoons hot water**
**1 cup coconut**
**1 cup chocolate chips**

OVEN 350–375°

Cream shortening and sugars. Add eggs, one at a time. Add baking soda dissolved in hot water or put it in with the flour. Add the rest of ingredients. Form into balls, flatten, and bake in moderate oven on greased cookie sheets for 12–15 minutes.

## OATMEAL-RAISIN COOKIES

Lois Scott, North Fryeburg, ME

**1 cup Crisco**
**2 cups brown sugar**
**2 eggs**
**1 teaspoon baking soda**
**1 teaspoon salt**
**2 cups flour**
**2 cups oats**
**1 cup raisins**

OVEN 375°

Cream shortening, sugar, and eggs. Mix in sifted baking soda, salt, and flour. After this is well mixed, add oats and raisins and mix well. Drop by teaspoonfuls onto cookie sheet. Bake for 10–12 minutes.

Makes 4 dozen.

## POWDERED OATMEAL COOKIES

Marilyn Schettle, Oshkosh, WI

*"These cookies pack well for mailing to someone special."*

**1½ cups shortening**
**3 cups brown sugar**
**3 eggs, beaten**
**1½ teaspoons vanilla**
**2¼ cups flour**
**¾ teaspoon salt**
**1½ teaspoons baking powder**
**1½ teaspoons baking soda**
**4½ cups oatmeal (dry)**
**Powdered sugar**

OVEN 350°

With a mixer beat shortening, brown sugar, eggs, and vanilla. Mix together flour, salt, baking powder, baking soda, and oatmeal; mix together with other ingredients. Chill overnight. Make balls and roll in powdered sugar. Grease cookie sheet. Bake for 8–10 minutes.

## OATMEAL CHOCOLATE CHIP COOKIES

Jean Gilbert, San Benito, TX

**1½ cups flour**
**2½ cups oatmeal**
**1 teaspoon salt**
**¾ cup brown sugar**
**¾ cup granulated sugar**
**1 cup Crisco**
**2 eggs**
**1 teaspoon vanilla**
**1 teaspoon baking soda**
**1 cup chocolate chips**
**½ cup chopped nuts**

OVEN 400°

Mix together flour, oatmeal, and salt. Cream sugars and shortening; add eggs, vanilla, and baking soda dissolved in hot water. Add chocolate chips and nuts. Bake until light brown.

## NO-BAKE OATMEAL FUDGE COOKIES

Mary Whisler, Vashon, WA

**½ cup margarine**
**½ cup milk**
**2 cups sugar**
**1 tablespoon cocoa**
**3 cups oats**
**¾ cup peanut butter**
**1 tablespoon vanilla**

Mix margarine, milk, sugar, and cocoa. Bring to a rolling boil. Boil 1 minute. Remove from heat and add rest of ingredients. Mix well, drop by tablespoonfuls onto waxed paper. Let cool and eat.

## COCOA OATMEAL CHOCOLATE CHIP

Laurie Haugen, Edmore, ND

**1¾ cups boiling water**
**1 cup quick oatmeal**
**1 cup brown sugar**
**1 cup granulated sugar**
**½ cup margarine**
**2 eggs**
**1¾ cups flour**
**1 teaspoon baking soda**
**1 teaspoon baking powder**
**1 tablespoon cocoa**
**¾ cup nuts**
**12-ounce package chocolate chips**

OVEN 350°

Pour water over oatmeal; let stand 10 minutes. Add sugars and margarine. Stir until melted. Add eggs. Add dry ingredients. Mix well. Add half of chips. Pour onto greased and floured 9x13-inch pan. Sprinkle nuts and rest of chips on top. Bake about 40 minutes.

## OATMEAL DROP COOKIES

Janet Hayman, Zephyrhills, FL

**2 cups sifted flour**
**1½ cups sugar**
**1 teaspoon baking powder**
**½ teaspoon baking soda**
**½ teaspoon salt**
**1 teaspoon cinnamon**
**3 cups rolled oats**
**1 cup raisins**
**¾ to 1 cup chocolate chips (optional)**
**1 cup oil**
**2 eggs**
**½ cup milk**

OVEN 375°

Sift flour, sugar, baking powder, baking soda, salt, and cinnamon. Mix in oats and raisins, also chocolate chips if desired. Add in order, oil, eggs, and milk. Mix until thoroughly blended. Drop from teaspoon onto cookie sheet. Bake for 10 minutes.

Makes about 6 dozen.

## OATMEAL COOKIES

Brenda Garrison, Gainesville, GA

*"My brother, who is now 48 years old, brought this recipe home from school when he was in grammar school. It is still one of my favorites and my children prefer it also."*

**2 cups sugar**
**½ cup sweet milk (condensed milk)**
**1 stick butter**
**3 tablespoons cocoa**
**½ cup peanut butter**
**2½ cups oatmeal**
**2 teaspoons vanilla**

Cook sugar, milk, butter, and cocoa for 1½ minutes (bring to a boil). Remove from stove, put in peanut butter, and stir well. Add oatmeal and vanilla. Stir well. Drop by spoonfuls on waxed paper. Cool until hard.

## HOLIDAY FRUIT DROP COOKIES

Elizabeth Hunt, Ithaca, MI

**1 cup shortening**
**2 cups brown sugar, packed**
**2 eggs**
**½ cup sour milk or ⅔ cup buttermilk**
**3½ cups flour**
**1 teaspoon baking soda**
**1 teaspoon salt**
**1 cup chopped nuts**
**2 cups candied cherries, cut into small pieces**
**2 cups dates cut into small pieces or 1 cup candied cherries and 1 cup dates**

OVEN 400°

Mix shortening, sugar, and eggs well. Stir in milk. Blend dry ingredients and stir into shortening mixture. Add nuts, dates, and cherries. Chill 1 hour. Heat oven. Drop dough by spoonfuls on greased baking sheet or make into balls. Bake 8–10 minutes.

Makes 8 dozen.

## CHRISTMAS COOKIES

Carolyn Roebuck, Massillon, OH

*"My family loved these cookies the best; so they are always baked at Christmas time."*

**2 cups sugar**
**½ teaspoon salt**
**1 cup shortening**
**1 ounce baking ammonia**
**1 tablespoon vanilla**
**2 cups sweet milk (condensed milk)**
**4 cups flour, just enough to stiffen**

OVEN 350°

Mix all ingredients together. Roll out about ½-inch thick, cut out with favorite cookie cutter. Bake 10 minutes. Ice with a vanilla icing and sugar sprinkles.

Makes about 11–12 dozen.

BAKER'S NOTE

Baking ammonia can be purchased through a baking catalog such as *King Arthur Flour's Baking Catalog*.

## CHRISTMAS EVE COOKIES

June Ferguson, Fairborn, OH

*"Smells like Christmas!"*

**1 cup sugar**
**½ cup butter**
**½ cup shortening**
**2 cups flour**
**½ teaspoon salt**
**1½ tablespoons cinnamon**
**1 egg, separated**
**1½ cups chopped nuts**

OVEN 325°

Grease and flour 10x15-inch pan. Cream sugar, butter, and shortening. Add egg yolk and dry ingredients. Press into pan. Beat egg white until foamy and spread very thinly over batter. Press on nuts. Bake for about 30 minutes. Cut into squares. Place on pretty plate with sprig of holly and a red bow.

## HOLLY COOKIES

Nichole Stiffler, Blairsville, PA

*"Adds a festive touch to your holiday platters, and doesn't take up needed refrigerator space."*

**⅓ cup butter**
**16 marshmallows**
**1 teaspoon vanilla**
**1 teaspoon green food coloring**
**2½ cups whole cornflakes**
**Red cinnamon candy**

Melt butter and marshmallows in double boiler. Blend in food coloring and vanilla. Place cornflakes in large bowl; pour mixture over cornflakes and mix lightly with fork. Drop cookies on waxed paper or form into wreath. Sprinkle with cinnamon candy and allow to set. No refrigeration needed.

## SOUR CREAM CHRISTMAS COOKIES

Carin Farnham, Hornell, NY

**1 cup Crisco**
**1 cup margarine**
**2 cups sugar**
**2 eggs**
**2 teaspoons baking soda**
**¾ teaspoon salt**
**1 teaspoon baking powder**
**2 teaspoons vanilla**
**1 teaspoon lemon juice**
**1 teaspoon nutmeg**
**6 cups flour**
**1 cup sour cream**
**1 cup buttermilk**

OVEN 375°

Melt Crisco and margarine together; cream with sugar, eggs, baking soda, salt, and baking powder; mix well. Add vanilla, lemon juice, and nutmeg. Alternately add flour, sour cream, and buttermilk. Chill overnight, uncovered. Roll and cut on floured surface. Bake for 5–8 minutes, or until soft in middle.

## PEANUT OATMEAL COOKIES

Lynn Glover, Washington, PA

**1 cup all-purpose flour**
**½ teaspoon baking soda**
**½ cup margarine or butter**
**½ cup peanut butter**
**⅓ cup granulated sugar**
**⅓ cup packed brown sugar**
**½ cup shredded carrot**
**2 egg whites**
**½ teaspoon vanilla**
**1 cup rolled oats**

OVEN 375°

In a bowl stir together flour and baking soda. In a large mixer bowl beat margarine with electric mixer on medium speed for 30 seconds. Add peanut butter, sugar, and brown sugar; beat until fluffy. Add carrot, egg whites, and vanilla; beat well. Add dry ingredients to beaten mixture; beat well. Stir in oats. Drop dough by rounded teaspoonfuls, 2 inches apart onto an ungreased cookie sheet. Bake about 10 minutes or until done. Remove cookies from cookie sheet. Cool on a wire rack.

## RIBBON CHRISTMAS COOKIES

Carol A. Blaylock, Duncanville, TX

**2 sticks butter**
**1¾ cups sugar**
**1 egg**
**1 teaspoon vanilla**
**2½ cups flour**
**1¼ teaspoons baking powder**
**¼ teaspoon salt**

**Add below ingredients to taste:**

**A few drops of green food coloring**
**Mint extract**
**Semisweet chocolate chips**
**Walnuts**
**Maraschino cherries**
**A few drops of red food coloring**

OVEN 375°

Cream butter and sugar. Add egg and vanilla, mix well. Mix together dry ingredients and add to butter mixture. Divide into 3 parts. Chill part 1, add green food coloring and mint flavoring. Part 2—add semisweet chocolate and walnuts. Part 3—maraschino cherries (and food coloring if needed). Place aluminum foil in bread pan. Pack dough one part at a time then chill overnight. Pull dough out of pan by holding onto foil. Cut in half lengthwise, then slice about ¼-inch thick. Bake for 8–10 minutes.

## EASY PEANUT BUTTER COOKIES

Beverly Lucero, Truth/Consequences, NM

**14-ounce can sweetened condensed milk**
**¾ to 1 cup peanut butter**
**1 egg**
**1 teaspoon vanilla extract**
**2 cups biscuit baking mix**

OVEN 350°

In large mixer bowl, beat sweetened condensed milk, peanut butter, egg, and vanilla until smooth. Add biscuit mix; mix well. Chill at least 1 hour. Shape into 1-inch balls. Place 2 inches apart on ungreased baking sheets. Flatten with fork. Bake 6–8 minutes or until lightly browned (do not overbake). Cool. Store tightly covered at room temperature.

## KOURABIEDES

(Greek Christmas Cookies)

Melanie Panagiotopoulos, Athens, Greece

*"When the pastry shops of Greece place these sugary delights in their windows. . .all know that Christmas isn't very far off! In* Christmas Baby*, Kristen Andrakos (*Odyssey of Love*) offers* kourabiedes *to the children who come to her home early on the morning of Christmas Eve singing the traditional Greek Christmas carol* "Kalanda." *The children go away with sugar-covered noses and chins, a common sight this time of the year!"* **Editor's Note:** *Kala Christouyenna!* "Happy Christmas!" Melanie was born in Virginia and now lives in Athens with her husband and two children. She is the author of books for Heartsong Presents.

**1 pound unsalted butter or margarine**
**3 tablespoons confectioners' sugar**
**2 egg yolks**
**1 teaspoon vanilla**
**5 cups flour, sifted**
**Confectioners' sugar for topping**

OVEN 375°

Cream butter until light and fluffy. Beat in sugar. Add egg yolks and vanilla. Gradually work in sifted flour to make a soft dough. . . you will need to discard the spoon and use your hands after a certain point, something children love to do. With floured hands shape into small crescents or oval shapes about half an inch thick. Place one inch apart on ungreased cookie sheet. Bake for about 20 minutes or until bottoms are very lightly browned. Place cookies on a plate and sift sugar over tops and sides. Cool thoroughly before storing.

## GRANDMA'S PEANUT BUTTER COOKIES

Claire Hudson, South Wales, NY

*"These are easy, good, and good for you. Try them, you will like them. They are different from other peanut butter cookies!"*

**1 cup butter or margarine**
**¾ cup brown sugar**
**¾ cup granulated sugar**
**1 teaspoon vanilla**
**2 eggs, beaten**
**1 cup peanut butter, smooth or crunchy**
**1 cup flour**
**1 cup bran**
**¾ cup rolled oats**
**2 teaspoons baking soda**

OVEN 350°

Melt butter or margarine; beat together with sugars, vanilla, eggs, and peanut butter. Combine flour, bran, oats, and baking soda. Stir flour mixture into butter mixture. Drop by teaspoonfuls onto ungreased cookie sheet. Bake for 15–18 minutes.

## QUICK AND EASY PEANUT BUTTER COOKIES

Alva Ford, Tyler, TX
Shirley J. Warren, Fox Island, WA

*"Believe it or not, these cookies take only 15 minutes to make, from start to finish. They're handy when you need a quick snack."*

**1 cup peanut butter (smooth or crunchy)**
**1 egg**
**1 cup granulated sugar**

OVEN 350°

Spray 2 cookie sheets with vegetable cooking spray. Mix ingredients together and drop by spoonfuls and bake about 8–12 minutes. Do not brown cookies on top as they will burn on bottoms.

Makes 36.

Variations: You may add nuts, M&M's, raisins, oatmeal, or coconut.

## COCOA PEANUT BUTTER CHEWYS

Debbie Jones, Midway, TN

**½ cup peanut butter**
**½ cup butter**
**1½ cups sugar**
**2 eggs**
**3 teaspoons cocoa**
**1 teaspoon vanilla**
**1 cup flour**
**1 cup pecans**

OVEN 350°

Grease and flour 9x13-inch pan. Melt peanut butter and butter in bowl over hot water. Add remaining ingredients and stir until blended. Bake for 25–30 minutes; cool and cut into squares.

Makes about 2 dozen.

## PEANUT BUTTER CORNFLAKE COOKIES

Georgia Hector, Swan Lake, NY

**1 cup sugar**
**1 cup light corn syrup**
**1½ cups peanut butter**
**1 teaspoon vanilla**
**8 cups cornflakes**

Put sugar and syrup in a saucepan, heat to full boil. Remove from heat and add peanut butter and vanilla. Beat until smooth. Pour over cornflakes, stir until flakes are completely coated. Drop by teaspoonfuls onto waxed paper.

Makes 3 dozen.

## PEANUT CLUSTERS
Loretta Boike, Saranac, MI

**1 pound chocolate almond bark**
**12-ounce package chocolate chips**
**1 cup chunky peanut butter**
**1 large (12–16 ounce) package salted peanuts**

Melt almond bark in microwave (about 3 minutes, adjust time for your microwave). Add chocolate chips, stir until melted. Add peanut butter and nuts, mix well. Drop from spoon onto waxed paper. Chill until set.

## PUMPKIN-BUTTERSCOTCH COOKIES
Margaret Moers, Fallbrook, CA

**1½ cups pumpkin**
**½ cup margarine**
**1 cup sugar**
**½ teaspoon salt**
**1 teaspoon vanilla**
**1 cup chopped walnuts**
**1 egg**
**2 cups unsifted flour**
**1 teaspoon salt**
**1 teaspoon baking powder**
**1 teaspoon cinnamon**
**1 package butterscotch chips**

OVEN 375°

Mix in all ingredients in order given; drop by spoonfuls onto greased cookie sheet. Bake for 12–14 minutes.

Makes 4 dozen.

Variations: Raisins, pecans, or coconut may be substituted for butterscotch chips. Also 3 ripe bananas can be substituted for pumpkin.

## PUMPKIN COOKIES
Lynn Campbell, Greensburg, PA

**1 cup margarine**
**2 cups sugar**
**2 cups pumpkin**
**1 cup chopped nuts or raisins**
**2 teaspoons vanilla**
**2 teaspoons cinnamon**
**2 teaspoons baking powder**
**2 teaspoons baking soda**
**4 cups flour**

OVEN 375°

Mix together margarine, sugar, pumpkin, nuts, and vanilla. Sift together other ingredients and mix together with pumpkin mixture. Drop on greased cookie sheet. Bake for 12–15 minutes.

## PUMPKIN NUT COOKIES

Nancy Keech, Williamsburg, MI

**¼ cup shortening**
**½ cup sugar**
**1 egg, beaten**
**½ cup cooked pumpkin**
**1 cup sifted all-purpose flour**
**½ teaspoon salt**
**2 teaspoons baking powder**
**1¼ teaspoons cinnamon**
**⅛ teaspoon ginger**
**¼ teaspoon nutmeg**
**½ cup raisins**
**½ cup chopped nuts**

OVEN 350°

Cream shortening, add sugar until light and fluffy. Add egg and pumpkin, mix well. Sift flour, baking powder, salt, and spices together. Stir in dry ingredients and mix. Add raisins and nuts. Drop by teaspoonfuls onto greased cookie sheet. Bake for 15 minutes.

Makes 2 dozen.

## SNICKERDOODLE COOKIES

Kathy Austin, Lodi, CA
Dorcas Walker, Jamestown, TN
Debbie Bragenzer, Petoskey, MI

**1 cup soft shortening (or ½ butter and ½ shortening)**
**1½ cups sugar**
**2 eggs**
**2¾ cups flour**
**2 teaspoons cream of tartar**
**1 teaspoon baking soda**
**¼ teaspoon salt**
**2 tablespoons sugar**
**2 teaspoons cinnamon**

OVEN 400°

Mix shortening, sugar, and eggs. Sift together flour, cream of tartar, baking soda, and salt. Stir into creamed mixture. Roll dough into balls the size of small walnuts. Mix 2 tablespoons sugar and cinnamon. Roll balls into mixture. Place 2 inches apart on ungreased cookie sheet. These cookies puff during baking, but flatten out. They are still soft when done. Bake for 8–10 minutes.

## SUGAR DROP COOKIES

Cherie Rivera, Port Charlotte, FL

**2½ cups all-purpose flour**
**1½ teaspoons baking powder**
**¾ teaspoon salt**
**1 cup sugar**
**¾ cup vegetable oil**
**2 eggs**
**1 teaspoon vanilla**
**Assorted colored sugars**

OVEN 350°

In small bowl combine flour, baking powder, and salt; set aside. In large bowl combine sugar and vegetable oil; mix well. Beat in eggs and vanilla. Gradually add flour mixture. Drop by rounded measuring teaspoonfuls onto ungreased cookie sheet. Shape into balls; roll in colored sugar. Bake 8–10 minutes.

## SOFT SUGAR COOKIES

Nora Spencer, Shaw Air Force Base, SC

**2½ cups Wondra Flour**
**1 teaspoon baking powder**
**½ teaspoon salt (optional)**
**¾ cup butter or margarine, softened**
**1 cup sugar**
**2 eggs**
**1 teaspoon vanilla**

OVEN 350°

Mix together flour, baking powder, salt, and butter or margarine. Add sugar, eggs, and vanilla. Mix together and let stand in refrigerator 1 hour. Roll out to ½-inch thickness. Cut into desired shapes. Bake for 8–10 minutes.

## CUT-OUT SUGAR COOKIES

Iva VanDeventer, Mound City, MO

**1 cup (2 sticks) butter, softened**
**1½ cups sugar**
**2 eggs**
**1½ teaspoons vanilla**
**4½ cups flour**
**1 teaspoon salt**
**1 teaspoon baking soda**
**1 teaspoon baking powder**
**½ teaspoon nutmeg**
**1 cup dairy sour cream**

OVEN 375°

Cream butter and sugar until light and fluffy. Beat in eggs and vanilla. Sift dry ingredients together and add alternately with sour cream, mixing well. Chill until firm enough to roll out on lightly floured surface, ½ inch thick. Cut with cookie cutter. Place on ungreased cookie sheet. Sprinkle with plain or colored sugar. Bake 8–10 minutes. Place on wire rack to cool.

Makes 5–6 dozen.

## SUGAR COOKIES

Sharon Gilmer, Brookfield, MO

**1¾ cups oil**
**2 eggs**
**Vanilla or almond extract (to taste)**
**4½–5 cups flour**
**2 cups powdered sugar**
**2 teaspoons cream of tartar**
**1 teaspoon baking soda**

OVEN 350°

Mix together oil and eggs, flavor to taste with vanilla or almond extract. In separate bowl, mix flour, powdered sugar, cream of tartar, and baking soda. Add oil mixture and stir well. Drop on cookie sheet. Flatten with glass or fork. Bake about 10 minutes. Sprinkle with cinnamon sugar before baking or decorate after baking.

## BEST DATE COOKIES

Arlene Warnwell

- **1 cup brown sugar**
- **2/3 cup butter or ½ butter and ½ Crisco**
- **1 egg**
- **1 teaspoon salt**
- **1 teaspoon baking soda**
- **¼ cup milk**
- **2 cups flour**
- **1 cup chopped dates**
- **½ cup chopped nuts**

OVEN 375°

Mix together ingredients and drop on cookie sheet. Bake for 15 minutes.

## DATE COOKIES

Rachel Schaffner, Bethlehem, PA

- **½ cup butter**
- **½ cup light brown sugar, packed**
- **½ cup granulated sugar**
- **½ teaspoon vanilla**
- **1 egg**
- **2 cups flour**
- **¼ teaspoon baking soda**

**Filling:**

- **7¼-ounce package chopped dates**
- **¼ cup granulated sugar**
- **½ teaspoon salt**
- **1/3 cup water**
- **1 cup chopped nuts**

OVEN 375°

Cream butter, add brown sugar, ½ cup granulated sugar, vanilla, and egg; beat until light. Add flour and baking soda. Chill until firm. Mix dates, ¼ cup granulated sugar, salt, and water. Simmer 5 minutes, stirring often. Add nuts. Divide dough in 2 equal parts. Roll each part on floured waxed paper, into 9x13-inch rectangles. Spread with filling, wrap in the waxed paper. Chill overnight. Cut in 1/8-inch slices. Bake for 10 minutes.

Makes 5–6 dozen.

## JAN HAGEL COOKIES

Marie van der Kaoy, Oceanside, CA

- **½ pound butter**
- **1 cup sugar**
- **1 egg yolk**
- **½ teaspoon cinnamon**
- **2 cups flour**
- **1 egg white**
- **Chopped almonds or walnuts**

OVEN 375°

Mix in order given, except egg white and nuts. Spread mixture on greased cookie sheet. Brush egg white on top of dough and sprinkle with chopped nuts. Bake for 20 minutes. Cut into strips while still warm.

## ZUCCHINI OAT COOKIES

Bonnie Tolly, La Cyane, KS

**1 cup brown sugar**
**1 cup white sugar**
**1/3 cup, less 1 tablespoon, oil**
**1 egg**
**1 cup zucchini, finely chopped or ground**
**2 cups, plus 1 tablespoon, flour**
**½ teaspoon salt**
**1 teaspoon baking soda**
**1 teaspoon cinnamon**
**1 cup quick oats**
**½ cup chopped nuts**

OVEN 350°

Lightly grease or spray cookie sheet. Mix together sugars, oil, egg, and zucchini. Sift and add flour, salt, baking soda, and cinnamon. Add oats and nuts. Bake for 10 to 12 minutes.

## GINGER SNAPS

Sharon Brown, North Little Rock, AR

*"Try them. They're delicious!"*

**2¼ cups all-purpose flour**
**2 teaspoons baking soda**
**1 teaspoon ground ginger**
**1 teaspoon ground cinnamon**
**½ teaspoon ground cloves**
**¼ teaspoon salt**
**1 cup light brown sugar, packed**
**¾ cup Crisco solid**
**¼ cup molasses**
**1 egg**

OVEN 375°

Sift together first 6 ingredients and set aside. Combine remaining ingredients and beat well. Add dry ingredients to beaten mixture. Form 1-inch balls. Roll in granulated sugar, if desired. Place 2 inches apart on ungreased cookie sheet. Bake for approximately 10 minutes.

Makes about 4 dozen.

## ORANGE SLICE COOKIES

Georgia Hawkins, Mackinaw, IL

**2 cups brown sugar**
**4 eggs, beaten**
**2 cups flour**
**2 teaspoons baking powder**
**1 teaspoon salt**
**20 orange slices**
**1 cup nuts (optional)**

OVEN 420°

Mix sugar and eggs in bowl. Add flour, baking powder, and salt. Cut orange into slices. Dip a pair of scissors in flour and cut sliced oranges in zigzag ridges along the peeling side. Add oranges to sugar mixture and mix well. Place in greased baking pan and smooth out. Bake for 30–35 minutes. Cut into small pieces and roll in powdered sugar while hot. May add nuts if desired. Store in very tight container.

## CREAM WAFERS

Lorraine Barclay, Findlay, OH

**1 cup butter**
**2 cups flour**
**1/3 cup whipping cream**

OVEN 370°

Mix ingredients. Cover and chill. Roll dough to 1/8-inch thickness. Cut into 1-inch circles. Roll both sides in sugar. Put on ungreased cookie sheet. Pierce 4 times with fork. Bake 7–9 minutes. Remove from pan, cool.

**Filling:**

**1/4 cup butter**
**3/4 cup powdered sugar**
**1 teaspoon vanilla**
**Food colorings of choice**

Mix first three ingredients. Divide and color with food colorings. Spread a small amount on one cookie and top with another cookie.

Color the filling with Christmas colors, Easter colors, or those to match a party color theme.

## JELL-O INSTANT PUDDING COOKIES

Deloris Berry, Basin, WY

**1 bar margarine**
**1/2 cup sugar**
**3.4-ounce package instant pudding**
**2 eggs, slightly beaten**
**1 1/2 cups flour**
**1/2 teaspoon baking soda**
**1/4 teaspoon salt**

OVEN 350°

Cream together margarine and sugar. Add pudding, eggs, flour, baking soda, and salt. Mix together well. Drop by teaspoonfuls onto baking sheet. Bake for 12 minutes or until lightly brown. Add nuts or frost if you like.

Makes 3 dozen.

## NO-BAKE COOKIES

Karen Felipe, Mante, CA

**1/2 cup milk**
**1/2 cup butter**
**1/4 cup baking cocoa**
**2 cups sugar**
**1 teaspoon vanilla extract**
**1/2 cup peanut butter**
**3 cups oats**

Combine milk, butter, cocoa, sugar, and vanilla in saucepan. Bring to a boil over medium heat. Cook for 1 minute, do not stir. Remove from heat. Stir in peanut butter and oats. Drop by spoonfuls onto waxed paper. Let stand until cool.

Makes 4 dozen.

## EASY COOKIES

Julia Taylor, Smith, AL

**2 cups of sugar**
**4 tablespoons cocoa**
**½ cup milk**
**1 stick of margarine**
**½ cup peanut butter**
**3 cups quick-cooking oats**
**½ cup nuts (optional)**

In saucepan mix first four ingredients; bring to boil over medium heat, and using a wire whisk, cook two minutes. Remove from heat. Stir in peanut butter and oats (and nuts if desired). Drop quickly onto waxed paper or cookie sheet (according to desired size).

## MELTING MOMENTS COOKIES

Marilyn Helfenstein, Milaca, MN

**1 scant cup flour**
**½ cup cornstarch**
**½ cup powdered sugar**
**¾ cup margarine**
**1 teaspoon vanilla**

OVEN 370°

Sift together flour, cornstarch, and powdered sugar. Add margarine and vanilla. Stir all together. Form into round bite-size balls. You may flatten the balls if you wish. Bake for 10–12 minutes.

## SUGAR-FREE APPLESAUCE COOKIES

Ruth Harner, Aurora, IL

**4 cups oat flour (make in blender or food processor)**
**2 cups oatmeal**
**2 teaspoons baking soda**
**2 teaspoons cinnamon**
**½ teaspoon nutmeg**
**½ teaspoon cloves**
**1 cup cooking oil**
**2 eggs**
**4 cups unsweetened applesauce**

**Optional:**
**1 cup unsweetened carob chips**
**½ cup nuts**
**½ cup dates**

OVEN 400°

Mix dry ingredients together, then add oil, eggs, and applesauce. Mix together. Drop by spoonfuls onto an ungreased cookie sheet. Bake 8–10 minutes.

Makes 6 dozen.

## C. C. COOKIE (CRISPIE)

Sandy Hagenbeck, Sturgeon Lake, MN

**1 cup granulated sugar**
**1 cup brown sugar**
**1 cup margarine**
**1 cup oil**
**2 eggs**
**1 teaspoon vanilla**
**4 cups flour (or substitute 1 cup oatmeal for ½ cup flour)**
**2 teaspoons baking soda**
**1 teaspoon salt**
**4 teaspoons cream of tartar**
**1 cup or small bag chocolate chips**

OVEN 350°

Cream together sugars, margarine, and oil. Add eggs and vanilla. Beat. Place flour on top, making hole in center. In hole, add baking soda, salt, and cream of tartar. Mix some flour together; then add chocolate chips. Bake 10–12 minutes.

## AUNT VIOLA'S BUTTERMILK COOKIES

Rachael Allen, Topeka, KS

**4 teaspoons baking powder**
**1 cup buttermilk**
**1 cup shortening**
**4 cups brown sugar**
**4 eggs**
**6 cups flour**

OVEN 350°

Dissolve the baking powder in the buttermilk. Mix ingredients together. Drop on lightly greased cookie sheet. Bake for 10 minutes.

## NO-BAKE CANDY COOKIE

Lisa Myers, Altoona, PA

**½ cup butter**
**2 cups sugar**
**½ teaspoon salt**
**2 tablespoons cocoa**
**½ cup milk**
**½ cup peanut butter**
**3 cups quick oats**

Melt butter in heavy pan. Stir in sugar, salt, cocoa, and milk. Bring to boil, exactly 2 minutes. Remove from heat and stir in peanut butter then oats; mix thoroughly and drop by rounded teaspoonfuls onto waxed paper. Cool then chill. Store in a tight container.

## RAISIN-FILLED SUGAR COOKIES

Beverly M. Camp, Montoursville, PA

**4 cups sugar**
**2 cups margarine**
**2 shakes of nutmeg**
**2 teaspoons vanilla**
**6 eggs**
**½ teaspoon salt**
**4 teaspoons baking powder**
**12 cups flour**
**2 cups buttermilk**
**2 teaspoons baking soda**
**2 teaspoons lemon juice**

**Filling:**
**2 boxes of raisins**
**4 cups water**
**1 cup sugar**
**¼ cup flour (approximately, to thicken)**

OVEN 400°

Mix and cream together margarine, sugar, nutmeg, vanilla, and eggs until blended. Put salt and baking powder in flour, set aside. Next pour buttermilk in container and add baking soda, stir, then add lemon juice. Alternate buttermilk mixture and flour mixture until thoroughly mixed. Roll out and cut with large cookie cutter. Put a tablespoon of filling on each cookie and cover with another cookie. Bake at 400° for 15–20 minutes.

Filling: In blender, chop raisins in water, then cook with sugar and flour to thicken. Cool then add 1 tablespoon of filling in each cookie.

## COOKIES IN A JIFFY

Mary Whisler, Vashon, WA

**9-ounce package yellow cake mix**
**⅔ cup quick-cooking oats**
**½ cup butter or margarine, melted**
**1 egg**
**½ cup M&M's or butterscotch chips**

OVEN 350°

In a mixing bowl, beat the first four ingredients. Stir in M&M's or chips. Drop by tablespoonfuls 2 inches apart onto ungreased baking sheet. Bake for 10–12 minutes or until lightly browned. Immediately remove to wire rack to cool.

Makes 2 dozen.

## BURIED-CHERRY COOKIES

Patricia Steward, Kennedy, NY

**½ cup margarine**
**1 cup sugar**
**1 egg**
**1½ teaspoons vanilla**
**1½ cups flour**
**⅓ cup cocoa**
**¼ teaspoon baking soda**
**¼ teaspoon baking powder**
**¼ teaspoon salt**
**6-ounce jar maraschino cherries, drained, juice reserved**

**Frosting:**

**½ cup real chocolate chips**
**¼ cup sweetened condensed milk**
**2 teaspoons cherry juice**

OVEN 350°

Cream sugar and margarine. Beat in egg and vanilla. Add dry ingredients and mix. Shape dough into 1-inch balls. Press down center with thumb. Put cherry in. Melt together frosting ingredients. Cover dough with frosting. Bake for 8–10 minutes.

## PIZZA COOKIES

Jessica Shires, Iron Station, NC

**¾ cup sugar**
**¾ cup brown sugar**
**½ cup butter**
**2 eggs**
**2¼ cups flour**
**1 teaspoon baking soda**
**1 teaspoon salt**
**1 teaspoon vanilla**
**12-ounce package chocolate chips**
**1 cup chopped nuts**

**Frosting:**

**6-ounce package chocolate chips**
**6-ounce package butterscotch chips**

OVEN 370°

In small bowl, mix together butter, sugars, and eggs. Add flour, baking soda, and salt. Add vanilla, 12 ounces chips, and nuts. Spread in two 14-inch pizza pans. Bake for 25 minutes. Remove and pour remaining chips over hot cookies. Let set 5 minutes, then spread chips to make frosting.

## PIZZA COOKIES

Arla Fry, Delta, OH

**½ cup margarine**
**½ cup peanut butter**
**1½ cups flour**
**½ cup sugar**
**½ cup brown sugar**
**1 egg**
**1 teaspoon vanilla**
**6-ounce package chocolate chips**
**2 cups mini marshmallows**
**Mini M&M's**

OVEN 370°

Mix together first seven ingredients. Press onto pizza pan. Bake 10 minutes. Remove from oven and sprinkle with chocolate chips and mini marshmallows. Return to oven and bake 5–8 minutes more. Do not overbake. Take out and sprinkle with mini M&M's.

Variation: To make in jelly roll pan, double ingredients.

## PIZZA COOKIE

Pat Walls, Greenwood, IN

*"You can use as many or few toppings, whatever your tastes are. Kids can help put toppings on and choose ones they like. This cookie is a hit with my 7 grandchildren."*

**Cookie Dough:**

- **1⅓ cups flour**
- **½ teaspoon baking powder**
- **½ teaspoon baking soda**
- **½ teaspoon salt**
- **⅓ cup melted margarine**
- **1 cup packed light brown sugar**
- **1 egg**
- **1 tablespoon hot water**
- **1 teaspoon vanilla**

**Topping selection:**

- **½ cup nuts, chopped**
- **1 cup chocolate chips**
- **½ cup M&M's**
- **½ cup jelly beans**
- **1 cup butterscotch chips**
- **1 cup peanut butter chips**
- **1 cup miniature marshmallows**

OVEN 350°

In a large bowl combine flour, baking powder, baking soda, and salt. Stir in melted margarine and brown sugar. In a separate bowl, combine egg, hot water, and vanilla. Stir into flour mixture. Grease 12-inch pizza pan. Flour hands and press dough evenly into pan. Sprinkle with selected toppings and top with miniature marshmallows. Bake 18 minutes.

## SNOWMEN COOKIES

Sharon Thursford, Sulphur Bluff, TX

*"These make cute snowmen for Christmas."*

- **Nutter Butter cookies**
- **White chocolate almond bark**
- **Mini chocolate chips, for eyes**

Take Nutter Butter cookies. Melt almond bark and spread the chocolate on the cookies. Place 2 mini chocolate chips side-by-side for the eyes.

## BROWNIE WAFFLE COOKIE

Vera Villinger, Newark, OH

- **⅓ cup margarine or butter**
- **1-ounce Nestle's Choco Bake**
- **½ cup sugar**
- **1 egg, lightly beaten**
- **½ teaspoon vanilla**
- **¾ cup flour**
- **½ teaspoon baking powder**
- **¼ teaspoon salt**
- **2 tablespoons milk**
- **1 cup finely chopped walnuts**

Stir butter and chocolate over a low heat until melted. Cool slightly. Add sugar, egg, and vanilla; beat well. Sift flour, baking powder, and salt together. Add to chocolate mix along with milk and ⅔ cup nuts. Mix well and drop by rounded teaspoonfuls onto greased preheated waffle baker. Sprinkle on top a few of the remaining nuts and bake 5–6 minutes.

Makes 18 cookies.

## GOBS (CAKE VERSION OF OREO COOKIES)

Jane Stewart, Phoenix, AZ

**1 cup shortening**
**2 cups sugar**
**3 eggs**
**1 cup milk**
**1 cup boiling water**
**2 teaspoons baking powder**
**1 teaspoon vanilla**
**4 cups flour**
**2 teaspoons baking soda**
**½ teaspoon salt**
**1 cup cocoa**

OVEN 350°

Cream together the sugar, shortening, and eggs. Add the rest of ingredients in a large bowl and beat until blended well. To bake, drop by teaspoonfuls on greased cookie sheet. Bake at 350° for 10–15 minutes.

**Filling:**

**2 cups powdered sugar**
**1 egg white**
**1 teaspoon vanilla**
**½ cup shortening**
**2 tablespoons flour**
**2 tablespoons milk**
**Food coloring of choice (optional)**

Cream well by hand or with beater. Put filling in between 2 of the oval cakes, as you would a sandwich.

## COWBOY COOKIES

Karin Dykes, Bokeelia, FL

**2 cups sifted flour**
**1 teaspoon baking soda**
**½ teaspoon salt**
**½ teaspoon baking powder**
**1 cup shortening**
**1 cup granulated sugar**
**1 cup brown sugar**
**2 eggs**
**2 cups rolled oats**
**1 teaspoon vanilla**
**1 cup semisweet chocolate bits**

OVEN 350°

Sift together flour, baking soda, salt, and baking powder. Set aside. Blend shortening and sugars. Add eggs and beat until light. Add flour mixture and mix well. Add rolled oats, vanilla, and chocolate bits. Drop by teaspoonfuls onto a greased cookie sheet. Bake 15 minutes.

Makes 11 dozen (can be doubled).

## DELICIOUS COOKIES

Alice McHarness, Salem, OR

**1 cup chopped nuts**
**1 cup coconut**
**1 cup quick oats**
**1 cup Rice Krispies cereal**
**1 cup butter**
**1 cup oil**
**1 cup brown sugar**
**1 cup granulated sugar**
**2 eggs**
**3½ cups flour**
**1 teaspoon cream of tartar**
**1 teaspoon baking soda**
**½ teaspoon salt**

OVEN 350°

In a bowl mix nuts, coconut, oatmeal, and Rice Krispies; set aside. Cream together butter, oil, and sugars. Beat in eggs. Sift and add flour, cream of tartar, baking soda, and salt. Add first mixture. Drop by teaspoonfuls on cookie sheet and flatten with fork. Bake for 8 minutes.

## COFFEE-CAKE COOKIES

Karin Blakeslee, Union City, PA

**4 cups flour**
**1 tablespoon dry quick yeast**
**1 teaspoon salt**
**¼ cup sugar**
**2 sticks margarine**
**2 eggs, beaten**
**1 cup scalded milk**
**¼ cup warm water**

**Filling:**
**2 tablespoons melted butter**
**½ cup brown sugar**
**1 teaspoon cinnamon**

**Glaze:**
**1½ cups powdered sugar**
**2 tablespoons butter**
**1 teaspoon vanilla**
**1–2 tablespoons warm water**

OVEN 350–370°

Separate 2 cups of flour, mix with yeast, and set aside. Mix salt, sugar, margarine, eggs, and 2 cups flour; add scalded milk, warm water, and the 2 cups of flour mixed with yeast. Mix lightly. Cover and refrigerate overnight.

Divide dough in two. Roll out and brush each half with melted butter. Sprinkle each with mixture of sugar and cinnamon. Roll up from long side. Slice each roll into 12 rolls. Bake for 12–15 minutes in a greased 9x13-inch pan. Mix glaze ingredients and frost with glaze.

## ANGEL COOKIES

Gloria Babish, Greenville, PA

**1 angel food cake mix**
**½ cup water**
**1 bag (8–12 ounce) dry mixed fruit, finely chopped**

OVEN 400°

Combine cake mix and water. Stir in fruit. Line cookie pan with foil. Drop by teaspoonfuls on foil. Bake 8–10 minutes. Bake until puffy and golden in color. Cool well before trying to remove from foil.

## PRALINE COOKIES

Evelyn Blair, Xenia, OH

**Graham crackers**
**1 cup margarine or butter**
**1 cup brown sugar**
**1 teaspoon vanilla**
**1 cup pecans, slightly chopped**

OVEN 350°

Layer rows of separated graham crackers on cookie sheet. Combine margarine or butter and brown sugar; bring to rolling boil then turn off heat. Add vanilla and pecans. Pour quickly over crackers and spread immediately. (It doesn't look like enough caramel but it is). Bake 10 minutes. Take out of pan and place on waxed paper. They set quickly so take them out immediately.

## SPRINGERLE COOKIES

Deanna McCoskey, Homestead, FL

*"Dad and grandfather's favorite cookies."*

**4 eggs**
**2 cups sugar**
**2 teaspoons crushed aniseed**
**3–3½ cups sifted flour**
**½ teaspoon baking powder**
**2 teaspoons anise extract (optional)**
**3–4 tablespoons whole aniseed to sprinkle in pan**

OVEN 300°

Beat eggs until light. Gradually stir in sugar, beat well after each addition. Stir in aniseed. Sift flour with baking powder. Add enough flour to make dough stiff enough to roll out to ⅓-inch thickness. These cookies are usually stamped with wooden mold or roller with picture on it. If you do not have a mold, cut into bars. Grease cookie sheet lightly and sprinkle with aniseed. Place cookies on sheet. Bake for 15 minutes or until lower part of cookies are pale yellow, tops will be white.

Makes 5 dozen.

## SOUR-MILK JUMBLES

Thelma Truax/Pat McAllister, Scotia, NY

**1 cup shortening**
**2 cups sugar**
**3 eggs, well beaten**
**6 cups all-purpose flour**
**2 teaspoons baking powder**
**½ teaspoon salt**
**½ teaspoon baking soda**
**¾ teaspoon ground nutmeg**
**1 cup sour milk**

OVEN 370°

Cream shortening with sugar. Add beaten eggs. Mix and sift dry ingredients, add to creamed mixture alternately with the sour milk. Roll out thick (about ¼-inch) on floured surface. Cut with desired cookie cutters. Lightly grease cookie sheet if not using Teflon sheets. Sprinkle cookie tops with granulated or colored sugar. Raisins can also be pressed into center of each cookie. Bake for approximately 8–10 minutes.

## LEMON SNOWBALLS

Carol Cox, Ash Fork, AZ

*"My grandmother baked these cookies. They were my favorite, surpassing chocolate chip!"*

**Editor's Note:** Carol has written *Journey toward Home* in the Heartsong Presents series.

**1 cup shortening**
**1⅓ cups sugar**
**4 teaspoons grated lemon rind**
**2 eggs**
**6 tablespoons lemon juice**
**2 tablespoons water**
**3½ cups flour**
**½ teaspoon soda**
**1 teaspoon salt**
**½ teaspoon cream of tartar**
**½ cup finely chopped nuts**

OVEN 350°

Thoroughly mix first four ingredients. Stir in lemon juice and water. Sift together rest of ingredients and stir in. Form into walnut-sized balls. Place about 1 inch apart on ungreased baking sheet. Bake about 10 minutes. Remove from baking sheet and roll in powdered sugar.

## GINGER-MOLASSES COOKIES

Marcee Riggan, Eagle, CO

*"These cookies freeze well, so you'll always have fresh cookies on hand to share with friends and neighbors."*

**2¼ cups softened margarine**
**1 cup, minus 1 tablespoon, molasses**
**3 cups sugar**
**3 eggs**
**7¾ cups flour**
**1 tablespoon ginger**
**1 tablespoon cinnamon**
**2 tablespoons baking soda**
**1½ teaspoons salt**

OVEN 350°

Mix together margarine, molasses, sugar, and eggs. Sift together flour, ginger, baking soda, cinnamon, and salt; add to molasses mixture. Roll into 1-inch balls. If desired, roll balls in a cinnamon/sugar mixture. Place on ungreased cookie sheets. Bake 8–10 minutes, until light brown.

## OLD-FASHIONED MOLASSES COOKIES

Verla L. Jones, Tucson, AZ

**1 cup sugar**
**1 cup shortening**
**1 teaspoon salt**
**1 cup molasses**
**½ teaspoon ground cloves**
**1 teaspoon cinnamon**
**½ teaspoon ginger**
**4 level teaspoons baking soda**
**1 cup sour milk**
**5–6 cups flour**

OVEN 400°

Mix sugar, shortening, and salt together. Add molasses and beat. Add cloves, cinnamon, ginger, and soda and beat. Add milk, then enough flour to make a soft dough (try 5 cups first and form a sample cookie). Add last cup of flour as needed. Drop by teaspoonfuls onto cookie sheet. Bake 8–10 minutes.

## CHOCOLATE PEPPERMINT CREAMS

Nina Hoover, Dillsburg, PA

**Cookies:**

**3 cups flour**
**1¼ teaspoons baking soda**
**½ teaspoon salt**
**¾ cup butter**
**1½ cups packed brown sugar**
**2 tablespoons water**
**2 cups chocolate chips**
**2 eggs**

**Peppermint Filling:**

**3 cups confectioners' sugar**
**⅓ cup soft butter**
**¼ teaspoon peppermint extract**
**¼ cup milk**
**5 drops green food coloring**

OVEN 350°

Cookies: Sift flour, baking soda, and salt together. In large saucepan, over low heat, melt butter with brown sugar and water. Add chocolate chips and stir until melted. Remove from heat, cool slightly. Beat in eggs. Add flour mixture and mix well. Drop by teaspoonfuls on greased cookie sheets. Bake for 8–10 minutes. Cool.

Filling: Blend ingredients together with mixer in small bowl. Pair together with 1 teaspoon filling.

Makes approximately 3 dozen filled.

Note: Chocolate chips, butter, and water can be heated in the microwave for two minutes on high, until chocolate melts (microwaves may vary). Add the brown sugar, mixing well.

## MOLASSES COOKIES

Jan Willman, Noblesville, IN

**¾ cup Crisco**
**1 cup brown sugar**
**1 egg**
**¼ cup molasses**
**1 teaspoon cinnamon**
**2¼ cups flour**
**¼ teaspoon salt**
**2 teaspoons baking soda**
**½ teaspoon cloves**
**1 teaspoon ginger**

OVEN 350°

Cream Crisco and sugar. Add egg and molasses and beat. Add dry ingredients. Mix well. Chill thoroughly. Roll into small balls. Dip in granulated sugar. Place sugar side up 2 inches apart on greased cookie sheets. Bake for 12–15 minutes.

## SUGARLESS SPICE COOKIES

Mary Sutley, Franklin, PA

**2 cups raisins**
**2 teaspoons cinnamon**
**½ teaspoon nutmeg**
**⅓ cup butter or shortening**
**1¼ cups water**
**2 eggs**
**2 cups sifted flour**
**½ teaspoon salt**
**1 teaspoon black walnut extract or vanilla extract**
**1 teaspoon baking soda**
**1 teaspoon baking powder**
**6 packets of Sweet-N-Low**

OVEN 350°

Boil together raisins, cinnamon, nutmeg, butter or shortening, and water for 3 minutes. Set aside to cool; then add eggs, flour, salt, walnut or vanilla extract, baking soda, baking powder, and Sweet-N-Low. Mix together. Spray cookie sheets with cooking spray. Drop by teaspoonfuls onto cookie sheets. Bake for 12–15 minutes.

# DESSERT BARS

# DESSERT BARS

## CHOCOLATE CHIP BLONDE BROWNIES

Ann Hashbargen, Foxhorne, MN

*"My grandkids love chocolate chip cookies, these come in as a close second.*

Meredity Mixson, Lodge, SC

**2/3 cup butter, melted**
**2 cups brown sugar**
**2 eggs**
**2 teaspoons vanilla**
**1–2 cups flour**
**1 teaspoon baking powder**
**¼ teaspoon baking soda**
**¼ teaspoon salt**
**½ cup chopped nuts (optional)**
**1 package chocolate chips**

OVEN 350°

Add brown sugar to melted butter, cool. Add eggs and vanilla to mixture and blend well. Add sifted ingredients gradually (flour, soda, baking powder, and salt). Stir in chopped nuts. Pour mixture into greased 8x12-inch pan. Sprinkle chocolate chips on top. Bake in 350° oven for 20–25 minutes. (Do not overcook.) Cut into squares.

## CHOCOLATE CHIP COOKIE DOUGH BROWNIES

Stefanie Nichols, Ashland, MO

**2 cups sugar**
**1½ cups all-purpose flour**
**½ cup baking cocoa**
**½ teaspoon salt**
**1 cup vegetable oil**
**4 eggs**
**2 teaspoons vanilla extract**
**½ cup chopped walnuts (optional)**

**Filling:**
**½ cup butter**
**½ cup packed brown sugar**
**¼ cup sugar**
**2 tablespoons milk**
**1 teaspoon vanilla extract**
**1 cup all-purpose flour**

**Glaze:**
**1 cup (6 ounces) semisweet chocolate chips**
**1 tablespoon shortening**
**¾ cup chopped walnuts**

OVEN 350°

In a mixing bowl, combine sugar, flour, cocoa, and salt. Add oil, eggs, and vanilla; beat at medium speed for 3 minutes. Stir in walnuts if desired. Pour into a greased 9x13-inch baking pan. Bake at 350° for 30 minutes or until brownies test done. Cool completely. For filling, cream butter and sugars in a mixing bowl. Add milk and vanilla; mix well. Beat in flour. Spread over the brownies; chill until firm. For glaze, melt chocolate chips and shortening in a saucepan, stirring until smooth. Spread over filling. Immediately sprinkle with nuts, pressing down slightly.

Yield: 3 dozen.

## BLACK AND WHITE BROWNIES

Kelly Hammer, Brownwood, TX

*"Family and friends all enjoy this."*

**2 eggs**
**1 cup sugar**
**1/3 cup butter, melted**
**2/3 cup flour**
**¾ teaspoon baking powder**
**¼ teaspoon salt**
**2/3 cup or 1½ ounces coconut**
**½ teaspoon almond or vanilla extract**
**2 squares melted chocolate or ½ cup melted chocolate chips (Chocolate is not necessary. Peanut butter or butterscotch chips are good substitutes.)**

OVEN 350°

Beat eggs and sugar. Blend in butter. Sift together dry ingredients. Stir into first mixture. Mix coconut and extract into 1/3 of batter. Blend chocolate in remaining batter. Pour chocolate batter into greased 8x8-inch pan. Spread vanilla batter on top. Bake at 350° for 25–30 minutes. Cool, cut into squares.

## CREAM CHEESE BROWNIES

Vivian Notz, Camp Hill, PA

**1 package Betty Crocker Brownie Mix (family size)**

**Filling:**

**8-ounce package cream cheese, softened**
**1/3 cup sugar**
**1 egg**
**1/8 teaspoon salt**

OVEN 350°

Prepare brownie mix according to package directions. Spread in 9x13-inch pan and set aside. Combine cream cheese, egg, sugar, and salt for filling. Space large spoonfuls of filling around brownies. Use a butter knife to form swirl designs. Bake at 350° for 30–35 minutes.

## CARAMEL BROWNIES

Shirley Tetz, Lynden, WA

*"This is heavenly, and very rich."*

**14-ounce package caramels**
**1 German chocolate cake mix**
**¾ cup margarine, melted**
**2/3 cup evaporated milk (divided)**
**1½ cups chopped walnuts or pecans**
**12-ounce package chocolate chips**

OVEN 350°

Combine 1/3 cup evaporated milk and caramels. Microwave for 6–7 minutes on medium. Stir after 3 minutes. Set aside. Grease 9x13-inch pan. In large bowl combine cake mix, melted margarine, 1/3 cup evaporated milk, and nuts. Stir by hand until mixed. Press ½ of dough into pan (reserve ½ for topping). It barely covers bottom of pan. Bake at 350° for 6 minutes. Sprinkle chocolate chips over hot crust. Pour caramel from spoon over chocolate chips until nearly covered. Press bits of reserved dough between fingers and making thin lay on top of caramel and chips. Bake 15–18 minutes at 350°. Cool and cut.

## HERSHEY SYRUP BROWNIES
Betty Schwartz, Hedrick, IA
Beverly Moorhead, International Falls, MN

**½ cup margarine**
**4 eggs**
**1 cup flour**
**1 teaspoon vanilla**
**1 cup sugar**
**16-ounce can chocolate syrup**
**½ teaspoon baking powder**
**1 cup nuts (optional)**

OVEN 350°

Blend margarine and sugar; mix in flour and baking powder; add eggs and vanilla. Beat. Add syrup. Mix nuts in after the syrup or sprinkle on the top. Pour into 11x15-inch pan and bake for 30 minutes.

**Frosting:**
**1⅓ cups sugar**
**6 tablespoons milk**
**6 tablespoons margarine**
**1 cup chocolate chips**

Boil ingredients one minute; beat and spread on brownies.

## BROWNIES
Lucille Cumba, Twisp, WA

**4 cups sugar**
**2 cups flour**
**8 eggs**
**1½ sticks margarine**
**¾ cup corn oil**
**6 tablespoons cocoa**
**2 teaspoons vanilla**
**1 cup pecans**

OVEN 350°

Beat eggs first; then mix dry ingredients, add rest. Beat well. Bake at 350° for 30 minutes.

**Icing:**
**1 box powdered sugar**
**1 stick margarine**
**2 tablespoons cocoa**
**1 teaspoon vanilla**

Mix and spread on warm brownies.

## SIMPLY DELICIOUS BROWNIES
Ollie Wadley, Jonesboro, AR

**1 stick margarine**
**1 cup sugar**
**2 tablespoons cocoa**
**1 cup self-rising flour**
**1 large egg (or 2 small eggs)**
**1 teaspoon vanilla flavoring**

OVEN 400°

Melt margarine in a 7½-inch baking pan, set aside. Blend together sugar, cocoa, and flour. Add melted margarine. Mix in beaten egg and vanilla. Mix well. Pour batter in the 7½-inch baking pan in which margarine was melted. Bake in oven at 400° for 15 minutes.

## BUTTERMILK FROSTED BROWNIES

Mrs. J. James, Portland, OR
Maxine Lucas, Gillette, WY

**1 stick margarine**
**3½ tablespoons cocoa**
**½ cup oil**
**1 cup water**
**1 teaspoon baking soda**
**1 teaspoon vanilla**
**2 cups nuts (optional)**
**2 cups sugar**
**2 cups flour**
**½ cup buttermilk**
**2 eggs**

OVEN 350°

Combine margarine, cocoa, oil, and water in pan, bring to boil mixing well. Add sugar and dissolve, then add flour, buttermilk, and eggs. Add soda, vanilla, and nuts. Pour into jelly roll pan and bake at 350° for 20 minutes.

**Frosting:**

**1 stick margarine**
**3½ tablespoons cocoa**
**⅓ cup evaporated milk or**
**5 tablespoons buttermilk**
**1 box powdered sugar**
**1 cup nuts**
**1 teaspoon vanilla**

Combine margarine, cocoa, and milk, bring to boil. Remove from heat and add powdered sugar, nuts, and vanilla. Beat and frost while brownies are still warm.

## BRICKLE BROWNIES

Marla Snyder, Washington, IN

**1 cup butter, softened**
**¾ cup brown sugar, packed**
**2¼ cups flour**
**½ teaspoon salt**
**¾ cup sugar**
**1 egg**
**1 teaspoon baking soda**
**1 package Heath Brickle Bits**

OVEN 350°

Mix butter, sugar, brown sugar, and egg. Stir in flour, soda, and salt; dough will be stiff. Stir in Heath Brickle Bits. Pour into 9x13-inch ungreased pan. Bake at 350° for 25 minutes. Let cool completely! Cut into squares.

Hint: You can substitute chocolate chips for Heath Brickle Bits.

# DESSERT BARS

## OLD-FASHIONED FROSTED BROWNIES

JoAnn A. Grote, Montevideo, MN

*"This is my grandmother's recipe for cake-type brownies. It is definitely at the top of the list of our family's favorite bars."*

**Editor's Note:** JoAnn has authored several Heartsong Presents romances, including *An Honest Love* and *Sweet Surrender.*

**1½ cups white sugar**
**Pinch of salt**
**3 tablespoons (approx.) butter**
**3 eggs**
**3 squares chocolate, melted**
**⅔ cup milk**
**1½ cups flour**
**⅔ teaspoon baking powder**
**½ cup walnuts, chopped**

OVEN 350°

Cream butter and sugar, add eggs, and beat until smooth. Add chocolate, should be cooled but still liquid. Mix together flour and baking powder. Add flour, baking powder, and milk alternately to mixture. Add walnuts. Bake in jelly roll pan or 2 small 8x8-inch pans at 350° for 30 minutes.

**Frosting:**

**1 box powdered sugar, sifted**
**4 tablespoons butter**
**4 tablespoons cocoa with a little hot coffee**
**1 teaspoon vanilla**
**Chopped walnuts (optional)**

Cream together butter and sifted powdered sugar, add cocoa and coffee a little at a time. Add vanilla; beat until smooth and spreading consistency. Spread on cooled brownies. Top with chopped nuts if desired.

## CHOCOLATE COOKIE BARS

Cathi DeRosier, Brainerd, MN

**1¾ cups flour**
**¾ cup sugar**
**¼ cup cocoa**
**1 cup butter**
**2 cups semisweet chocolate chips, divided**
**14-ounce can sweetened condensed milk**
**1 teaspoon vanilla**
**1 cup chopped nuts**

OVEN 350°

In medium bowl, stir together flour, sugar, and cocoa; cut in butter until crumbly (mixture will be dry). Press firmly on bottom of 9x13-inch baking pan. Bake 15 minutes. Meanwhile in medium saucepan, combine 1 cup chocolate chips, milk, and vanilla. Cook over medium heat, stirring constantly until chips are melted. Pour over crust, top with nuts and 1 cup chocolate chips. Bake 20 minutes.

## MILK CHOCOLATE CHIP AND PEANUT BUTTER BARS

Peggy L. Self, Sedalia, MO

**½ cup (1 stick) butter or margarine**
**½ cup creamy peanut butter**
**¾ cup granulated sugar**
**¾ cup packed light brown sugar**
**1 teaspoon vanilla extract**
**3 eggs**
**1¾ cups all-purpose flour**
**1½ teaspoons baking powder**
**½ teaspoon salt**
**2 cups (11.5-ounce package) milk chocolate chips**

OVEN 350°

Grease 9x13-inch baking pan. In large bowl, beat butter and peanut butter; add granulated sugar, brown sugar, and vanilla, beat until well blended. Add eggs; beat well. Stir together flour, baking powder, and salt; add to butter mixture, beating until blended. Stir in milk chocolate chips. Spread batter in prepared pan. Bake 40 minutes or until browned. Cool and cut into bars.

## CHOCOLATE REVEL BARS

Irene E. Burton, Wellsville, NY

**3 cups quick-cooking rolled oats**
**2½ cups all-purpose flour**
**1 teaspoon baking soda**
**1 teaspoon salt**
**1 cup butter or margarine**
**2 cups packed brown sugar**
**4 teaspoons vanilla**
**2 eggs**
**14-ounce can (1⅓ cups) sweetened condensed milk**
**1½ cups semisweet chocolate pieces**
**2 tablespoons butter or margarine**
**½ teaspoon salt**
**½ cup chopped walnuts**

OVEN 350°

Combine oats, flour, soda, and salt. Beat 1 cup butter for 30 seconds. Add brown sugar and beat until fluffy. Add eggs and 2 teaspoons vanilla; beat well. Stir dry ingredients gradually into beaten mixture, stirring until well combined. In saucepan heat chocolate, sweetened milk, 2 tablespoons butter, and ½ teaspoon salt over low heat, stirring until smooth. Remove from heat. Stir in nuts and 2 teaspoons vanilla. Pat ⅔ mixture in bottom of ungreased 10x15-inch baking pan. Spread chocolate over mixture. Dot with remaining oat mixture. Bake at 350° for 25–30 minutes. Cool on wire rack. Cut into bars.

Makes 72 bars.

## RICE KRISPIE TREATS

(without marshmallows)

Ruth Hagemeier, Hillsdale, WY

**1 cup sugar**
**1 cup light corn syrup**
**1 cup peanut butter**
**5–6 cups Rice Krispies cereal**

Bring sugar and syrup to boil. Remove from heat. Add peanut butter, mix together. Add Rice Krispies and stir. Place in 9x13-inch pan. Let cool.

## EASY BARS

Rosella Hawkins, North English, IA

**3 eggs**
**¾ cup brown sugar**
**¾ cup white sugar**
**1 cup oil**
**1 heaping teaspoon baking soda**
**2 teaspoons vanilla**
**1 level teaspoon salt**
**2 tablespoons peanut butter**
**2 scant cups flour**
**2 cups quick oats**

OVEN 350°

Combine and bake at 350° for 15 minutes or until center is done. Spread in oiled cookie sheet. While still hot drip icing over bars.

**Icing:**
**1 cup confectioners' sugar**
**1 teaspoon vanilla**
**Water**

Combine sugar and vanilla; add water until thin enough to drip.

Variations:
**1 tablespoon salad dressing or 2 tablespoons honey**
**1 cup raisins**
**1 cup nuts**
**Reese's chips or chocolate chips**

## O'HENRY BARS

Peggy L. Self, Sedalia, MO

**6 cups Rice Krispies**
**1 cup peanut butter**
**1 cup white syrup**
**1 cup sugar**

**Topping:**
**1 cup chocolate chips**
**1 cup butterscotch chips**

Combine sugar and white syrup in a saucepan and bring just to a boil. Stir in peanut butter. Then stir in Rice Krispies and spread in a 9x13-inch pan. Topping: Melt butterscotch and chocolate chips together, then spread on top.

## NUTRITIOUS CRISPY BARS

Pamela Karges, Ava, MO
*"Tasty and nutritious snack!"*

**½ cup butter or margarine**
**4½ cups miniature marshmallows**
**½ cup peanut butter, chunky**
**1 teaspoon vanilla**
**4 cups Rice Krispies cereal**
**½ package chocolate chips**
**1½ cups Rice Puffs (optional)**
**½ cup dried bananas**
**½ cup dried apricots**
**¼ cup raisins**
**1½ cups granola cereal**
**¼ cup dried apples**

Melt butter or margarine and marshmallows until creamy. Add vanilla and peanut butter. Remove from heat. Mix dry ingredients in bowl. Stir in melted marshmallow mixture. Press in pans and chill. Then cut and serve.

## CHOCOLATE NUT CARAMEL BARS

Ruth Drew, Nauvoo, IL

- **2 cups chocolate chips**
- **2 tablespoons vegetable shortening**
- **40 caramel pieces**
- **5 tablespoons margarine**
- **2 tablespoons water**
- **1 cups chopped peanuts**

Melt over hot water, chocolate chips and 2 tablespoons vegetable oil. Stir until smooth. Pour half into 8x8-inch pan, spreading evenly. Refrigerate until firm. Combine caramel, margarine, and 2 tablespoons of water on heat until smooth. Add nuts and pour over chocolate mix that has hardened. Then reheat your half mix of chocolate and oil and cover the caramel layer. Set several hours until hard.

## PEANUT BUTTER CEREAL BARS

Eunice Van Der Hoef, Englewood, CO

- **½ cup sugar**
- **½ cup white syrup**
- **¾ cup peanut butter**
- **1 teaspoon vanilla**
- **3 cups Special K cereal**
- **1 package butterscotch chips**
- **2 squares chocolate**

Boil together sugar and white syrup, but not very long or bars get hard, just until sugar dissolves. Remove from stove and add peanut butter and vanilla. Mix thoroughly and add Special K cereal. Spread thinly in buttered pan. Melt butterscotch chips and chocolate squares and frost the bars with this. Allow this to cool. Cut into bars.

## CHEWY PEANUT BUTTER BARS

Sarah Millican, Detroit, AL

*"Great with milk. A great snack."*

- **1 stick margarine**
- **1½ cups sugar**
- **½ teaspoon vanilla flavoring**
- **½ cup peanut butter**
- **1 cup self-rising flour**
- **2 eggs well beaten**

OVEN 350°

In a small boiler over low heat, melt the margarine, add the peanut butter; stir well. Add flour, sugar, eggs, and vanilla; stir well. Spread evenly into a square baking pan. Bake at 350° until golden brown. Cool; then cut into squares.

# DESSERT BARS

## PEANUT BUTTER & JELLY BARS

Bessie Jacot, St. Maries, ID

**1 package Super-Moist vanilla cake mix**
**½ cup (1 stick) margarine or butter, softened**
**2 eggs**
**12-ounce jar strawberry jelly (1 cup)**
**10-ounce package peanut butter chips**

OVEN 375°

Grease a 9x13-inch pan. Mix cake mix (dry), margarine, and eggs in large bowl using spoon (mixture will be stiff). Spread evenly in pan. Spread jelly evenly in pan to within ½- inch of edges. Sprinkle with peanut butter chips. Bake about 25 minutes or until golden brown around edges. Cool completely. Cut into 2½-inch bars. For ease in cutting use sharp or wet knife.

## QUICK PEANUT BUTTER BARS

Marie Johnson, West Des Moines, IA

**1 cup granulated sugar, less 2 tablespoons**
**⅔ cup white corn syrup**
**1½ cups creamy peanut butter, less 2 tablespoons (I prefer Skippy)**
**3¾ cups Cheerios cereal**

Cook sugar in corn syrup until dissolved, very short time. Add peanut butter and mix until smooth. Stir in Cheerios and spread in greased 9x13-inch pan. You may add frosting and cut into bars.

## SPICY PUMPKIN BARS

Jacqueline VanDyk, Kalamazoo, MI

**4 large eggs, beaten until frothy**
**1¾ cups sugar**
**1 cup corn oil**
**2 cups (16 ounces) solid pack pumpkin**
**2 cups all-purpose flour**
**2 teaspoons baking powder**
**1 teaspoon salt**
**2 teaspoons pumpkin pie spice**
**1 cup golden raisins**

OVEN 350°

Add sugar to eggs and beat for 2 minutes. Beat in the oil and pumpkin. Sift dry ingredients over the raisins and fold dry mixture into the egg mixture. Do not overmix. Pour into a greased and floured 9x13-inch pan. Bake in the oven for 35–40 minutes or until done through. Cool on rack and cut into 24 squares.

Makes 24 bars.

## PUMPKIN BARS

Olive M. Jefferies, Jamison, PA

- **4 eggs**
- **1⅔ cups sugar**
- **1 cup oil or applesauce**
- **2 cups cooked pumpkin**
- **2 cups flour (may use 1 cup whole wheat and 1 cup white)**
- **2 teaspoons baking powder**
- **1 teaspoon baking soda**
- **2 teaspoons cinnamon**
- **½ teaspoon nutmeg**
- **¼ teaspoon ginger**
- **⅛ teaspoon ground cloves**
- **1 teaspoon salt**
- **½ cup raisins (optional)**

OVEN 350°

Beat eggs, sugar, oil, and pumpkin until light and fluffy. Stir together dry ingredients. Add to pumpkin mixture and mix well. Spread batter in ungreased 10x15-inch baking sheet. If desired, sprinkle batter with raisins. Bake at 350° for 30 minutes.

Yields 24 bars.

When cool, frost with canned cream cheese frosting or make frosting by mixing together:

- **3-ounce package cream cheese, softened**
- **½ cup butter**
- **1 teaspoon vanilla**
- **2 cups powdered sugar**

## MIXED NUT BARS

Nellie Knox, Presque Isle, ME
Virginia Hart, Janesville, WI

- **1 cup soft butter or margarine**
- **1 cup brown sugar**
- **1 egg yolk**
- **2 cups flour**
- **¼ teaspoon salt**
- **1 teaspoon vanilla**
- **12-ounce package butterscotch bits**
- **½ cup light corn syrup**
- **2 tablespoons butter**
- **1 tablespoon water**
- **13-ounce can of mixed nuts (one with less peanuts is best)**

OVEN 350°

Mix 1 cup butter or margarine, brown sugar, egg yolk, flour, salt, and vanilla until crumbly. Press into ungreased 9x13-inch pan. Bake at 350° for 20–25 minutes. Melt in double boiler, butterscotch bits, corn syrup, 2 tablespoons butter, and water. Pour over base and cover with nuts, press. Refrigerate until set. Cut into squares.

# DESSERT BARS

## PECAN PIE BARS

Betty Ogle, Paris, KY

**1 package yellow cake mix**
**½ cup margarine or butter, softened**
**1 egg**
**1 cup chopped pecans**

**Filling:**
**⅔ cup reserved cake mix**
**½ cup brown sugar**
**1½ cups dark corn syrup**
**1 teaspoon vanilla**
**3 eggs**

OVEN 350°

Generously grease bottom and sides of 9x13-inch pan. Reserve ⅔ cup dry cake mix filling. In large mixing bowl combine margarine, remaining cake mix, and 1 egg. Mix until crumbly. Press into pan. Bake at 350° for 15–20 minutes until light golden brown. Mix together filling ingredients and pour over partially baked crust. Sprinkle with pecans. Return to oven and bake for 30–35 minutes until filling is set. Cool. Cut into bars.

## DAVY CROCKETT BARS

Elaine Jolliff, Yukon, OK
Tammy Marks, Richmond, KY

**2 cups flour**
**1 cup sugar**
**1 teaspoon salt**
**1 teaspoon baking powder**
**1 teaspoon baking soda**
**1 cup brown sugar**
**1¾–2 cups quick-cooking oatmeal**
**6-ounce package chocolate chips**
**2 eggs**
**1 cup vegetable oil**
**1 teaspoon vanilla**
**1 cup nuts (optional)**

OVEN 350°

Mix flour, sugar, salt, baking powder, and baking soda. Mix in brown sugar, oatmeal, and chocolate chips, and nuts if desired. Combine eggs, oil, and vanilla; add to oatmeal mixture, then stir into dry mixture. Press into ungreased jelly roll pan. Bake at 350° for 15 minutes or until lightly browned. Do not overbake. Cool slightly before cutting.

## GREEN TOMATO BARS

Ady Walburg, Brookings, SD

**4 cups green tomatoes, chopped finely**
**1 cup brown sugar**

Simmer for 20–25 minutes.

**¾ cup soft margarine**
**1 cup brown sugar**
**1½ cups flour**
**1 teaspoon baking soda**
**1 teaspoon salt**
**2 cups oatmeal**
**½ cup nut meats**

OVEN 375°

Mix and press 2½ cups of above in bottom of a 9x13-inch pan. Spread the tomato mixture on top. Spread on remaining crumbs. Bake at 375° for 30–35 minutes.

## FUDGE NUT BARS

Karla Kolle, Redwing, MN

**12 ounces chocolate chips (I use milk chocolate)**
**1 can Eagle brand sweetened condensed milk**
**3 tablespoons butter or margarine**
**¾ cup chopped nut meats**
**2 teaspoons vanilla**
**1 teaspoon Burns sugar flavoring**

OVEN 350°

Over hot water in a double boiler add condensed milk, chocolate chips, and butter, stir until melted; add the nuts, vanilla, and sugar flavoring. Set aside. (I use nonstick pan.)

**1 cup margarine**
**2 cups brown sugar**
**2 eggs**
**1 teaspoon vanilla flavoring**
**2½ cups sifted flour**
**1 teaspoon baking soda**
**1 teaspoon salt**
**3 cups oatmeal**
**¼ cup chopped nut meats**

Combine the margarine, brown sugar, eggs, vanilla, and mix well. Sift together flour, baking soda, and salt; add to creamed mixture. Work in the oatmeal and nuts. Grease a 10x16-inch jelly roll pan. Press ⅔ of this mixture into the pan and pat down. Pour reserved fudge mixture over the top and sprinkle remaining oatmeal mixture over top. Bake at 350° for 20–25 minutes.

If you leave this on the jelly roll pan indefinitely it tends to dry out. So after the first day or so, store in a closed container.

## CREME DE MENTHE BARS

Betty Peterson, Pocatello, ID

**1 cup sugar**
**⅓ cup butter**
**4 eggs**
**1 can Hershey's syrup**
**1 cup flour**

OVEN 350°

Cream together butter and sugar. Add eggs, Hershey's syrup, and flour. Spread in greased and floured 9x13-inch cookie sheet. Bake 20–25 minutes at 350°. Cool.

**Filling:**

**4 cups powdered sugar**
**2 tablespoons milk**
**1 cup soft butter**
**1 teaspoon peppermint extract**
**2 ounces (½ cup) Creme de Menthe**
**Dash of green food coloring**

Combine and spread on top of first layer. Refrigerate for 2 hours.

**Topping:**

**12-ounce package semisweet chocolate chips**
**4 tablespoons oil**

Melt semisweet chocolate chips and oil. Beat. Spread on top. Better if refrigerated.

# DESSERT BARS

## HONEY BARS

Sharon Robinson, Edgemont, AR

**1 cup sugar**
**¾ cup oil**
**¼ cup honey**
**1 egg**
**½ teaspoon salt**
**1 teaspoon cinnamon**
**2 cups flour**
**1 cup nuts**

**Icing:**
**1 cup powdered sugar**
**1 tablespoon water**
**2 tablespoons milk**
**2 teaspoons vanilla**

OVEN 300°

Beat egg, oil, honey, and sugar. Add salt, cinnamon, and flour. Mix well. Fold in nuts. Pat dough out on cookie sheet. Bake 20 minutes at 300°. While hot, top with icing. Icing: combine all ingredients.

## NUT GOODIE BARS

Rebecca S. Hohulin, Fort Scott, KS

*"I have entered this candy in our annual fair, and have won a blue ribbon each year for many years!"*

**12-ounce package milk chocolate chips**
**12-ounce package butterscotch chips**
**2 cups peanut butter (creamy or chunky)**
**1 cup butter**
**½ cup evaporated milk**
**¼ cup vanilla pudding mix (Do not use instant!)**
**2 tablespoons powdered sugar**
**½ teaspoon Kitchen Klatter maple flavoring**
**2 cups salted peanuts**

Melt the chocolate chips, butterscotch chips, and peanut butter in double boiler. Put ½ of the mixture in buttered 10x15-inch jelly roll pan. Freeze. Combine butter, milk, and dry pudding. Boil one minute (this is your pudding mixture). Place the powdered sugar in a large bowl and spread pudding mixture over it. Beat until smooth. Add flavoring. Spread this mixture evenly over hardened chocolate layer that was previously in the freezer. Put in freezer again. Reheat the remaining chocolate mixture and add the peanuts. Spread over powdered sugar layer. Freeze. Let thaw 15–20 minutes before cutting and serving. Keep frozen or in refrigerator until time to serve.

## CHEERIO BARS

Hermine Ellison, Mead, NE

**1 cup white syrup**
**1 cup sugar**
**1 cup peanut butter**
**1 cup peanuts, dry roasted or salted**
**1 cup coconut**
**6–8 cups Cheerios**

Bring syrup and sugar to boiling point. Add peanut butter, peanuts, and coconut. Mix in Cheerios. Refrigerate.

## CINNAMON COFFEE BARS

Lois Shaw, Lake Stevens, WA

**¼ cup soft shortening**
**1 cup packed brown sugar**
**1 egg**
**½ cup hot coffee**
**1½ cups flour**
**1 teaspoon baking powder**
**¼ teaspoon baking soda**
**¼ teaspoon salt**
**1 teaspoon cinnamon**
**½ cup raisins**
**¼ cup nuts**

OVEN 350°

Cream together thoroughly, shortening, brown sugar, and egg. Stir in hot coffee. Sift together dry ingredients. Add to first mixture. Blend in raisins and nuts. Spread in greased 9x13-inch pan. Bake at 350° for 18–20 minutes.

**Glaze:**
Mix together: 1 cup powdered sugar, 1 teaspoon vanilla, 1½ tablespoons milk; spread on hot bars. Cool and cut.

Makes about 2 dozen bars.

## QUICK GRAHAM BARS

Belvadine Lecher, Chardon, NE

**½ cup (1 stick) margarine**
**1 cup sugar**
**2 beaten eggs**
**2½ cups ground graham cracker crumbs**
**2 cups miniature marshmallows**
**12-ounce package semisweet chocolate chips**
**3 tablespoons peanut butter**

Melt margarine; add sugar and eggs; bring to boil. Boil until thick, from 2½ to 3 minutes, stirring occasionally. Cool slightly. Add ground graham cracker crumbs, marshmallows, and mix thoroughly. Press into 9x13-inch greased cake pan. Melt chocolate chips with peanut butter. Spread over graham cracker crust. Refrigerate until chocolate starts to harden. Cut into squares. Will keep in the freezer for several months.

Makes 30 squares.

## FILLED DATE BARS

Norene Morris, Ashtabula, OH

**Editor's Note:** Norene is a grandmother who has penned four successful romances for Heartsong Presents, including *A Heart for Home.*

**Filling:**
**3 cups (1 box) pitted dates, cut, chopped**
**⅓ cup sugar**
**1½ cups water**

Cook over low heat 10 minutes. Cool.

**Crust:**
**¾ cup shortening**
**1 cup brown sugar (dark is best)**
**1¾ cups sifted flour**
**½ teaspoon baking soda**
**1 teaspoon salt**
**1 cup rolled oats**

OVEN 400°

Work crust together with hands like pie dough. Pat ½ into greased and floured 9x13-inch pan. Spread filling, pat remaining crumbs on top. Bake at 400° for 20–30 minutes. When cooled, sprinkle with powdered sugar and cut.

## HOLIDAY CHERRY CHEESE BARS

Virgie M. McIntyre, Columbus, NC

**Crust:**

**1 cup walnut pieces, divided**
**1¼ cups all-purpose flour**
**½ cup firmly packed brown sugar**
**½ cup butter-flavored shortening**
**½ cup flake coconut**
**½ cup nuts**

**Filling:**

**2 packages 8 ounce cream cheese, softened**
**⅔ cup granulated sugar**
**2 eggs**
**2 teaspoons vanilla**
**21 ounce can cherry pie filling**

OVEN 350°

Grease 9x13-inch pan. Set aside. Chop ½ cup nuts, coarsely, for topping. Set aside. Chop remaining ½ cup finely.

Crust:

Combine flour and brown sugar. Cut in shortening until fine crumbs form. Add ½ cup finely chopped nuts and coconut. Mix well. Remove ½ cup. Set aside. Press remaining crumbs in bottom of pan. Bake for 12–15 minutes, until edges slightly brown.

Filling:

Beat cream cheese, eggs, vanilla, and granulated sugar in a small bowl, with electric mixer at medium speed, until smooth. Sprad over hot baked crust. Return to oven. Bake 15 minutes.

Spread cherry pie filling over cheese layer. Combine reserved coarsely chopped nuts and crumbs. Sprinkle over cherries. Return to over and bake 15 minutes. Cool. refrigerate several hours. Cut into bars.

## CASHEW CARAMEL CRUNCH SQUARES

Jennifer Mann, Chapel Hill, NC

**1 bag (14-ounce) caramels**
**2 tablespoons butter**
**2 tablespoons water**
**6 cups Kellogg's Cocoa Krispies cereal**
**1 cup cashew nuts**
**1 cup white chocolate chips**

Grease a 9x13-inch pan. Put the caramels, butter, and water into a large saucepan or microwave-safe bowl. Place over medium-low heat and cook for 18 minutes, stirring occasionally, or microwave on high from 3–4 minutes, stirring every minute, until caramels melt and mixture is smooth. Stir in cereal and nuts, let cool 1 minute, then stir in white chocolate chips. Press into prepared pan and let cool. Invert onto cutting board. Cut into 2-inch squares.

Makes 24 squares.

## LEMON COCONUT SQUARES

DiAnn Mills, Houston, TX

**Editor's Note:** DiAnn debuted in the Heartsong Presents series with *Rehoboth.*

**1½ cups sifted flour**
**½ cup brown sugar**
**½ cup butter**

OVEN 300°

Mix and pat into bottom of buttered 9x13 pan. Bake at 300° for 15 minutes.

**Filling:**
**2 eggs, beaten**
**1 cup brown sugar**
**1½ cups coconut**
**1 cup chopped nuts**
**2 tablespoons flour**
**½ teaspoon baking powder**
**¼ teaspoon salt**
**½ teaspoon vanilla**

OVEN 350°

Combine filling and pour into baked crust. Bake at 350° for 15 minutes.

**Frosting:**
**1 cup powdered sugar**
**1 tablespoon melted butter**
**Juice of one lemon**

Mix and spread over cookie while still warm.

## TEA TIME TASSIES

Claire Hudson, South Wales, NY

**1 cup margarine or butter**
**3 ounces cream cheese**
**1 cup flour**
**Nuts, chopped**

OVEN 325°

Cream together margarine or butter and cream cheese. Add flour, mix well; chill 1 hour. Shape into 24 balls, press into ungreased mini-tart pans. Sprinkle with chopped nuts.

**Filling:**
**1 beaten egg**
**1 tablespoon butter, melted**
**1 teaspoon vanilla**
**½ cup chopped nuts (optional)**
**¾ cup brown sugar**

Combine filling ingredients and fill tart shells. Bake at 325° for 25 minutes.

Yields: 2 dozen small tarts.

## PECAN TARTS
Ellen Scott, Meadow Creek, WV

**½ cup butter or margarine**
**8 ounces cream cheese**
**1 cup flour**

OVEN 350°

Let butter and cream cheese soften at room temperature, then mix well; add flour, mix and chill one hour. Layer tart cups with dough.

**Filling:**
**1 teaspoon melted butter**
**¾ cup brown sugar**
**1 large or 2 small eggs**
**1 teaspoon vanilla**
**½ to 1 cup chopped pecans**

Mix all ingredients well, fill tart ¾ full. Bake at 350° for 15 minutes, then 250° for 30 minutes until brown. Cool and eat.

## FELIX KING'S "POISON" BERRY TARTS
Sara Wekh, Meadow Vista, CA

**1 package vanilla pudding**
**Raspberries or strawberries**
**1 cup all-purpose flour**
**½ cup soft butter**
**¼ cup powdered sugar**
**12 medium muffin cups**

OVEN 350°

Mix flour, butter, and powdered sugar. Divide dough into 12 equal pieces. Press each piece against bottom and sides of ungreased medium sized muffin cups. Do not allow dough to extend above tops of cups. Bake tart shells 8–10 minutes, or until golden brown. Cool. Carefully remove shells from cups with top of knife. Filling: Follow directions for pudding on package. Spoon pudding into cooled tart shells, using about three to four tablespoons in each. Top with berries.

Makes a dozen tarts.

## PEPPERMINT STICK BARS
Rita F. Maust, Millmont, PA

**3 cups sugar**
**1 cup shortening**
**2 cups milk**
**3 cups flour**
**3 teaspoons baking soda**
**¾ cup cocoa**
**4 medium eggs**

OVEN 300°

Cream sugar and shortening together, then add milk, alternating with combined sifted flour, baking soda, and cocoa. Add eggs. Put in greased 9x13 pan. Bake 30 minutes or until done.

Suggested topping: In the last two minutes of baking time, sprinkle white chocolate chips on top of brownies. Spread the chocolate and immediately sprinkle 4–6 crushed pepermint sticks on top. (If it is your passion, substitute semi-sweet chocolate chips for the white.)

# CANDIES

## CHOCOLATE FUDGE

Shirley A. Rendon, Albuquerque, NM

**3 cups semisweet chocolate chips**
**14-ounce sweetened condensed milk (not evaporated milk)**
**Dash salt**
**1 cup chopped walnuts**
**1½ teaspoons vanilla extract**

In heavy saucepan, over low heat, melt chips with sweetened condensed milk and salt. Remove from heat, stir in walnuts and vanilla. Spread evenly into aluminum-foil-lined 8- or 9-inch square pan. Chill 2 hours or until firm. Turn fudge onto cutting board, peel off foil, and cut into squares. Store, loosely wrapped, at room temperature.

Makes about 2 pounds.

## FUDGE

Elinor Wingrove, Parkersburg, WV

*"Good instant fudge!"*

**1 can vanilla or chocolate ready mix frosting**
**18-ounce jar peanut butter**
**Nuts (optional)**

Mix together frosting and peanut butter. Chill. Add nuts.

## QUICK 'N EASY FUDGE

Elaine Morrison, Ft. Lauderdale, FL

**2 8-ounce boxes semisweet chocolate squares**
**14-ounce sweetened condensed milk**
**1 cup chopped walnuts**
**2 teaspoons vanilla**

Melt chocolate and milk in microwave, stir often. Add vanilla and nuts, stir, pour into buttered 9x9-inch pan. Refrigerate and serve.

## CHOCOLATE FUDGE

Faye Harrell, Edenton, NC

**3 cups sugar**
**6 tablespoons cocoa**
**⅛ teaspoon salt**
**1 cup milk**
**3 tablespoons light corn syrup**
**3 tablespoons butter**
**1½ teaspoons vanilla**
**¾ cup chopped nuts**

Combine sugar, cocoa, salt, milk, and syrup in a saucepan. Cook until forms soft ball when dropped in cold water. Remove from heat and add butter, vanilla, and nuts. Beat until it loses part of shine. Pour into buttered pan. Let harden and cut into squares.

Makes 1½ pounds.

## CONFECTIONERS' SUGAR PEANUT BUTTER FUDGE

Rachel E. Miller, Sunbury, PA

**1 pound confectioners' sugar (10x)**
**½ cup milk**
**12-ounce jar creamy peanut butter**
**7- or 8-ounce jar marshmallow creme**

Mix together sugar and milk in saucepan. Bring to rolling boil on high heat. Reduce heat to medium and boil 5 minutes, stirring all the time. Remove from heat and add peanut butter and marshmallow. Mix thoroughly. (Work fast or it will harden in pan.) Pour into buttered pan. When cooled cut into bite-size pieces.

## CHOCOLATE-SCOTCH FUDGE

Elizabeth Hunt, Ithaca, MI

**12-ounce package chocolate chips**
**12-ounce package butterscotch chips**
**1 cup condensed milk (recipe below)**
**1 teaspoon vanilla**
**1 cup chopped nuts**

Heat chips and milk together, stirring often. When melted, add vanilla and chopped nuts. Pour into buttered pan, 9x13-inch or smaller. Put into refrigerator. When cooled cut into pieces.

**Condensed milk:**

**½ cup warm water**
**1 cup, plus 2 tablespoons, instant non-fat dry milk**
**¾ cup sugar**

Pour water into blender. Add dry milk and sugar. When blended, use or store in refrigerator. Will keep several months in the refrigerator.

## PEANUT BUTTER FUDGE

Jessie Passino, South Glens Falls, NY

**3 cups granulated sugar**
**A piece of butter the size of an egg**
**⅔ cup evaporated milk**
**3 tablespoons peanut butter**
**1 teaspoon vanilla**
**3 teaspoons marshmallows**

Boil together sugar, butter, and canned milk until it forms a hot ball in cold water. Add peanut butter, vanilla, and marshmallows; beat and pour into well-greased pan.

## EASY PEANUT BUTTER FUDGE

Melissa Barefoot, Alum Bank, PA

**1 stick margarine**
**12-ounce jar peanut butter (1½ cups)**
**1 teaspoon vanilla**
**1 pound powdered sugar**

Melt margarine; add peanut butter, vanilla, and powdered sugar. Mix well with hands. Spread in greased 9-inch square pan.

## MARSHMALLOW CREME PEANUT BUTTER FUDGE

Mrs. J. C. Hutchinson, Coventry, RI

**3 cups sugar**
**1 cup milk**
**1 pint marshmallow creme**
**1½ cups peanut butter**
**1 teaspoon vanilla**

Cook sugar and milk to soft ball stage. Remove from heat. Add other ingredients. Mix, then refrigerate until hard. Cut and serve.

## CHOCOLATE-DRIZZLED PEANUT BUTTER FUDGE

Angela Spaulding, Elkhorn, WI

**1½ cups sugar**
**1 cup (5 ounces) evaporated milk**
**¼ cup butter**
**1 jar marshmallow creme**
**1 cup chunky peanut butter**
**1 teaspoon vanilla**
**2 squares (1 ounce each) semisweet chocolate**

Grease 8- or 9-inch square pan. Melt sugar, milk, and butter. (Can microwave on high for 6 minutes, stirring after 3 minutes.) Cook 4–6 minutes more or until small amount of sugar forms soft ball when dropped in water, or until it reaches 236°. Add the rest of ingredients, except chocolate; beat until well blended. Pour in pan. Cool 30 minutes. Melt chocolate 1–2 minutes. Stir after 30 seconds. Drizzle over top.

## PECAN PEANUT BUTTER FUDGE

Denise Dittberner, Andrews, TX

**2 cups sugar**
**⅔ cup evaporated milk**
**1 cup peanut butter**
**1 small jar marshmallow creme**
**1 cup pecans**

Bring sugar and milk to a soft ball stage (about 4½ minutes on reduced heat after it comes to a boil). Add peanut butter. Mix well. Add marshmallow creme. Mix well. Add nuts and pour into a 9x9-inch buttered dish.

## NO-COOK PEANUT BUTTER FUDGE

Mrs. Dolores Reiner, Arcade, NY

**1 cup butter-flavored Crisco**
**1 cup peanut butter**
**1 tablespoon vanilla**
**4 cups confectioners' sugar**
**Walnuts**

Melt Crisco, add peanut butter, stirring until melted also, add vanilla. Pour melted mixture into confectioners' sugar, mix well. Put in 8x8-inch pan and decorate with walnuts.

## PEANUT BUTTER FUDGE

Nellie Hicks, Diamond, OH

**2 cups sugar**
**⅓ cup milk**
**1 pint marshmallow creme (or 2 cups miniature marshmallows)**
**1 cup peanut butter**
**1 teaspoon vanilla**

Combine sugar and milk in a saucepan and cook to the soft ball stage (234°). Remove from heat. Add marshmallow, peanut butter, and vanilla. Mix well. Pour into a buttered 6x10-inch pan. Cool and cut into squares.

## FANTASY FUDGE

Lori Reed, Hutchinson, KS

**3 cups sugar**
**¾ cup margarine**
**⅓ cup (small can) evaporated milk**
**12-ounce package chocolate bits**
**7-ounce jar marshmallow creme**
**1 teaspoon vanilla**
**1 cup nuts**

Butter 8-inch square pan. Put sugar, margarine, and milk in heavy saucepan. Bring to full boil, boil 5 minutes, remove from heat. Beat in rest of ingredients, just until well blended. Pour into pan. Cool, cut into squares.

## SOUR-CREAM FUDGE

Rose Miller, Falls, PA

**2 cups sugar**
**½ teaspoon salt**
**1 cup dairy sour cream**
**2 tablespoons butter or margarine**
**½ cup broken pecans or other nuts**

Combine sugar, salt, and sour cream in heavy saucepan. Cook, stirring occasionally (over not too high heat, as it will scorch) until a little dropped into cold water forms a soft ball (or 236° on candy thermometer). Add butter or margarine. Let cool at room temperature without stirring until mixture is lukewarm (110°). Beat mixture until it loses gloss, add nuts. Spread in buttered 9x9-inch pan. When firm, cut into squares.

Makes a small amount, about 24 pieces, but is very rich.

Note: Boiling time is approximately 6 or 7 minutes. Follow directions exactly.

## TWO-TONE FUDGE

Myra Felton, Richland Center, WI

**2 cups brown sugar, firmly packed**
**1 cup granulated sugar**
**1 cup evaporated milk**
**½ cup butter**
**7 ounces marshmallow fluff**
**1 teaspoon vanilla**
**6-ounce package butterscotch chips**
**6-ounce package chocolate chips**
**1 cup nuts**

Combine sugars, milk, and butter. Bring to a full boil over medium heat, stirring constantly. Boil 10 minutes over medium heat, stirring occasionally (if using candy thermometer, cook to soft ball stage). Remove from heat and add marshmallow fluff and vanilla. Stir until mixture is smooth. To ½ add butterscotch chips and ½ cup nuts, stir until smooth. Pour evenly in pan. To other ½ add chocolate chips and ½ cup nuts, stir until smooth. Pour over butterscotch mixture.

## BLUE RIBBON PEANUT BRITTLE

Ilene Oatney, Donnelly, ID

*"This recipe has won many blue ribbons at our country fair and is a favorite candy of many friends."*

**3 cups sugar**
**1 cup light corn syrup**
**½ cup water**
**1 teaspoon salt**
**1 pound raw peanuts**
**1 teaspoon baking soda**
**1 teaspoon vanilla**

Boil together in heavy saucepan, sugar, syrup, water, and salt, until it reaches 240°. Add peanuts and cook to 290°. Remove from heat and add baking soda and vanilla. Stir well and pour onto buttered sheet pan. Break into pieces when cool.

## PEANUT BRITTLE CANDY

Barbara Ray, Ray City, GA

**¼ cup water**
**3 cups sugar**
**1 cup light corn syrup**
**4 cups raw peanuts**
**3 teaspoons baking soda**

Mix water, sugar, and syrup; bring to a boil, add peanuts and boil about 10 minutes (on medium-high heat) or until golden brown. Remove from heat and stir in baking soda. It will foam and turn white. Stir until it is the color you want. The more it is stirred, the darker it gets. Pour out onto buttered heavy-duty aluminum foil or cookie sheet. Spread as thin as you can. Cool and break into pieces.

## PEANUT BUTTER TREATS

Carla Moore, Wichita, KS
Kyndra Shedd, Clearwater, SC

**½ cup butter, softened**
**½ cup brown sugar**
**½ cup granulated sugar**
**1 egg**
**½ cup creamy peanut butter**
**½ teaspoon vanilla**
**1¼ cups all-purpose flour**
**¾ teaspoon baking soda**
**½ teaspoon salt**
**36 miniature Reese's Peanut Butter Cups**

OVEN 370°

Combine butter, sugars, egg, peanut butter, and vanilla; beat until smooth. Combine flour, baking soda, and salt; add to mixture. Roll in small balls and place each in miniature muffin tins. Bake for 8–9 minutes. Remove from oven and immediately put Reese's cup in each. Cool in pan. Can be stored in refrigerator for 1 week.

# CANDIES

## PEANUT BUTTER CORNFLAKE TREATS

Joyce Todd, Pasco, WA

**1 cup sugar**
**1 cup corn syrup**
**2 cups peanut butter**
**4½ cups cornflakes**

Boil together sugar and syrup for 1 minute. Add peanut butter and cornflakes. Drop by tablespoonfuls onto buttered cookie sheet, and cool in refrigerator.

## PEANUT BUTTER CHEWIE CAKES

Janice Lowrey, Anacoco, LA

**1 stick butter**
**1 cup peanut butter**
**2 cups brown sugar**
**3 eggs**
**2 cups flour**
**1 teaspoon vanilla**
**2 cups chopped nuts (optional)**

OVEN 350°

Mix butter, peanut butter, and brown sugar. Mix in eggs and flour. Add vanilla and nuts if desired. Bake at 350° for 40 minutes.

## HOMEMADE PEANUT BUTTER CUPS

Lilly Menezes, Seaside, CA

**1 cup peanut butter**
**1 pound box powdered sugar**
**¼ pound butter, melted and cooled**
**1 cup crushed graham crackers**
**1½-ounce Hershey chocolate bar**

Mix together peanut butter, sugar, butter, and graham crackers. Mix well. Use your hands to pat into a 9x13-inch pan. It is a dry mixture, so pat in the pan and take your time. Melt chocolate and spread on top. Cut into squares.

## CANDIED PECANS

Alice Faye Mahoney, Beebe, AR

*"This is really easy and popular for Christmas."*

**¼ cup butter or margarine**
**½ cup brown sugar**
**1 teaspoon cinnamon**
**2 cups pecan halves**
**Salt (optional)**

Use a heavy skillet or pan. Cook ingredients over medium-low heat, stirring constantly until nuts are coated, and sugar is golden brown (about 5 minutes). Spread on aluminum foil, sprinkle lightly with salt, if desired. Cool.

## SPICED PECANS

Lorna Marsh, Alamo, TX

**1 egg white**
**1 teaspoon cold water**
**1 pound pecan halves**
**½ cup sugar**
**¼ teaspoon salt**
**1 teaspoon cinnamon**
**½ teaspoon nutmeg**
**½ teaspoon (scant) cloves**

OVEN 270°

Beat egg white and water until frothy. Add and mix nuts thoroughly. Mix dry ingredients, coat nuts. Bake on buttered cookie sheet for 1 hour, stirring every 15 minutes. Dry on paper towels. Store in airtight container.

## SOUTHERN SALTED PECANS

Virginia Emmon, Jonesboro, AR

**⅓ cup butter**
**4 cups pecans**
**1 tablespoon salt**

OVEN 200°

Melt butter in large skillet. Stir in salt and pecans. Pour into 9x13-inch pan and bake for 1 hour, stirring every 15 minutes. Drain on absorbent paper towel.

## SUGAR AND SPICE PECANS

Deborah McCreery, Beaumont, TX

**1 cup firmly packed brown sugar**
**1/3 cup boiling water**
**1/2 teaspoon cinnamon**
**1/2 teaspoon ginger**
**1/8 teaspoon allspice**
**1/8 teaspoon nutmeg**
**2 cups pecan halves**
**1/4 teaspoon maple flavoring**

Lightly butter a 10x15-inch jelly roll pan. In heavy 3-quart saucepan, combine brown sugar, water, and spices. Bring mixture to full boil over medium-high heat, stirring occasionally. Boil without stirring for 5 minutes. Remove from heat. Add nuts and flavoring. Stir until coating on nuts begins to sugar, approximately 2½–3 minutes. Pour into prepared pan and quickly separate nuts. Cool completely. Store in airtight container in cool dry place.

## MICROWAVE CARAMEL CORN

Teresa A. Martin, Rogue River, OR

**1 cup brown sugar**
**1/4 cup light corn syrup**
**1 stick butter**
**1/4 teaspoon salt**
**1/2 teaspoon baking soda**
**1 teaspoon vanilla**
**1/2 cup popcorn, popped**

Bring brown sugar, corn syrup, butter, and salt to a boil in a 2-quart microwave-safe bowl. Boil for 2 minutes. Add baking soda and vanilla, stir. Pour mixture over popped corn; microwave on high for 1 minute. Stir well, and repeat 3 additional minutes, stirring after each minute. Cool on a cookie sheet.

## CARAMEL POPCORN

Carla Moore, Wichita, KS

**2 sticks butter**
**1/2 cup light corn syrup**
**2 cups brown sugar**
**1/4 teaspoon cream of tartar**
**1/4 teaspoon salt**
**1 teaspoon vanilla**
**1 teaspoon baking soda**
**8 quarts popped corn**

OVEN 220°

Mix butter, syrup, and sugar; bring to boiling point. Let boil 6 minutes and keep stirring. Take off heat and add cream of tartar, salt, vanilla, and baking soda. Stir until foamy and quickly pour on popped corn, stirring as pouring. Spread this in large flat pans and bake for 1 hour. Stir 2 or 3 times. Store in tightly closed containers. Can be made in advance and kept in refrigerator. Peanuts or any nuts can also be added as desired.

## POTATO CANDY

Sarah Schale, Goldendale, WA

**2/3 cup hot cooked potatoes**
**2 teaspoons butter, melted**
**1 box powdered sugar, sifted**
**2½ tablespoons cocoa**
**1 teaspoon vanilla**
**Dash of salt**
**2 cups (½ pound) moist coconut**

Put potatoes through a ricer. Add butter and powdered sugar, beat until well blended. Add cocoa; beat thoroughly. Mix in vanilla, salt, and coconut. Drop by teaspoonfuls onto waxed paper. Refrigerate to harden. Hardened candy should be kept in a tightly covered container once it has set.

Makes 1½ pounds.

## MASHED POTATO CANDY

Betty Lombardo, Valrico, FL

*"I have been making this candy since I was a young girl. At home I made it for my children. Now I'm making it for my grandchildren and great-grandchildren."*

**½ cup potatoes, mashed**
**2½ boxes confectioners' sugar**
**2 sticks margarine**
**Peanut butter**

Beat together potatoes, sugar, and margarine. Roll out into a ¼-inch-thick square. Spread with peanut butter and roll up like a jelly roll. Cut into 1-inch pieces.

## BAKED POTATO CANDY

Doris Schwanke, Porter, TX

**1 medium potato baked (not red or yellow potato)**
**1 pound confectioners' sugar**
**Creamy peanut butter**

Cool potato until you can hold it in your hand. Remove peel and mash well with a fork in a medium-size bowl. Add powdered sugar gradually, stirring well until a stiff dough forms. Turn out on a board covered with powered sugar. Roll into rectangle about ¼-inch thick. Spread with peanut butter. Roll into tight roll, using a spatula to help lift the dough, beginning with the long side. Let dry for about an hour, then slice into ¼-inch slices and spread out on a plate with waxed paper between layers. Cover lightly. Dough can be tinted with food coloring or 2 tablespoons of cocoa may be added before rolling.

# CANDIES

## HAYSTACKS

Sylvia Smeltzer, Bristol, TN

**2 packages butterscotch pieces**
**1 can potato sticks**
**1 cup salted peanuts**

Melt butterscotch pieces into a pan, at low temperature. Add potato sticks and peanuts. Stir until well coated. Drop from teaspoon onto waxed paper to form clusters.

## CHOW MEIN HAYSTACKS

Bernice Howard, Gauley Bridge, WV

**6 ounces butterscotch morsels**
**½ cup chunky peanut butter**
**1 cup miniature marshmallows**
**3-ounce can chow mein noodles**

In the top part of a double boiler over hot, not boiling, water, melt together butterscotch morsels and peanut butter. Add marshmallows, stirring constantly until mix is smooth. Gently fold in noodles. Blend well. Drop mixture by teaspoonfuls onto waxed paper. Let cool until set.

## OHIO BUCKEYES

Louise Letter, Washougal, WA

**2 sticks margarine, melted**
**2 cups peanut butter**
**4 cups powdered sugar**
**1 teaspoon vanilla**
**2x2-inch piece of paraffin**
**3 cups chocolate chips (not imitation chocolate)**

Cream together all ingredients except paraffin and chocolate. Chill in refrigerator a few hours, then roll into balls approximately ¾-inch in diameter. Chill the balls in refrigerator at least 8 hours. Melt paraffin and chocolate in double boiler. Using a toothpick, dip each ball into the chocolate mixture, twirling off excess chocolate. Place on waxed paper to set up.

## NO-BAKE CHOCOLATE DAINTIES

Joyce Francis, Gurdon, AR

**2 cups sugar**
**1 stick margarine**
**½ cup evaporated milk**
**2 cups quick oats**
**⅓ cup cocoa**
**½ cup coconut**
**1 teaspoon vanilla**

Mix sugar, margarine, and milk together. Boil 4 minutes. Remove from heat and stir in oats, cocoa, coconut, and vanilla. Beat and drop by spoonfuls on waxed paper. Let sit until cool.

## DING-A-LINGS

Annamae Laumb, Tolley, ND

**1 package almond bark**
**1½ cups Peanut Butter Crunch by Captain Crunch**
**1¼ cups cashews**
**1¼ cups mixed nuts**
**1½ cups miniature marshmallows**

Melt almond bark. In a big bowl add Peanut Butter Crunch, cashews, mixed nuts, and marshmallows. Pour almond bark over and drop by spoonfuls onto waxed paper.

## CARAMEL APPLE PIECES

Nina Hoover, Dillsburg, PA

**½ cup brown sugar**
**4 teaspoons flour**
**4 tablespoons butter**
**4 teaspoons milk**
**1 teaspoon vanilla**
**4 medium apples, cored, and cut into ⅛-inch pieces (peel if for small children)**
**Chopped nuts**

In small saucepan mix together brown sugar, flour, butter, and milk. Stir constantly on medium heat until thick and bubbly. Remove from heat and add vanilla. Let cool. Spoon caramel sauce over apples. Sprinkle with chopped nuts if desired.

## SWEET THINGS

Terry Hudman, Magnolia, AR

**1 cup dates, chopped**
**1 cup fat-free Eagle Brand condensed milk**
**1 cup pecans, chopped**
**Reduced-fat Ritz crackers**

**Frosting:**
**1 3-ounce package fat-free cream cheese**
**½ cup reduced-fat margarine**
**1½ cups powdered sugar**
**1 teaspoon vanilla**

OVEN 320°

Mix dates and milk in saucepan. Cook on medium heat until thick. Mix in pecans. Spread Ritz crackers on cookie sheet and cover with date mixture. Bake for 8 minutes. Mix together frosting ingredients. Frost. Cover and refrigerate.

## GRAHAM GEMS

Imagene Davis, Freedom, PA

**¼ cup sugar**
**½ teaspoon salt**
**½ cup all-purpose flour**
**2 teaspoons baking powder**
**1 cup whole wheat flour**
**1 cup milk**
**2 tablespoons sour cream**
**1 egg, beaten**

OVEN 420°

In mixing bowl, stir together first 5 ingredients, make a well in center. In another bowl combine milk, sour cream, and egg. Add to first ingredients, stirring just until blended. Pour into greased muffin cups. Bake for 15–20 minutes until lightly browned. Serve with butter, margarine, or honey.

## MERINGUE SURPRISES

Jeannie Hash, Northeast, MD

**2 egg whites**
**1 teaspoon vanilla**
**⅛ teaspoon salt**
**½ cup sugar**
**6 ounces chocolate chips**

OVEN 300°

Combine egg whites, vanilla, and salt. Beat until stiff. Beat in sugar gradually until stiff and satiny. Fold in chocolate chips. Drop by teaspoonfuls onto greased cookie sheet and bake 30 minutes.

## DIVINITY CANDY

Andrea Watts, Hixson, TN

**2 cups sugar**
**½ cup light corn syrup**
**½ cup hot water**
**¼ teaspoon salt**
**2 egg whites**
**¾ cup nuts**
**1 teaspoon vanilla**

Mix together sugar, syrup, water, and salt. Cook until hard ball forms in water. Beat whites stiff, pour hot syrup slowly over whites. Beat high speed for 5 minutes; then add nuts and vanilla. Spoon onto waxed paper.

## PEPPERMINT DIVINITY

Janice Lowrey, Anacoco, LA

**2⅔ cups sugar**
**⅔ cup light corn syrup**
**½ cup water**
**2 egg whites**
**2 teaspoons peppermint extract**
**Pink food coloring**
**⅔ cup broken nuts (optional)**

Heat sugar, corn syrup, and water in 2-quart saucepan over low heat, stirring constantly until sugar is dissolved. Cook, with stirring, to 260° on candy thermometer, or until small amount of mixture dropped into very cold water forms a hard ball. Remove from heat. Beat egg whites until stiff peaks form, continue beating while pouring hot syrup in a thin stream into egg whites. Add peppermint extract and food coloring. The mixture should hold its shape. Add nuts if desired. Drop from spoon onto waxed paper.

## RICE KRISPIE CANDY

Mary Chessor, Savannah, TN

*"A good snack and easy to fix."*

**½ cup sugar**
**½ cup light corn syrup**
**¾ cup peanut butter**
**3 cups Rice Krispies cereal**

Bring sugar and corn syrup to boil. Remove from heat, add peanut butter, mix well, and stir in cereal. Drop by spoonfuls onto waxed paper.

## PARTY FAVORITES

Ludia Love, Dudley, MO

**Ritz crackers**
**Peanut butter**
**Chocolate chips**

Put water in a pan and put another pan on top, creating double boiler. Put chocolate chips in top pan and heat until melted. Spread peanut butter on cracker, place another cracker on top. Dip into chocolate. Place on waxed paper to dry, then refrigerate.

## CORN POP SQUARES

Jean Haun, Simcoe, Ontario

**¼ cup margarine**
**1 teaspoon vanilla**
**1 package marshmallows**
**6 cups Sugar Corn Pops cereal**
**1 package M&M Chocolate candies (to taste)**

Melt margarine and marshmallows in microwave. Add vanilla. Reserve a few M&M's for sprinkling on top. Mix M&M's and Sugar Pops with the marshmallow mixture; put in 8x11-inch dish to cool and harden. Cut into squares and serve.

## ENGLISH TOFFEE

Lynn Burton, Gilbert, AZ

**1 cup sugar**
**1 cup butter**
**1 teaspoon vanilla**
**6 1½-ounce Hershey Bars**
**Chopped pecans**

Cover a cookie sheet with foil and spray with nonstick cooking spray. Cook sugar and butter to hard crack, on medium heat until they turn brown. Add vanilla. Pour ingredients onto pan and spread out ⅛- to ¼-inch thick. Break up Hershey Bars, lay on top of hot toffee. Spread. Sprinkle with nuts. Cool and break into pieces.

## OLD-TIME TAFFY

Birdie L. Etchison, Ocean Park, WA

*"This is the recipe Pearl, in* Love's Tender Path, *made and took to school for the Christmas party. Takes two or more to make. Try it!"*

**Editor's Note:** Birdie has written several books for the Heartsong Presents series, including *The Heart Has Its Reasons* and *Albert's Destiny*. She loves to research family history and her findings are often part of her stories.

**1 cup sugar**
**1 cup dark corn syrup**
**2 tablespoons water**
**1 tablespoon apple cider vinegar**
**Butter, the size of a peanut**
**½ teaspoon baking soda**

Place first 5 ingredients in a pan; bring to a boil. Boil until it forms a hard ball in a cup of cold water. Then add baking soda; stir well. Pour on buttered pan and, when cooled, pull until shiny and ready to cut.

## STRAWBERRY CANDIES

Janice Lowrey, Anacoco, LA

**12-ounce package coconut**
**1 can condensed milk**
**2 packages strawberry Jell-O (maybe more)**
**1 teaspoon almond extract**
**1½ cups chopped almonds (optional)**

Mix coconut, milk, extract, nuts, and 1 package of Jell-O. Mixture will be sticky. Shape into candies that look like strawberries, roll in one box of Jell-O (may need more). Green icing can be piped on top for leaves. Chill before eating.

Variations: Use blueberry Jell-O or another favorite flavor.

# INDEX

## APPETIZERS



## BREADS

## BREAKFAST

## CAKES

## CANDIES

## COOKIES

## DESSERT BARS



## DESSERTS

## MAIN DISHES

## SALADS

## PIES